Financial Advisor Series: Product Essentials

ESSENTIALS OF BUSINESS INSURANCE

Glenn E. Stevick, Jr., CLU, ChFC, LUTCF

FA251.02.1

This publication is designed to provide accurate and authoritative information about the subject covered. While every precaution has been taken in the preparation of this material, the authors, and The American College assume no liability for damages resulting from the use of the information contained in this publication. The American College is not engaged in rendering legal, accounting, or other professional advice. If legal or other expert advice is required, the services of an appropriate professional should be sought.

© 2010 The American College Press
270 S. Bryn Mawr Avenue
Bryn Mawr, PA 19010
(888) AMERCOL (263–7265)
ISBN-10: 1-932819-98-3
ISBN-13: 978-1-932819-98-4
Library of Congress Control Number 2009911643
theamericancollege.edu
Printed in the United States of America

Sales Skills Techniques

Techniques for Exploring Personal Markets

Techniques for Meeting Client Needs

Techniques for Prospecting: Prospect or Perish

Women and Money—Matters of Trust

Product Essentials

Essentials of Annuities

Essentials of Business Insurance

Essentials of Disability Income Insurance

Essentials of Life Insurance Products

Essentials of Long–Term Care Insurance

Essentials of Multiline Insurance Products

Planning Foundations

Foundations of Estate Planning

Foundations of Retirement Planning

Foundations of Financial Planning: An Overview

Foundations of Financial Planning: The Process

Foundations of Investment Planning

The American College® is an independent, nonprofit, accredited institution founded in 1927 that offers professional certification and graduate-degree distance education to men and women seeking career growth in financial services.

The Center for Financial Advisor Education at The American College offers both the LUTCF and the Financial Services Specialist (FSS) professional designations to introduce students in a classroom environment to the technical side of financial services, while at the same time providing them with the requisite sales-training skills.

The Solomon S. Huebner School® of The American College administers the Chartered Life Underwriter (CLU®); the Chartered Financial Consultant (ChFC®); the Chartered Advisor for Senior Living (CASL®); the Registered Health Underwriter (RHU®); the Registered Employee Benefits Consultant (REBC®); and the Chartered Leadership Fellow® (CLF®) professional designation programs. In addition, the Huebner School also administers The College's CFP Board—registered education program for those individuals interested in pursuing CFP® certification, the CFP® Certification Curriculum.[1]

The Richard D. Irwin Graduate School® of The American College offers the master of science in financial services (MSFS) degree, the Graduate Financial Planning Track (another CFP Board-registered education program), and several graduate-level certificates that concentrate on specific subject areas. It also offers the Chartered Advisor in Philanthropy (CAP®) and the master of science in management (MSM), a one-year program with an emphasis in leadership. The National Association of Estate Planners & Councils has named The College as the provider of the education required to earn its prestigious AEP designation.

The American College is accredited by:

The Middle States Commission on Higher Education

3624 Market Street

Philadelphia, PA 19104

267.284.5000

The Middle States Commission on Higher Education is a regional accrediting agency recognized by the U.S. Secretary of Education and the Commission on Recognition of

---

1. Certified Financial Planner Board of Standards, Inc., owns the certification marks CFP®, CERTIFIED FINANCIAL PLANNER™, and CFP (with flame logo)®, which it awards to individuals who successfully complete initial and ongoing certification requirements.

Postsecondary Accreditation. Middle States accreditation is an expression of confidence in an institution's mission and goals, performance, and resources. It attests that in the judgment of the Commission on Higher Education, based on the results of an internal institutional self-study and an evaluation by a team of outside peer observers assigned by the Commission, an institution is guided by well-defined and appropriate goals; that it has established conditions and procedures under which its goals can be realized; that it is accomplishing them substantially; that it is so organized, staffed, and supported that it can be expected to continue to do so; and that it meets the standards of the Middle States Association. The American College has been accredited since 1978.

The American College does not discriminate on the basis of race, religion, sex, handicap, or national and ethnic origin in its admissions policies, educational programs and activities, or employment policies.

The American College is located at 270 S. Bryn Mawr Avenue, Bryn Mawr, PA 19010. The toll-free number of the Office of Professional Education is (888) AMERCOL (263-7265); the fax number is (610) 526-1465; and the home page address is theamericancollege.edu.

CONTENTS

The mission of this book is to develop your professionalism as a financial advisor counseling prospects and clients about the need for business insurance. We intend to do this by teaching you about the benefits of business insurance, by enhancing your *marketing and sales skills*, and by stressing the importance of planning foundations in shaping your performance as a successful advisor. It is our hope that this book has the right blend of sales skills techniques, product essentials, and *planning foundations* to accomplish this mission.

While much of the text material will be new to you, some will, no doubt, refresh knowledge you acquired in the past. In either case, all of the text material is both valuable and necessary if you aspire to be successful in the business marketplace. The benefits you gain from studying the text material will be directly proportional to the effort you expend. So read each chapter carefully and answer both the essay and multiple choice review questions for the chapter (preferably before looking in the back of the book for the answers); to do less would be to deprive yourself of a unique opportunity to become familiar with business insurance and to learn more about selling it.

The book includes numerous features designed to help you focus your study of business insurance. Among the features found in each chapter of the book are

- an overview and learning objectives
- a chapter outline, examples, quotes, and lists
- key terms and concepts
- review questions (essay format)
- self-test questions (multiple choice format)

The back of the book includes a glossary, answers to self-test questions, and an index.

Finally, all of the individuals noted on the acknowledgments page made this a better book, and we are grateful. However, in spite of the help of all of these fine folks, some errors have undoubtedly been successful in eluding our eyes. For these we are solely responsible. At the same time, however, we accept full credit for giving those of you who find these errors the exhilarating intellectual experience produced by such discovery.

ACKNOWLEDGMENTS

This book was written by Glenn Stevick, Jr., LUTC author/editor at The American College.

For their valuable contribution to the development of this book, appreciation is extended to Todd Denton and Jane Hassinger for production assistance, and Patricia Cheers, Permissions Editor.

Very special thanks to Alan Meagher, retired from LUTC, who maintained the previous version of this book for over 30 years. Also, special thanks to Dr. Laurence Barton for providing guidance and encouragement to continue the LUTC tradition at The American College.

The College would also like to thank the following individuals for their substantial contributions to this book:

William Lister	Jack Eulitt
Thomas Horn	Richard Costello
Joel Goodhart	Randy Clemens
James Penn	Sid Bradshaw
Hank Donaghy	Hampton Durbin
Tim McDonald	George Hibsman
M. Jay Einstein	Leo Meadows
Curtis Babich	Ray Patsy
Chuck Short	Sal Gagliardi
Roddy Read	

To all of these individuals, without whom this book would not have been possible, the College expresses its sincere appreciation and gratitude.

Walt J. Woerheide
Executive Vice President and Dean of Academic Affairs
The American College

Glenn E. Stevick, Jr., LUTCF, CLU, ChFC, is an author/editor and assistant professor of insurance at The American College. His responsibilities at The College include writing and preparing text materials for the LUTCF and FSS programs. He also teaches insurance and financial planning courses at The College.

Mr. Stevick is co-author of *Essentials of Long-Term Care Insurance, Techniques for Exploring Personal Markets,* Foundations of Financial Planning: The Process,and Techniques for Prospecting: Prospect or Perish. He is author of *Techniques for Meeting Client Needs, Essentials of Life Insurance Products,* and *Foundations of Estate Planning,* published by The American College. Mr. Stevick also writes articles for *Advisor Today,* the national magazine distributed to members of NAIFA.

Before joining The College, Mr. Stevick worked for New York Life as a training supervisor for 15 years in its South Jersey office. He also served as an agent with New York Life for more than 2 years. Prior to his insurance industry experience, Mr. Stevick taught psychology at the college level and worked in various educational and mental health programs. Mr. Stevick earned his BA degree from Villanova University and his MA degree from Duquesne University.

Text Materials Disclaimer

This publication is designed to provide accurate and authoritative information about the subject covered. While every precaution has been taken in the preparation of this material to insure that it is both accurate and up-to-date, it is still possible that some errors eluded detection. Moreover, some material may become inaccurate and/or outdated either because it is time sensitive or because new legislation will make it so. Still other material may be viewed as inaccurate because your company's products and procedures are different from those described in the book. Therefore, the authors and The American College assume no liability for damages resulting from the use of the information contained in this book. The American College is not engaged in rendering legal, accounting, or other professional advice. If legal or other expert advice is required, the services of an appropriate professional should be sought.

Caution Regarding Use of Illustrations

The illustrations, sales ideas and approaches in this book are not to be used with the public unless you have obtained approval from your company. Your company's general support of The American College's programs for training and educational purposes does not constitute blanket approval of the sales ideas and approaches presented in this book, unless so communicated in writing by your company.

Use of the Term Financial Advisor or Advisor

Use of the term "Financial Advisor" as it appears in this book is intended as the generic reference to professional members of our reading audience. It is used interchangeably with the term "Advisor" so as to avoid unnecessary redundancy. Financial Advisor takes the place of the following terms:

Account Executive	Life Insurance Agent
Agent	Life Underwriter
Associate	Planner
Broker (stock or insurance)	Practitioner
Financial Consultant	Producer
Financial Planner	Property & Casualty Agent
Financial Planning Professional	Registered Investment Advisor
Financial Services Professional	Registered Representative

Health Underwriter   Senior Advisor

Insurance Professional

Answers to the Questions in the Book

The answers to all essay and multiple-choice questions in this book are based on the text materials as written.

ABOUT THE FINANCIAL ADVISOR SERIES

The mission of The American College is to raise the level of professionalism of its students and, by extension, the financial services industry as a whole. As an educational product of The College, the Financial Advisor Series shares in this mission. Because knowledge is the key to professionalism, a thorough and comprehensive reading of each book in the series will help the practitioner-advisor to better service his or her clients—a task made all the more difficult because the typical client is becoming more financially sophisticated every day and demands that his or her financial advisor be knowledgeable about the latest products and planning methodologies. By providing practitioner-advisors in the financial services industry with up-to-date, authoritative information about various marketing and sales techniques, product knowledge, and planning considerations, the books of the Financial Advisor Series will enable many practitioner-advisors to continue their studies so as to develop and maintain a high level of professional competence.

The Financial Advisor Series encompasses 16 titles spread across three separate subseries, each with a special focus. The first subseries, *Sales Skills Techniques,* focuses on enhancing the practitioner-advisor's marketing and sales skills but also covers product knowledge and planning considerations. The second subseries, *Product Essentials,* focuses on product knowledge but will also delve into marketing and sales skills, as well as planning considerations. The third subseries, *Planning Foundations,* focuses on planning considerations and processes that form the foundation of a successful career as a financial services professional.

Essentials of Business Insurance focuses on the problems, and the solutions to those problems, that may result from the death or disability of a business owner or a key employee. A major theme is succession planning, discussing ways that a business owner can retain and continue the value of the business in the case of death, disability, or retirement from the business.

To accomplish this, the text covers the forms of business organization in Chapter 1. An understanding of business forms, how they are organized and taxed, and what advantages and disadvantages they possess is critical to understanding the problems which can result of the death or disability of a business owner. Emphasis is placed on being able to communicate these issues with business owners. Chapter 2 looks at the business owner's perspective, covering concerns he or she may have in running a business. A review of financial statements and key accounting terms is also covered.

Chapter 3 discusses prospecting for approaching business prospects. Chapter 4 covers fact-finding and sets the stage for a discussion of buy-sell arrangements by discussing the problems that can result for those involved with and dependent on a business in the case of a death or disability to an owner or key employee.

Chapter 5 develops a detailed discussion of the types of buy sell agreements, their advantages and disadvantages, tax consequences, and discusses prospect's objections to and concerns about buy-sell agreements.

Chapter 6 looks at specific problems that are presented in family-owned business situations. There are a number of income tax issues that make the family business succession problems different from other businesses. This chapter also discuses business valuation and the problems that can result from the disability of an owner or key employee. Disability buyouts and business overhead expense policies are discussed.

Key employee insurance is the topic of Chapter 7. The chapter focuses on problems that result for the business from the death of a key employee and possible solutions. Additionally, the tax aspects and valuation of key employees are covered.

Last, in Chapter 8, estate planning for the business owner is covered. The basic concepts of estate planning, and principles of planning that would effect business owners' estate and business succession are the topics of this chapter.

Learning Objectives

An understanding of the material in this chapter should enable the student to

1. Describe the life cycle of a business.

2. Explain how the advisor is a businessperson who shares many common concerns with business owners.

3. Describe 10 different forms of business organization, and identify the distinguishing characteristics of each form.

4. Describe the major advantages and disadvantages of each form of business organization.

This chapter looks at the business owner and the challenges facing the financial advisor who enters the business insurance market. It asks you to view yourself as a business owner and realize you have much in common with the business owners you wish to approach. It looks at the life cycle of a business and discusses 10 forms of business ownership, examining the advantages, disadvantages, and tax implications of each form.

THE BUSINESS INSURANCE MARKET

There are over 23 million small businesses in the United States, according to the U.S. Census Bureau. That means there are 23 million prospects with business insurance needs. In this book we will examine those needs and discuss how you can successfully help businesses meet them.

The complex business environment is filled with the pressures of running a business, such as product or service considerations, profit margins, government regulations, constant decision-making, worry about the future, changing market conditions, and countless other things. Each type of business also has its own unique challenges. A dry cleaning firm is different from a car dealership; an architecture firm is different from a physician's practice, a manufacturing plant is different from a consulting firm.

This book focuses on what a financial advisor (see Special Notes to Advisors page for an explanation of the terms *financial advisor* and *advisor* as used in this book) needs to know to work with business owners in planning for the continuation of their businesses in the event of the death or disability of an owner or key employee. Working in the business market is not easy. It takes an understanding of accounting principles, tax law, and employment law. It takes an understanding of businesspeople and their psychology: what makes them tick. It also takes time. Developing a business case is not a one-interview process. It takes weeks—sometimes even months or years to bring a case to conclusion. But for those who are successful, it is well worth the effort.

The Business Life Cycle

In working in the personal market, you learned that there is a life cycle common to most of your clients. It begins when they are young singles and continues through retirement to their long-term care needs. You learned that at each stage in the life cycle, their needs are different. For the young single person, disability insurance is the greatest need. A young couple with children needs life insurance. Empty nesters focus on saving and investing for their retirement.

Like individuals, businesses also experience a life cycle. The over 23 million small businesses in the United States are operating at varying stages of the business life cycle. A newly started business has different needs than a well-established, mature one. Understanding the general business cycle of different businesses can help you understand the insurance needs of a particular business and help you focus your prospecting efforts.

The life cycle of a business has three stages:

1. new or emerging business
2. successfully operating/growing business
3. mature/successful business

New or Emerging Business

A new business operates in a survival mode. It is the culmination of an idea put into action. With the original investment used simply to open the doors, the business is often short of cash. It is fast-paced, with the owner(s) and a few key people often doing everything because the business is understaffed. Its primary focus is to develop customers and meet their needs.

Insurance needs are likely to be a secondary consideration to the other financial demands of the fledgling business. Owners of new businesses are not looking ahead to retirement. They are working hard to make it to the next week. There are, however, some insurance plans they should consider.

For a new business with employees, group insurance plans make sense. They provide a valuable benefit for the employees and for the owners. They also make employment with the business more attractive, enabling it to hire the employees it needs to succeed.

For the individual entrepreneur, personal disability and life insurance coverage can be critical. Often the success of the business depends on the efforts of the owner. If he or she becomes disabled or dies, the business will almost certainly fail. While it may be impossible to insure the success of a new business, personal policies can protect its owner and his or her family.

Successfully Operating/Growing Business

As the business achieves success, its complexion changes. With positive cash flow and established customers, it may hire additional staff, spreading the workload. And as it grows, its insurance needs change.

The group plans initiated in stage one need to be reviewed and improved. Options for employees offered by a cafeteria plan may be appropriate. A qualified retirement plan should be considered as should nonqualified salary continuation and deferred compensation plans.

For the owner(s), increased cash flow and salary may cause personal needs to grow. Personal policies need to be supplemented with additional business life insurance using executive carve-out and executive bonus plans.

The continued success of the business will also become an issue, leading to consideration of a buy-sell agreement and key employee insurance. A business overhead expense policy should be put in place to protect against losses associated with the disability of an owner.

Mature/Successful Business

As the business continues to grow and prosper, its insurance needs also grow. As the owners approach retirement age, their focus changes to securing retirement and stabilizing the business. They must then begin to address the eventual transfer of their business to others.

The business's insurance needs may become more complicated and sophisticated in this stage. Cafeteria and medical expense plans need to be reviewed and should be updated when necessary. Benefit packages must be matched with those offered by competitors. Key employee insurance and deferred compensation plans may also need review and updating. Comprehensive retirement planning is needed for the owner(s) and the key employees who are reaching retirement age. The owner(s) must also address individual estate planning goals.

These are just a few examples of the changing needs in the life cycle of a business. As such, your ongoing advice and service are valuable components of the sales process.

In addition to the life cycle of a business, there may also be an annual business cycle. This is the cycle that controls a business's cash flow and workload. Many businesses are seasonal in nature. Many retail stores depend heavily on the December holiday season for their success. A landscaping business will be extremely busy in the spring and summer and may have relatively little to do in the winter months.

Understanding the annual cycle of a business you are working with is important in your planning. Does an appointment with a retailer a week before Christmas make sense? How about an appointment with an accountant in early April? Do you think you will get their undivided attention to your proposals? Understanding the annual business cycles of different businesses can help you focus your prospecting attention.

FORMS OF BUSINESS ORGANIZATION

We begin our education of the business market with a review of the different forms a business can take. The form is fundamental to the way the business operates; how it is taxed; what liability its owners have; how expenses, compensation and benefits are treated; and the problems that the business owner may encounter.

Businesses in the United States can be organized in one of three basic legal forms:

- Sole proprietorships
- Partnerships
- Corporations

To complicate matters, there are variations of each of these forms. In addition, a hybrid form known as a limited liability company, with characteristics of both a corporation and a partnership, is now available in all states.

The following list identifies the 10 forms of business found in the United States.

1. Sole proprietorship
2. General partnership
3. Limited partnership
4. Family limited partnership
5. Professional partnership
6. C corporation
7. S corporation
8. Limited liability company
9. Professional corporation
10. Personal service corporation

To a financial advisor working in the business market, understanding the differences between business forms is important but not necessarily easy. The differences are not always apparent to the outside observer. In fact, in deciding how a business will be taxed, the Internal Revenue Service looks at how a business operates instead of what it calls itself, and taxes it accordingly.

There are eight primary factors that define how a business is structured and operates. These factors are:

1. creation—how the business is started
2. management—how it is managed and operates on a daily basis
3. ownership—who owns the business's property and assets
4. profit—how the business's profits and losses are distributed
5. liability—who is accountable for the business's legal responsibilities
6. taxation—how the business is taxed
7. continuity—the length of the business's life
8. termination—how the business can be terminated

Familiarity with each of these areas will help you understand the unique problems facing your business prospects. A working knowledge of the elements of the business will help you understand what the owner(s) has invested, not just in financial terms, but also in time, energy and emotion. You will develop a better understanding of what your clients have at risk, the concerns they have, and the conflicts they face. This working knowledge of the elements of business will also help you focus your clients on the need to plan for the future.

The better you understand the various types of business organizations—their characteristics, advantages, and disadvantages—the better you can identify needs and create solutions. Knowledge breeds confidence, trust, and success.

Problems of Closely Held Businesses

This book focuses on the closely held business, which is defined as a business not traded on a securities exchange and where ownership is not typically available through shares offered for public sale. The business is controlled by a small group of people who are generally involved in the day-to-day operation of the business and who provide services for the business.

The owners of a closely held business face numerous problems. Some are inherent in the organizational structure of the small business and others exist in enterprises of all sizes. Many problems facing the business owner, such as survival in the marketplace, are obvious. The business owner may not recognize other problems, such as the reduction in business income resulting from the loss of a key employee due to death or disability, until the incident occurs.

Many problems facing the business owner can be avoided, or at least reduced, through proper planning. To plan intelligently to avoid or handle future problems, it is necessary to identify the potential problems and form objectives.

Your role as a financial services professional is to help business owners or professionals recognize these problems and to assist in formulating plans that are appropriate for the special needs of each client. The purpose of this chapter is to discuss typical problems faced by the closely held business owner or professional. Possible solutions to these problems will be discussed in subsequent chapters.

Choosing the Form of Business Organization

Business owners are faced with a number of choices when selecting the form of enterprise. They may elect to operate unincorporated, as a sole proprietorship, a partnership, or a limited-liability company (LLC); or they may incorporate as a regular (C) corporation or as an S corporation. The choice of ownership form is not irrevocable, and owners of existing businesses often decide to change the form as circumstances dictate. For example, the sole proprietor might wonder if the benefits of switching to the corporate form of ownership are worth the costs of incorporation. Or perhaps the owners of an existing closely held corporation are considering what the tax advantages would be if they switched to a subchapter S form of business.

The choice of a form of ownership is a complex decision facing all business owners because it will have a significant impact on the initial start-up cost, the control and flexibility in management, the taxation of the business and individual owners, the ability of the firm to raise capital, and the business risks absorbed by the individual owners.

Business Owner Objectives. Owners often have several objectives when selecting the form of ownership under which the business will operate:

- start-up costs and formalities of operation
- control of the business and management
- flexibility in business operations
- ability of the business to raise funds
- limiting the liability of owners from business operations
- overall tax burden
- business continuity and termination
- compensation and fringe benefits

The priority ranking of these goals will differ from one individual to the next, but the typical business owner or professional shares all to some extent. The following discussion of forms of business organization will examine how each form of business impacts these objectives.

The Sole Proprietorship

sole proprietorship

It is natural to begin with sole proprietorships because they are the simplest and most numerous form of business. There are over 17 million sole proprietorships in this country, representing over 73 percent of all businesses. Thousands of new ones begin each year. More than 90 percent of all sole proprietorships are one-person operations. Most others have a very small number of employees. Less than 8 percent have more than eight employees.

Background on Sole Proprietorship

By definition, a sole proprietorship is an unincorporated business owned by one person. A sole proprietor may run the business directly or may hire others to run it, but ultimately it is the sole proprietor's decisions that determine the firm's destiny. Typically, a sole proprietor performs most of the major functions such as overall manager, sales manager and finance manager. Since the proprietor is the sole owner of the business, there is generally no need for any agreements or formalities.

The proprietorship has its roots in the earliest days of commerce. In primitive economic society, each person depended for survival on his or her own work. This system gave way to the first age of specialization.

In those days, there was no such thing as life insurance and disability income insurance. When the proprietor became disabled or died, the family was suddenly destitute. There were no alternatives, no preplanned solutions.

Today's proprietor lives a much more complex life precisely because specialization has created a highly interdependent business community. Although an electrical contractor may be self-employed, he or she cannot survive without the work of thousands of other people in hundreds of other organizations that produce tools and equipment that are a contractor's stock in trade.

The interdependence of business organizations provides you with the greatest opportunity for endless-chain prospecting among business owners. You can get referrals to a proprietor's suppliers, to the supplier's customers, and to their suppliers, without end. There is a large existing network that can be tapped.

Distinguishing Characteristic of Sole Proprietorship

The majority of sole proprietorships today operate on a relatively small scale, where the capital and credit of one person is adequate. The real distinguishing feature of a sole proprietorship is not size; it is the unlimited and unshared responsibility of the sole owner.

Advantages of Sole Proprietorship

Why choose this form of business rather than another? What are the advantages of sole proprietorships?

- **Simplicity**—Starting a sole proprietorship is relatively simple. This is probably why such a large proportion of all businesses are proprietorships. The only legal formalities are applying for appropriate state or local permits and licenses and filing a special certificate if the sole proprietor intends to operate the business under a name other than his or her own.

  Similarly, no legal action is required to terminate a sole proprietorship. When a sole proprietor wants to quit for whatever reason, he or she simply satisfies any outstanding contracts and financial obligations and takes on no new business.

- **Autonomy**—Autonomy is one of the hallmarks of the sole proprietorship. Far more than any other form of business, the sole proprietorship exemplifies one of the advantages and glittering attractions of going into business alone: freedom of action.

  There is no boss to criticize a sole proprietor's work. There is no partner who must be consulted on decisions and who may begrudge splitting the profits. There is no board of directors to second-guess the decisions of the sole proprietor or enforce a distasteful policy. Neither is there a partnership agreement, a corporate charter from the state, or corporate bylaws to limit the scope of the sole proprietor's powers.

  At will, the owner may expand operations or contract them, move to another location, seize or ignore opportunities, sell or liquidate. In short, the proprietor may do virtually whatever he or she wants.

- **Sole Gain**—Related to this aspect of the proprietorship is the fact that all profits belong to the sole owner. Just as all of the responsibilities of the business fall solely on the owner, so do all the benefits. There are no partners to share the proceeds. There are no stockholders to claim dividends.

- **Single Tax**—The sole proprietor and the sole proprietor's business are taxed as a single unit. The sole proprietor files Form 1040, and along with it Schedule C ("Profit or Loss from Business or Profession"). All profits of the business are personal income to the sole proprietor even any portion not withdrawn. There is no separate federal income tax reporting for the proprietorship. This is known as pass-through taxation.

- **Shelter Income**—Along with other forms of business, the sole proprietor enjoys the tax advantage of reducing taxable income by charging off costs of doing business as "expenses."

Not all "expenses" are actual expenditures. Depreciation expenses are the best example of this advantage. A business may have a profit of $25,000 in terms of actual gain over actual operating costs. On the tax report, however, the owner can deduct depreciation of buildings and equipment.

Depreciation doesn't necessarily mean the equipment or building is wearing out; it just means that the business owner can deduct the cost of the equipment over a prescribed period of time. If depreciation totals $10,000 this year, the proprietor pays income tax on only $15,000 instead of $25,000.

Disadvantages of Sole Proprietorship

Operating as a sole proprietorship has a number of disadvantages. Most of these disadvantages spring from the very feature that makes the sole proprietorship form of business so attractive-the complete identity of the business with its owner.

- **Limited Resources**—One disadvantage is that of limited resources. The capital available to a sole proprietorship is limited by the personal financial resources of the owner and his or her ability to obtain credit and borrow money.

  The sole proprietor has no way to raise funds from outside investors without ceasing to be a sole proprietorship. For this reason, sole proprietorships generally are not practical in large business ventures that demand major capital inputs.

  The sole proprietorship form also is limited in terms of business talent and ability. The success of the business generally is tied to the ingenuity, initiative, resourcefulness, and managerial abilities of the sole owner.

  Even if a sole proprietor is a skilled manager, the business probably will decline any time this person is sick or disabled. In addition, a sole proprietor typically would be reluctant to undertake projects that require a variety of specialized technical skills.

- **Unlimited and Unshared Liability**—Another drawback to the sole proprietorship form of business is that the sole proprietor's financial liability is unlimited and unshared.

  There is no distinction between the sole proprietor's business assets and liabilities and his or her personal assets and liabilities.

In the event of business failure, creditors can come after personal assets and business assets, as they are one and the same.

If the sole proprietor dies or becomes disabled, and if there isn't adequate insurance or other funds to pay off the debts and pay an income to the family, the family can be completely wiped out financially. There is no legal protection against the claims of business creditors.

While the law permits creditors to make claims on all of the sole proprietor's material assets, it protects the owner's family by protecting the owner's life insurance. Both the death benefits and the cash values of the policies are generally untouchable by creditors-with the U.S. Government being the major exception. This could literally be the only asset the proprietor is allowed to keep. This protection against the claims of creditors is strong motivation toward the purchase of life insurance, especially cash value life insurance.

Business Dies with the Sole Proprietor. No disadvantage of a sole proprietorship could be more significant to a financial advisor than the fact that—without planning—the business dies when the sole proprietor dies. This means that the family's source of income is cut off.

The sole proprietor's need here is life insurance to continue the family's income. It doesn't matter whether this is called personal insurance or business insurance; it is life insurance that allows the family to maintain itself and meet its financial obligations.

In general, state laws provide that all of a sole proprietor's business activities cease at the owner's death. Unless the sole proprietor's Last Will and Testament expressly states that the business may be continued, it almost certainly will be terminated at the owner's death.

Even with a will, the business may not survive without planning. All assets pass into the exclusive possession of the personal representative of the deceased's estate to be administered under the supervision of the appropriate courts.

The laws provide further that the personal representative must pay all of the business and personal debts of the proprietor and liquidate any remaining assets. (*Personal representative* is a generic term used instead of *executor, executrix, administrator, or administratrix.*)

Only essential transactions are permitted after the owner's death. If the personal representative continues to run the business and enters into transactions not approved by the courts, the representative is held personally liable for any losses incurred as a result. If the deceased had included a 'hold harmless' clause in the will, the personal representative will not be held liable for losses incurred.

Whose Price?
"Business owner, if you were in a position today where you had to sell your business, you would want to do it at your price rather than at the buyer's price. Isn't that so?
"Chances are you don't want to sell out, but the day might come when your family must sell. When that day comes, they would rather sell at their price. But unless you take action while you're here, they might have no choice but to sell at the buyer's price.
"Wouldn't it make sense to guarantee your price so this won't happen?"

Given these facts, the personal representative is not likely to want to continue the business. In the absence of advance planning and legal authorization, it is unlikely that the business will be sold as a going concern (an intact operating business). Lack of planning, therefore, usually means heavy financial losses because assets must generally be sold piecemeal under forced-sale circumstances.

Buyers hold all the advantages in a forced-sale situation. The deceased's personal representative needs cash to settle the estate and therefore must sell the assets.

Life insurance on the sole proprietor will provide the personal representative with cash to settle the estate taxes and other debts. This means that there will now be time to sell the business. The pressure will be off, and the personal representative can get a better price for the business.

As mentioned, the business can be continued if the deceased's will gives such authorization. Without authorization in the owner's will or through a court, the personal representative would be foolish to try to continue the business because it is a no-win situation. That is, the personal representative would be personally responsible for any losses but could not pocket any gains.

Barring authorization through the will, the business legally could be continued only if all of the proprietor's heirs are adults who agree to the continuation, and if there is enough cash to pay administration costs and death taxes. If one or more of the heirs is a minor, continuation of the business would require assent of the trustee/guardian and authorization by the courts.

Even with authorization, the heirs might do a bad job of running the business. For example, considering the heirs' lack of experience, suppliers may not extend credit. Customers may not come back.

Despite this, someone may decide to continue the decedent's business, even without legal authorization. This might be the decedent's personal representative, a family member, an employee, or some combination of interested individuals.

Only rarely, however, does a sole proprietorship continue to operate profitably after losing the experience and expertise of its owner. Even if the heirs have the legal authority to continue the business, they may have little or no practical chance to succeed.

Partnerships in the U.S.

There are approximately 1,350,000 partnerships currently operating in the United States. The vast majority of all partnerships are commercial partnerships (companies that manufacture or sell products), as contrasted with professional partnerships such as those in law and medicine. Though most of the insurance-related problems are similar, the professional partnership does have a few peculiar problems, which will be discussed later.

Background on Partnerships

When two or more people agree to combine their resources and skills for mutual profit, they have formed a partnership. It is just about as simple as that. The Uniform Partnership Act defines a partnership as "an association of two or more persons to carry on as co-owners of a business for profit." The definition given by Chancellor Kent in Corpus Juris says: "A contract of two or more competent persons, to place their money, effects, labor and skill, or some or all of them, in lawful commerce or business, and to divide the profit and bear the loss, in certain proportions."

A partnership, then, is a voluntary association of two or more persons, each contributing money, property, skills, labor, or goodwill as the capital of the new firm. The partners must agree on a division of ownership and profits based on the relative value of each partner's contributions.

Types of Partnerships

There are two basic types of partnerships: general partnerships and limited partnerships.

- **General Partnership**—A general partnership is the usual type where each partner is fully active in the firm with a voice in its management. Each is an agent of the other partner (or partners) with full authority to act for the firm within the scope of its business activities. Each is fully liable for the debts of the business, and each shares in the profits.

- **Limited Partnership**—Every limited partnership has at least one limited partner and one general partner. The limited partner is not legally liable for all the financial obligations of the firm. Instead, this partner's liability is limited to the amount of his or her investment in the venture. A limited partner has no voice in management, no involvement in the day-to-day running of the business. In essence, the limited partner is largely an investor in the firm. A general partner is one who has unlimited liability and is active in managing the partnership.

Legal Facts about General Partnerships

The following are additional facts concerning general partnerships:

- **Oral or Written**—A partnership is created by an oral or written contract between the partners. This agreement indicates the basis on which the partners agree to operate. Although oral contracts may be upheld in court, prudent business practice calls for the agreement to be placed in writing in the form of articles of partnership for the full protection of each partner. Articles of partnership usually include the following items of special interest for our purposes:

  - Names of the partners
  - Name of the partnership
  - Nature of the business to be conducted
  - Capital and property of the firm
  - Capital contribution of each partner
  - Share of each partner in the profits and losses
  - Provisions for settling differences
  - Drawing account arrangements (technically, partners do not receive a salary)

- Duration of the partnership and provisions for dissolution and closure of the firm under circumstances not provided for elsewhere

How can knowledge about such a topic as articles of partnership help you in establishing relationships with partnerships? Here are a few ways:

- **Create Confidence**—One of your hardest but most important jobs in selling insurance and other financial products is helping prospects gain confidence in you. One way to do this is to ask pertinent questions that also exhibit your knowledge. These could be asked in the preapproach, approach or fact-finding.

Here, for example, are a few questions to ask in a partnership situation: *Do you have articles of partnership? Do they define the circumstances where your partnership will be dissolved? Do they speak specifically about what happens at death or disability? What do they say on these points? Did you consult your attorney in drawing up the articles of partnership? Do you have any other written agreements that address these contingencies?*

- **Get Facts**—During the fact-finding process, ask for a copy of the articles of partnership. They can provide helpful facts and insights.

For example, you will probably discover the age of the partnership, the relative "values" of capital contributed to the firm by each partner, and the shares of profit to be taken from the firm. It also lets you know which partner, if any, has more say (or a larger stake) than the others.

- **Changes**—You can get a brief history of the organization and thereby gain a feel for its current status.

For example, are there now more partners than initially? Fewer? Has the nature and scope of the business changed since its inception? How? Perhaps other businesses have spun off from this one? Have former partners started their own business? Who are these businesses? Can you get referrals to them?

- **Confidence Test**—When you ask to see one or more of a prospect's business documents, a positive response is generally a sign of confidence and trust in you.

As co-owners, the partners have equal rights to possession of the partnership assets, but only for partnership purposes. For example, they cannot assign, sell, or transfer their individual shares of this ownership.

Contrast this with a stockowner's ease of selling his or her stock to another person. When a partner dies or withdraws from the firm, this tenancy in partnership ceases to exist, and ownership of the assets of the firm is vested in (belongs to) remaining partners as liquidating trustees who are generally required (in the absence of an agreement to the contrary) to dissolve the business.

The primary exception to the requirement that the partnership be liquidated occurs when the partners have executed a buy-sell agreement. This agreement specifies that the surviving partner(s) must buy the deceased partner's interest from the heirs and that the heirs must sell this interest. Funding the buy-sell agreement with life insurance adds certainty that the surviving partners will be able to fulfill their promises.

Helping partners to assure the survival of their business is one of the important services you can provide your clients. Business continuation options and buy-sell agreements for partnerships are covered in detail later in the course.

When a partner dies, the deceased's partnership interest passes to the decedent's personal representative. But ownership as such does not pass to the personal representative; that is, the personal representative does not become a partner. By the same token, heirs cannot become partners by way of a dead partner's will.

Partnerships are formed only when living people consent to become partners. The personal representative receives from the surviving partner(s) the deceased's share of any profits and surplus remaining after liquidation of the business. The personal representative then distributes these funds to the deceased's heirs. The heirs of the deceased partner are legally entitled to get cash for the decedent's share of the business. If necessary, they can force the issue through court action. Even if the remaining partners want to continue the business, they may have to sell out just to raise cash to pay off the dead partner's heirs. With a little forethought (a written agreement and a source of buy-sell funds), this potentially devastating situation can be readily avoided to everyone's satisfaction.

- **Authority**—Each partner is a principal and has equal authority with the other partner(s), unless the articles of partnership specifically limit such authority. In partnerships of more than two members, the majority usually will rule. Unanimous consent is required for unusual decisions of major or vital importance.

  Each partner becomes an agent of the other associates. Unless specifically restricted in the articles of partnership, each partner may transact business on behalf of the firm and bind the other partners so long as the transaction is within the ordinary scope of the firm's business.

  However, a partner does *not* have authority in the following areas which are of special interest for our purposes: a partner cannot assign or sell partnership property, admit another to the firm without the consent of all associates, or sell his or her interest to another without the consent of the partners.
- **Share**—Partners share in agreed proportions in the net profits and undistributed capital of the firm and in any losses that may be incurred. In the absence of a formal agreement, the partners are assumed to share equally in any profits or losses.
- **Unlimited Personal Liability**—Each general partner is subject to unlimited personal liability for the firm's obligations. As with sole proprietorships, this is a key planning issue. If the firm becomes insolvent for any reason, including death or disability of a general partner, each partner is individually liable for *all* of the firm's debts. Consequently, business debts can eat up not only all of the assets of the firm, but every cent of the personal estates of *all* partners.

  However, partners are entitled to have business assets applied in satisfaction of business debts insofar as such assets are adequate. This, in itself, offers a very good reason for insuring the lives of the owners, with the partnership being the applicant, premium payer, and beneficiary of what is, in essence, key person life insurance. Any indebtedness not covered by business assets will be made up from the personal estates of the partners.

  Likewise, the personal insolvency of any partner can jeopardize the entire partnership business. The personal assets of the insolvent partner must be used first to satisfy his or her personal creditors. But if such assets are inadequate, the personal creditors can force a liquidation of the partnership interest in order to satisfy their claims! It's no wonder the law will not allow anyone to become a member of a partnership except by the mutual consent of all other partners!

Your Problem
"Business owner, if you had died yesterday, would your family need the money you have invested in this business? Would your partner be able to pay them in cash as soon as your family needs it?"

Common law holds that lawsuits may not be brought against the partnership, as such, but rather are to be brought against the partners as individuals. However, under the laws of some states a partnership is considered an entity (a separate being) for specified limited purposes and can sue and be sued.

If a partner dies, retires, sells his or her interest, or goes into bankruptcy, the partnership is *dissolved* immediately. The Uniform Partnership Act defines dissolution as "the change in a relation of the partners caused by any partner ceasing to be associated in the carrying on as distinguished from the winding up of the business." The partnership is not *terminated* until the surviving partners have folded the business and equitably distributed the net proceeds.

Under arrangements that are explained later in the course, the business may be continued under a new structure. But the old firm has been dissolved, and a new one will have taken its place.

- **Taxation**—A partnership as such is not subject to federal income tax. A partnership is required to file an information return (Form 1065) that reports gross partnership income, business deductions, and net taxable income. However, a partnership is a pass-through entity, not a separate taxable entity, and thus no federal income tax is imposed on the partnership itself.

As part of its reporting responsibilities, the partnership must provide each partner with a copy of Schedule K of the Form 1065. On an individual income tax return, each partner then must include his or her share of the profits—*whether or not actually distributed during the taxable year.* Partners can also take advantage of partnership losses to offset their other personal income.

Advantages and Disadvantages of General Partnerships

general partnership

Following are several advantages and disadvantages of general partnerships. (Limited partnerships have slightly different rules, and will be mentioned shortly.)

Advantages of General Partnerships. First, the partners get all the profits. Unlike corporations, there are no stockholders with whom to share the earnings of the business.

Second, unlike corporations the partnership itself is free from federal income tax. Also, partnerships are not subject to the accumulated earnings tax, as some C corporations are.

Third, any losses or profits of the partnership pass directly to the partners as personal income for federal income tax purposes. This means that any partnership losses can be used by the partners to offset income from other sources, thereby reducing their individual federal income tax bill. This is unlike a corporation, where corporate losses can be used only to offset the past or future profits of the company. This treatment of partnership losses can be particularly important to partners who have significant income from other sources.

Finally, as contrasted with sole proprietorships, partnerships permit a pooling of capital and talent and a sharing of risk. For example, two people may decide to open a wholesale distributorship. They pool their financial resources to lease space and purchase inventory. One partner may have a knack for dealing effectively with people. The other is more detail oriented and excels at the bookkeeping.

Disadvantages of Partnerships. First, the death of a partner may automatically end the partnership—with serious consequences to all concerned. These consequences can be avoided if an *ownership transfer plan* (buy-sell agreement) is implemented and funded.

The second major disadvantage lies in the unlimited personal liability of the partners. Business debts can devour all of the business assets. If the debts cannot be satisfied out of these partnership assets, creditors can attack the personal assets of every partner.

Limited Partnerships

limited partnership   The Uniform Limited Partnership Act defines a limited partnership as "a partnership formed by two or more persons having as members one or more general partners and one or more limited partners. The limited partners as such shall not be bound by the [financial] obligations of the partnership beyond the extent of their investment."

To grasp the concept of limited partnership, think of limited partners as investors. This is, in fact, what they are—namely, investment vehicles, as opposed to regular business partnerships. They put their money into the partnership as a financial investment, taking none of the day-to-day responsibilities for managing the business. In addition, their limited liability keeps them from losing more than they invest.

Your Price
"Business owner, if your partner had died yesterday, do you think the heirs would sell their interest to you at a price you would consider fair? (Wait for a response.) How would you go about setting a price that both you and the heirs would consider fair?"

The general partners conduct the day-to-day business for the entire partnership and have *unlimited liability* for the firm's obligations. Most limited partnerships deal in investment ventures such as oil and gas drilling, cattle breeding, and real estate.

Legal Facts Concerning Limited Partnerships. The purpose of the limited partnership is to enable a person who has money to enter into partnership with others, without being exposed to the unlimited liabilities of a general partner. If the business fails, the limited partner can lose no more than the capital invested in the firm.

- The limited partner cannot be active in the management of the firm.
- Usually the limited partner receives a specified share of the profits.
- The partnership interest of a limited partner may be reached (attached) by any of his or her creditors.
- Upon dissolution of the partnership, the limited partner's share has priority over funds due the general partners, but is subordinate to claims of the firm's creditors.
- Upon death, the limited partner's personal representative is entitled to the deceased's portion of assets and deferred profits in order to

settle the estate. Death of the limited partner does not dissolve the partnership. However, the death of a general partner can end the business unless the partnership agreement stipulates otherwise.

If a limited partnership develops too many characteristics of a corporation—even though it calls itself a partnership—it will be taxed as a corporation. Four major corporation characteristics are considered in determining whether or not a limited partnership will be classified by the IRS as a corporation for tax purposes. If the limited partnership has more than two of the following characteristics, it probably will be taxed as a corporation:

- Freely transferable ownership interests
- Continuing of life
- Participation of limited partners in management of the partnership
- Limited liability of the limited partners for debts of the partnership

There are many gray areas concerning what constitutes each of these four characteristics. Thus, the limited partnership agreement must be carefully drawn—and followed—to avoid corporate tax status.

family limited partnership

Family Limited Partnership. A version of the limited partnership, the family limited partnership (FLP) is sometimes used in estate planning, especially when there is a family business interest. In a family limited partnership, a property-owning family member transfers property such as real estate and stocks to the partnership, receiving partnership units in exchange. Younger generations receive limited partnership units while the senior, donor member(s) receive general partnership units, maintaining control of the assets. Ultimately, the majority of the ownership interest is transferred to the limited partner, with the general partner retaining only a minimal number of units but retaining, as the general partner, management and responsibility for the assets.

A family limited partnership is a legal agreement that allows business owners and their children to address several business-succession and estate planning needs all at once. It works like this: Mother and father create a limited partnership in which mother and father are the general partners, and their children (and/or grandchildren) are the limited partners.

Mother and father transfer property to this partnership. The property may be stocks, bonds, cash, the family farm or stock in the family C corporation. Mother and father no longer own these assets. In exchange for their contributions of property to the limited partnership, they receive units of ownership in the family limited partnership.

Over time, mother and father will give ownership of most of the partnership to the children, following a "planned gifting" program. But they will not give up control over the partnership until both have died.

Understanding what happens as a result of setting up such a limited family partnership requires an understanding of some tax laws that are beyond the scope of this course. In essence, however, the primary benefit is its ability to reduce the size of mother and father's taxable estate, thereby reducing the amount of federal estate tax at death. This benefit comes as a result of the planned gifting program and is based on tax laws allowing less-than-asset value to be placed on the C-corporation stock of the business held by the children. The reduced value is based the fact that non-marketable stock and minority interest stock are allowed to be discounted for IRS purposes. This discounted price results in lower gift tax at time of giving and lower estate tax at death.

The limited partnership arrangement lets mother and father, as the general partners, control the business despite the fact that they may own less than 1 percent interest in the limited partnership.

There is a lot more to know about family limited partnerships, but this basic information provides enough of a foundation for you to be familiar with the concept and to ask your family-owned C-corporation owners if they have examined the concept with their legal advisers and accountants.

professional partnership
Professional Partnerships. Another way of differentiating partnerships is to divide them into commercial (business) partnerships and professional (personal service) partnerships.

Typical professional or personal service partnerships are legal, medical, engineering, architectural, accounting, dental, advertising, consulting firms, realtors, and brokers. Though most of the characteristics of professional partnerships and commercial partnerships are the same, professional partnerships do have a few distinctive characteristics.

Partners often meet the challenge of work a little better and to make more money in a partnership than working alone. For example, a survey by the National Income Division of the Office of Business Economics shows that lawyers operating in partnerships earn more on average than lawyers operating alone. Surveys among other professional groups would undoubtedly indicate the same situation. Because this is true, an obligation is created. The partners owe each other some measure of responsibility for their enhanced positions.

When one of the partners dies, the survivors are keenly aware of this debt. Your opportunity is to help partners realize this obligation before one of them dies, while there is still time to use the best solution.

The Difference between Partnerships. How does a professional partnership differ from a commercial partnership? An important difference lies in the character of assets. Most commercial partnerships are capital intensive. That is, a substantial part of the value of the firm is represented by its physical assets such as real estate, machinery, fixtures, equipment, materials, supplies, inventory, and so forth. In short, tangible assets are an essential part of the business. These capital assets constitute a large part of the value of each partner's interest in the business, directly or indirectly. The more capital intensive, the more likely there is debt.

With professional partnerships, the situation is quite different. They are usually not capital intensive. The real value of the typical personal service partnership lies in the training, knowledge, skill, experience, character, and reputation of the individual members of the firm. As a consequence, the firm's income is derived almost entirely from the personal services rendered by the partners.

Capital, in the form of tangible assets, is generally incidental to the operation of most professional partnerships. Little, if any, income results from these physical or tangible assets.

Similarly, commercial partnerships frequently allow a good-sized portion of their profits to remain in the business. Partners in personal service firms are far more likely to withdraw the bulk of the earnings. The result is often minimal working capital within the professional partnership.

A Key Difference for Professional Partnerships. There is one additional way in which commercial and professional partnerships differ. Partners must be qualified members of a given profession. A deceased partner's heirs cannot come into the business as partners unless they too are qualified professionals in the same field.

Under the Uniform Partnership Act, professional partnerships face the same threat of liquidation after a partner's death as do commercial partnerships. The need for a solution to the problem is just as urgent and vital with professional partnerships as with commercial partnerships.

Corporations

A corporation has been defined by Ames and Ames in their authoritative work *Private Corporations* as "a body, created by law, composed of individuals united under a common name, the members of which succeed each other, so that the body continues the same notwithstanding the change of individuals who compose it, and is, for certain purposes, considered as a natural person." From this definition, we may derive the following important facts about the corporate form:

- A corporation is created by law.
- A corporation is invisible and intangible. It cannot be seen, as can the buildings and machinery owned by the corporation.
- A corporation is an intangible artificial being—an entity separate and independent from the owners of its capital stock. As an entity, it is viewed as an artificial person and is subject to many of the privileges and restrictions of a natural person.

Corporations are divided into two classes: (1) those organized and conducted for profit and (2) not-for-profit (nonprofit) organizations, which are generally created for educational, charitable, religious, or public purposes. Nonprofits generally pay no federal income taxes. Corporations organized for profit are the only ones to be considered here. They include all corporations organized for business purposes.

C corporation

closely held corporation

There are a few kinds of "for profit" corporations. Most corporations are *C corporations,* named after subsection C of the Internal Revenue Code. C corporations not traded on the stock market are referred to as *closely held corporations.* Corporations traded on the stock markets are referred to as publicly held corporations.

S corporation

Second are *S corporations,* which resemble partnerships in many ways, including some tax aspects.

**personal service
corporation**

**professional
corporation**

Third are *personal-service corporations,* which are primarily service oriented as opposed to product oriented. They are taxed somewhat differently than C corporations. One variety of personal service corporation is the *professional corporation,* operating in such services as dentistry, medicine, and accounting.

Chief Characteristics of Corporations

Because a corporation is a separate legal entity, certain characteristics distinguish it from the sole proprietorship and the partnership.

1. **Limited liability of stockholders**

   The corporate form of business enables persons to own part of a business and yet limit their losses (in case of failure) to the amount of their investment in the capital stock. This is true even if the assets of the corporation are not sufficient to pay its own debts. (Sometimes creditors will not extend credit to the corporation; they will insist that stockholders sign *personal notes.* This calls for life insurance to cover the debt, which will be discussed later.)

   The corporation itself is responsible for its own actions and liabilities; creditors have no claim to the personal assets of a stockholder to satisfy claims that are strictly against the corporation.

2. **Continuity of existence**

   Corporations can go on indefinitely. An owner's death, withdrawal, mental incompetence, or bankruptcy does not in itself interrupt the corporation's continued existence. The same is true in the event of a stockholder's retirement or change in the corporation's stockholders, directors, or officers.

3. **Ease of transferability of interest**

   A stockholder is an owner of part of a corporation. Ownership is evidenced by a stock certificate issued by the corporation. Unless restricted by contractual agreement, such a share of stock may be transferred from person to person simply by an endorsement on the certificate by the owner, without necessarily affecting the operations of the corporation. It can also be transferred at death through the stockholder's will.

4. **Capital may be increased**

It is a common occurrence today for corporations to increase their capital stock for expansion purposes. Issuing new shares of stock for this purpose can affect the proportion of ownership among stockholders. This, in turn, can affect who controls the company. As will be discussed later, life insurance can play a key role in providing money to the corporation so that ownership and control need not change at the death of an owner.

Advantages of Corporations

Following are some f the corporate form of doing business. Included are contrasts with proprietorships and partnerships.

- **Tax Status**—The decision to incorporate is often influenced by the fact that owner-employees of C corporations can buy tax-deductible fringe benefits for *themselves*. Except for contributions to their own retirement plans, and their own group health insurance premiums, such deductions are not generally available to sole proprietors, or partners, or to most owners of S corporations.

  For example, if two *partners* buy group life insurance to cover themselves and their three other employees, they can deduct only about three-fifths of the premium for federal income tax purposes. Specifically, sole proprietors, partners and S corporations employees who own more than 2 percent of the outstanding stock or more than 2 percent of the voting power of the corporation can deduct the portion of the group life insurance premium that covers the three other employees, but not the portion that covers them. In general, only the cost of fringe benefits covering employees is income tax deductible by the business.

  If the two partners incorporated the business, they could deduct the entire premium, including the portion that covers their own lives. The law's rationale is that corporate owners who work for their own corporation are generally considered employees of the corporation for federal income tax purposes. Partners in a partnership, sole proprietors and S corporation owners are not considered to be employees.

- **Income Tax Levels**—Many corporations manage to pay little or no income tax. This is possible if times are bad, and expenses exceed income. It is especially likely to happen if there are major items of depreciation, deductible fringe benefits, tax credits, and high salaries.

The corporate alternative minimum tax helps assure that large corporations with real economic income will pay at least a minimum amount of income tax. The alternative minimum tax is discussed at the end of this chapter.

- **Continuity**—With partnerships, even when there is a written agreement to continue, the technical fact of dissolution always occurs when a partner dies. Death of a sole proprietor has a similar result. This is not true of corporations. Legally, even the deaths of all the stockholders at once would cause no dissolution of the corporation.

  Obviously, legal considerations are not the sole considerations. The death of a key executive-and almost certainly the deaths of all the key executives-would shake the business to its foundations.

- **Limited Liability**—Every cent owned by a sole proprietor or partner is subject to the debts of the business. But the owner of a corporation is not liable for any corporate debts (if incurred legitimately).

  If the business folds, the stockholder might lose every cent invested in the business, but no more. The owner's house and all personal property, including shares of stock in other businesses, are safe from the creditors of the failing corporation. This is a key advantage of the corporate form. Only the corporate assets themselves are subject to the claims of creditors.

  As a practical matter, however, the protection of limited liability is lessened in corporations which are relatively new or whose financial situations are somewhat unstable. Lenders often require one or more stockholders in these corporations to sign personal notes for business loans. Such debts become their personal responsibility if the corporation defaults.

  Not all corporate credit is arranged this formally, of course. Customary trade credits, for example, would usually not be a legal responsibility of the owner personally if the corporation defaults.

Whether it is personal or corporate credit, there is often a need for life insurance whenever there is debt. Common reasons for incurring debt are to buy materials for inventory, loans for expansion of the business, and purchase of equipment. Life insurance on the owners or other key people is not only a prudent move; the creditor sometimes requires it.

Since business loans, including normal trade credits, are continuing factors in most businesses, there is almost always a continuous level of substantial debt. This means continuous life insurance to cover the debt, either permanent insurance or renewable term insurance.

Ownership Transfer of Partnerships

No one can legally force an unwanted partner on a partnership. If a partner wants to withdraw from the business, he cannot simply sell his share to someone else without regard to the other partners. They can refuse or accept the offered partner.

Here is a distinct difference for a stockholder. The stockholder has complete freedom legally to transfer shares to *anyone*. The stockholder may give away shares, will them, or sell them at any price—all without legal interference from the other owners of the corporation. They, too, enjoy this same flexibility of ownership. The corporation is blind to the identity of its owners.

Disadvantages of Corporations

Following are some drawbacks of the corporate form of business.

- **Double Taxation on Dividends**—Most publicly held corporations (and some that are closely held) distribute net earnings as dividends to stockholders. Net earnings are profit left after paying corporate taxes. A stockholder receiving such dividends must report them as taxable income on that year's Form 1040. Thus, the earnings are taxed again as personal income to the stockholder. An accompanying illustration demonstrates double taxation.

- **Ease of Transfer**—The ease with which stockholders can transfer shares of stock to others is an advantage. The ease with which a stockholder's associates can transfer his or her shares of stock to others may be a disadvantage to that shareholder.

  Consider a two-person corporation in which one owns 60 percent and the other 40 percent of the shares. The business runs smoothly; the owners like and respect each other. Then the majority owner, for whatever reason, transfers ownership to someone else.

  What happens to the minority stockholder's position then? It certainly won't be the same as before. The minority stockholder might even be voted out of a job. Worse yet, the minority stockholder might have little choice but to remain on the job despite an intolerable new boss. Legally, the minority stockholder is free to sell out, but who would buy into this position that the minority stockholder is trying to escape?

Double Taxation* Example		
Corporate Income Tax	Corporate Earnings	$85,000
	Less Income Taxes Paid by Corporation (34% marginal bracket)	−10,900
	Earnings Available to Stockholders	$74,100
Individual Income Tax	Dividends to Stockholders	$74,100
	Less Personal Taxes Paid by Stockholders (28% marginal bracket)	−20,748
	Net to Stockholders	$53,352
*2010 income tax rates.		

- **Regulations**—A price is often paid for any advantage. The owner who incorporates will pay at least the price of increased "red tape" in the form of government reports and regulations.

Creation of a Corporation

Most states pattern at least part of their incorporation laws after the Model Business Corporation Act. This act is a uniform code that may be adopted with or without modifications-or not at all-by the states.

As a rule, firms seek incorporation in the state in which their principal activities will be conducted. However, companies doing a large interstate business usually incorporate in a state where the laws are most favorable. Some of the considerations governing the choice of the state in which to incorporate are the following:

Taxes and Corporations. States or municipalities generally levy a franchise tax, a real property tax, and a personal property tax. Most states also have a corporate income tax. Some states have more favorable corporate taxes than others and thus have become favorites for those seeking corporate charters.

Powers Granted to a Corporation. The powers granted to a corporation are specified in its charter, which is to a corporation what a constitution is to a state. The application for a charter is called the *articles of incorporation*. The charter is granted when the articles of incorporation (the application) are approved by the proper state official (usually the Secretary of State).

As soon as the charter is granted, the corporation may be authorized to operate its business. The incorporators issue capital stock certificates to the original stockholders and call the first meeting of the stockholders. At this meeting, the stockholders usually elect corporate officers and a board of directors, and adopt bylaws.

Corporate Management

Some corporations have hundreds or thousands of stockholders. Some have only one or two. In large corporations, the vote of all stockholders on matters of daily routine would be impossible. The exercise of authority is therefore divided among three groups: stockholders, directors, and officers. The stockholders elect the board of directors. The directors formulate company policies and elect the officers. The officers execute the company policies.

In most closely held corporations, the scope is much smaller. The same individuals may hold several positions. For example, closely held corporations typically have a president, a vice president, and a secretary-treasurer. These three officers might also be the directors of the closely held corporation. The same three are probably stockholders as well, quite possibly the only stockholders.

Stockholders of Corporations. The stockholders are the people who own the capital stock of a corporation and therefore own an interest in its assets. Stockholders as such do not necessarily participate actively in the management of the company. They do not have to be employees of the corporation.

A stockholder has certain basic rights in the corporation, including the following:

- sell or transfer shares of stock
- subscribe for additional issues of capital stock if and when issued (*preemptive right*)
- receive dividends, if declared, in proportion to the number of shares of stock owned
- in the event of liquidation, share in the assets in proportion to the number of shares of stock owned

- attend and vote at stockholder's meetings. Note, however, that not all kinds of stock have voting rights. Usually "common stock" has this right.

Board of Directors of a Corporation. The board of directors is elected by the stockholders and constitutes the managing body of the corporation. The directors can act only as a group. As individuals, they are without power to transact the business of the company.

The board meets at least as often as called for in the bylaws. It selects the administrative officers and thus delegates its management authority to the company officials.

The official decisions of the board are recorded in the minutes of its meetings. These minutes are the corporation accountant's authority for certain entries pertaining to the corporate capital. Quite often, decisions relating to the purchase of insurance need to be authorized by the directors and officially documented in the minutes of the board of directors meeting.

Corporation Officers. The bylaws of a corporation generally provide that certain officers are to be elected by the corporation. Corporate officers and their functions might typically be as follows:

- The president is usually the chairman of the board of directors and is the chief executive officer. The president generally presides at meetings of the stockholders and directors and makes appointments as needed.
- There may be one or more vice presidents. They are responsible for specified operations, such as engineering, production, or sales.
- The secretary keeps the official records of the corporation, including minutes of meetings.
- The treasurer is the custodian of company funds and supervises their receipt and disbursement.

Capital Stock

The charter of the corporation gives it the power to issue a specified number of shares of capital stock, which is another way of saying "stock." (The two terms are interchangeable.) The amount of stock originally authorized is determined largely by how much the incorporators want to raise as initial capital.

The corporation does not need to issue the entire number of shares authorized at any one time, or ever. But if it does issue all of this stock and then desires to issue more later, it must first receive approval of the state.

Authorized capital stock may be sold for money, property, or service. When it is sold and certificates issued, the authorized stock is known as *issued capital stock.* Capital stock that is authorized, but not issued, is called *unissued* capital stock.

> ***Par or No-Par Value Stock in Corporations.*** Each share of capital stock may have a par value or it may be of no-par value, according to specifications in the charter. Par value is simply a nominal figure. It has no necessary relationship to the real value of the stock. It is merely the amount at which it is recorded on the books of the company. For example, many companies set par value at $1.

Originally issued stock may be sold by the company at par or above par value. If state regulations permit, it may even be sold below par. If no-par stock is issued, it is carried on the books at the amounts for which it is sold.

> ***Classes of Capital Stock.*** The two most usual classes of stock are common and preferred. If a corporation issues only one class of stock, it is called common stock. Practically all common stocks carry the privilege of voting for all stockholders. Since the claims of the common stockholders are subordinate to the claims of other classes of stockholders, relatively greater risk is attached to the ownership of common stock.

However, the power to declare dividends rests with the board of directors, who are elected by the common stockholders. Thus, the greater risk may be rewarded with larger dividends. Most closely held corporations issue only one class of stock.

Preferred stock usually does not carry the right to vote, but it normally enjoys the right to receive dividends before dividends are paid on the common stock. In the event of liquidation of the corporation, the preferred stockholders will receive the return of their investment before the common stockholders receive anything.

Closely Held C Corporations

This text deals primarily with closely held corporations as contrasted with publicly held corporations. Also known as *closed corporations and close corporations*, closely held corporations constitute the vast majority of all corporations. They are seldom owned by more than a handful of people, each of whom is engaged actively in the day-to-day management of the business. The stock is not listed on the stock exchanges and rarely changes hands except at death, retirement, or a major realignment within the firm.

There is a tendency to view corporations as formal business organizations—rigidly structured, managed, and administered. The fact is that many closely held corporations are not this way at all. Some corporations are little more than sole proprietorships with "incorporated" added to the name. Although a sole proprietor might have become president by incorporating, nothing substantial has changed in the day-to-day operation of the business. He or she is the sole stockholder and therefore continues to make all of the decisions just as before.

Other corporations might be partnerships turned corporate. The old partners are now stockholders, but the business goes on much as before despite the fact that one is now president and others are vice presidents. One noticeable difference is that certain major decisions must be recorded and annual meetings of the stockholders must be held. Such annual meetings are also likely to be informal, perhaps taking place at a dinner table over a cup of coffee.

Characteristics of Closely Held Corporations

The general characteristics of a corporation apply to both closely held and publicly traded corporations. However, the personal structure and the methods of operation of the typical closely held corporation bring about some important differences. Understanding these distinguishing characteristics will help you come to know the closely held corporation's needs for business life insurance.

- **Union of Ownership and Management**—In closely held corporations, each stockholder usually has a threefold role as a director, an officer, and an employee as well. The owners are the managers. Therefore, death of an owner means death of a key employee of the corporation.

- **No Ready Market for the Stock**—A characteristic of a public corporation is that its shares may be bought and sold on the stock exchanges. In closely held corporations, however, a few employees are the major stockholders.

Ordinarily, the only persons interested in buying the shares of a deceased closely held stockholder are the surviving stockholders or possibly a competitor. The stock owned by the deceased stockholder's family generally is worthless to them unless it is sold or unless they own enough of the stock that they can use their influence to hire themselves as paid employees.

In and of itself, stock of a closely held corporation generally provides no income for the family. As will be discussed later, this is a key reason why having a buy-sell agreement is so important for all stockholders of closely held corporations. Here is where your "sale" will be made, and funding the buy-sell is where insurance enters the picture.

- **Limited Liability: Theory Versus Reality**—Many creditors will insist that loan notes be signed not only by the appropriate corporate officer of a closely held corporation, but also by the corporate owners personally. If the corporation cannot repay the loan, the owners are personally responsible to repay it. Thus, the legal limit of a shareholder's liability is meaningless in such cases. Insurance to cover these personal notes is just as important to the stockholder's family as is insurance on a homeowner's life to cover the mortgage.

- **Dividends and Unreasonable Compensation**—In virtually all closely held C corporations, the owners are also salaried employees of the corporation. In theory and in practice, they can set their own salaries at whatever levels they wish. If given free choice, it would be foolish for owners to pay themselves dividends instead of salaries because salaries are tax deductible by the corporation while dividends are not. Closely held corporations generally pay no dividends.

  Were it not for a provision of the law dealing with *reasonableness of compensation*, the owner-employees of a corporation could reduce or even eliminate corporate taxable income simply by paying themselves extremely large (and tax-deductible) salaries. The reasonable compensation provision allows the government, in effect, to force the corporation to treat a portion of the owner's salary as a dividend.

In cases where the IRS audits a corporation's tax returns and is successful in challenging the reasonableness of compensation, it will limit the corporation's tax deduction for that owner's salary to a certain dollar amount. The balance of what had been treated as salary must then be "un-deducted" by the corporation and reported instead as taxable corporate income.

In general, the IRS determines reasonableness of compensation by reviewing the entire compensation package (including fringe benefits) of the owner-employees. The IRS compares this total compensation with that paid in comparable companies.

S Corporations

Someday you will be talking with a prospective client who will tell you that his or her business organization is an S corporation. This section covers much of what you need to know about this form of business organization—its structure, ownership, tax status, the impact of death, and other insurance-related considerations.

S corporations get their name from that part of the Internal Revenue Code that gave them birth, namely, *Subchapter S of Chapter 1 of the Internal Revenue Code*. Although 1982 legislation officially designated them as "S corporations," you might run into their older names of Subchapter S corporations, Sub S corporations, or simply Sub S. The form used by S corporations for reporting their income is Form 1120S. (C corporations use Form 1120.)

Similarity to Partnerships

Although S corporations have some of the important features of closely held corporations, they are taxed in part like partnerships and in part like corporations. Here's how they resemble a partnership:

- As with partnerships, there is generally no federal income tax levied on S corporations. (Certain levels of capital gain and passive income such as interest are taxable if certain conditions exist.)
- As with partnerships, S corporations are pass-through forms of business. The owners of S corporations are taxed on their proportionate share of the earnings of the corporation.

It does not matter whether the earnings are actually distributed to the owners or remain with the corporation as undistributed earnings. Either way, the owners must report earnings personally. Expenses and losses are passed through directly to the shareholders.

The popularity of S corporations fluctuates with changes in income tax law and the tax status of individuals and their businesses. Corporate tax rates can sometimes exceed individual rates, and individual rates can exceed corporate rates at different income levels. Decisions to incorporate as a C or S corporation will often vary based on the relative income tax brackets of the individual owner(s) and the corporation. At certain income levels, business owners would rather have income taxed to a C corporation, rather than have it passed through to their individual taxes via an S corporation structure.

For example, if there are good business tax deductions, such as in the start-up phase of the business, an S-corporation can be a more favorable organization from a tax standpoint during the early loss years. An "S" election allows corporate losses to be deducted on the returns of individual shareholders. When the business becomes more profitable, the S election may be changed to a C corporation to have profits taxed to the corporation rather than the individual owner(s). Additionally, losses of an S corporation may be used to offset income earned outside the business if this is desirable from an income tax perspective.

- Because all earnings-even undistributed earnings-are reportable by the shareholders, S corporations are not subject to the accumulated earnings tax. (The accumulated earnings tax, covered later in detail, is a tax on certain levels of profit retained by closely held corporations.)
- There is no such thing as unreasonable compensation in S corporations. As you recall, the concept of unreasonable compensation is the way by which the IRS makes sure that tax-deductible salary is not really a disguised dividend. In S corporations (as in partnerships and sole proprietorships), there is no tax on the corporation itself, since it is a pass-through form of business. This allows the stockowner to take out all corporate income without the normal double taxation on C corporate profits.

Similarity to Corporations

S corporations resemble closely held corporations in the following ways:

- Both S corporations and closely held corporations have continuity of life. They can legally continue as going concerns despite death of a shareholder.
- Each shareholder's liability is limited to the amount of his or her investment. This is true in both closely held corporations and S corporations.
- Legally, shares of ownership are readily transferable. In practice, however, since S corporations cannot have more than 100

- shareholders, their shares lack marketability as do those in most other closely held corporations.
- Some states impose corporate taxes on S corporations just as if they were regular corporations.

Distinct Characteristics of S Corporations

S corporations differ from closely held corporations or partnerships in the following ways:

- The legal limit of shareholders in an S corporation is 100. In C corporations the number is unlimited.
- Shareholders of S corporations may be any individuals except nonresident aliens. (This prohibition against nonresident aliens exists because nonresident aliens pay no income tax to the U.S. Government.) In addition to individuals, estates, and certain trusts also are eligible to be shareholders.
- Amounts contributed by the S corporation to qualified retirement plans are generally deductible. This is true regardless of whether or not the employee is a shareholder. Amounts paid by the corporation for other fringe benefits such as group term life insurance or disability income insurance are deductible by the corporation for coverage on all employees except those employees owning more than 2 percent of the corporation. In addition, such over-2-percent-shareholder employees must report these corporate payments as taxable income. This is not the case with C corporations.

Regular corporations are generally referred to as C corporations, taken from the Internal Revenue Code subchapter that establishes them. This terminology is useful, especially to distinguish S corporations from C corporations.

- To become an S corporation, all the shareholders of a corporation must vote in favor of it.
- Revoking the status of an S corporation requires consent of one or more shareholders owning 50 percent or more of the voting stock.
- The corporation must be domestic.
- There can be only a single class of stock.
- Certain events cause the S status of a corporation to be terminated. These disqualifying events include having more than 100 shareholders or having an ineligible shareholder.

Why Use an S Corporation?

The most important reason why S corporation status is elected is that the owners can take advantage of corporate expenses and losses to reduce and offset their other personal income at tax time each year. In this respect, S corporations are similar to partnerships: business losses and expenses pass through to the owners personally as offsets against current income.

Since it is usually new businesses that anticipate losses, it is therefore new businesses that most frequently elect S status as opposed to regular corporate status. And because such losses are typically "paper losses" brought about primarily by cost recovery (depreciation) of capital assets, it is often new businesses with substantial capital investments that elect S status.

According to the IRS, about 40 percent of all S corporations report net losses. To understand why losses are so important for tax purposes, look at an S shareholder's ownership as a tax-sheltered investment.

Two characteristics of many tax shelters are that they produce a real dollar income to the investor, while also providing paper losses for federal income tax purposes. For example, an S shareholder might receive, say, $30,000 in distributed earnings while his or her share of depreciation losses might come to $20,000. The result would be taxable income of only $10,000 instead of $30,000.

By way of comparison, losses in a C corporation do not pass through to the stockholders. Even the corporation itself cannot deduct such losses in the current year; it must wait until a year in which it has a taxable gain to offset.

There is one notable limitation relating to the pass through of losses of an S corporation. Each shareholder can deduct losses only to the extent of his or her basis. Basis is the amount invested in the business. The higher the basis, the more a shareholder can deduct.

Why Not Partnership?

A question to ask at this point is why not just become a partnership? While partners can benefit from a pass-through of losses, partnerships do not have the advantages of continuity of life, limited liability, and ease of ownership transfer that S corporations have.

Table 1-1 S Corporation Compared with Partnerships		
	S Corporation	**Partnership**
Liability	Shareholders' liability is limited to the amount of investment	Unlimited for general partners; limited for limited partners as long as they retain their status as limited partners
Management	Board of Directors with specific authorities	Extent of authority between general and limited partners may be vague
Shareholders	Limited to 100	Unlimited participation
Dividends	Typically none are paid	No such thing
Unreasonable Compensation	No such thing	No such thing
Accumulated Earnings Tax	No such thing	No such thing
Federal Income Taxation	All losses and earnings of the S corporation pass through to shareholders. The shareholder is taxed; The corporation is not taxed.	All losses and earnings of the partnership pass through to partners. Partners are taxed as individuals. The partnership is not taxed.
Transferability	Stocks transferred by endorsement	May be more complicated, especially with limited partnerships
Formation	Specific requirements under federal law	Usually defined under state law. Same as S corporation
Taxable Years	December 31 or by approval under federal law	Same as S corporation
Deductibility of payments for group insurance and other fringe benefits (other than qualified retirement plans where contributions are deductible even for coverage of owners/partners)	Only deductible for employees holding 2% or less of the company's stock. S corporation's owners can deduct 100% of the cost of fringe benefits on non-shareholder employees, but generally not on themselves.	Can deduct 100% for nonpartner employees. Partners can generally deduct a specified portion of the group health premiums covering themselves.

Another appealing feature of S corporation status is that it allows the stockholders to vote to go back into a regular corporate form. Usually, the intent is to do this once the major tax losses and high early expenses are used up.

Limited Liability Companies (LLCs)

limited liability company

An important innovation in forms of business organizations is the limited liability company (LLC). All states now allow LLCs, and their numbers are mushrooming nationally into the hundreds of thousands. LLCs are very similar to limited liability partnerships (LLPs are partnerships in which all partners are sheltered from liability for partnership activities).

A limited liability company combines some basic concepts of partnerships, C corporations, and S corporations. Owners of LLCs are called members. In many respects, a limited liability company is like an S corporation, but has some additional advantages, and fewer disadvantages.

Limited liability companies combine the personal liability protection of a corporation with the tax benefits and simplicity of a partnership. In other words, LLCs have the benefit of being taxed only once on their profits, and the owners of the LLC, or "members," are not personally liable for the LLC's debts and liabilities. In addition, LLCs are more flexible and require less ongoing paperwork than an S corporation.

Here are some of the characteristics that make LLCs so popular.

Membership in LLCs

- Unlike S corporations, which have a limit of 100 owners, limited liability companies have no limit on the number of members. Members may be individuals or entities. Generally, start-up costs will exceed those of a simple partnership or corporation due to the more complex nature of the operating agreement.

- Unlike S corporations, which prohibit nonresident aliens as owners, limited liability companies have no restrictions on foreign ownership.

- Unlike S corporations, which allow only one class of ownership, limited liability companies allow different classes of ownership.

- LLCs are attractive to family businesses that want to keep control in the family. How is this accomplished? Generally, ownership interests cannot be transferred without the consent of other members.

Limited Liability of LLCs

Unlike general partners who have unlimited liability for debts of the partnership, the financial liability of LLC members is limited in the same way that shareholders of C and S corporations are limited. That is, a member's financial liability for debts of the business is limited to his or her contribution to the LLC. Unlike limited partners, LLC members can be active in the management of the business.

A limited liability company is valuable for professionals because it protects the assets of each member against the negligence of the other members. There is no shelter from liability for an individual's own actions.

LLCs are Taxed as Sole Proprietor, Partnership, or Corporation

For federal income tax purposes, LLCs may be treated as a sole proprietorship, partnership, or corporation. Tax regulations provide rules to determine how a business entity is classified for tax purposes. If a business has a preponderance of the characteristics of a regular (C) corporation, it will be treated for federal income tax purposes as a corporation.

A business with only one owner can elect to be taxed as a sole proprietorship or as a corporation. Businesses with two or more owners can elect a partnership or corporate tax status. The tax filing status will determine other characteristics, benefits and disadvantages of the business entity as described throughout this chapter. Most of the discussion on LLCs in this section assumes the use of the corporate form of organization.

LLCs in General

LLCs are most useful for new businesses that are just forming, or for partnerships that want to become LLCs. Existing partnerships or S corporations converting to LLC status may do so tax-free. There will be no gain or loss recognized on the transfer of assets and liabilities so long as each partner's or owner's percentage of profits, losses and capital remains the same after the conversion.

If an existing C corporation elects to become an LLC, it will be a taxable event for federal income tax purposes. The corporate shareholders will be responsible for any taxes due on corporate gains, because they will be taxed as though the C corporation assets had been distributed to them.

In most states, dissolution of the LLC is brought about by several events, including death. However, most states allow the remaining members of the LLC to vote to continue the LLC. Depending on the state law and the LLC's operating agreement, this election to continue may require approval of all members, or only a stipulated percentage of them.

Professional Corporations and Professional Associations

At times, an individual practitioner or a group of practitioners of the same profession decide to incorporate. In most states, C corporations that provide professional services, in areas such as dentistry, accounting, engineering, actuarial science, performing arts, architecture, law, consulting, or medicine, are required to form a *professional corporation*. State laws define what constitutes a professional service, but they typically require a license to operate in that state. They are owned, organized, and operated by licensed practitioners of a common profession as an individual or group corporate practice rather than as a sole proprietorship or partnership.

Some states use the term "association" rather than "corporation." When you see "John Jones, M.D., P.A.," the P.A. stands for Professional Association and has the same meaning as incorporated. "Ltd." (Limited) is sometimes used as well. State laws establish these terms, so there are variations by state.

Some professional corporations are also personal service corporations. The term *personal service corporation* is a federal income tax categorization used by the Internal Revenue Service to describe corporations in which the principal business activity is performing personal services and where those services are performed mostly by owner-employees.

The main difference in these terms, then, is that the term *professional corporations* refers to state regulation and licensing, whereas the term *personal service corporation* refers to the federal income tax treatment of professional corporations.

Of course, not all professionals choose to incorporate. Some find it more advantageous to function as sole practitioners or as partners, while others elect S corporation status.

Characteristics of a Professional Corporation

Although state laws are not uniform, there are a few basic ways in which virtually all professional corporations differ from other closely held corporations.

Ownership of Professional Corporations. Ownership is limited to licensed practitioners in a given profession. For example, only licensed dentists may be shareholders in a corporation established to practice dentistry. This stipulation applies to initial shareholders and future owners alike.

However, when a shareholder dies, the decedent's estate can legally be the shareholder for a specified duration, while the estate is being settled. The estate cannot vote or participate in management decisions, however.

When a shareholder of a professional corporation dies, the surviving owners may purchase the deceased's stock within a specified period of time—usually a few months. If they choose not to buy the stock within that time and if no other qualified buyer is found, the corporation itself must acquire it—usually within 6 months. This legal requirement makes it critically important for every professional corporation to have a buy-sell agreement specifying how the price will be determined and how funds will be provided.

Scope of Operations of a Professional Corporation. The practice of a professional corporation is generally limited to one field of endeavor. For example, if several optometrists incorporate, they could not expand into unrelated products or services.

Limited Liability of Professional Corporations. Although no professional is protected against his or her own negligence, a professional corporation can protect a practitioner against liability for the negligence of an associate. Since the primary risk of a practice is malpractice liability, this limitation can be significant.

Board Membership in Professional Corporations. Only practitioners may be officers or board members. They do not have to be shareholders.

Prospects for Professional Corporations. State laws are not uniform as to which professions may incorporate. Some states restrict the eligible professions to as few as four, while other states allow incorporation or association by practitioners of any profession that requires licensing by the state. Among the professionals who may generally incorporate are the following:

- Physicians
- Surgeons
- Attorneys
- Accountants
- Dentists
- Optometrists
- Engineers
- Architects
- Chiropractors
- Osteopaths

- Actuaries
- Psychiatrists
- Podiatrists
- Radiologists
- Pathologists
- Opthamologists
- Pharmacists
- Psychologists
- Social Workers
- Marriage Counselors

- Veterinarians   - Chiropodists

Since there is a wide variance as to who may form a professional corporation or association, check your own state laws to determine your prospects in this area.

Insurance Needs of Professional Corporations

Professional corporations and associations offer about the same advantages as closely held commercial corporations, including tax deductibility of insurance-related fringe benefits for the owner-practitioners.

- The rules for qualified retirement plans for professional corporations are the same as for all other corporations. There are key people to be insured to cover losses that will be incurred as a result of their death or disability.

- Establishing buy-sell agreements is the only sound and prudent way to handle the orderly transfer of ownership at death of a shareholder-practitioner. Life insurance remains the surest, simplest, and most cost-efficient way to fund the agreement.

- Definite plans should be established as to what will be done if an owner becomes disabled for an extended period of time. Funding for these plans should include disability income insurance on the owners' lives.

The personal life and disability income insurance of each owner must be considered.

Personal Service Corporations

As described above under professional corporations, a personal service corporation's principal business activity is performing personal services. At least 95 percent of the stock must be owned by employees performing the personal services. Corporations in this category are those engaged in accounting, actuarial science, architectural, consulting, engineering, health, law, and performing arts. Many professional corporations are also personal service corporations and are taxed accordingly. IRS takes the position that it is what the company does rather than who the shareholders are or what they call themselves that determines the tax status.

Federal Income Tax Rates Personal Service Corporation		
Tax Year 2010 Taxable Income	Personal Services Tax Rate	Corporate Tax Rate
$0 to $50,000	35%	15%
$50,001 to $75,000	35%	25%
$75,001 to $100,000	35%	35%
$100,001 to $335,000	35%	39%
$335,001 to $10,000,000	35%	34%
All personal service corporations are taxed at 35 percent on all taxable income, starting with the first dollar. Regular corporation tax rates are graduated, but they are not for personal service corporations.		

There are two key points about taxation of personal service corporations. First, there is a flat tax rate paid on profits at the corporate (entity) level. That is, every dollar of income is taxed at the same 35 percent. Second, at most levels of income, they are taxed higher than C corporations, since the benefit of the graduated corporate income tax rates is not available. Because of this, professional corporations are not as popular as they once were. Corporations try to distribute all profits in the form of wages to the employee-shareholders performing the services. This in effect can eliminate the negative results caused by the flat 35 percent tax.

Joint Ventures

A joint venture is a business relationship resembling a partnership. Joint ventures may exist between individuals, corporations, partnerships, or any combination of these. When persons or groups come together in a joint venture they do so for their mutual advantage.

One may bring special skill, knowledge, or judgment; another may contribute property; another may be the source of money. Each person is important. Without this pooling of money, material, and service, the specific project could not be handled adequately.

Syndications

Syndications are much like joint ventures in that they are the joining together of two or more individuals or entities. As a matter of fact, a syndication can be a joint venture. A syndication may also take the form of a general partnership, a limited partnership, a regular corporation, or an S corporation.

Comparison of Five Types of Business Organizations					
Comparison Item	Sole Proprietor	Partnership	C Corporation	S Corporation	Limited Liability Company
How Established	No formal document needed. Local business license.	May use either oral or written agreement. Local business license.	Certificate of incorporation must be filed with state. Local business license.	Certificate of incorporation must be filed with state.	Articles of organization filed with state
Length of Life	Dies with sole proprietor. Can be sold by beneficiary.	Death of any general partner dissolves partnership.	Perpetual—Not affected by death of a stockholder.	Perpetual—Not affected by death of a stockholder.	Continuity generally disrupted by death, retirement, or resignation. (See applicable state law)
How Managed	Entirely by the sole proprietor.	Jointly by the partners, but one partner can obligate the partnership.	By board of directors (elected by shareholders) through officers appointed by the board.	Same as regular corporation.	Jointly by members if so specified by operating agent.
Ownership of Business Property	Title held by sole proprietor.	Title held by partnership entity. Not assignable by individual partners.	Title held by corporate entity.	Same as regular corporation.	Title held by LLC entity.
Business Liabilities	Sole proprietor fully personally responsible.	Each partner fully liable for all the partnership debts. If partner A can't pay share, partner B must pay all.	Corporation is liable for all debts incurred, and for all employee acts when acting for the corporation. Stockholders are not liable above their investment.	Same as regular corporation.	Limited liability of members.
Income Taxation	All income taxable to sole proprietor.	A partnership is not subject to income taxation, but is required to file an informational return.	Corporation pays corporate tax on income over expenses, before paying dividends to stockholders.	Income taxes shareholders-employees similar to partnership. No regular corporate taxes.	Each member pays taxes on share of LLC income designated a noncorporate entity

Comparison of Five Types of Business Organizations					
How Profit is Distributed	Sole proprietor gets it all.	Partners share in proportion to their partnership interest.	Board of directors determines the amount of dividends to be paid and profit to be retained.	All income is taxed to shareholders. Any amount retained for business purpose is after-tax dollars.	Members share proportion to their interest.
Termination of Business	Sole proprietor closes door and settles accounts.	Death of a partner dissolves partnership. If one partner wants out, partnership must be dissolved.	Vote of stockholders, bankruptcy, violation of certificate of incorporation (by court).	Same as regular corporation.	Operating agreement can require a number to obtain interest beyond transferring interest.

The limited partnership is the most popular form. This is probably because a limited partnership offers the limited partners the advantages of limited financial liability, tax-deductibility of depreciation and other business losses on their individual tax returns, and noninvolvement in the management of the project.

Most syndications are the joining together of a relatively small group of investors for the purchase and development of a large financial undertaking—generally the purchase and development of real estate. They are usually formed by a developer (syndicator) needing investors to put up cash to accomplish the investment objectives.

Additionally, however, there are professional, ongoing syndications—organizations whose only reason for being is to act as syndicators. Their twofold function is to (1) seek out people with large sums of money to invest and (2) seek out investment opportunities that meet the investors' goals for rate of return and level of risk.

Income Taxation of Businesses

A few summary facts about business taxation follow. They are presented here as a brief overview. The text will also include a discussion of tax information as planning ideas are discussed.

Taxation of Sole Proprietorships, Partnerships and S Corporations

With sole proprietorships and partnerships, the proprietor or partners are the only taxpaying entities. The business itself pays no income tax. All business income and expenses are passed through to the owner(s) for income tax purposes.

In general, sole proprietors, partners and S corporation owners are taxed directly on the net income of the business. By law, the gains and losses of the business pass through to the owners without the business itself being subject to tax. In computing the net income subject to tax, the owners' salaries are generally not deductible. In general, sole proprietors, partners and S corporation owners may deduct the entire cost of group insurance and other fringe benefits on their employees. Starting in 2003, the premiums for health insurance on the owners and their dependents are fully deductible. Contributions to a qualified retirement plan are fully tax deductible, as long as they are reasonable and meet plan requirements.

It helps to think of partnerships, sole proprietorships, and S corporations as pass-through businesses, because the income from the business passes through to the owners and is taxable to them as individuals. The business itself is not taxed. In contrast, C corporations are taxable entities.

Taxation of Corporations

With corporations, there are two possible taxpaying entities to pay life insurance premiums. One is the corporation itself. The other is the owner(s) as an individual(s). Having the entity with the lowest taxable income pay nondeductible premiums is the least-expensive option.

By law, C corporations are taxed on the net income of the business; gains and losses are not simply passed through to the shareholders. In computing the net income subject to tax, all salaries and fringe benefit costs are generally deductible by the corporation. This includes salaries and fringe benefits for shareholders who are also employees. What remains after all deductions is the profit of the business, upon which the corporation is taxed.

If a C corporation later distributes these profits to the shareholders, the result will be a dividend. Dividends are taxable as ordinary income to the shareholders and are not deductible by the corporation. For this reason, owner-employees try to avoid or minimize dividend treatment through a number of devices. One way is through deductible items such as salaries and fringe benefits for shareholder-employees.

Through various penalties and restrictions, the IRS tries to force distribution of corporate profits as dividends, because dividends aren't deductible by the C corporation. Among these techniques are disallowing deductions for excessively high salaries and fringe benefits for the shareholder-employees, and imposing penalty taxes on corporations that accumulate too much profit without distributing it.

S corporations are taxed in a manner similar to partnerships. Professional corporations are generally personal service corporations taxed at 35 percent on all taxable income; there are no graduated tax rates.

Federal Income Tax Rates for C Corporations	
Taxable Income	Tax Rate
$0 to $50,000	15%
$50,001 to $75,000	25%
$75,001 to $100,000	34%
$100,001 to $335,000	39% *
$335,001 to $10 million	34%
Over $10 million	35%

* The 39% rate from $100,001 to $335,000 of income is called a bubble because it is preceded and followed by 34% rates. This seemingly illogical 5% temporary blip has the purpose of recapturing from the corporation the dollar benefit of the 15% and 25% tax rates. That is, a corporation with taxable income of exactly $335,000 will have paid tax of $113,900, which is exactly 34% of $335,000. A second bubble kicks in at 38% from $15 million to $181.3 million. Then the rate returns to 35%.

Alternative Minimum Tax (AMT)

alternative minimum tax

The corporate alternative minimum tax (AMT) is an income tax that attempts to make certain C corporations pay a "fair" amount of tax despite deductions, credits, and other tax preference items that reduce their regular income tax to a small amount. Tax preferences are tax items that allow larger than normal deductions, or exemptions for certain types of income, from regular tax rules. A corporate AMT must be paid instead of the corporation's regular tax if the AMT amount is higher. The tax applies only to C corporations, not to S corporations.

Until 1998, C corporations could be subjected to the AMT regardless of size. Beginning in 1998, however, "small" corporations are exempt from the tax. A "small" corporation is a C corporation with no more than $7.5 million in average annual gross receipts for the 3 previous tax years. For corporations in existence less than 3 years, the initial qualification for exemption involves average annual gross receipts of no more than $5 million. Generally, a corporation will be exempt from the AMT in its first years of existence.

Determining the alternative minimum tax is a complex procedure. Alternative minimum taxable income (AMTI) is the corporation's regular taxable income, increased by adjustments for tax preferences. These preferences included certain excess depreciation, tax exempt interest, life insurance cash value increases that exceed annual premiums, and death benefits received in excess of the policyowner's basis. Seven-five percent (75%) of AMTI is subject to a flat 20 percent tax. Since 20 percent of 75 percent is 15 percent, you can think of the tax as 15 percent of AMTI. To the extent that the alternative minimum tax paid exceeds the regular income tax for the year, the corporation may use this excess to offset regular tax liability in future years.

The corporate alternative minimum tax can have an adverse effect on key person life insurance. Urge your corporate clients who may be subject to this tax to increase the amount of life insurance they plan to buy on key employees. If the tax comes into play at the key employee's death, there will be enough after-tax proceeds to meet the firm's needs. For example, if the amount of needed key person life insurance is $1 million, add $150,000 to it for a face amount totaling $1,150,000. Then, following the key person's death, if there is a tax at all, it will be a maximum of 15 percent, and so the net proceeds would be $1 million.

Project: Feedback

Are you looking for a way to speed up the process of learning about business and business insurance? If so, try this project.

From businesses you currently do business with, choose three individuals with whom you have a good relationship. Go to those three people and explain that you are interested in business insurance and that you would like to discuss ideas you will be studying.

KEYS TO SUCCESS

To be successful in the business market, you need to follow a process, understand the prospect, and see yourself as a businessperson.

Follow a Process

The business owner is a challenging prospect. For many, their businesses not only provide income, but are the consuming passion of their lives. It is not uncommon for the owners of small businesses to invest most of their time, energy and money in the development of the business. Faced with constant challenges in the daily activities of their businesses, it is often difficult to get them to take time to discuss how you can help them. This book will offer many ideas on how you can overcome this problem.

To be successful in this market, you must be able to help the business owner establish realistic financial goals, gather relevant information about the owner's current situation, analyze the situation, devise a plan that bridges the gap between the present reality and desired future, implement the plan, and then monitor it. In some ways, marketing to business owners is very much like marketing in the personal market. After you have identified the prospect, you must

1. establish financial goals
2. gather relevant data
3. analyze the data
4. develop a plan for achieving goals
5. implement the plan
6. monitor the plan

Despite the similarities, there are differences. However, business situations are often more complicated than personal ones, balancing the needs of the owner, the business, and its employees with tax and profit considerations. To be successful, you must not only understand your products and how they can be applied to meet your prospect's needs, but you must also understand the prospect's business and the business environment in which those needs exist.

Understand the Prospect

To be successful in this market, you must understand what is important to business owners. You need to use all your relationship skills to get the owners to take a realistic look at what they are creating and what will happen to their businesses in the future. As with other prospects, you must learn to listen carefully to what owners are saying to you. You must ask probing questions to determine their goals, not just for themselves, but also for their businesses.

> ### Exit Strategy
>
> "Business owner, what is your exit strategy from your business? How are you going to get out? Do you have any plans for leaving your business for retirement, or for what may happen if you die or become totally disabled? This is the kind of work I do. Let me help you with this."

To be successful, you must also be able to speak the language of business owners. You must be knowledgeable enough about the specifics of their businesses to make them feel confident in talking to you. You must also be knowledgeable about business structures and taxation to help them identify problems they might not otherwise notice.

Your understanding of business structures and what will happen in the event of an owner's death, disability, or retirement will allow you to help owners plan for these events. In this regard, the continuity or termination of businesses are of the greatest importance.

As an insurance expert and financial advisor, helping your business prospects plan for the distribution of their business assets can be the most valuable service you provide. For many owners, the business represents not only the way they generate income for themselves and their families, but also their major investment for the future and, often, a way of life.

For business prospects, the issues of life, death, disability, and retirement become even more critical. The element that makes their businesses valuable—their personal involvement-depends on their continued ability to work.

These are only some of the reasons why business owners need the advice of trained financial advisors. Insurance and other financial products can provide the solution to many of the problems created by the death or disability of a business owner. They can also provide at least part of the solution to the transfer of business assets when a business owner decides to retire. Equally important, your role as a financial advisor, working in conjunction with the business owner's other professional advisors, can encourage the owner to address these critical issues before it is too late.

See Yourself as a Businessperson

Reflect on your experience as a financial advisor. Where have you had your greatest success? If you are like most financial advisors, your greatest success comes from your natural market—people who think like you, act like you, and share common values with you—in other words, people like you. If you want to relate to business owners, you will need to see yourself as a businessperson–an entrepreneur. It is your identity as a businessperson that will help you relate to business owners because you have so much in common with them.

Strategic Planning

It does not matter what you call yourself because, in the final analysis, you are a businessperson. Do you think of yourself as a businessperson? What is your business? What do you want your business to be? Who are your customers? Who would you like to have as customers? What are your goals for your business? To maximize your successes, you need to answer questions like these.

When you think of successful people, you can almost always identify some common characteristics. Generally, successful people have a clear sense of direction, and they develop and effectively implement their plans. This rarely happens by accident.

In your role as a financial advisor, you ask your prospects to establish financial goals and participate in the fact-finding process. The purpose of fact finding is to determine where your prospects are, so you can analyze their situation and develop a plan that will help them achieve their goals. This may involve recommending products and services to your prospects in order to implement the plan.

Engaging in this process for your business activities is called strategic planning. Strategic planning involves developing a comprehensive plan and strategies for the future of a business. It is establishing long-term direction, setting specific performance objectives and standards, developing strategies and action plans to achieve objectives, executing action plans, and evaluating results.

The process of strategic planning is a fundamental and important aspect of managing a business. The product of the strategic planning process is a detailed plan for business direction and course of action. The advantages of strategic planning are that it

- focuses your thinking
- provides you with a clear sense of direction
- guides you in setting specific, quantifiable goals

- helps you recognize and respond to opportunities and threats that affect your goal achievement
- aids you in coordinating and prioritizing your activities
- helps you establish realistic strategies
- positions you to be proactive rather than reactive

Your Business Plan

Anyone thinking of starting a business would not attempt it without a sound business plan If one needed to obtain financing, it would be almost unthinkable to approach a bank or potential financial backer without a plan that would lead to success, and subsequently repay the debt. As a businessperson, you should have a working business plan and follow it.

It is important to plan, and most people do plan, at least informally. You may do year-end planning as part of making goals for the New Year. Or you may plan because you want to reach a specific income goal or because the primary company you write for requires you to have a production plan for the coming year. Perhaps you plan because you want to buy a house or a car, fund college educations for your children, or save for retirement.

But have you ever written a plan that spans more than one year-a plan aimed at defining and achieving your long-range goals for the future? Have you taken the time to complete a fact finder on yourself? Do you know where you want to be both personally and professionally in 5 or 10 years? Establishing and achieving your personal and professional goals requires you to decide where you want to be, look at where you are now, and develop a plan that will move you toward your goals.

In its simplest form, a business plan is a written document that lists your business goals and describes how you will achieve them. But it should be much more than that. It should be the end result of strategic planning. It should be a dynamic, flexible document that guides you toward achieving your business goals. It is your blueprint for success.

It is not the intent of this book to review the concept of a business plan. It is simply to make the point that you are a businessperson and have much in common with other business owners that you approach. You need to think of yourself as a business owner and you need to act like one. That means developing and following a business plan, as well as investing a great deal of time, energy, and money into making your business successful, just like your prospects do.

In this book we will cover the skills you need to survive in the highly competitive business market. You will learn

- about business people and the things that are important to them
- how they make decisions and how to guide them to the right decisions
- how to analyze their financial situations to define needs and develop solutions to the problems they face
- the tax ramifications of different approaches to their problems
- ways to present your solutions that will help you establish business clients

---

Ben Feldman, Legendary Insurance Salesman

Careful planning, methodical organization, dogged prospecting, detailed research, innovative approaches, and relentless persistence made the late Ben Feldman synonymous with sustained sales greatness. He was called the most successful life insurance advisor of all time, and he may have been the most remarkable salesman in sales history. In July 1974, Fortune magazine pointed out that Ben Feldman had sold more life insurance than most of the nation's 1,800 insurance companies had on their books.

When Feldman died in 1993, he left a record that almost defies belief. His lifetime sales volume exceeded $1 billion of insurance—a career average of more than $20 million per year. His peak year exceeded $100 million, and his record for a single day was a $20 million sale. He worked in the business market, selling the types of plans discussed in this book. Moreover, Feldman did not work in a large metropolitan area, corporate center, or wealthy retirement playground; he worked in East Liverpool, Ohio, a river town of 20,000 near where Ohio, Pennsylvania and West Virginia converge.

CHAPTER REVIEW

Key terms and concepts are explained in the Glossary. Answers to the Review Questions and Self-Test Questions are found in the back of the book following the Glossary.

Key Terms and Concepts

sole proprietorship	C corporation
general partnership	closely held corporation
limited partnership	S corporation
family limited partnership	personal service corporation
professional partnership	professional corporation

limited liability company   alternative minimum tax

Review Questions

1.   List the distinguishing characteristics of sole proprietorships.

2.   Explain the differences between a general partnership and a limited partnership.

3.   Name three ways in which closely held C corporations can be distinguished from publicly held C corporations.

4.   Compare the federal income taxation of an S corporation with that of a partnership.

5.   List three characteristics of limited liability companies.

6.   Look at the chart "Comparison of Five Types of Business Organization."
     a. What is the federal income tax status of C corporations?
     b. What is the length of life of a C corporation?
     c. What is the length of life for an S corporation?

7.   What are the 10 forms of business in the United States?

8.   Is it legal for a business to change from its initial form? For example, can a partnership become a C corporation? Briefly explain your answer.

9.   Which of the 10 forms of business pays federal income tax?

10. Compare the advantages and disadvantages of a general partnership and closely held C corporation for small business owners.

Self Test Questions

Instructions: Read chapter one first, then answer the following questions to test your knowledge. There are 10 questions. Circle the correct answer, then check your answers with the answer key in the back of the book.

11. Which of the following statements about sole proprietorships is true?

     (A) The sole proprietorship form is advantageous for small firms; incorporation is advisable in any case where the business is large enough to qualify for a charter.
     (B) Operations are more restricted than in the case of a limited partnership.
     (C) Sole proprietors are not eligible for qualified retirement plans.
     (D) The sole proprietor's financial liability is unlimited and unshared.

12. An S Corporation is

    (A) a corporation which is taxed like an unincorporated business
    (B) any business which elects to have earnings taxed as a distribution of dividends
    (C) a subsidiary corporation with a nonprofit tax status
    (D) normally owned by 90 or more stockholders

13. Which of the following is characteristic of limited liability companies?

    (A) They are taxed as corporations.
    (B) They allow only one class of ownership.
    (C) Members cannot be active in the management of the business.
    (D) They have no restrictions on foreign ownership.

14. A joint venture most closely resembles

    (A) a partnership
    (B) an S corporation
    (C) a sole proprietorship
    (D) a professional corporation

15. Which of the following is true with regard to a limited partnership?

    (A) The income is taxed at corporate levels.
    (B) Both limited and general partners enjoy limited liability equal to their capital contributions.
    (C) The partnership interest of the limited partner can be reached by any of his or her creditors.
    (D) Upon dissolution of the partnership, the general partner has priority in obtaining any assets before the limited partners are paid.

16. A professional corporation differs from other closely held corporations in which of the following ways?

    (A) There may be only 35 stockholders in a professional corporation.
    (B) A professional corporation is taxed at special lower income tax rates.
    (C) Ownership is limited to licensed practitioners in a given profession.
    (D) A buy-sell agreement is not needed with professional corporations.

17.   Which of the following is (are) a true statement regarding federal taxation as it applies to corporations?

    I. Dividends are paid out of profits that have already been taxed as corporate income.
    II. All undistributed earnings are taxed at capital gains rates.

    (A) I only
    (B) II only
    (C) Both I and II
    (D) Neither I nor II

18.   Which of the following statement about partnerships is correct?

    I. Each partner must obtain the consent of all other partners for each business transaction.
    II. Each partner can sell his or her interest to a third party without the consent of the other partners.

    (A) I only
    (B) II only
    (C) Both I and II
    (D) Neither I nor II

READ THE FOLLOWING DIRECTIONS BEFORE CONTINUING

The questions below differ from the preceding questions in that they all contain the word EXCEPT. So you understand fully the basis used in selecting each answer, be sure to read each question carefully.

---

19.   All of the following are characteristics of the corporate form of business EXCEPT

    (A) unlimited life
    (B) lack of transferability
    (C) limited liability
    (D) centralized management

20. All of the following statements about partnerships are correct EXCEPT

   (A) In a general partnership, the partners bear personal liability for the firm's obligations.

   (B) A general partnership is essentially two or more individuals operating a business for profit.

   (C) A partnership can be incorporated or unincorporated depending on the number of partners.

   (D) A limited partnership is simply an unincorporated organization with at least one general and one limited partner.

Learning Objectives

An understanding of the material in this chapter should enable the student to

1. List day-to-day concerns of business owners.

2. Describe the impact of an owner's death on a business's capital, suppliers, and employees.

3. Name three financial statements used by business owners.

4. List four ways that knowledge of financial statements could be beneficial to you.

5. Define a balance sheet and list its three main components.

6. Define an income statement and list its two main components.

7. Explain cash flow and why it is important to a business.

This chapter introduces the potential problems that may result from the death or disability of a business owner for the business, its employees and the business owner's family. It then reviews the business owner's concerns about the day-to-day operation and long-range goals of the business. Financial statements and how the advisor can use basic accounting statements to analyze the business' strengths and weaknesses and uncover problems that insurance can solve are also discussed.

THE EFFECTS OF THE BUSINESS OWNER'S DEATH OR DISABILITY

Your success in the business insurance market will increase as you begin to understand the unique concerns and problems of business owners. This textbook focuses on three main areas of planning opportunities with business owners: insured buy-sell agreements, key person insurance, and some basic estate planning topics.

This section will help you identify the business owner's risks that can be solved by business life insurance. In addition, it will increase your knowledge of the non-insurance-related concerns that impact business owners and can affect business insurance-related problems. Your understanding of how business owners think and your ability to effectively communicate how your products can meet their needs will help you encourage them to take action.

Problems Resulting From the Death of the Business Owner

There is a very simple reason why the death of the business owner often means the end of the firm. No business can run without money. Working capital is needed every day to keep the doors open. It doesn't matter whether they are service businesses, retail establishments, manufacturing companies, or any other kind. They need money to pay such things as insurance premiums, utility bills, and printing costs; to make rent or mortgage payments and meet the payroll; to buy telephones, fax machines, and photocopiers and to keep them in good repair; to pay for cleaning services, waste removal, carpet cleaning, and general building maintenance. There are taxes and business licenses. They need supplies and furniture, and computer hardware and software—the list goes on and on.

If they are in a product business, as opposed to a service business, they need money to buy inventory. If they are in the manufacturing business, they also need money to buy raw materials and machinery.

When business owners are alive, cash to finance these purchases and pay these expenses usually comes from two sources. One is suppliers who will provide needed credit. Suppliers generally give an extension of time to pay the bill. The second source is banks or other financial institutions that will loan money to the business for a variety of purposes. Such bank loans may be automatic in the sense that they are authorized in advance up to a certain dollar limit. Then, whenever the business needs to purchase something or, say, meet a payroll, it writes a check on its line of credit at the bank.

Loss of Credit

However, business owners often overlook the fact that their deaths destroy the main source of new money—credit. When business owners consider the consequences of death, their natural inclination is to think in terms of control of the business. They want to make sure that no "outsiders" wrest the helm from the family. But no one lends money to a dead person. Likewise, seldom does anyone lend money to a dead person's business or to a dead person's estate unless there are valid reasons to believe that the business will continue to operate.

The Effect on Goodwill

In business circles, goodwill is an asset. It is the extra value of a business resulting from its good reputation, its prestige or its acceptance in the community. If a business is sold as a going concern, part of the sale price will be based on the estimated value of its goodwill. It is a value over and above the value of the tangible assets of the business.

However, all of the value of goodwill is lost entirely if the business shuts its doors and stops doing business, and then sells the assets piecemeal. That is, *goodwill has value only if the business continues to operate*. Averting this potential loss is another good reason for business owners to make plans for the sale or transfer of the business as a going concern upon the death of an owner.

The Response of Creditors

As soon as a business owner dies, suppliers will generally suspend deliveries, customers will cancel orders, and banks will cancel the line of credit to the business. But this is not all.

Suppliers do not fade away; they come to call, with palms upturned. They want to be paid what they are owed. If the business has outstanding loans, bankers also come to collect.

The only persons who will not come to call are those who could render help to a dying business—the old customers and the employees. The customers would like to help, but they have their own businesses to concern them. They cannot wait for delivery of goods; they need them today. So they must place their orders elsewhere. The employees—the workers, the technicians, and the salespeople—also would like to help. But after all, they have their own families and responsibilities. They cannot wait to see if their jobs will be available tomorrow. They must know today, so they may take their services elsewhere.

Even if a business has sufficient cash on hand to honor its debts, pay its loans, and meet its payrolls, it has so little chance for survival without its leader that most state laws discourage continuation after the owner dies. While it is possible that someone else could take over in the crisis and restore life to the business, this is usually unlikely.

Consider this example: the chief financial officer of a communication consulting firm tried to continue running the company after the death of its owner. Unfortunately, the chief financial officer lacked the deceased owner's marketing skills and customer contacts. Within a year, new contracts had declined drastically. The surviving spouse of the deceased owner was forced to sell the company at a drastic reduction in the underlying value.

Legal Implications

State probate laws usually make it unattractive for someone else to continue a business by holding such an individual personally liable for any losses. The state's long experience dictates the need to protect the creditors of the business and the deceased owner's family. It is worthwhile to note that protection of creditors comes first; the family gets what is left, if anything.

Naturally state laws make an exception if a deceased owner had provided for the business to be continued, but many business owners are not well enough aware of the consequences of death to have made such effective plans.

Other Possible Problems

The problem of death obviously has been oversimplified in this short discussion. There are different results, for example, when a business has more than one owner. In some cases, the death of a key employee other than the owner may have more disastrous results than the death of the owner. Federal estate taxes at death will weigh more heavily on the families of some business owners than others, depending on the size of the estate and whether or not there is a surviving spouse.

Problems Resulting from the Disability of a Business Owner

The disability of a business owner or other key person is even more likely to occur than death. The consequences can be financially disastrous to the business and to the owner's family.

A stroke could take away an owner's ability to walk, talk, or travel to the place of business. Such a disabled person probably could not perform the necessary duties of running the business. This would mean coming up with extra money to hire someone to run it. Without this, the business would likely begin to fail.

In addition—and unlike the results of death—the continued disability of an owner or other key person means that the family's financial resources will be severely drained by ongoing medical bills and living expenses of the disabled person.

The impact on employees, creditors, and suppliers is much the same with the "living death" of disability as those that arise with the actual death of a business owner. Uncertainty about the future of the business will lead employees to look elsewhere for employment. Creditors will likely want their money quickly and probably will extend no more credit. Suppliers are likely to demand cash if new orders are to be delivered. In addition, the business owner's retirement plans are likely to be derailed.

As with the problems that result from the death of a business owner, the problems of disability generally can be met and overcome if plans are made and adequately funded before catastrophe strikes. It is in the funding process that life insurance and disability insurance play the starring role. In Chapter 6 we will examine the problems created by disability that can be solved through insurance.

Solutions Take Money

With planning, the business owner can solve or lessen the problems caused by death and by disability. Almost invariably these solutions require money, in large amounts, immediately.

By safeguarding a business against the potentially disastrous financial results caused by death and disability, the family's standard of living is protected. So, too, is the standard of living of the families of the employees and the families of the creditors.

It is easy to see the tragedy caused by the death or disability of a business owner. Why, then, do so many business owners not make appropriate plans? There are two likely reasons:

- No one has explained the problems to the business owners or convinced them of the importance of planning to avoid these problems.
- Business owners are too involved with day-to-day problems of running a business to even think about long-range problems—and for most business owners, death or disability is considered a long-range problem. They think it happens only to others tomorrow, not to them today.

CONCERNS OF THE BUSINESS OWNER

Consider the day-to-day concerns of a business owner. If you understand how a business owner thinks and what he or she thinks about, you should be able to explain long-range problems and solutions in a manner they will understand.

Profit

The purpose of business is profits. Income should exceed expenses, or the business is on its way to bankruptcy. In the pursuit of profit the business owner is concerned with every element of the business: rent, employee wages and benefits, cost of products, cost of credit, inventory, sales promotion and advertising, state and federal regulations, selling costs, prices, competition, taxes, contributions and general overhead, employee relations, and customer relations.

All of these elements have a bearing on profits. Unless the business owner has a thorough knowledge and control of all these integral aspects of the business, profits will be affected adversely, income will suffer, the owner and the owner's family will face financial difficulty, and so will the business.

Credit

Obtaining credit is one of the chief preoccupations of all business owners. They work hard to keep their credit rating in good condition. The credit "markets" are frequented not only by the small business owner but by the giants of industry as well. Every bond listed on the stock exchange represents a loan that was made to a business. These account for only a small fraction of the total loans needed by businesses every year. A sudden halt to the ordinary trade credits between a business owner and suppliers or customers could result in the collapse of many businesses.

Operations

Operational problems are acute in this competitive era. Automation and imports from countries with low labor costs are playing havoc with many businesses in this country. Efficient production and service operations are essential to survival, and new, improved methods must be a constant concern and objective. Technology improves and changes incessantly. Production costs affect prices. In turn, prices affect sales in a competitive market. Poor sales mean low profits.

Cash Needs

In any growing business, cash is always needed for payroll, payables, inventory, equipment, and the like. As the business grows, so do the cash needs. There never seems to be excess cash in a growing, successful business. This provides you with an opportunity to emphasize the need for your products. Without business insurance, the business is not likely to survive the cash-drain emergencies that typically follow the disability or death of the owner or other key employee.

Competition

Competition is the very heart of the free enterprise system. It necessitates wise and efficient control of every element of the business. Quality of goods and services, prices, sales promotion, and advertising are of the utmost importance in a competitive market.

In the competitive market, the courage, imagination, and ingenuity of the business owner or manager is especially vital. Many companies have floundered because their owners and managers lacked the imagination to foresee trends in new products, style, and price. Other firms have gained prominence and prestige because their management exhibited "vision."

Success attracts competition. Competition, in turn, creates pressure to keep costs down while maintaining profit margins. This is a source of concern for many business owners. If profit margins are minimal now, what will happen to the profit margin if a key person dies or becomes disabled? What will happen to the profitability of the business if inexperienced family members take over at the owner's death? Life and disability insurance proceeds would provide welcome financial relief in such situations.

Service

Customer service is, of course, of paramount importance. People will discontinue patronizing a business from which service is poor and/or delivered in an inconsiderate manner. In order to attract and retain customers, all successful businesses know that a business must provide quick, efficient, and pleasant service. The company that foolishly disregards this basic success factor soon will lose business and profits.

Personnel

These can be the most serious of all management problems. Every individual in the company will view every decision that affects a company's employees differently. The same policy that is welcomed by half of the employees might be intolerable to the other half.

For example, a company decision to offer child day-care benefits might be enthusiastically received by employees with preschool age children, but not by those older employees who have parents living with them and would much prefer an elder-care program.

Every unresolved personnel problem affects the welfare of the organization and intensifies all the other seemingly unrelated problems of the business. Some of the more common personnel problems are absenteeism, inefficiency, unreliability, high turnover, and, of course, compensation inequities. Every human problem must be handled with fairness, tact, and firmness.

Labor

Akin to personnel problems are labor relations. Personnel management deals with employees as individuals; labor relations deals with employees as a group. A fair and cooperative attitude by both management and labor is a company asset of inestimable value. A good labor-relations environment does not just happen. It is a prize that must be won through careful planning, fair-mindedness, and hard work.

Good labor relations are of vital importance not only to management and labor, but to the public as well. In some cases labor disputes can be so serious as to threaten the health and welfare of the whole nation. Consider, for example, labor disputes in such important industries as food, communications, defense production, automobile, steel, transportation, and shipping.

Economics

Economic conditions and trends are a constant threat and worry to the business owner. If general business conditions are good and the foreseeable future is favorable, the business owner can expand the firm's credit and inventory and carry on a vigorous and progressive business program.

If the outlook is doubtful and the long-term trend is unfavorable, then credit often is tightened and inventories curtailed. The wrong judgment on economic conditions and trends can do great harm to a business and often bring financial disaster.

Consider, for example, a business that plans to open new branch offices or begin marketing a new product line. In large part, these plans are based on projections of the strength of the national or regional economy. If the projections prove incorrect, the new ventures could harm company profits or lead to significant losses.

Consider a business that decides to borrow large sums from a bank in order to acquire new equipment or build a new plant. The decision may be based on an assumption that current interest rates will remain reasonably stable. If interest rates rise significantly higher than projected, interest expenses could impair the firm's ability to meet the loan obligations.

Public Relations and Business Ethics

Business owners cannot afford to ignore the communities they serve or the effects of their products and services on the general public. Products must be safe. Business practices must be consistent with efforts to conserve or improve the environment. Advertising must be presented accurately and fairly. Credit charges must be fully disclosed. Company accounting practices must be beyond reproach. Business ethics has found its way from the business pages to the front pages over the last few years.

While a consumer-oriented attitude makes good sense for any business owner, such an attitude demands conscious thought, planning, and effort.

Government

Rulings and regulations of federal, state, and local governments, though generally constructive in purpose, can nonetheless be very harmful to a business or industry. Examples of regulations that could harm industries include those with praiseworthy purposes such as prohibiting the use of certain coloring dyes in foods and certain chemicals in clothing, and requiring conformity to certain non-pollution or safety standards.

Then there are the numerous and often complicated reports which businesses must file with various government agencies. Often these reports are a time-consuming and expensive burden to complete.

For example, manufacturing companies and others must file complicated reports that permit the appropriate government agencies to monitor their compliance with the Occupational Safety and Health Act (OSHA). Businesses that institute certain retirement programs must fulfill the reporting requirements and restrictions of the Employee Retirement Income Security Act (ERISA). Recent legislation to curtail or prevent unethical business conduct or terrorism can exact a heavy burden on daily business practices and the cost of doing business.

Dynamic Markets and Technology

Think of the business owner who owns an obsolete computer or whose inventory is full of goods that have been rendered useless by a new product. Risks and frustrations of this sort can weigh heavily on the minds of business owners. Consider the potential problems faced by heirs of a business owner who dies during a period of major technological or economic change.

Tax Laws

Business owners are concerned about the implications of new tax legislation, which is being amended constantly. How will it affect them? They will welcome any assistance you can provide. You will want to clearly demonstrate how your products and services can help them take advantage of the tax laws.

Your Challenge

These and other problems become burdens and worries on the mind of a business owner. They are relentless, persistent problems that affect the success of the business and ultimately the financial well being of the owner and the owner's family. These are the things that are on the owner's mind when the financial advisor shows up at his or her office.

With all these daily problems to manage, few business owners stop to give serious consideration to the problems that would arise in the event of their death or disability, or the death or disability of one of their key employees.

Skill and preparation are required for an advisor to capture the attention and imagination of a business owner who is preoccupied with so many everyday problems. Yet none of these day-to-day problems is as serious and potentially destructive as the problems to which the owner gives little thought—the problems caused by the termination of the owner's own economic value through death, disability, or old age.

In every business insurance situation you will be translating the lost economic value caused by the owner's death or disability into specific problems and solutions. You will be showing how life insurance is the best means of providing money for these solutions:

- to pay debts
- to buy a deceased owner's share of the business
- to provide cash flow when a key profit maker has died
- to find and hire a replacement for a deceased key employee
- to keep the family of a deceased owner financially sound
- to provide retirement benefits and pre-retirement death benefits
- to pay an income to loyal employees who no longer can work because of disability

These are the reasons why the story of business life and disability insurance is of such great and vital importance to business owners. These are the reasons why business life insurance is of such compelling interest when your prospects understand its purpose.

OVERVIEW OF BUSINESS AND ESTATE PROBLEMS AND SOLUTIONS OF THE BUSINESS OWNER

Regardless of the size of a business, the death or disability of an owner or a key employee can devastate the firm. Larger, national organizations often have backup managerial systems that help them survive the death of a key employee.

Medium and small firms typically are not as fortunate. These businesses, which represent the vast majority of your potential business clients, depend heavily on the business owners or a few key employees. Many sole proprietorships, partnerships, and closely held corporations have been forced into liquidation following a death or disability of one of these key people.

Death or Disability Triggers Questions

The death or disability of an owner or key employee triggers some critical questions; for example:

- Can the business survive or must it be sold or liquidated in some fashion?

- How can the spouse and/or children of the deceased or disabled owner realize the economic benefits of the entity which generally represents the largest single estate asset—the business?

Therefore the sale, liquidation, or continuation of the business should be of interest to any business owner.

Retirement Planning Questions

As the owner grows older and the business shows signs of stability, another type of planning becomes important as well—planning for eventual retirement. The owner begins to ponder questions such as:

- If I decide to retire, how will the business provide my family with an adequate income?
- How can I transfer ownership of my business to my children or grandchildren or to new owners?
- Do I have one or more family members who are sufficiently interested and competent to take over management of the company? If not, who will purchase the company?

As you continue to develop your business insurance market, you will discover that one of your primary tasks is helping business owners recognize the urgency of addressing these critical questions. Your nonthreatening manner, probing questions, and well-developed listening skills will help your business prospects conclude that these problems are indeed pressing and have affordable solutions.

The fact that a business owner can solve these problems in an affordable fashion is especially important to communicate. Many business owners have given some initial thought to the need for planning for their death, disability, or retirement, but they sometimes assume that practical solutions are beyond their financial means.

As you progress in marketing business insurance, you will increasingly be able to meet your prospect's concerns with affordable solutions. You will learn how to help the business owner appreciate the severe problems that result when an owner does not make plans for the results of death, disability, and retirement.

Estate Planning Problems and Solutions

A business is often the largest asset in a person's estate. Proper integration of business insurance planning and estate planning thus becomes essential in achieving the business owner's lifetime goals for his or her business and heirs.

Estate planning deals with the creation, administration, and disposition of an estate. An *estate* is the sum of a person's assets—real estate, stocks, insurance, property, savings, business interests, and so on.

Purpose of Estate Planning

The primary purpose of estate planning is to help the estate owner achieve his or her goals for the distribution of assets following death. A secondary purpose is to minimize estate taxes. The common tools of effective estate planning include wills, trusts, gifts, life insurance, and business agreements.

As noted before, when a business owner dies without planning for business continuation, the business may have to be liquidated in a forced sale. The great disparity between the value of the business as a going concern and its value in a forced liquidation emphasizes the need for proper business and estate planning.

Legal Aspects. With sole proprietorships and partnerships, if there is no provision in the owner's will (allowing others to continue operating the business) or through a buy-sell agreement, the business will likely come to an end soon after an owner dies. There is too much potential liability for someone to operate the business without legal "permission" and it is not wise to do so.

In the absence of either of these methods, the deceased owner's heirs could get permission from the court to continue the business. This could be a positive outcome, but it's uncertain whether or not the court will grant permission. With corporations, the business can—legally at least—be continued without express authorization of a will or without a buy-sell agreement.

Funded Agreement. As a matter of financial fact, however, continuation might be unrealistic or impossible. This is especially true in the absence of a written agreement clearly transferring control of the business to someone with the ability and desire to continue it. Adequate funds must be readily available to implement this agreement and to provide the extra cash flow usually required in any transition to new management.

The estate planning problems for business interests differ somewhat depending on the organizational structure of the business. Sole proprietorships, partnerships, and corporations each have unique planning requirements.

The major technical differences for business and estate planning between these three forms of business ownership will be discussed in detail in Chapter 5. Here, however, is a quick look at the special estate planning and business insurance needs of each major form of business.

Sole Proprietorships

In a sole proprietorship the owner typically provides the main source of management skill. The owner usually is the business, for he or she is usually the only person with the drive and desire to make the business prosper. Upon the death of the owner, his or her heirs will likely assume control of the business. However, these heirs may not have the time, desire, or competence to manage the business successfully.

Conflicting interests are likely to arise among the heirs. Those heirs who are not involved in the day-to-day management of the business often push for the business to be liquidated so that they can receive the cash proceeds. This pressure often compounds the problems of those heirs who are trying to continue the business despite the recent loss of its owner. In most instances, the conflict is only resolved by liquidating or selling the company.

As a sole proprietorship grows, the owner often employs others to assist them in managing the firm. In these instances, the owners may count on the key employees to guide the business safely through a change in ownership when the sole proprietor dies.

However, the owner may have overlooked the fact these employees might be unwilling to hold the business together if they have no financial interest in the success of the business beyond their own job security. To retain these employees, the owner may find it desirable, or necessary, to provide either equity interests (ownership) or other significant financial rewards for these persons.

Partnerships

Partnerships face at least two potential problems at the death of a partner.

First, the laws of most states require that a partnership be dissolved upon the death of any partner unless there is a contrary provision in a written partnership agreement. All business must cease, except for the completion of existing contracts. The surviving partners then must liquidate all partnership assets, pay all partnership debts, and distribute the remaining capital.

Even if a partnership agreement has a provision to prevent this dissolution, a second problem may arise if the deceased partner has a surviving spouse. Although the spouse may inherit the business interest, he or she is often unable or unwilling to take an active part in the management of the business.

Another potential problem is where a special license or particular skill is necessary to be a partner. If the spouse does not have the necessary license or skill, he or she will not be able to contribute to the day-to-day functioning of the business. If the surviving spouse had not previously been active in the business, his or her objectives will probably be at odds with those partners who are continuing the business.

The surviving spouse typically is interested in realizing the maximum possible return on his or her share of the business. Thus, the surviving spouse will generally favor distribution of the business earnings.

The surviving partners, on the other hand, tend to be interested in reinvesting earnings in order to expand capacity and improve operating methods. Such disagreements often lead to a deadlock and prevent the partnership from achieving meaningful accomplishments.

Corporations

A corporation is a legal entity in and of itself. As such, the corporation does not automatically terminate at the death of a shareholder, even if that shareholder owns 100 percent of the outstanding stock. The ownership interest in a corporation, represented by shares of the corporation's stock, passes to the estate of the deceased owner.

Owners Are Key Employees

The typical closely held corporation, however, is usually managed by a few shareholders who are also the principal employees of the corporation. In such cases, the death of a major shareholder is also the death of a key corporate executive. The stabilizing force of experienced management is removed.

Struggle for Survival

"Business Owner, is there anyone in your organization who is more capable than you—or even as capable—in handling the day-to-day problems of this business, such as meeting competition, maintaining good employee relations, generating business, keeping customers and getting the job done?" *(Wait for a response.)*

"Have you taken a two or three month vacation during the past year or two?" *(Wait for a response, which will usually be something like "Of course not!")*

"Do you plan on taking a one, or 2, or 3 month vacation this year?" *(Wait for a response.)*

"If you're reluctant to take a lengthy vacation, do you think the business would survive your absence for a year or more if you became disabled?"

"Would it survive your death?"

"How well will your family manage when its income is cut off while the business struggles for survival under new, inexperienced management?" *(Wait for a response.)*

"This problem surely will occur someday. Doesn't it make sense to plan for it now?"

Without such leadership, the company may struggle as the ownership interest of the deceased major shareholder passes to his or her heirs. The heirs and the surviving shareholders may hold different business philosophies, different risk preferences, or different needs for income. Resolving these differences without the leadership of the deceased key executive is usually very difficult.

Friction with New Shareholders

The new shareholders may pressure the corporation to declare dividends. After all, the new shareholders are not getting salaries from the corporation because they are not employees of the corporation. The continuing shareholders, however, will probably want to maintain a policy of retaining earnings rather than paying them out as dividends. Such competing interests can be highly disruptive to normal business, and detrimental to profits. If the competing groups each hold equivalent amounts of stock, the conflict can lead to a deadlock and virtually immobilize the business.

Stock of a closely held corporation is not traded on stock markets, so the heirs of the deceased stockholder are usually not able to sell their business interest quickly, or perhaps at all.

The heirs may face an even more serious problem in the case of professional corporations such as those prevalent in medicine, law, and accounting. State laws dictate who can own stock in a professional corporation, and these laws prevent the heirs (and other non-licensed professionals) from retaining the stock. This fact further limits the possibility of selling the stock to others.

Changing Management Style

As a business grows, so does its management style. At first, all decisions are made by the owner-employees. They directly supervise their employees and have a hands-on management style. As the business grows, it gets compartmentalized. The owners cannot do everything, manage and supervise everyone, or make all decisions. New nonowner decision makers begin to appear. As the business grows even more, specialists are hired to perform various jobs and management functions. Many decisions begin and end with managers who are not owners. Year by year the owners tend to become more removed from the workers and from the day-to-day management decisions. When you approach businesses, find out who the decision maker(s) is with regard to your products.

Formal Ownership Transfer Plan (Buy-Sell Agreement)

ownership transfer plan The more a business owner knows about the pitfalls which can accompany disposition of a business interest at death, the more the business owner will be receptive to solutions that avoid these pitfalls.

One widely accepted and practical solution involves establishing an ownership transfer agreement that becomes effective at a shareholder's death, disability, retirement, or withdrawal at some earlier time or event. In essence, the agreement establishes a guaranteed and ready market for the business interest.

This is done by a contractual arrangement with either the business or the other owners for the automatic purchase of the decedent's business interest at a predetermined price or with a predetermined formula to obtain the price. This contractual arrangement, commonly known as a buy-sell agreement, will be discussed in detail later in the text. Several commonly used terms for this arrangement, *business continuity*, *business succession* and *buy/sell agreements* are considered synonymous.

A properly arranged buy-sell agreement provides a strong measure of certainty to all interested parties. Each owner knows that his or her heirs will receive an equitable settlement in exchange for the business interest. The surviving owners are assured that they will retain control of the company.

Funding to facilitate the settlement is almost always best accomplished by using life insurance and disability income insurance. With insurance, the funds are available precisely in the amount that is needed when they are needed, namely, at the time of death or in the early stages of a long-term disability

OVERVIEW OF PERSONAL FINANCIAL MANAGEMENT PROBLEMS AND SOLUTIONS

In addition to coordinating solutions to business insurance and estate planning problems, the advisor often assists business owners in personal financial management. All three areas of planning need to work in unison if the business owner and the owner's family are to maximize the benefits of business ownership.

Handling Choices

Perhaps the one factor that has the greatest effect on the personal financial position of any business owner is how well that individual handles economic choice. Making wise economic choices is extremely important, especially to new business owners who frequently invest the bulk of their financial resources in their new business venture.

As a result, the financial success or failure of the business owner's family is tied to the business. Even as the business grows and evolves into a successful venture, owners often continue to reinvest their earnings back into the business to meet its capital needs.

Rewards

Most people go into business for themselves in hopes of obtaining financial rewards. They are optimistic that their businesses will generate significant gains, thereby justifying the investment risks.

The business owners' actions follow one of the cardinal tenets of investing: the risk-return trade-off. This principle states that higher investment returns can be expected only if risks are greater. The risks associated with a new business are significantly greater than those inherent in many alternative investments, but the business enterprise offers larger potential gains as well.

Diversification

Although the typical business owner follows one important investment principle, he or she often violates another equally important rule of personal financial planning—the principle of diversification of assets to reduce risk. With most if not all assets locked into a business, the owner often lacks sufficient liquidity to meet occasional financial setbacks.

As a result, careful insurance planning becomes crucial. Inadequate life, health, and/or disability insurance could prove financially disastrous to both the business and the family. For example, the business could incur severe cash flow problems if sufficient insurance dollars are not available to offset financial losses arising at the death or disability of a business owner. This is an important reason why business insurance advisors stress the need for periodic reviews with their clients. Coverage that was sufficient when initially purchased is likely to be inadequate when a loss occurs 5 or 10 years later.

Although concentrating their assets in their businesses increases the risks to their personal financial position, it also can lead to unique personal financial planning opportunities. For example, business dollars sometimes can be used to meet personal needs, including funding personal insurance programs for the business owner and the key employees. Such funding often is not only feasible but is prudent from a financial and tax planning perspective.

OVERVIEW OF EMPLOYEE PROBLEMS AND SOLUTIONS

As a business grows, the owners come to depend more and more on the performance of the employees. Business owners must recruit, train, and retain valuable employees whose technical and behavioral skills contribute to the growth and profitability of the business. Just as the owner has pressing financial needs, so do the employees.

Good employees may willingly exert extraordinary efforts on behalf of the business, but they do so in large measure because they anticipate rewards and opportunities for personal financial security.

Here is where you can be of tremendous service to a business owner. More than any other advisor, you are well equipped to help the business owner meet the personal financial needs of the firm's valuable employees. Most likely you have spent the initial phase of your financial services career working in the personal markets. As a result, you know the personal needs of many different types of individuals.

Personal Planning Opportunities

You have developed an ability to solve many of these needs and to communicate your solutions clearly to your clients. Thus, by assisting employees with their personal financial needs, your products and your skills now can be valuable assets to business owners with whom you work.

You are already aware of the critical need for income when death or disability strikes a wage earner. You understand that few people have adequate insurance or other cash resources available to meet these contingencies. You are also aware of the perils of not preparing adequately for retirement income needs.

You are in a position to help the business owners meet some of these employee needs through various benefit programs, such as qualified retirement plans, group insurance, and selective executive benefits such as split dollar or deferred compensation.

Payroll Deduction

You can also help employees understand their personal responsibility for their own financial security. To facilitate implementation of this security, many employers set up payroll deduction programs that allow employees to purchase life and health insurance and other financial products in a convenient and cost-saving fashion.

You generally meet with the employees at the business location during regular business hours. Thus, you can save the time and expense of traveling to each employee's home.

Employee benefit programs usually are selected by a firm's owners and/or top managers. Nonetheless, the implementation of these programs typically gives the advisor an opportunity to meet with every employee of the business. This is good chance to acquire large numbers of new personal insurance clients under very efficient and favorable conditions.

What Can Be Used Where						
	Sole Proprietor	Partnership	Limited Liability company	S corp.	C corp.	Public corp.
Personal insurance	Yes	Yes	Yes	Yes	Yes	Yes
Section 162 bonus	Yes*	Yes*	Yes*	Yes*	Yes	Yes*
Buy-sell Key person	Yes	Yes	Yes	Yes	Yes	No
Estate planning	Yes	Yes	Yes	Yes	Yes	Yes
Group insurance	Yes	Yes	Yes	Yes	Yes	Yes
Split dollar	Yes*	Yes*	Yes*	Yes*	Yes	Yes
Disability income	Yes	Yes	Yes	Yes	Yes	Yes
Nonqualified deferred compensation	Yes*	Yes*	Yes*	Yes*	Yes	Yes
303	Yes	No	Yes	No**	Yes	No
IRA	Yes	Yes	Yes	Yes	Yes	Yes
Pension/profit sharing	Yes	Yes	Yes	Yes	Yes	Yes
403(b)	***	***	***	***	***	No
SEP	Yes	Yes	Yes	Yes	Yes	Yes
Payroll Deduction	Yes	Yes	Yes	Yes	Yes	Yes

*Yes, if on nonowner employees. But not generally advantageous on owners in this form of business

**Although it is possible for this plan to be adopted by an S corporation, it is not recommended

***403(b)s are in most nonprofit organizations and school systems.

BASICS OF FINANCIAL STATEMENTS

balance sheet

income statement

This section presents a few basic accounting concepts, with emphasis on two key financial statements used by all businesses: the balance sheet and the income statement

Relevance

Are you surprised to find accounting in a business insurance course? None of the information in this chapter is critical to placing financial and insurance products with businesses. It is useful, however, for many reasons. It gives you insights about the financial health of the firm, its needs for insurance, its value, and its ability to pay premiums. Also, if you are eventually to become a competent adviser to your business clients, it will benefit them and you if you understand financial statements.

The following are ways in which you can gain through an understanding of accounting and business financial statements:

- **Talk intelligently**. With an understanding of business accounting statements, you can talk more intelligently about many financial matters with your prospects, their accountants, and attorneys.

- **Show professionalism.** To be a competent financial advisor to business owners, you need at least some knowledge of certain key topics such as accounting.

- **Be viewed as an equal.** When prospects know you are knowledgeable about business-related subjects such as accounting, they will treat you as a fellow businessperson and will be more likely to do business with you.

- **Show signs of confidence**. Your knowledge of accounting can make prospects comfortable enough to let you study their financial statements (and/or take them with you for review). This willingness is a sign of confidence in you.

- **Understand size, profitability, and growth patterns**. By studying a firm's financial statements, you can get a picture of the business—particularly its size, profitability, and growth patterns.

- **Stress the impact of insurance**. You will be able to tell your prospects what impact business-owned life insurance has on their financial statements and demonstrate the cost in terms they can understand.

- **Make key selling points**. Certain financial facts can be key selling points for you.

- **Recognize insurance needs.** You can sometimes spot potential insurance needs by reviewing a firm's financial statements.

- **Understand premium money.** You can get a feel for the firm's cash position, which reflects on their premium-paying ability.

- **Research the fringe benefits.** From financial statements, you can sometimes find out things about the company's pension and fringe benefits, possibly including existing cash values and premiums being paid.

- **Know the terminology.** Familiarity with accounting practices may save you from embarrassment and possible loss of prestige.

- **Estimate the value of the business.** As you discuss the business, pay attention to clues about sales volume and the relative values of key individuals.

- **Ask motivating questions.** The more you understand accounting, the better able you are to ask tough, pertinent questions of your prospects. Such questions are often key factors in the sales process. They can force your prospect to face important issues, problems, and needs.

- **Develop a comfort level.** Learning about accounting leads to understanding many other practical aspects of business. When this happens, you develop a comfort level in business situations. As this confidence is communicated to business owners, they become comfortable with you. Sales are more likely to result in such an atmosphere.

- **Establish target markets.** If you are seriously seeking to establish target markets, your knowledge of accounting can play an important part in gaining in-depth insights into your target groups. A full understanding of a particular business is not possible without insights into its financial matters.

- **Manage your own business.** Your knowledge of financial statements will help you manage your own insurance business in a financially sound and intelligent manner.

Why Businesses Keep Financial Records

Why do businesses keep financial records? Knowing the reasons will help you develop close ties with your business insurance prospects. This closeness implies a developing level of trust, and trust is one of the key ingredients that encourage business owners to deal with you. Business owners use accounting to

- determine their future cash needs
- prepare tax returns
- comply with government requirements for withholding, workers' compensation, and so on
- determine if they can pay their bills when due
- keep track of profitability
- know how much money is tied up in inventory
- determine if too much is tied up in inventory
- know if inventory is turning over fast enough
- decide if dividends should be paid, and how much

- see if any part of the business is unprofitable
- know what is causing profit or lack of profit
- keep stockholders informed
- determine various ratios of profitability
- track accounts payable
- track accounts receivable

The Balance Sheet

The balance sheet is a formal statement of the assets, liabilities, and owners' equity at the close of business on a given date, often the last day of a year or the last day of a quarter. Many financial statements apply to 12-month time periods other than the calendar year. For example, many companies operate on a fiscal year, which starts July 1 and ends 12 months later on June 30.

owner's equity   A balance sheet is made up of three basic items:

- assets
- liabilities
- owners' equity

Assets

Assets are the values of all rights and property owned by the business. They are customarily divided into *current assets*, *fixed assets*, and *other assets*.

Current Assets

assets   Current assets are "liquid" or working assets. Included under this heading are cash and any items that will be converted into cash under normal operations within a short period of time—usually one year. Current assets include cash, marketable securities, accounts receivable, notes receivable, inventories, and sometimes other items.

Cash includes coins and currency on hand and money on deposit in a bank. While most assets on a balance sheet are estimates, cash is an exact value. (This is also true of life insurance cash values, which is treated under *Other Assets*.)

cash flow   Cash is the beginning and end of most business transactions. You may hear accountants speak of the "cash flow" through the cycle of: cash, inventory, sales, receivables, and, again, cash. This means that cash is spent to buy inventory; inventories when sold become accounts receivable; and receivables upon collection become cash.

Marketable securities are the securities such as bonds, stock, commercial paper, or debentures of other firms and governments held by the business. Commercial paper is short-term, usually low-risk debt issued by large corporations with very strong credit ratings. Debentures are unsecured debt obligations of large corporations, backed by the issuer's full faith and credit.

Most marketable securities held by a business have very short maturities—typically less than one year. Marketable securities are sometimes referred to as *near-cash assets* because they can be converted into cash in a very short period of time.

When added together, cash and near-cash marketable securities are known as *liquid assets*. If a business has cash on hand that may not be needed for a few months, the business owner may convert the cash into marketable securities in order to increase the return on this temporary liquid asset. This is done routinely by seasonal businesses.

Accounts Receivable. These are monies owed to the business by its customers. Practically all business done today involves a temporary extension of credit. In fact, trade credit and accounts receivable have grown to the point where the liquidity of U.S. corporations is concentrated largely in these two categories.

Notes receivable are debts owed to the business and evidenced by the unconditional written promises of customers or others to pay a specified amount at a specified time, or on demand.

Inventories are the goods that the company plans to sell to customers. This item does not include other items of value, such as office supplies, that are not for sale.

In a merchandising business, stock on hand is usually ready for sale; hence, it is usually shown as merchandise inventory.

In a company that buys raw materials and manufactures a product, the goods that are in the plant for ultimate sale are usually in various stages of production. These firms use three separate listings for inventory—one for raw materials, one for goods in process, and one for finished goods.

As a matter of normal practice, accountants value inventory at the lower of cost or market value—that is, either the lower of how much the manufacturer actually paid for the raw materials or how much it would cost now to replace the inventory.

LIFO

FIFO

In an attempt to reduce the time, effort, and cost required to place a precise value on inventory, accountants have adopted some shortcut methods. Two of these methods have well-known names: LIFO and FIFO (pronounced life-o and fife-o). LIFO is the abbreviation for *last in, first out*. FIFO stands for *first in, first out*.

Under LIFO, goods most recently bought or produced are treated as those first sold. Thus, goods on hand at the close of the year are treated as those bought or produced earliest.

Under FIFO, goods purchased first or produced first are treated as the first goods sold. Thus, goods on hand at the close of the year are treated as those bought or produced latest.

Valuation of inventory is an important and complex problem for accountants and business owners. Part of its importance lies in the fact that the method used to determine value will directly affect the income statement and balance sheet.

It can be the cause of a conservative or liberal estimate of a firm's financial situation. If it is conservative, the firm may actually be making more profit than the financial statements show. In turn, then, there may be more money available for insurance premiums than you first thought.

Fixed Assets

Fixed assets are those that a company expects to use for a number of years. These are not assets intended for sale; rather, they are used over and over again in the process of manufacturing, displaying, warehousing, or transporting the product. Items usually listed under fixed assets are real property (land), buildings, machinery, heavy equipment, cars, trucks, furnishings, and fixtures. Except for land, these assets are typically shown at cost with an indication for tax purposes of cost recovery (depreciation).

For example, buildings may be shown at an original cost figure of $2 million. Below this entry may be an allowance for depreciation, or accumulated depreciation, of $600,000, followed by a net asset valuation of $1,400,000 for buildings. The original cost figure is just that. The current market value of the buildings may be several times greater than the original cost.

The purpose of making three entries for fixed assets instead of simply showing the net figure is to make clear how much of the original value has been written off for tax purposes.

Thus, the $1,400,000 above means this amount of the purchase price of the buildings is still to be deducted or "expensed" for tax purposes.

For our purposes, *depreciation* and *cost recovery* are synonymous terms. Both terms describe a way of showing that an asset's cost is being deducted, for federal income tax purposes, over a number of years instead of being deducted entirely in the year of purchase. They describe ways of indicating that part of an asset's value has been written off as a business expense under federal income tax law.

Other Assets

Some assets do not fit neatly into the categories mentioned so far. They are often included on the balance sheet under the heading of *other assets*. One such asset is the cash value of life insurance owned by the business. This asset is not intended for routine business use, as cash, nor is it normally intended to be used as collateral for loans, although its value as collateral is unsurpassed.

Sometimes life insurance is not expressly mentioned in a balance sheet but is included instead under a general heading of other assets or miscellaneous assets. If insurance cash values are expressly mentioned on a financial statement, you know that your prospect already has positive feelings about the value of life insurance for business purposes. This is reassuring knowledge for you.

Intangible Assets

Even more difficult to assign to a slot as "current" or "fixed" assets are such intangible assets as leases, patents, copyrights, and franchises, all of which have a limited life, and assets such as goodwill and trademarks, which might have an unlimited life.

Although these intangible assets have no physical existence, they do have substantial value to the company. In practice, many companies do not attempt to establish a true dollar figure for intangibles. Instead, they simply assign a value of one dollar to all intangibles. Other companies use a figure that, while still arbitrary, more accurately represents their estimate of the value of intangibles.

Liabilities

liabilities   The liabilities of a business represent claims on asset values by persons other than the owners. In short, liabilities are the debts of the business as of the date the balance sheet is prepared. They are generally separated into current liabilities and long-term liabilities.

Current Liabilities

Debts due now or within one year are usually considered *current liabilities*, including:

Accounts Payable. This item corresponds to accounts receivable. It represents amounts owed to other businesses for the purchase of goods and services.

Notes Payable. This item represents notes given by the company. They may be trade notes given in the normal course of business or promises to pay for other reasons, such as on loans from banks.

Accrued Items. Debts already incurred but not yet due are placed under this heading. For example, if the date of the balance sheet is halfway between employee paydays, half the payroll is a debt accrued though not yet due. A semiannual tax of $10,000 due on June 30 would be shown on the previous March 31 as an accrued tax of $5,000.

Keep in mind that the money to pay current debts comes from current assets. Thus, the relationship between these two items is not only important, but revealing; namely, is there enough to pay bills as they come due? If so, is there much breathing room?

Long-Term Liabilities

Long-term liabilities are generally debts that will not fall due within a year's time. Sometimes they are termed *fixed obligations*, *funded debts*, or *long-term obligations*.

A common listing under this heading would be *mortgage on buildings*. Depending on the type of business, you might also find such titles as *long-term notes payable* and *bonds payable*. As in family situations, large amounts of indebtedness often reflect a need to insure the lives of the key profit makers.

Owners Equity

net worth

Owner's equity (also known as *net worth*) is the excess of assets over liabilities. It is the portion of value to which owners—rather than creditors—have claim. The equity shown for the owners is only as accurate as the asset values and bookkeeping mechanics from which it is calculated. A negative owners equity on a balance sheet is referred to as a *deficit*.

In a partnership balance sheet, the equity or owner's equity figure may be subdivided according to the respective shares of the partners. In a corporation, owners equity is generally divided into two categories: capital stock and retained earnings.

Capital Stock

capital stock

Capital stock may include different kinds of stock (common, preferred, treasury, and others). The value shown for shares of stock depends partly on whether market value, par value, book value, or liquidating value is used.

par value

book value

face value

- *Market value* reflects the current selling price in the market.

- *Par value,* sometimes called *face value,* is the dollar amount printed on the face of the stock certificates (often a very low figure like one dollar, $5, or $10).
- *Book value* of a share is the owners equity of the corporation divided by the number of shares.

- *Liquidating value* shows how much each share would be worth if the company sold its assets, paid its liabilities, and retired (bought back) the stock.

Retained Earnings

When speaking of "profits that have been plowed back into the business," a corporate owner is describing *retained earnings,* which are profits that have already been taxed to the corporation. The retained earnings account is part of the owner's equity portion of the balance sheet.

Dividends are paid out of retained earnings. If a corporation has no retained earnings, it cannot pay dividends. If a corporation pays out all of its profits as dividends each year, it would have no retained earnings. Retained earnings are also known as *retained income*, *retained profit*, *accumulated earnings*, *earnings retained for use in the business*, *surplus*, and *earned surplus*.

Some of the retained earnings are usually earmarked as a sinking fund, perhaps for plant expansion or for the future purchase of machinery and equipment. Some of it may be designated as a reserve for other specific contingencies or simply as a reserve for general contingencies.

It is important to remember that retained earnings (even when it is called surplus) is not an asset nor a sum of cash. As a practical matter, retained earnings are simply an accounting measure of how much of the business value is not represented by liabilities or capital stock. To say it another way, retained earnings are determined by subtracting capital stock from the owner's equity.

Retained earnings do not exist in balance sheets of sole proprietorships or partnerships, only in corporations.

Insolvency

A company is considered insolvent when it cannot pay its debts on time. This happens when a company has more current debts than it can handle currently—when the bills coming in are more than the cash coming in. Conversely, solvency is the ability to pay current debts as they come due.

A company with a strong retained earnings position might have very little cash. Theoretically, it could be insolvent despite hundreds of thousands in the retained earnings account. A company could also be solvent despite having more liabilities than assets. The basic factor that determines insolvency is whether the business can pay its bills on time.

Retained earnings simply show that the value of the business has increased as a result of its operations. Creditors, on the other hand, want cash.

Other Terms

Among other terms that make the analysis of the balance sheet more meaningful are the following:

- *Credit transactions* are sales of goods or services for which full payment is not made at the time of delivery.
- *Net working capital* is the excess of current assets over current liabilities. It is the lifeblood of the business. When current liabilities exceed current assets, the ability to pay bills is seriously impaired.
- *Profit* is the excess of income over expenses during a period of time. (Profit is discussed in detail later.)
- *Withdrawals* and *dividends* are personal distributions to the owners. Strictly speaking, sole proprietors and partners do not receive salaries, they simply withdraw money.

A sole proprietor or the members of a partnership may withdraw all of a firm's profits for the year (or even more) or may leave some of the profits in the business.

A corporation, likewise, may declare dividends for its stockholders in an amount equal to, less than, or in excess of profits. Dividends are not usually declared in excess of profits. In fact, some states do not allow dividends to be declared in excess of that year's profits. It is not unusual for a closely held corporation to retain all profits for use in the business.

Balance Sheet Equation

As complex as a balance sheet may become, it remains a picture of what the business has to work with (assets), what claims of creditors exist against them (liabilities), and how much is left for the owners' share (owners' equity). It can be expressed as an equation: Assets = Liabilities + Owners' Equity.

Balance Sheet Example

The following is a brief illustration of a balance sheet and how it works.

Assume Smith owns a house valued at $200,000 and a car worth $20,000. Furniture, sailboat, and other personal property are worth $38,000. Smith's cash values in life insurance, money in bank accounts, mutual funds, and money market funds total $42,000. Thus, the dollar value of what Smith owns (the assets) totals $300,000.

The mortgage on Smith's house stands at $120,000. Smith owes $14,000 on the car, $4,000 on furniture, and $7,000 on the sailboat. The total amount owed (the liabilities) is $145,000.

Smith could list these items as follows:

Present Dollar Value of Things I Own	
House	$200,000
Car	20,000
Personal property	38,000
Cash, investment, and so on	42,000
Total values	$300,000

Present Dollar Value of What I Owe		
Mortgage	$120,000	
Note on car	14,000	
Furniture company	4,000	
Loan for boat	7,000	$145,000
Value really owned (owner's equity)		$155,000
		$300,000

In accounting terminology, Smith has assets totaling $300,000, liabilities totaling $145,000, and owner's equity of $155,000.

Notice that owner's equity ($155,000) added to liabilities ($145,000) equals assets ($300,000). This is true not only in this example, but must hold true—by definition—in all situations.

Effect of Borrowing

Let us see what happens if Smith borrows $2,000.

As shown below, total assets would increase by $2,000. Liabilities would increase by $2,000. Smiths equity would remain unchanged because the difference between assets and liabilities is still $155,000.

Assets (minus) liabilities = owners equity

$302,000 − $147,000 = $155,000

What happens next depends on what Smith does with the $2,000. If Smith spends the $2,000 on goods or services that are used up immediately (for example, a vacation), the $2,000 asset would be consumed while the liability (the outstanding loan) would remain. Hence, Smith's new financial position would become

Assets (minus) liabilities = owner's equity

$300,000 – $147,000 = $153,000

As you can see, Smith's assets declined by $2,000. The liabilities are still at $147,000. Smith's equity (the difference between assets and liabilities) is reduced by $2,000.

Now, assume that Smith had not spent the $2,000 on a vacation. Instead, assume Smith had invested the borrowed $2,000.

For example, suppose Smith bought an acre of farmland at the bargain price of $2,000 and the value of the land doubled overnight.

Recall that Smith's assets had already increased to $302,000 as a result of the borrowed money. When Smith exchanged the $2,000 for farmland, the assets remained at $302,000.

But the next day, when the land appreciated from $2,000 to $4,000, Smith's assets increased to $304,000 without any corresponding increase in liabilities. Therefore, Smith's owner's equity also increased by $2,000.

Assets (minus) liabilities = owner's equity

$304,000 – $147,000 = $157,000

In this transaction, Smith succeeded in increasing his equity, partly by taking on a liability—a loan from the bank. Business owners try to do the very same thing. They borrow money and "invest it" by buying raw materials that eventually become inventory to be sold—it is hoped—at a profit. If kept in the business, profit increases owners' equity.

Look for the Loss

When you are reviewing a financial statement or talking with a business owner, always try to *look for the loss.* Finding a problem that your products can solve is the essence of every sale.

- What financial loss will occur to the business if this owner dies or becomes disabled?
- Are there other persons in this business whose death or disability would cause a severe financial loss? What amount of loss would occur?
- Would the firm's income be affected seriously by the death or disability of a key person? Could insurance reduce or eliminate that loss?
- Are current assets sufficient to pay off current liabilities if income is affected seriously by death? Could life insurance offset that loss?
- Will control of the company be in jeopardy if an owner dies?
- Will the value of the company be in jeopardy at the death of an owner?
- Are there other key people whose resignation would cause a financial loss? Is there any way that insurance products can be used as a strong incentive for key people to remain with the firm?
- What amount would be lost from an owner's estate if the heirs had to sacrifice the business at a forced sale in order to pay estate taxes?

Obtaining the Data

Balance sheets for extremely large companies are usually available from Dunn and Bradstreet Reports, Industry Mercantile Agencies, and financial publishers such as Moody's, Fitch, and Standard and Poor's. Keep in mind that this information may be limited and/or dated, so it should be used only as background before an initial call on a prospect.

Balance Sheets and Financial Statements

For most of your business prospects, you will need to obtain the balance sheets and income statements directly from prospects.

Tax Returns

Owners of small businesses may not have annual financial statements. Ask these prospects for copies of their tax returns. Through careful examination of the business tax returns, you will find some of the information that is contained in formal financial statements.

Computer Programs

Many small business owners use one of a growing number of accounting software packages to maintain financial statements. In this case, your prospect should be able to print out current financial statements quickly and easily.

Try to obtain financial statements covering the most recent 3 years. As you compare specific items from year to year, this financial history reveals trends and patterns.

Trust

Obtaining financial statements from a prospect is not a matter to be taken casually, but it does not need to be a difficult task. If you have established trust and confidence with your prospect, he or she will provide the needed financial statements without reservation. If the prospect has agreed to a fact-finding interview, trust has been established.

To request financial statements, simply say, "I will need copies of your balance sheets and income statements for the past 3 years. Can I get them from your bookkeeper or accountant?"

Some prospects may ask why you need the financial statements. Here are some appropriate responses:

- "They provide me with detailed background information about your business that I could not get without asking you dozens of specific questions. They help me understand your business—where you have been and where you are now."

- "Some specific items on financial statements can indicate areas that may be problems if an owner or a key employee dies or becomes disabled. These are problems that can be alleviated or eliminated with planning. For example, I pay particular attention to the amount of indebtedness and the amount of working capital relative to the needs of the company."

- "If insurance is eventually proposed, my company wants documentation from me that the amount of insurance is reasonable in relation to the size and financial status of the business."

- "When I study a company's financial statements, I can ask more pertinent questions. In essence, the financial statements help me do a better job of helping you."

SALES USE OF THE BALANCE SHEET

Total Assets

The first thing to check on a balance sheet is the total assets figure. This indicates the size of the business. One caveat is important when reviewing the total assets figure. Many closely held businesses, especially professional corporations, lease most of their office space and equipment from a separate leasing company established by one or more of the business owners. These assets appear on the books of their leasing company rather than those of their professional corporation. Ask your prospect, "Do you or any of your business associates own office space (including warehouses or manufacturing plants) or equipment that is leased to your business?"

Cash Position
"Prospect, as a business owner you know the importance of cash. A strong cash position—or good liquidity—is what your bank and your creditors look for in your financial statements. Right?
"What effect would there be on the financial position of your business if you or your associate had died or become disabled yesterday?" *(Wait for a response.)*
"If I could show you how to increase the company's liquidity on a tax free basis, would you like to hear more?"

Equity

You can estimate a firm's strength by looking at its equity. If its equity exceeds liabilities by a good margin, the company probably has a good credit rating and basically is in a strong position. Where liabilities exceed equity, the business can be hurt badly by unexpected contingencies, such as a sudden loss in sales, changes in its markets, or a sharp increase in costs. Life and disability income insurance add to the strength of such a company and to its ability to borrow because these policies guarantee funds in the event of a key employee's death or disability.

Net Working Capital and Current Ratio

working capital

current ratio

The third item to check is net working capital, the excess of current assets over current liabilities. This is an indicator of the debt-paying ability of the business and is often expressed as a ratio (current ratio) computed by dividing current assets by current liabilities.

COMPUTER INNOVATIONS, INC.
Balance Sheet
(At Close of Business October 31)
ASSETS

CURRENT ASSETS

Cash		$97,435
Accounts Receivable		481,969
Notes Receivable		30,764
Inventory		
Raw Materials		127,865
Goods in Process		218,790
Finished Good		105,734
Total Current Assets		**$1,062.557**

FIXED ASSETS

Property		98,500
Plant	$265,098	
Allowance for Depreciation	186,700	
		78,398
Equipment	345,670	
Allowance for Depreciation	212,560	
		133,110
Total fixed Assets		**$310,008**

OTHER ASSETS

Insurance Cash Values	95,943	
Trademarks and Patents	128,790	
Total Other Assets		**224,733**
Total Assets		**$1,597,298**

LIABILITIES AND OWNERS' EQUITY

CURRENT LIABILITIES

Accounts Payable	$345,980	
Less: Discounts	6,919	
	$339,061	
Notes Payable	158,518	
Accrued Expenses	94,240	
Accrued Taxes	63,892	
Other Current Liabilities	67,865	
Total Current Liabilities		**723,576**

LONG-TERM LIABILITIES

Long-Term Debt	196,467	
Mortgage	68,435	
Other Long-Term Liabilities	21,015	
Total Long-Term Liabilities		**285,917**

OWNERS' EQUITY

Reserves for New Plant Facility	240,090	
Common Stock ($100 Par)	248,067	
Retained Earnings	69,648	
Total Owners' Equity		**557,805**
Total Liabilities and Owners' Equity		**$1,597,298**

In the Computer Innovations, Inc. example, net working capital is $338,981 ($1,062,557 - $723,576). This figure is more revealing when it is considered with the current ratio, which shows that Computer Innovations, Inc. has about $1.47 of current assets for every $1 of current liabilities.

Bankers generally consider a current ratio of two-to-one a positive sign. However, this ratio should not be applied arbitrarily; nor should it be considered alone as a final indication of a company's condition. The current ratio varies among different types of businesses and also may depend on economic conditions and trends of business activity. A current ratio of two-to-one may be the proper yardstick for a business with large inventories and accounts receivable, but not for a "cash-and-carry" business with normally small inventories and few accounts receivable.

In general, however, the minimum amount of current assets needed is an amount somewhat in excess of the current liabilities. The stronger the current ratio, the better the company's position to pay bills when due. A current ratio of less than two-to-one could indicate a weakness in working capital and a need for life insurance.

If a key person dies or becomes disabled, the company's marginal working capital position could become a serious financial problem. The key people should be insured to strengthen the company's credit.

Computing the Acid-Test Ratio
The acid-test ratio is calculated by dividing quick assets by total current liabilities.
Quick assets ÷ current liabilities = acid-test ratio
Quick assets are those assets that can be converted rather quickly to cash without losing value. They are often called *near-cash assets*. They usually consist of cash, marketable securities, and net receivables.

Too high a current ratio can indicate an inappropriate use of funds. In essence, too much money may be sitting around to pay bills. It could be used more productively. Look for a life insurance use here, such as key person insurance or a Section 162 bonus plan.

Acid Test Ratio

acid test ratio Another indicator of a company's financial condition is the so-called acid-test ratio. The acid-test ratio indicates how well a business is able to cover its short-term obligations. This is a comparison of current debts with "quick assets" or near-cash assets (cash, marketable securities, and net receivables) found by dividing near-cash assets by total current liability. This eliminates inventories, goods in process, and other current assets that might bring less than their stated value.

The acid-test ratio for Computer Innovations, Inc. is .80 ($579,404 in cash and receivables divided by the total current liability of $723,576).

A company's acid-test ratio will, by definition, be less than its current ratio. A concentration of assets in goods or inventories—which are difficult to move quickly at reasonable prices—might expose a business to heavy losses if a sudden need for cash arises. Such a need could occur when an owner dies and creditors demand payment. In such an instance, losses can be reduced or offset completely by life insurance.

A related item is the comparison of certain current assets to fixed assets. Generally, a business with a very high percentage of its assets in inventories and receivables may not be on a solid foundation. It may be building up liabilities rather than establishing a foundation of permanent capital. On the other hand, a heavy concentration in fixed as compared with current assets may indicate stagnation of business. Capital may be turning too slowly, with a resultant loss of profitability.

Life Insurance

If a balance sheet shows life insurance cash values under other assets, you know your prospect already has an appreciation of the business needs for insurance. Such a company should be a good prospect for the same reason that it is easier to sell a policy owner more life insurance than it is to sell the first policy. Find out the purpose of the present insurance. It can tell you a lot.

An owner who already has business life insurance knows that the entire premium is not a cost, if it is permanent or cash value life insurance. For example, when a business pays out $8,000 for the next premium, this is deducted from the current asset of cash. This reduces its owner's equity by the same amount. But then the increase in cash value for that year, for example $6,400, is added to other assets, and owner's equity is increased by $6,400. So, although the company paid out $8,000, its assets and equity were reduced by only $1,600 net—a small net expense in that year.

As a permanent life insurance policy grows older, the change in the financial picture becomes attractive. When the increase in cash value exceeds the net premium, the assets and equity increase with each premium payment.

This is important to keep in mind when a business owner or an accountant insists on term insurance because of the "cost" of cash value life insurance. In fact, the accountant may already be familiar with this method of accounting for business owner cash value insurance because it is the one established by the American Institute of Certified Public Accountants (AICPA).

In the same balance sheet listing as life insurance cash values, you might find an indication of money that the company has advanced to officers or other key people (loans or advanced salaries). What happens when the debtor dies? How will the company recover the money advanced? Clearly, here is another need for key person life insurance, or perhaps a split-dollar arrangement.

Footnotes

The next item to examine in a balance sheet is the footnotes. Among other things, the footnotes indicate any contingent liabilities. Does the company have the money to meet such contingencies when they arise?

While not all contingent (or estimated) liabilities require funding, there are some that naturally lend themselves to life insurance funding. For example, many companies have key people whom they could ill afford to lose to competitors. To retain the services of these key employees, the company may have given them Supplemental Executive Retirement Plans (SERPs), which promise salary continuation for a number of years after retirement and also pay the surviving spouse a certain percentage of a deceased employee's income for a number of years.

informal funding   Such an agreement is risky to both parties unless adequately funded on an informal basis. (*Informal funding* means money is set aside for a specific purpose but it is not directly tied to that purpose. That is, for tax purposes, the fund is not contractually linked to the specific purpose.) Here is a good use of life insurance.

The footnotes often list any buy-sell agreements. If none are shown, you might have the greatest sales opportunity of all. Do the owners have such a contract? Is it woefully out of date, as many are? Certainly the existence of such a contract calls for adequate funding. Is it adequately funded? If there is an agreement noted, when was it last reviewed?

Among other possible footnotes might be an indication of a pending lawsuit, a contingent liability. If the pending lawsuit materializes at the same time a key person dies or becomes disabled, the company could be in very serious financial trouble. Why not insure against this contingency?

The footnotes might also indicate the method used to value inventory and include the auditor's endorsement. The method used in estimating inventory may reveal the overall picture, because the listed values would vary accordingly. An endorsement by an auditor (usually a CPA) indicates that the figures have been prepared in accordance with generally accepted accounting procedures (GAAP).

Accumulated-Earnings Tax

accumulated earnings tax

retained earnings

If your prospect is a closely held corporation, look at the retained earnings account. Corporations that do not fully distribute profits may be charged with tax penalties in the form of an accumulated-earnings tax. This occurs when the Internal Revenue Service judges that the corporation is attempting to minimize the personal income taxes of its stockholders by retaining (accumulating) earnings rather than distributing them as dividends.

The accumulated-earnings tax is imposed when annual profit is retained beyond the reasonable future needs of the business. Any part of this year's profit retained for reasonable future needs of the business serves as a credit for this year. In addition, there is an aggregate credit (past and present earnings combined) of $250,000 for most C corporations. However, for professional corporations, the aggregate credit is only $150,000. The tax was 15 percent for 2006 through 2008 of the current year's unreasonable accumulations. In 2009, the tax reverted back to the highest individual tax rate of 35 percent.

If a corporation can show that accumulations above $250,000 are for definite and reasonable business purposes, the tax can be avoided. For purposes of the accumulated-earnings tax, life insurance is sometimes viewed as a reasonable need of the corporation.

For tax purposes, key person life insurance is well established as a reasonable need for the accumulation of funds. The same acceptance generally holds true for deferred compensation.

Not as well settled is whether a stock redemption buy-sell plan is a reasonable need of the business. The IRS tends to say that stock redemption plans serve the needs of the owners, not the business. Some cases have been favorably decided, while others have not. The wording of the corporate resolution and the documentation to back it up are important elements in arguing the case.

If the buy-sell agreement is a cross-purchase plan, there is no question about accumulated earnings. That is, the corporation does not own the policies, so the cash values do not appear on the corporation's financial statements. Individuals own the policies and the policy cash values.

COMPUTER INNOVATIONS, INC.
Income Statement

INCOME

Sales		$3,662,514
Less: Discounts, Returns, and Allowances		71,814
Net Sales		**$3,590,700**

COST OF GOODS SOLD

Beginning Inventory		$ 423,284
Purchases	$1,297,698	
Less: Discounts	25,954	
Total Purchases		1,271,744
Total		1,695,028
Less: Ending Inventory		448,567
Cost of Merchandise		1,246,461
Manufacturing Expenses		967,895
Cost of Goods Sold		**$2,214,356**

GROSS PROFITS FROM SALES		**$1,376,344**

EXPENSES

Selling Expenses		$ 240,846
Advertising Expenses		456,032
General & Admin. Expenses		320,178
Bad Debt Expense		112,890
Depreciation		97,192
Other Expenses		79,876
Total Expenses		**$1,307,014**

NET PROFIT BEFORE TAXES		69,330
Less: Taxes		12,332
NET PROFIT AFTER TAXES		**$ 56,998**

The accumulated-earnings tax applies only to C corporations. It does not apply to sole proprietorships, partnerships, or S corporations, because there is no such thing as accumulated earnings in these kinds of businesses. They are pass-through businesses. It does not matter whether profits are kept in the business or paid out to the proprietor partners/owners. For tax purposes in these forms of businesses, it is all taxed as though it had been paid out.

Premiums

Finally, a balance sheet provides clues as to whether a business can find the money for premiums. The cash and near-cash account are the first indications, but there are others that may be less obvious. The acid-test ratio and current ratio show an ability to meet expenses.

In addition, some property may be depreciated far below its true worth. Such assets, when sold, are a source of more cash than the value shown on the balance sheet.

Sometimes your prospects will be seriously looking for a source of money to fund death benefits, retirement plans, and other insured benefits. In that case, it is appropriate to ask if consideration has been given to assets such as CDs or other securities owned by the business, converting them to premiums.

Also look for old mortgages. Refinancing high interest loans can produce new cash flow for life insurance premiums.

THE INCOME STATEMENT

The purpose of the income statement is to compare the income earned during a certain period of time—usually annually—with the expenses incurred during that same period. The income statement summarizes income and expense items. Hence, it measures how successfully the business has been managed.

Total income less total expenses equals net income for the period. If expenses exceed income, the deficit is called net loss. Unlike the balance sheet, the income statement is a summary of what has taken place (regarding income and expenses) over a period of time.

The Bottom Line

If you want to see how profitably a business has been run over the past year, simply look at the bottom line of the income statement. The bottom line shows the net profit or net loss after taxes.

In general, businesses that deal exclusively in services have an income statement with only two major categories: income and expenses. Manufacturers, wholesalers, and others who deal with products have a third major category, known as cost of goods sold. For wholesalers and retailers, cost of goods sold generally includes only the cost of inventory. For manufacturing firms, however, it includes manufacturing expenses as well as the cost of inventory.

If the business is not managed wisely, profits may evaporate in interest paid to creditors, tax deductions lost, misdirected advertising, poor selection of markets, and various other items of wasted expense.

Key People

Many of the elements of profit depend on people at all levels in the business. The smaller the business, the more likely it is that the margin of profit depends on the ability of a few people. Without them, the business may continue to function, but at reduced profits or even at a loss—at least until new talent can be substituted and trained. A high turnover of salespeople or key people in the labor force or executives with management talent could easily be the difference between profit and loss. A business that shows high operating expenses or poor profits in relation to sales might need to solve a basic problem of retaining its people. Life insurance on key people can help solve this problem—both in preventing it from becoming serious and in filling the gap caused by it if new key employees must be hired.

Insuring the Human Money Maker

"Business owner, the book value of your sole proprietorship appears to be about $100,000. At 10 percent interest, this would be earning $10,000 a year.

"Your own personal earnings from this business were $45,000 last year, indicating that your management ability accounted for the difference of $35,000.

"To put it another way, your ability was worth more than three times again as much as the 10 percent. You might say that the $100,000 earned $10,000, while you made it earn an additional $35,000.

"Now, if you are worth three times as much as the interest earnings, doesn't that also indicate that you are worth three times as much as the $100,000? Isn't your current value as a money maker actually $300,000?

"Let's carry this one step further. If you had a $300,000 piece of equipment—a machine—wouldn't you insure a substantial part of the value of this asset against loss?

"Doesn't it make even better sense to insure the value of the human money maker—the asset that really produces the profits here—yet an asset that must surely die?"

Computer Innovations, Inc. Income Statement

Look at the income statement for the Computer Innovations, Inc. All of the company's income ($3,662,514) came from just one source—the sale of products the company manufactures.

Toward the middle of the page, you will notice that the cost of the products sold was $2,214,356. Manufacturing expenses accounted for $967,895 of that total. The remaining $1,246,461 is the cost of the inventory (shown here as cost of merchandise).

As you will notice, several calculations were performed to derive the $1,246,461 cost of merchandise. It involved three major factors: (1) inventory on hand at the beginning of the year, (2) additional purchases made throughout the year, and (3) how much inventory remained at the end of the year.

Look at the expenses shown on the income statement for Computer Innovations, Inc. They are typical of those you will find on many income statements.

Inventory Turnover

Business owners are particularly interested in several items revealed by the income statement. One of these is turnover of inventory.

If inventory is $97,000 at the beginning of the year and $103,000 at the end of the year, then average inventory is said to be $100,000. If the cost of goods sold is $800,000, then the inventory turnover rate is eight times per year (cost divided by average inventory). Turnover of inventory tells the business owner how much inventory is needed to produce a given volume of sales.

Most industries have associations that collect, compile, and publish statistical information such as average rates of turnover. Business owners can compare their own results with these averages to see how efficiently they are operating.

Ratio Data

If you are serious about developing target markets, you will want to learn all you can about the industries you are targeting. For example, Robert Morris and Associates publishes a reference book entitled *Annual Statements,* which contains financial ratio data for most major industries. Learning to use this data could prove helpful as you attempt to analyze the financial status and needs of your prospects and clients. Check your local library.

Business owners are also interested in

- operating expenses per dollar of sales
- profits per dollar of sales (gross and net before taxes)
- profits per dollar of owner's equity

The operating expenses of a business have a direct effect on net profits, yet one who has not studied the elements of accounting might ignore them.

If the business is not managed wisely, profits can evaporate in interest paid to creditors, tax deductions lost, misdirected advertising, poor selection of markets, and a hundred other items of possible wasted expense.

Business owners must constantly study what it costs to sell their products. By comparing their ratio of expenses to sales with those of similar businesses, business owners can discover whether their business is operating on a sound basis.

The ratio of gross profits to sales is the other side of the coin. This indicates how much it costs to manufacture or buy a product in relation to the gross revenue it brings into the company. For a manufacturer, this ratio helps show how efficiently labor, machinery, and raw materials are being brought together and how prudently the product is being priced.

RETURN ON INVESTMENT

The ratio of profits divided by owner's equity indicates the return the owners are getting for their investment. It is computed by dividing net profits by owner's equity (usually after subtracting intangibles).

The Computer Innovations, Inc. balance sheet shows a net profit after taxes of $56,998. Its owner's equity (on the balance sheet) is $557,806. The ratio of profits to owner's equity is, therefore, about 10.22 percent ($56,998 ÷ $557,806).

When business owners shy away from life insurance because they "can do better with their money," you can ask about their return on investment. They might not know, or they may not be doing as well with their money in the business as they might wish. The before-tax ratio shows an 12.43 percent return ($69,330 ÷ $557,806).

Risk and Return

Business owners take a great deal of risk with their money and certainly anticipate a better return than could be expected in a "safe" investment. Generally, the greater the risk, the higher the return that can be expected on the investor's capital.

Determining the rate of return may be more involved than just dividing profits by owner's equity. For example, this formula ignores how high a salary an owner is paying himself or herself. It also ignores the possibility that the owner's spouse or other family members might be on the payroll at salaries intentionally higher than would be the case if they were not related.

In the final analysis, profitability is proof of the value of the human factor in business. The return on investment—over the return that could be realized in a bank account—is one indication of how valuable management talent is to a business. A low figure may be due to many factors, but high profitability almost certainly is due to good management.

When profits are good, business owners are likely to be especially interested in implementing or increasing tax-deductible fringe benefits, such as group life and health insurance and pension or profit-sharing plans.

If they do know their return on investment, and if it is good, then use this result to emphasize how important key people are in producing this result. Ask who the profit makers are. Are they insured as other income-producing assets are insured?

Cash Flow

Although most businesses have many receipts and expenditures that remain fairly constant, they also have a variety of receipts and expenditures that vary greatly from month to month and from year to year. Because of these variations, efficient business owners look ahead and analyze cash needs over the coming months and years, matching these needs against projected receipts and expenditures.

This is a very important process for business owners because they need to know how much cash is likely to be available for use in the near future. It can forewarn them of the need to borrow money on a short-term basis or can give them advance notice of an ability to do such things as purchasing needed items of inventory or equipment, or repaying loans.

Cash Budget

This projection normally is referred to as a *cash budget*, and actual receipts minus expenditures is generally termed *cash flow*. A cash flow statement can be helpful to you because it is generally a better indicator of a firm's ability to pay premiums than is the income statement. In addition, if cash flow statement shows a healthy cash position, it indicates that one or more key people are doing a good job of controlling income and expenses. When a business has sufficient cash flow to meet all financial obligations as they fall due, it is said to be solvent. For insurance purposes, assume that the owner-employees are always key people. In addition, ask the owners who else in the organization contributes significantly to the firm's profitability (high income and controlled expenses). These are key people whom the owners may want to insure to offset the financial loss that would likely occur as a result of their death.

If the cash flow is negative (more expenditures than receipts) or only marginally positive, the business owner may feel unable to afford new insurance. Much like the family insurance prospect who says "I can't afford it," this business owner is very likely to be in great need of life insurance. The death of a key person could quickly cause a severe loss of profitability and even an inability to pay bills when due (insolvency).

Example

Notice the $97,192 expense item for depreciation in the Computer Innovation, Inc.'s income statement. Although this shows as an expense, it is basically just an accounting transaction; it is possible that none of the $97,192 has been paid out. This means the cash flow could actually be $97,192 higher than the $56,998 net profit after taxes as shown on the income statement. This is how writing off, or depreciating, an asset over a period of time can actually increase cash flow or profit over the same period of time.

Profit Goes to Owner's Equity

The income statement has an interlocking connection with the balance sheet. When the income statement shows a profit for any period, owner's equity on the balance sheet increases by that same amount. In a corporation, this means an increase in the retained-earnings category of owner's equity. Similarly, a net loss for the period decreases the retained earnings.

Tax Return Shows Financial Statements

Most people do not know it but the corporate tax return, Form 1120, gives a balance sheet for the corporation via Schedule L. (You can get a "Tax Guide for Small Business" from any Internal Revenue office. It is also known as Publication 334. There is no charge for it. You can also download it from www.irs.gov.)

Form 1120 also provides an income statement via lines one through 31, as well as Schedules A and M-1 on the second page of the form.

Do you also want to know who the corporate officers are and how much they are paid? Look at Schedule E of Form 1120. If you want to know how much money is being put into retirement plans and other employee benefit plans, read Form 1120, lines 24 and 25. For a rough idea of how much debt the business has, review the line item called *Cost of Goods Sold*. This is how much money the company has invested in inventory. Until it is sold, it is debt. Also, does the company have a mortgage? It, too, calls for key person life insurance as a way of transferring the risk from the owners to the insurance company.

Business Insurance Guide

	Business Insurance Guide				
	Plan Payor	**Objective Family**	**Premium Aspects**	**Owner**	**Beneficiary**
1	Cross-purchase buy-sell agreement funded with life insurance.	Disposal of business interest upon death of an owner, by transferring ownership to surviving co-owners who continue business.	Each partner or stockholder pays premiums for policy on the life of partner(s) or costockowner(s).	Each partner or stock-holder owns policy on the life of partner(s) or costockowner(s).	Each partner of stockholder is beneficiary of policy on life of partner(s) or costockowner(s). Proceeds used to buy interest from deceased owner's estate.
2	Business Continuation—Stock Retirement or Entity.	Disposal of business interest upon death of an owner, by having business purchase deceased's interest.	Business	Business	Business—Proceeds used to buy interest from deceased owner's estate.
3	Stock redemption buy-sell agreement funded with life insurance.	Transfer stockowner's interest at stockowner's death to his or her heirs, and have partial stock redemption, providing estate with cash to pay settlement costs.	Corporation	Corporation	Corporation. Proceeds are used to purchase stock from estate of deceased stockowner in an amount not exceeding estate settlement costs.
4	Key Employee Life Insurance	Provide protection to offset financial losses to a business due to death of valuable employee.	Business	Business	Business. Proceeds offset reduced profits and help pay for replacement upon key employee death.
5	Disability Income for Key Employees	Provide salary continuation plan for selected employee during period of disability.	Business	Covered employee	Covered employee—Benefits offset salary lost while unable to work.
6	Split Dollar (Conventional Method)	Retention of key selected employee by helping him or her purchase life insurance at relatively low cost.	Business pays portion of premium equal to increase in cash value—Key employee pays balance.	Corporation or insured or third party.	Business collects amount equal to policy cash value—Balance of proceeds payable to key employee's beneficiary.
7	Nonqualified Deferred Compensation	Retention of key executive by deferring taxable income and providing salary continuation plan.	Business	Business	Business—Proceeds used to fund key executive's salary continuation plan.
	This Guide does not address the corporate alternative minimum tax of FASB 109 concerning tax accounting.				

Income Tax Aspects			Estate Tax
Business	**Employee**	**Deceased's**	**Estate Tax**
1	Premiums not deductible—Proceeds not taxable.	"Step-up" in basis usually applies if payments do not exceed stepped-up basis, there is no tax	Purchase price paid for deceased's business interest is included in the gross estate. This usually equals amount of policy proceeds.
2 Premiums not deductible—Proceeds not taxable		"Step-up" in basis usually applies. If payments do not exceed stepped-up basis, there is no tax.	Purchase price paid for deceased's business interest is included in the gross estate. This usually equals amount of policy proceeds.
3 Premiums are not deductible. Proceeds are not taxable, except for potential alternative minimum tax (AMT) liability in a C corporation		"Step-up" in basis usually applies. If payments do not exceed stepped-up basis, there is no tax.	Payments received by estate in exchange for stock not included in gross estate, but value of decedent's stocks will be.
4 Premiums are not deductible. Proceeds not taxable, except for potential alternative minimum tax (AMT) liability in C corps.	No impact	No impact	Proceeds not taxable. But valuate of business is increased by the proceeds. Therefore, value of owner's estate is increased too.
5 Premiums deductible	Employer-paid premiums not taxable income—Benefits taxable.		No impact
6 The premium is not deductible. Proceeds are not usually taxable.	Taxed on economic benefit received as a result of employer paid premiums. Premiums paid by employee offset this taxable amount.	Proceeds not taxable.	Proceeds may be included in employee's gross estate due to incidents of ownership, e.g., right to designate and change beneficiary.
7 Premiums are not deductible. Proceeds are usually not taxable. Benefit payments are deductible if deemed to be "reasonable compensation"	Employer-paid premiums not treated as taxable income. Taxes deferred until executive receives benefits, which are considered ordinary income.	Benefit payments taxable as ordinary income when received.	Commuted value of benefit payments included in executive's gross estate.

	Plan Payor	Objective Family	Premium Aspects	Owner	Beneficiary
	Business Insurance Guide, continued				
8	Section 162 Plan	Retention of key selected employee by providing life insurance and retirement benefits.	Business	Covered employee	As designated by covered employee
9	Qualified Pension Plan	Provide retirement benefits for employees, including stockholder-employees, on a tax-favored basis.	Business	Trust—Vesting schedule determines covered employee's ownership rights.	As designed by covered employee, subject to qualified joint and survivor and preretirement survivor annuity requirements, including consent of spouse.
10	Qualified Profit Sharing Plan	Provide for employees, including stockholder employees, to share in the profits of the business on a tax-favored basis.	Business	Trust—Vesting schedule determines covered employee's ownership rights.	As designated by covered employee, subject to qualified joint and survivor annuity and preretirement survivor annuity requirements, including consent of spouse.
11	Traditional Individual Retirement Annuity (IRA)	Provide retirement benefits. Current tax deductible, tax-free buildup.	Individual or individual's spouse.	Annuitant	As designated by the individual.
12	Group Life	Provide life insurance death benefit for employee's family.	Business	Business	As designated by covered employee.
13	Medical Expense and/or Major Medical	Provide basic and/or more extensive coverage for hospital, surgical, and other medical expenses incurred due to sickness or accident	Business	Business	Covered employee
This Guide does not address the corporate alternative minimum tax of FASB 109 concerning tax accounting.					

	Income Tax Aspects		Deceased's	Estate Tax
	Business	**Employee**	**Deceased's**	**Estate Tax**
8	Premiums deductible	Employer-paid premiums considered taxable income. Benefits are not taxable.	Proceeds not taxable.	Proceeds included in covered employee's gross estate due to policy ownership.
9	Contributions deductible provided they meet the "reasonable compensation" test of the Internal Revenue Code and do not exceed the limits of Code Section 415.	Employee contributions not considered taxable income, except one-year term cost of insurance protection. Income taxes are deferred until benefits are received. Employee contributions (including PS 58 costs) are recovered income tax free.	The portion of payout representing employer contributions is taxable. Employee contributions (including PS 58 costs) are received tax free.	Life insurance proceeds and present value of annuities may be subject to estate tax.
10	Contributions up to 25 percent of the compensation of all plan participants are deductible each year. The maximum annual compensation taken into account is $245,000.*	Employee contributions not considered taxable income to employee, except one-year term cost of insurance protection. Income taxes are deferred until benefits are received.	The portion of payout representing employer contributions is taxable. Employee contributions (including PS 58 costs) are received tax free.	Life insurance proceeds and present value of annuities may be subject to estate tax.
11		Individuals who are not active participants in an employer-maintained plan can make deductible contributions up to $4,000 in year 2006.**	IRA distributions are taxed as ordinary income. A spouse can roll over the IRA into his or her own IRA.	IRA proceeds are subject to estate tax.
12	If plan if discriminatory, key employee must include cost of group life insurance in taxable income.	Employer-paid premiums in nondiscriminatory plans not taxable income up to $50,000. Cost of coverage in excess of $50,000 is taxable income	Proceeds normally not taxable.	Proceeds included in employee's gross estate, unless an absolute assignment of ownership has been made more than 3 years before death.
13	Premiums deductible.	Employer-paid premiums not taxable and benefits not taxable. Insured medical plans are not currently subject to nondiscrimination requirements. But if self-insured plans discriminate, benefits paid to highly compensation employees are taxable income to them.		

*The Section 415 annual additions limit per participant in 2010 is the lesser of 100 percent of compensation or $49,000.
**An additional $1,000 is allowed as a "catch-up" contribution if age 50 or older.

ONE APPROACH TO BUSINESS OWNERS

Funded buy-sell agreements and key person life insurance are the two most popular reasons why businesses buy life insurance. Here is a single-need approach that can spark a discussion with a business owner concerning a possible need for a buy-sell agreement, funded with life insurance.

What to Say

Begin by asking the business owner some thought-provoking questions. Here is the suggested initial question for this single-need approach to a business owner. It is powerful and gets right to the heart of a crucial issue that will eventually be faced by all successful businesses.

"What do you want to happen to your business when you die or retire?"

There are tens of thousands of small business owners who have not thought seriously about this important issue. Or, if they have thought about it, they have not made any decisions about it. Or, if they have made decisions, they have not made plans to implement their decisions. Or, if they have made plans to implement their decisions, they have not established a funding mechanism that most such plans require. Or, if they have established a funding mechanism, they have not updated it for growth and inflation.

In short, most business owners have either been generally ignorant of the potential problem or have procrastinated at one or more points in the process of doing anything about it. They generally have only vague ideas about what they want to happen to their business, and they have no formalized plans to make it happen.

Essentially, there are only three alternatives available to business owners regarding disposition of a business at the death of one owner:

- Keep it.
- Sell it.
- Liquidate it.

Keep It

Keeping the business generally means keeping that ownership portion in the family. Usually this would mean passing it on at the owner's death by will to the other family members. In the case of retirement, it would usually mean giving away or selling ownership at retirement.

Sell It

This means selling the business as a going concern. Most often the business would be sold to the remaining owners, as opposed to outsiders.

Liquidate It

In this context, liquidate means to sell the assets after shutting down the business. This is in contrast to selling the business as a going concern.

If the business owner does not know what to do with the business, or does not know the options, you will have to spell them out. If you feel unqualified to discuss the options, just tell your prospects that you want to discuss these options with them at a later date. Then come back at a later date with someone who can help you. Or, study up and come back with some information written out for your prospects. You can stop practically anywhere, tell the prospect that you would like to come back later, and then do whatever is necessary to prepare for the second meeting.

For example, assume you have asked the initial question, "What do you want to happen to your business when you die or retire?" Let's say that your prospect says he/she is not sure, or has not made any plans, or does not know what the options are. You can stop the interview at that point and arrange to come back later, perhaps with an advisor who is experienced in business insurance. You might say something like this, "Prospect, I would like to pursue this with you more fully at a later date. What I have in mind is asking my business specialist to join us next time. How does that sound to you?" Or, "I would like to give you some printed information that spells out the options available to business owners in planning for contingencies such as death and retirement, and then discuss these options with you."

> **"Business owner, what do you want to happen to your business when you die or retire?"**
>
> By committing this initial question to memory, you will have an effective business insurance approach with you at all times.

Another stopping point is after you tell your prospect the three main options of keep, liquidate, and sell. Or, you can discuss the options a little bit and then stop the interview. Or, you can go further into the interview by asking some questions. You can use questions from the fact finders found later in this book, or use your company's business insurance fact finder. Then, at some point, stop the interview as discussed above and come back later.

Another alternative, following your prospect's response about what he/she wants to happen to the business at death or retirement, is to ask: "Have you made any legal and financial arrangements to carry out your desires in this regard?" If no, then the response is, "let me come back later and give you some specific information about what is normally done in situations like this."

The main thing to understand is that you can stop at a point when you feel you are about to get in over your head. Do not be afraid to start for fear of going beyond your knowledge level. It's always an option to gracefully end the interview, gather your resources, and come back at a later date.

CASE HISTORY: AN EARLY START

Agent

Bob Wesson is a college graduate, age 31, married, and has two children. Bob was an Air Force navigator and played semiprofessional baseball for a short while before entering the insurance business 4 years ago. He is a leading agent for his company.

Prospect

I found the prospect while reading a newspaper article about the death of one of the community's leading businessmen. The deceased man's brother is a client of mine whom I had met while playing baseball in the local summer league. I immediately called my client to express my sympathy and to ask if his brother had an insurance agent.

As it turned out, the deceased hadn't bought any insurance for over five years due to his uninsurability. The agent he last bought from never came back. Through my client, I offered to assist the widow in settling the estate. My offer was accepted.

In due course, I met the deceased's son, Steve. He was 24, a college graduate, single, and would eventually fill his father's shoes as president of the family's metal fabrication company. Steve had been sales manager for the past three years. He apparently was quite successful because the company's production was almost always at full capacity.

Facts

Steve's father was only 48 when he died. He left $450,000 of personal life insurance and a business interest conservatively valued at $1,000,000. The home was valued at $425,000, with a $200,000 mortgage. There were bonds and cash totaling $20,000.

The corporation owned $500,000 of key person insurance on the life of Steve's father, with the proceeds payable to the firm. His personal insurance was payable to his wife under the interest option with full withdrawal privileges.

Under his will, drawn just one year before his death, all property was left to the wife. Upon her death or upon Steve's 25th birthday—whichever occurred sooner—the business interest was to go to Steve. This represented 95 percent of the company's stock. (This also means that the widow is having a large amount of security "taken" from her. The whole business value goes to Steve.)

Preapproach

After the estate was settled, I asked Steve if we could get together over lunch to discuss some ideas which I felt would be of interest to him concerning his eventual majority ownership of the business. He agreed.

We met for lunch about a week later and spent the time getting better acquainted and discussing some of the business problems he might face now that his father was gone. Steve was aware that his father would be hard to replace, especially in connection with the "inside" operations of the firm. In the meantime, he knew losses were bound to occur until he became fully acquainted with his new duties.

However, since he had been active in the business for the last 3 years, he felt confident that it would not be too long before he would be ready to step in and take full charge.

We discussed the effect his father's death would have on the credit position of the firm. Fortunately, there were not any immediate problems because Steve's dad had the foresight to purchase key person insurance on himself.

Steve answered a few more questions about the operation of the business, leaving me with the impression that it would continue to run fairly smoothly, with some losses to be expected, until he was fully experienced as head of the firm.

I decided not to dig any deeper at this time as I try not to turn a luncheon appointment into a sales interview. I used it as a convenient way to establish rapport with my prospect and to obtain some facts about him and his business.

After lunch I drove Steve back to his office and spent about 15 minutes discussing his personal program in an effort to ascertain his reaction to buying insurance at this time.

As I was ready to leave, I asked if I could talk with him at another time about a plan with guaranteed insurability features. Steve was very receptive to this idea because his dad had been uninsurable for the last 5 years of his life due to recurring heart attacks. My plan was to get Steve started on his personal insurance program before delving again into any business insurance needs. I suggested that we get together one day at lunchtime at his home.

Interview

Our appointment was 3 weeks later. Steve's mother sat with us at the dining room table, and we got right into the discussion. It resulted in a recommendation of $550,000 of permanent insurance with a guaranteed purchase option.

Steve asked quite a few questions during the presentation. When I finished, I asked if he had any more questions. He said, "No, I think you've covered everything."

"Well then, Steve, do you have any objections to getting this plan started now?"

"Don't get me wrong, Bob," he said. I am interested in the idea... but right now I'm very busy at the company. I'd like to put off making any decisions."

"That's okay, Steve. I understand. But to be sure I've made myself clear, would you mind if I quickly run over the highlights of this plan again?"

"Sure, go ahead," he replied.

I didn't want Steve to think I was pushing him, so I directed most of my attention to his mother. I was hoping that she would be impressed with the insurability features of the plan. When I concluded, I turned my attention back to Steve.

Before I could say anything, he said, "It's not that I'm against owning insurance, Bob. But I do feel that at my age and being single, $550,000 is too much."

This was his real objection. I answered, "This may be true now, Steve, but your needs are going to change quite rapidly. As you take over the business, your insurance needs will increase proportionately. I'm suggesting is that you take advantage of an opportunity to get an early start in the right direction—at a premium rate you will never be able to get again—plus the guaranteed right to buy significant amounts of additional life insurance between now and age 40."

Close

At this point, I asked Steve's mother what she thought of the idea of protecting Steve's insurability. His mother looked at him and said, "Steve, I think it's about time that you did something! What does it cost, Bob?"

"How do you want to handle the premium payments?" I asked.

"Well, let's say twice a year," said Steve

I quoted him the amount of the premium. Since he was "short of cash" I accepted a binder, with the balance to be collected upon delivery of the policy.

A Second Sale

Five months after the policy was delivered, I suggested to Steve that he consider having the business pay the premiums. He was interested and asked how it could be arranged.

I explained that the premium would represent compensation and that he would need only pay the federal income tax on this as if he had received the increase in his paycheck. My purpose for suggesting this arrangement was to get Steve used to the idea of the company's paying for insurance premiums.

We met in Steve's office, and I commented on how well the business seemed to be running. I was impressed with his ability to keep the business together after his father's death. Then I asked, "Have you ever given much thought to what may happen to your business if you were to die suddenly?"

"No, I haven't, but I guess things would get pretty rough," he answered. I suppose my key person, John, could keep things going for a while, but eventually the company could run into serious marketing and production problems and eventually be out of business."

I asked, "Is your mother dependent on the business?"

"My gosh, yes," he replied. Most of her income is from being employed with the company. You may recall, when we were settling Dad's estate, you said that it would be smart for her not to use the remaining $250,000 of insurance proceeds until she retires and starts to receive Social Security and her company pension. It would supplement her Social Security and pension income."

"That's right," I continued. "Now suppose you die before then—and the business dies with you—then what happens to her income?"

"I guess she would have to start using the insurance. I'm afraid it wouldn't stretch very far. She'd have to find employment somewhere else."

"Steve, what do you think we ought to do about this problem that's likely to come about if you die prematurely?"

"I've been thinking about training one of the men in the sales end of the business, something like Dad had me do for the 3 years before he died. That might keep the business going," he admitted.

"That's a good idea, Steve. This business was probably saved by the fact that your dad had the opportunity to train you to take over at his death. But there is no way to guarantee that you will have the same time to do likewise—is there?"

"Maybe not," he said. I'll just have to hope for the best. What else can I do?"

"I'm sure everything will turn out all right, Steve. It will go well if you plan it that way."

"What do you mean?" he asked.

"About 6 years ago, your dad bought some life insurance that was paid to the business when he died. Tell me, did the money help make things any easier for you in keeping the company open for business?"

"Help? I'll say! It helped me meet many a payroll until I could get things rolling again," Steve replied, "That's it! Why can't I do the same thing?"

Comments

This sale was for $500,000 with the company as owner, beneficiary, and premium payer. I believe both sales came as a direct result of my low-pressure tactics combined with high-pressure ideas. I concentrated as much as possible on the problems.

By letting Steve and his mother talk, I learned all I needed to know. Selling the "service concept" to Steve's mother in the beginning and having an opportunity to demonstrate my ability to handle the settlement of her husband's estate were contributing factors to the success of both sales.

CHAPTER REVIEW

Key terms and concepts are explained in the Glossary. Answers to the Review Questions and Self-Test Questions are found in the back of the book following the Glossary.

Key Terms and Concepts

ownership transfer plan	capital stock
balance sheet	par value
income statement	book value
owner's equity	face value
assets	working capital
cash flow	current ratio
LIFO	acid test ratio
FIFO	informal funding
liabilities	accumulated earnings tax
net worth	retained earnings

Review Questions

1. List 10 day-to-day concerns of business owners.

2. In one word, what is the essential ingredient mentioned in this chapter if a business is to stand a chance of surviving the death of a key owner?

3. Briefly define *Ownership Transfer Plan*.

4. Briefly describe the impact of a business owner's death on a business's capital, suppliers, and employees.

5. Name three financial statements used by business owners.

6. Briefly define assets.

7.   Briefly define liabilities.

8.   Briefly define owner's equity.

9.   What is shown on the bottom line of an income statement?
      The following questions pertain to the Business Insurance Guide.

10.   The "Business Insurance Guide" is a matrix covering four text pages. The left column shows various plans for using life and disability insurance in a business setting. Name the eight specific aspects discussed for each of these plans. In other words, what are the eight categories mentioned at the top of each column?

11.   What is the objective of key employee life insurance?

12.   If a cross-purchase buy-sell agreement is funded with life insurance, what are the income tax implications for the employee?

13.   Who is the owner of a Section 162 plan?
      The following questions pertain to "An Early Start."

14.   What were Bob's low-pressure tactics and high-pressure ideas?

15.   The business will pay the premium on the policy purchased by Steve. What are the income tax consequences to Steve and the company?
      The following questions pertain to "One Approach to Business Owners.

16.   Name the three alternatives available to business owners regarding disposition of the business at the death of one owner. Give a one-sentence description of each alternative.

17.   Write the words of the approach (suggested in this chapter) to a business owner.

18.   Suppose you get over your level of knowledge in talking with a business owner. What does the text suggest in such a situation?

Self Test Questions

Instructions: Read the chapter first, then answer the following questions to test your knowledge. There are 10 questions. Circle the correct answer, then check your answers with the answer key in the back of the book.

19.   Retained earnings, accumulated earnings, and retained income are terms variously used interchangeably with

      (A)   current assets or fixed assets
      (B)   surplus
      (C)   intangible assets
      (D)   unreasonable compensation

20. Where are key person life insurance cash values generally listed on the balance sheet?

    (A) other assets
    (B) liability
    (C) net worth
    (D) cash

21. Working capital is

    (A) net sales
    (B) gross sales
    (C) profits before taxes
    (D) excess of current assets over current liabilities

22. Cash flow addresses:

    (A) the status of the firm's debts
    (B) the efficiency of a firm's operations
    (C) the timing of actual cash transactions
    (D) the rate at which inventory can be converted to cash

23. The primary purpose of estate planning is the help the estate owner:

    (A) achieve his or her goals for the distribution of assets following death
    (B) minimize the costs of transferring the estate under all circumstances
    (C) arrange for the purchase of a decedent's business interest at a predetermined price
    (D) guarantee that the sole proprietorship can continue after the owner's death

24. What is the formula for determining owner's equity on a balance sheet?

    (A) earnings plus assets equals owner's equity
    (B) assets minus liabilities equals owner's equity
    (C) assets divided by liabilities equals owner's equity
    (D) liabilities multiplied by assets equals owner's equity

25. Goods most recently bought or produced are treated as those first sold is an example of:

    (A) FIFO (first in, first out)
    (B) LIFO (last in, first out)
    (C) FOFI (first out, first in)
    (D) LOLI (last out, last in)

26.   Which of the following is (are) correct about the balance sheet:

   I. It summarizes the income and expenses of a business over a period
       of time.
   II. It represents a snapshot of the financial status of a business at a point
       in time.

   (A) I only
   (B) II only
   (C) Both I and II
   (D) Neither I nor II

27.   Which of the following statements concerning the income statement is (are)
       correct?

   I. It summarizes the income and expenses of a business over a period
       of time.
   II. It represents a snapshot of the financial status of a business at a point
       in time.

   (A) I only
   (B) II only
   (C) Both I and II
   (D) Neither I nor II

READ THE FOLLOWING DIRECTIONS BEFORE CONTINUING

The questions below differ from the preceding questions in that they all
contain the word EXCEPT. So you understand fully the basis used in
selecting each answer, be sure to read each question carefully.

_____

28.   On a balance sheet all of the following are considered current assets EXCEPT

   (A) cash
   (B) inventory
   (C) equipment
   (D) accounts receivable

Learning Objectives

An understanding of the material in this chapter should enable the student to

1. Identify the steps of the sales process (sales cycle)

2. Discuss differences that may be found between the personal and business insurance markets

3. Identify prospect sources and methods of obtaining business prospects

4. Explain preapproach and approach techniques to use with business owners

5. Describe ways of developing a positive public image

6. Explain advantages and disadvantages of approach techniques using direct mail and the telephone

This chapter looks at the sales process and focuses on prospecting for business insurance clients. Prospecting methods as they apply to the business market are the main emphasis, and suggested scripts are included. Preapproach and approach techniques are reviewed with suggestions on how to use them with prospects.

WORKING IN THE BUSINESS MARKET

This chapter will address key subjects for the advisor working in the business market. It will focus on prospecting for and approaching business owners. Topics covered will include prospecting sources, the skills and information you need to know, setting production goals and how to become an established business advisor.

A Familiar Sales Pattern

selling/planning process

Although you will learn many new concepts, the planning process for selling business insurance remains the same as in the personal markets. As you may recall, the selling/planning process includes these steps:

1. **Identify the prospect.** Identify whom you are going to contact, and have one or two good reasons to contact that person. Precondition the prospect to create an expectation that you are going to call for an appointment. Sending a letter is usually appropriate, whether it comes from you or a person who is referring you.

2. **Approach the prospect** and ask for the interview, typically face-to-face or by telephone.

3. **Meet the prospect** in an initial interview. Establish rapport, explain your business purpose, ask some thought-provoking questions, and get agreement to proceed with gathering pertinent information about the prospect.

4. **Gather information and establish goals.** Conduct a fact-finding process and ask questions that uncover the prospect's situation, including information about goals, attitudes, and priorities, not just facts and figures. Establish and prioritize goals. Acknowledge the need to gain acceptance to work together to achieve the goals.

5. **Analyze the information.** Identify the real problems and needs that you can solve with your products and services.

6. **Develop and present the plan.** Your recommendations should meet the prospect's needs and support the decision to act now. Isolate and answer real objections.

7. **Implement the plan.** Ask for a commitment to your recommendations and get an answer. Complete necessary paperwork and underwriting. Deliver policies and documents.

8. **Service the plan.** Provide excellent service and conduct periodic plan reviews. Develop cross-selling opportunities and referrals.

Don't Wait
Don't wait until you know everything. Don't delay your entry into the business insurance market. Let the prospects see you. Know enough to create interest. Then come back with help.

You already possess many of the skills critical for success in the business market. As your knowledge improves, your confidence, technical skills, and sales performance should expand dramatically as you pull together the tools for success in the business market.

Building from Your Current Skills

Few people begin a career in the insurance and financial services industry lacking the desire for a high level of financial independence that we associate with owning a successful business. In fact, one of the most widely recognized benefits of a career in insurance and financial services sales is the ability to gradually build a successful business enterprise without a substantial initial capital investment by the advisor.

Desire for financial independence, however, is only one of the ingredients for a successful sales career. Starting and nurturing a business is a very challenging task. It requires long hours of work and meticulous attention to many conflicting needs. In order to be successful, an advisor must be willing to make many of the same personal and financial sacrifices as any new entrepreneur.

Along your path to success in your markets, you have been learning numerous critical business skills and developing professional habits that continue to contribute to your economic growth. These skills and habits are transferable and will assist as you move into the business insurance field.

You are in the process of becoming a competent small business owner. You have worked hard to cover an expanding overhead while simultaneously trying to keep the bottom line of your business growing. You have made those lonely, critical decisions that entail the careful evaluation of many business risks. You have experienced the high "highs" and the low "lows" of running your own business!

Now you have an opportunity to apply your growing business experience and know-how to broader marketing of your products in a new marketplace. As you enter the business insurance market, you will be calling on businesspeople with whom you have much in common.

You will be able to identify with the multitude of problems and frustrations that can keep a business owner awake at night. This understanding will allow you to express genuine empathy for the business owner. Combined with your growing business skills, this ability to understand how the business owner thinks gives you an extremely valuable advantage as you work in the business insurance market.

Your people skills and your ability to build relationships of trust are often more important to your sales success than are your strictly technical skills. Your understanding of the problems of the business owner should help you to overcome those initial communication problems that so often occur in sales work.

You may not realize at first just how important your experience as a business owner can be to success in this market. As the size and complexity of your own practice grows, your business and management skills will expand by necessity. You will gain a better ability to meet the needs of other business owners in your community. You and your new clients will grow profitably together!

Consequences of Inadequate Life Insurance Planning

One of the more dramatic reasons for an optimistic outlook for the business life insurance market is that few business owners could afford to die without business life insurance. Disaster awaits businesses and families for those business owners who have not planned for such a contingency.

Why? In general, most of the assets of the sole proprietor, the partner, or the stockholder in a closely held corporation are tied up in the business. Should the business owner die, numerous consequences to the business could cause severe—if not catastrophic—problems for the business and the business owner's family.

For example, the company's key customers who had close relationships with the owner may now take their business elsewhere. Or a competent manager who understands the inner workings of the company and who could replace the deceased owner may be unavailable or too expensive. Consider also that the company's operating costs may skyrocket once the owner's unique cost-control skills are gone. Credit lines may disappear as lenders reevaluate the firm's credit position. If the business should fail, the family's financial position also may suffer disastrous consequences.

Sole Proprietorship Buyout

If an unincorporated proprietor does not leave a will (or other legal provision) containing definite instructions for the orderly disposition or continuance of his or her business, the business may have to be sold.

This generally will be a forced sale, often a piecemeal liquidation. The assets of the business will be converted to cash by selling them to the highest bidders. Forced piecemeal liquidations usually result in business assets being sold at less than half their value when the company was a going concern. Potential buyers have the advantage, and they know it. A prearranged buyout agreement, funded by a life insurance policy, is a good solution for many sole proprietors.

Partnership Buyout

Think also of the partnership's dilemma if one of the partners dies. If there is no business continuation agreement, the partnership is dissolved automatically by law. Unless the affairs of the business are wound up without delay, those who carry it on do so at their own financial peril.

This often results in the same kind of forced sale mentioned in the case of the sole proprietorship. Losses are almost inevitable. Since the firm usually does not exist as an entity separate from its owners, this situation also could be disastrous to the personal estates of the partners. The value of the business interest and business assets could plummet, or not be available to heirs. If you were a partner, would you want that to happen to your business?

Once again, a buy-sell agreement among the partners is a good solution. Using life insurance policies to fund this solution is wise, prudent, and economical, as we will see.

Corporation Buy-Sell

The small, closely held corporation is very much like a partnership, with many of the same problems. However, the closely held corporation does not dissolve automatically when a stockholder dies. The deceased stockholder legally could transfer his or her shares of stock to surviving family members or other heirs.

The heirs and the surviving stockholders usually have competing interests. Typically, the heirs have neither the desire nor the ability to participate in the management of the company. The result could be an inability of the surviving stockholder-executives to exercise full control of the company.

Furthermore, the new owners may request that the company start paying dividends. If the new owners hold a majority interest in the business, they can demand that dividends be paid. The surviving stockholders, on the other hand, may favor reinvesting any profits in the growth of the business.

A buy-sell agreement funded with life insurance is often the ideal solution. It satisfactorily resolves the competing interests of both the deceased's heirs and the surviving stockholders.

Key Persons

Lastly think of the problems that often arise in any type of business upon the loss of a key person. A firm's profits frequently depend heavily on those with managerial or special skills and experience. The death of a key employee is often a major disaster to a business.

The most effective offset to the loss of a key person is cash—cash to pay or train a replacement, to pay debts, and to keep the company solvent during the critical recovery period following the key person's death.

The impact is often greatest for small businesses, since they generally have no plan to meet such problems. They are even more vulnerable than larger businesses because they lack reserve assets—both human and material—to survive the crises that follow the unexpected death of a business owner or a key employee. Similar problems occur when an owner or key person becomes disabled. A good solution for many businesses is to insure the life of the key person, with the business as beneficiary.

An Extension of Your Personal Insurance Business

Life insurance policies sold for business insurance purposes are the same ones that you sell to meet personal insurance needs. You do not have to learn about new policies. Business insurance needs are simply other needs for the same products.

Becoming involved in business insurance markets does not mean neglecting your personal insurance markets. Look at your involvement as a transition, not an abrupt jump. Remember, too, that personal insurance sales can lead to business life insurance, and vice versa. One begets the other. In fact, some of your personal insurance clients may own a business interest. Much life insurance sold to businesses and business owners is, in fact, personal insurance funded by the business.

While you are learning about business life insurance, plan to contact all of your current clients who have a business interest. Expand your business contacts gradually by asking for referrals. This practice can pay off in a big way! Making the transition from your existing personal insurance markets into business insurance markets is usually less difficult than the average financial advisor imagines.

Your involvement in both personal and business life insurance will not only increase your income but will also increase your job satisfaction and prestige with your clients.

Setting Your Goals

Your goals for growth in the business market should be both challenging and realistic. They must be worthy of the sacrifices and efforts you will make, but not so challenging as to guarantee frustration and impair your continued success in the markets which you have developed to date.

As you enter the business insurance market, you should establish goals for your work in this market. The following illustrates a set of goals devised by a typical financial advisor for entering the business insurance market:

- Each week, obtain the names of at least three prospects (ideally more) for an approach on business insurance needs.
- Each week, hold face-to-face, preliminary opening interviews with at least two prospects.
- Hold opening interviews with at least 10 business insurance prospects in the next 2 months.
- Conduct at least one business fact-finding interview each week.
- Hold at least one closing interview with a business prospect each week.
- Secure at least two new business clients who are willing to provide referrals to other business prospects. Plan to have at least one such client in the next 2 months.
- Allocate no more than 20 percent of your time to develop your new business insurance market. Accomplishing these goals within this constraint means that you will need to devote even more time to productive selling activities and to manage your time even more efficiently. You must continue to be consistently productive in your personal markets.
- Allocate adequate time for additional study of business insurance.

What should I do if I identify a prospect?
As you are learning about business insurance, you may develop some good business prospects but not feel competent to handle fact-finding or closing interviews. You have several choices in working with these early "hot prospects:" • Seek assistance from your agency or company support staff. • Ask an established financial advisor to work with you on a joint basis. • Refrain from taking any action with these prospects until you acquire the necessary knowledge and skills. Obviously, the last option could prove fatal to client development. Thus, one of your immediate tasks should be to explore the first two options. Be careful, however. Don't allow yourself to become dependent on help from others. Eventually, the best way to learn is to do it yourself. You will note that the illustrative goals listed above do not relate to insurance volume, premiums, or commissions. Instead, during the developmental stages of entry into business markets, establishing and building relationships with new business clients is essential to your ultimate success in the business insurance field. Initial sales are not as critical as developing strong, trusting client/advisor relationships. You will be pleasantly surprised how just a few successful business relationships like these can help you to grow rapidly in the business market.

Prospecting Sources

As you begin working in the business insurance market, one of your first questions undoubtedly will be: Where do I begin prospecting for business clients? You might have guessed that one good place to start may be with your current client files.

However, to succeed in the business markets you will need to develop prospecting sources beyond your current clients. These sources are listed below and then discussed in the balance of this section.

- Current clients
- Businesses you and your family patronize
- Referrals
- Centers of influence
- Tips Clubs
- Your community contacts
- Canvassing
- Prospecting Using the Internet and Social Networking
- Lists, reference books, directories, and public records

Experiment with all these sources while you are building your business clientele. Don't limit yourself to just one or two prospecting sources. Although you are unlikely to use all of these sources with equally rewarding results, experience and record keeping will teach you which of these prospecting sources are best for you.

Keep records of how many people you actually see as a result of each method, how many are seen on a favorable basis, and how many become clients. Before long, you will be in a position to decide which sources have been the most productive for you in generating prospects and new clients. Good record keeping allows you to analyze the results you obtain from each sources, so that you can truly benefit from your experience in trying alternative prospecting sources.

Good Bet

When I ask a successful business owner for referrals, I put it this way: *"Think for a moment of the people you know in our business community. If you had to bet $100 on the one person you expect to see at the very top in his or her field in a few years, who would it be?"*

Again and again this approach has yielded excellent leads. It works because I challenge them to demonstrate their knowledge of the way the wind blows in the local business community. It's a chance for them to show how familiar they are with the up-and-coming business owners. It is a great compliment to their business sense.

Current Clients

Even if you have been in the financial services business only a short time, some of your current policy owners are probably business owners or are key employees who can open doors for you.

Transforming clients from your personal markets into business clients is a natural step. These clients already have expressed confidence in your abilities. They will grant you an interview and listen to you. Clients who become prospects for your business insurance services are still the same people—not strangers!

When you identify current personal clients who are business owners or key employees, try saying something like

> *"John, I believe you have been pleased with the service I have provided you and your family. I would like the opportunity to explain*

another service I can provide—business insurance planning."

Another way of bringing up this subject is to say

> *"Mary, I need your help. As you know, my company has worked hard to meet your personal financial needs in a cost-effective manner. We also have an excellent reputation for helping business people solve the insurance problems they face. I'd like an opportunity to be of service to you in this area."*

Businesses That You and Your Family Patronize

It is a rare day when you or a family member does not patronize a business. Is there any reason why you should concede these potential business insurance clients to some other advisor? Who has a better right than a customer to ask for an interview? Why shouldn't a business owner devote some attention to a good customer who wants to discuss something important with that owner?

The businesses that you and your family patronize are a good reservoir of business prospects. These are natural markets that many advisors ignore to some degree. Certainly, no advisor should expect to make a life insurance sale in exchange for, say, buying a new television set or having a suit cleaned. But there is no reason why you can't ask the business owner for an interview and for referrals. Others will ask. Why shouldn't it be you—a customer of the prospect? If you are a steady customer, the business owner may be pleased to have a chance to reciprocate. Most business owners prefer doing business with their loyal customers rather than with strangers. Can you imagine their frustration (and yours) if—shortly after purchasing business life insurance from a stranger—they learn that you handle business insurance?

Referrals

Obtaining referrals on a regular basis plays a key role in the success of most advisors selling in the personal markets. Continuing to ask clients and prospects for the names of others in the same line of business will become a key way to build your inventory of new business prospects.

The more you ask, the quicker you build your inventory. Try to form the habit of asking one person each day for a referral to a business owner. Many advisors use questions such as the following when asking for referrals:

3-2-1

What is the biggest reason why people don't get referrals? Right—they don't ask for them! You have to be prepared. You shouldn't find yourself in the car after an interview saying, "Oh gee, I forgot to ask for a referral."

I've got a sure fire method guaranteed to get referrals. I hand a client a piece of stationery marked with his or her name and the numbers one, two, and three. I generally say:

"Well, Bill, you're a successful person and I've really enjoyed doing business with you over the years.

"You know all my clients now are personal referrals. If you'll recall, the way I met you was on a very favorable basis.

"You remember that Thomas Referrer suggested I get in touch with you. If it hadn't been for Thomas, you wouldn't have the fine financial program you now have.

"Just as Thomas got us together, I would like to know if there are two or three people you do business with who are the same caliber of person and who you think I might be able to help."

He says, "O.K., there's Tom Jones." Now I don't put Tom up in the number one spot. I put him in the number three spot. Mentally, it really works. Put the first name at number three, and I guarantee you'll get the other two. If you start at number one, you may get one, possibly two. You'll probably never get three names.

And when the client is giving me names, I don't want to know anything about Tom Jones. I want the other two names first. Then I've got time to hear a little bit about Tom. He plays golf; he's a good guy—all the information that you normally want.

- *John, much of your service business depends on referrals from your good customers. So does mine. Whom should I visit? (Or, who are the five most successful business owners you know?)*

- *Mary, I need your help. Who in the local business world do you most respect?*

- *Carl, I have enjoyed working with you very much. You have a thriving business, and I would like to meet some other successful people in your industry. Will you help me?*

- *Bill, can you help me to identify the leaders of a few rapidly growing businesses here in our community?*

- *Susan, with your help, I would like to learn about the businesses in our community that are adding new employees.*

- *Jim, I need your help to identify any business owners who have recently brought a son or daughter into their successful company.*

- *Cathy, I'd like your help. Do you feel that any of your associates or clients could benefit from my services?*

- *Mark, I'd appreciate your help. Who are the five best-known, best liked, and most respected individuals in this community?*

Asking for Help—Be Referable

Note that the key words in these questions relate to "help." When you ask for referrals, basically you are asking your client, prospect, or friend to help you.

Helping others gives most of us a good feeling! We seldom decline when someone asks us directly for help, especially if that help is easy to provide. How many times have you said no to someone who asked for help? But remember that you must be of value to the client—you must be referable. That means that the client must want to pass the benefit of your services to people they value.

The questions you ask when seeking referrals probe for persons whom your client respects or who are successful in business. By asking questions of this type, you do far more than generate names; you get quality referrals.

After you have asked for referrals, your potential referrer is likely to say, "Well, I'll be happy to help you. Let me think about it and provide you with a list in a few days (or a few weeks). I'll put the list in the mail to you." Your potential referrer is expressing a willingness to help (or hoping to get out of his or her commitment to help).

But, as you know, procrastination or failure to follow through occurs all too often. Try helping your client by saying: *"That's very thoughtful of you. I will call you in 3 days (or a week) when you have the list together and drop by to pick it up. I really appreciate your assistance."* At this point, you may also wish to ask *"In the meantime, do you know John Smith over at Apex Widget?"* or *"Do you do business with Mary Jones down the street at XYZ Corporation?"*

If you have enough preselected names to mention at this point, your client will probably know at least one of the people about whom you ask. When your client recognizes a name, the client often will say: "Oh yes, I know John, but I don't think he needs life insurance."

You will find it helpful to reassure your referrer that you would never imply to the new prospect that the referrer felt something should be purchased. You simply would like to meet the prospect on a favorable basis to determine if you might be of service.

You might add: *"Client, when I next see John, do you mind if I mention that I handled (or serviced) your account?"* When your client says this would be acceptable, you have a useful referral.

Sometimes you are seeking referrals from new clients. If you determine that the prior advisor no longer is in the financial services business, you might ask your new client who referred the previous advisor. After some thought, the client is likely to say, "Oh, yes, it was Harry who referred me to Advisor X."

You can simply ask: *"Do you mind referring me back to Harry? Like you, Harry may need the services of an advisor but not have anyone currently servicing his account."*

You must be careful in this area of referrals so as not to betray your professionalism by being negative about another advisor. Uncomplimentary comments can only serve to hurt your image and that of the industry.

I Need Your Help

"Client, I need your help. I am looking for people who are responsible individuals like you. I would like the names of the people with whom you associate—business acquaintances and associates and business people for whom you have respect. I'd like to call on these people to see if I may be of some assistance to them. I realize that you can't know what other people's insurance or financial needs are. I will simply work with the people you recommend exactly the same way I did with you. I'll contact them to see if I can arrange an initial interview. If they say no, I will not contact them again. Is that fair enough?"

Associations

Another way to seek valuable referrals is to ask clients or friends about their involvements with local professional or industry associations. Business owners are often on boards and active in local organizations.

When you learn that your contact is a member of an organization, you might ask: *"Mary, do you know the president or vice president of (your association) personally?"* If you can obtain a referral to an association officer and ultimately obtain this respected individual as a client, your prestige with other association members will be very high. Your ability to meet with additional group members will be enhanced significantly.

Sometimes your contact will be unable to refer you to any of the key officers of an organization. Try probing gently for referrals to other group members. Many successful advisors develop "nests" within particular industry or professional groups in this manner.

When your source gives you a name, the ice is broken. He or she will then generally give you lots of additional information if you ask for it. *Do* ask for it. Find out everything the referrer knows about this person.

Suppliers

If asked to do so, your clients can often supply very powerful referrals to the businesses that are their suppliers. Try asking, *"Jack, who are your biggest suppliers?"* Jack will probably give you the names of one or more firms or individuals.

Business owners usually are not hesitant to provide the names of their suppliers. Next, ask Jack for permission to mention to Mr. Smith at Smith, Inc. (a supplier Jack just mentioned) that you handled Jack's account (or have provided some service to him). Jack probably will find your request quite acceptable, especially because Mr. Smith is a supplier—not a customer or a "superior."

Centers of Influence
My centers of influence are the backbone of my prospecting system. I make a point of seeing them frequently and find out if anyone comes to mind that I can help. I send thank-you notes if I see the referral. If the referral is not receptive, I keep it low-key with my center.

You then can contact Mr. Smith and say, *"Hello, I recently had an opportunity to be of help to Jack Brown at Brown Corporation and during our conversation your name came up..."* Your chances of obtaining a fact-finding appointment are high! Suppliers won't casually offend a good customer by refusing to see you.

Helping Your Helpers

Individuals often need assistance to comply with your request for referrals. They often show signs of wanting to help, but they may struggle in giving you names. Most advisors have found that assisting individuals in learning how to provide referrals often plays an important role in a successful prospecting system.

One stumbling block your potential referrers may have is an inappropriate definition of a "good prospect." Many clients think you are looking for someone who needs insurance or financial products, and, of course, they do not know any such person. Clients aren't likely to consider the many business insurance needs when pondering referrals to give you.

How can you help your clients and other contact persons to provide the referrals you seek? You need to clarify your definition of the type of person whom you want to meet. Share a profile of your "ideal prospect" with your client and/or emphasize that you simply wish to meet other individuals who are as successful as your client. Explain that neither you nor your client can know at this time whether the men and women your client refers have any need for your services.

Another method often used is to ask your client to look through their business calendars, professional association directories, address books, or rosters of service or social clubs for names. Some advisors develop and provide to the prospect or client a list of business prospects to whom they would like a referral. These names could come from these same types of sources, but the advisor has done the research. The advisors ask their clients which people on the list they know and qualify the prospect from there. Because a referrer is not volunteering the names as candidates for sales calls, there may be less reluctance on the client's part. The advisor has simply offered the names as people the advisors wants to meet. Nonetheless, when the advisor calls on these people, he or she can mention that both the advisor and the prospect know someone in common.

Help from Established Clients

New clients are not the sole source for referrals. In fact, your best referrals are likely to come from established clients. These clients will already have "referral education" and will know the type of people you would like to meet. You have worked with the client over time to develop the client/advisor relationship and have become referable. The client knows what you are looking for in a potential client and knows what you can do.

As you visit with all of your existing clients on a regular basis to provide necessary services and/or to update their coverage, ask for referrals. You have earned the respect of your satisfied clients because of the valuable professional service you have rendered. Referrals can become a regular part of your relationship as a function of the value you bring to the client.

An Endless Chain

A natural outgrowth of referred lead prospecting for business leads is an endless chain—one interview points directly to other interviews. This is prospecting at its very best! Each new interview becomes a connecting link that gives continuity to the prospecting process and maintains an endless flow of prospects. In fact, every prospect becomes part of the referral chain—whether you sell something to that prospect or not. Even when someone doesn't buy from you, ask for referred leads. Try to keep the chain unbroken.

Qualify the Names

No matter what method you use to obtain referrals, remember that you want to obtain more than just names from your referrers. After a referrer has given you a name, ask for information about the prospect. Discovering interests and experiences that you have in common with your new prospect will help you obtain an interview on a favorable basis. Often your referrer can give you a head start on obtaining this information.

Follow-up on the Referral

Obtaining a referral is important and valuable. Of equal importance is a quick contact to the new prospect. Business people are always talking to each other. The referrer may have mentioned the referral to the prospect. If you delay your contact too long, both the prospect and the referrer may wonder why you made no contact and draw a negative inference about you. You should also keep the referrer informed of your contact results.

Centers of Influence

center of
influence

The concept of centers of influence is the same in the business market as it is with personal markets. Although everyone who gives you referrals could be thought of as a center of influence, true centers usually have three additional attributes. Typically, centers of influence are individuals with

- high prestige in the community, in their industry or profession, or in organizations to which they belong
- more than a passing interest in your business success;
- access to or knowledge of a wide circle of successful people on a regular and ongoing basis

A center of influence can provide you with a continuous source of leads in the business market. Keep in mind that a center of influence does not have to be a client, nor even a business owner.

The key is the willingness of the center of influence to help you on a continuous basis and his or her ability to provide information on quality prospects. If you can develop just a few effective centers of influence that provide quality referrals, you will find yourself off to an excellent start in business insurance.

Many business insurance advisors have found accountants to be very valuable centers of influence. Accountants generally have contact with their clients throughout the year as the business prepares its quarterly financial statements and undertakes its annual tax planning. In addition, clients frequently turn to their accountants for advice on many different types of business proposals, including those relating to insurance and financial products.

Many business insurance advisors make a concentrated effort to cultivate the accountants in their community. The advisors' primary purpose is to build rapport and to explain the type of work they do, recognizing that the accountant may some day review proposals they have submitted to their clients. These advisors recognize, too, that accountants can provide powerful referrals to large numbers of business prospects. Other potentially important centers of influence include lawyers, bank loan officers, politicians, and bank trust officers.

Lawyers and accountants can be good sources of referrals because they are likely to be familiar with the financial needs of their clients. Try developing two or three lawyers or accountants with the idea that you will be their financial services resource person. That is, whenever they have a question about financial products, they can feel free to call you. Eventually this will pay off. The attorney will start recommending you when his/her clients are looking for a reliable financial services advisor.

The more centers of influence you cultivate and the longer they cooperate with you, the more firmly you will become established in the business field. Centers of influence greatly expand your contacts, multiply your prospecting sources, and increase your prestige.

Of course, good centers of influence don't just magically appear. You must find, develop, and nurture them. In your early stages in the business market, it will be well worth your time to go through your personal telephone book, your prospect and client files, and any other name sources to locate potential centers of influence.

Developing centers is not unlike the sales procedure you already know. There are six general steps to developing good centers of influence.

1. Find names of people you believe are potential centers of influence.

2. Arrange an appointment to talk with each of these potential centers of influence about helping you. Emphasize the importance of this process to your overall practice and your goal of helping them and helping them help others they care about.

3. Determine in advance what you will say and do to "sell" your prospective centers on providing referrals. Get agreement of your value and benefit to them. Who you are, what you do and how you help them is vital to getting referrals.

4. Tell your new centers what you want them to do for you. If possible, ask a center to introduce you personally to prospects. If a personal introduction cannot be arranged, then a telephone call from the center introducing you to the prospect can be very powerful. If your center is reluctant to provide either a personal or phone introduction, ask the center to write letters or complimentary notes of introduction. Sometimes it will not be feasible for direct contact to occur between the center and the prospects. In these cases, try to obtain permission from the center of influence to use his or her name with the prospect.

Report Back

I ask my centers of influence for new names almost every time I see them. I also give them a follow-up report on past names. Then we discuss new names. One center of influence provided names that resulted in 20 percent of my first year sales. And all those clients are still with me.

---

5. Establish a plan to remain in regular contact with the new center of influence. This can be by phone or mail, but visiting your centers in person generally will be most effective. Regular contact is an important element in developing cooperative centers of influence. You need to provide value regularly. Most centers like to be helpful to the people they like and who are appreciative.

6. Devise and implement procedures to keep your centers of influence informed of your progress with the names they have given you—especially the successes.

The more you cultivate your centers of influence, the more cooperative they usually become—especially if you faithfully report back on the results of your calls and show sincere appreciation for their assistance.

Keep in mind that the center of influence does not necessarily need to know the people whose names he or she gives you. For example, the center may provide you with a list of new businesses in town, a list of club members, or any other list of prospects—none of whom may be known personally to the center of influence. Even in these situations, however, the prestige of the center of influence can be valuable because it allows you to start a letter or introductory comments to the prospect like this: *"I understand from Michael Brown that you recently opened a new office here in town."*

Sample Referral Objections, and Suggested Responses

Objection: I don't know that many people.

Response: Tom, you and I have spent a lot of time together, and you're obviously knowledgeable about our local business community.

(Then ask questions that direct your referrer's attention to specific types of business owners whom you wish to meet. Alternatively, you can show your referrer a list of prospects and ask if any of the persons on the list are business or professional contacts. *Another way to help your referrer start is to ask about others in the same business:* "What other restaurant suppliers do you know?" *Another starter:* "What's the name of your doctor?")

Objection: You can see Jane, but don't use my name. *(This is a serious objection that you may encounter regularly with individuals who are not comfortable in giving referrals.)*

Response: Tom, if Jane walked into this room right now, you would introduce me, wouldn't you? *(Wait for response.)* Well, it's in this same context that I want to use your name . . . just to tell her when I introduce myself that I know you. OK?

Another response: Tom, all I need to do with your name is tell Jane that I'm your financial advisor. Would that be OK?

Another response: Tom, being able to mention your name to Jane is important to me because you are well respected for your good judgment. I promise to be tactful and prudent in using your name. OK?

Another response: I'll wait till next week to call Jane if you think it's better for you to call her first and tell her who I am.

Objection: I'd like to contact Mike before you call him.

Response: One way to respond to this objection is to suggest that you prepare a letter to Mike on Sally's stationery for her review and signature. This could turn an objection into an even stronger referral. If your relationship with the referrer is strong, you can even suggest that Sally give Mike a call while you are sitting in her office. Sally's introduction of you over the phone while you are in the office can be exceptionally powerful. *(An alternative way to handle this is to say: "Good. I'll be calling Mike the day after tomorrow. That should give you enough time. OK?")*

To help get more referrals, you might provide and review lists of businesses or business owners with your centers of influence. You can gather these lists from:

- yellow pages
- personal observations
- help wanted advertisements
- tax assessment records found at your City Hall or in your local library
- business directories which are available in many cities

Ask your center leading questions that can elicit referrals. Helpful questions include:

- *Do you know any of the owners of these businesses?*
- *Which ones do you think could especially use my services?*
- *Are there any firms you know in this line of business that are not on this list?*
- *Are there any firms on this list I should not spend my time trying to see?*

Tips Clubs (Sales Club or Professional Club)

A Tips Club is composed of local salespersons who represent such diverse industries as insurance, real estate, banking, office products/furniture, and so on. The club is formed solely for the regular exchange of information on business prospects. Each member of the Tips Club shares his or her own expertise and business and social contacts with the group. The resulting exchange of ideas and leads can multiply each member's referred leads.

Usually a Tips Club has only one member per industry. Each member must come to the meeting with at least one prospect for someone. If a member misses three meetings in a row or attends three in a row without a prospect, he or she is no longer a member of the club.

You may want to start your own Tips Club, or ask other successful salespeople in your community if they belong to a Tips Club you might join.

Community Involvement

If you have built good relationships with people in your neighborhood, in clubs, and in civic, religious, and charitable organizations, you may have another excellent source of business prospects.

Membership in the same organization or participation in the same social function often makes it easier to meet people and to obtain interviews on a favorable basis. This is especially true when your approach is clearly to discuss business insurance. With personal insurance, prospects sometimes have an artificial psychological barrier to granting an interview. Business owners often treat business dealings in a way that is detached from their personal affairs. You may find that you are more comfortable in approaching social and organizational contacts about business insurance as opposed to personal life insurance.

You can gain valuable contacts through your participation in various organizations because the more successful business owners in your community are often among the leaders of these community groups. They have learned that success involves contributing to the good of the community.

Active participation in these groups offers an opportunity to meet people from a broad segment of the business community. Within these organizations, friendships are readily formed with business people who are eager to build goodwill. The active members of these groups frequently have outgoing personalities and have a large number of acquaintances.

Many of the most successful financial advisors have given generously of their time and talents to the benefit of social, civic, and charitable groups. As a side benefit, they have harvested bountifully in the business markets.

It is wise to remember, however, that only those who are willing to give first will then receive. Your prestige can be enhanced greatly if you make a definite effort to be a very active and hard working member of the organizations you join—a member who truly wants to devote time and talents to a worthy cause. **You would make a grave error if you try to "use" organizations solely for prospecting purposes.** Your career as a business insurance advisor will be impaired severely if the leaders in the business community believe you are a person who will abuse the privilege or honor associated with membership in social or civic organizations.

Canvassing

There are many prospects with whom you share no mutual acquaintances, but this is no reason to ignore these prospects. They should be located and contacted. One way is with canvassing.

Canvassing in the business market is a common practice for both new and experienced insurance advisors. They can be spontaneous or can be done with some degree of preplanning and prior knowledge about the firm and/or the owners.

Spontaneous canvassing can be done wherever businesses are located. This might mean going from door to door or building to building in an industrial park, or from door to door and floor to floor in an office building. You can canvass by car simply by pulling off the road as you see various business establishments. Or you can explore among the fringes of a downtown section where you are likely to find businesses other than retail establishments with which you are familiar.

The most serious drawback to spontaneous canvassing is that you will not be able to ask for the owner by name. Instead, you have to ask to speak with "the owner." However you can gain the name of a business owner from the next-door business neighbor with whom you talk. Before leaving one business establishment to go to another, ask who owns the business located next door (or in the next office, or in the next building down the road).

An even better way to canvass is to do some preplanning. For example, a week or two before canvassing in an office building, visit the office building and copy the names of the businesses from the directory at the main entranceway. Then visit a library to find the names of the owners or managers. By sending a letter or brochure to each of these organizations several days prior to making your calls, you'll find calls are not as "cold." You can call the business, asking for the owner's name so that you can mail him or her a letter. Then mail the letter and follow up in person.

You may be reluctant to canvass because you are uncertain what to say in the first few minutes. Here are some words you might try,

> *"Business Owner, I was in your area and I wanted to introduce myself and tell you the kind of work I do."*

Here's another way to get started:

> *"Business Owner, I'm with the XYZ insurance agency over on Main Street. I'd like to discuss your insurance with you. Would that be okay?"*

Be ready with at least a few questions to ask immediately after introducing yourself to the owner. Initially, pick questions with which you are comfortable, then keep refining your list of questions until you have ones that seem to work well for you.

For example, your questions might be

> *"Do you have a group health insurance plan? Are you satisfied with the coverage it provides? Are you satisfied with the cost? When is its renewal date? Do you usually shop around at renewal time? Do you often change carriers? (If yes, you've got a one-year client.) If you'll show me your coverage, I'll be back to show you if I can save you some premium cost."*

When canvassing you will sometimes catch a business owner or key employee at a time when he or she is really just too busy to talk with you. You can make a good impression by indicating your awareness of the prospect's time constraints and coming back a few days later.

Information Packets

To canvass effectively, you may prepare information kits to leave with your intended prospects. The ideal kit will introduce you and the services you provide along with information about the specific idea you want to discuss with the prospect. This can be a company or personal brochure or any other information you think will be of interest.

Your personal information packet can be a valuable resource in all of your business sales activities. It is an easy way to introduce you and the services you provide.

For your introduction, develop a brief biographical resume or brochure of your professional background and experience. Include a list of the business insurance needs that you address and information about your company.

Company brochures on specific issues are a good addition to your package. Your company's health insurance brochures, for example, or brochures on key person insurance and buy-sell agreements, give the prospect something to think about before your initial approach. Remember to get approval from your home office for all sales materials you plan to use in your packet.

When canvassing, ask to see the owner, manager, or person in charge. Of course, since you won't have an appointment, the person you want to see may not be available, but it opens the door for you to leave the packet.

Canvassing is a preapproach technique, but it can move directly into an approach if the owner is available. You need to be prepared to make a brief presentation of the material in the packet and be able to answer basic questions. Your goal at this stage is to get an extended appointment.

X-Dating

X-dating is a prospecting technique common in the property/casualty field. It is the process of contacting prospects to determine when their existing coverage is due to renew or expire, and it can be used effectively in the medical insurance area as a door-opener to a discussion of other insurance needs.

Businesses that provide health insurance for their employees are very sensitive to changing insurance rates. It is not uncommon for the premium to increase significantly at the renewal period. This provides you with an opportunity to make a proposal for the plans you offer.

The X-date preapproach is a simple one. It involves contacting a prospect and asking when his or her insurance plan is scheduled for renewal and asking for permission to call again at that time to offer a competitive proposal.

"(Prospect), may I call you 45 days or so before your renewal date to offer you a plan that may be more satisfactory than the one you have now?"

This technique requires you to maintain an excellent "tickler" (tracking) system to make sure you follow up at the appropriate time. In the meantime, you may want to put the prospect on your mailing list and send an introductory packet.

Prospecting Using the Internet and Social Networking

Today, it is possible that financial consultants could create their own shared networks and niche markets. The popularity and broad expansion of social networking sites like Twitter, Facebook, MySpace, and LinkedIn create new opportunities through "social networking." These new tools make it possible for individuals and groups to form their own networks. An amazing innovation in community building is taking place right before our very eyes.

Within the life insurance producer community, a recent article in the "Million Dollar Round Table" (MDRT) magazine summarized these best practice opportunities for social networking that may provide helpful perspective and ideas:

More than Socializing

Social networking builds connections with prospective clients and referral sources.

"Social networking isn't just for kids. Fifty-eight million baby boomers are joining social networks like MySpace, Twitter, Facebook, and LinkedIn to connect and learn more about their friends and business associates. What many might not realize, however, is that with the right approach, these networking sites can be a great resource to interact with current and prospective clients.

Gaining trust Adding clients, referral sources, and colleagues to your online social network is the first step. You can use these sites to see who they associate with and if they are connected to anyone you are seeking to do business with.

David E. Appel, CLU, ChFC, a 13-year MDRT member from Newton, Massachusetts, told Round the Table magazine that he uses LinkedIn as a means to gain the trust of potential new clients. "If I get a referral from someone, I used LinkedIn to see if we have anything in common," Appel said.

"I also use it to back up referrals I've already been given by mentioning the names of the connections when I call. If I can help potential new clients realize there are more connections with whom to check on me, I think it builds a level of trust."

Connect through groups Facebook, MySpace, and LinkedIn enable you to join groups based on your professional interests, which can assist you in making online connections. Joining online groups related to professional organizations can offer benefits as well.

Promote your business Social networking sites increase the ability to share information. As a financial advisor, you can use these sites to offer yourself as a resource and promote your business, but each site requires a different approach.

Twitter is especially useful for displaying your knowledge through expertise. Although the posts are limited to 140 characters, some people use this space to write about a specific interest and link to articles about the subject.

The most professional of social networking sites, LinkedIn offers the opportunity to post discussion topics and answer other people's questions. By answering a question, you can display your expertise and possibly connect with a new client. LinkedIn users can also seek recommendations from people they've done business with. These recommendations are displayed on the LinkedIn profile. Having a large number of recommendations helps other users to perceive you as a trustworthy professional.

MySpace pages include an embedded blog. You can use this blog to write about different financial trends you see in the industry and just give general advice. Broadcasting your knowledge makes it more likely that a prospect will consider doing business with you in the future.

Appel lists his company location and specialties on his Facebook profile. He also uploads photographs from conferences he attends and his speaking engagements.

> Connecting with the people you already know on Twitter, MySpace, Facebook, and LinkedIn is easy. If you take the right approach, these connections could easily lead to new business prospects."

Excerpts from: <u>More than Socializing</u>, Round the Table Magazine, Samuelson, April, May/June 2009.

<u>*Caveat:*</u> *Social networking has created new challenges for many a compliance officer. Please note that since use of these sites may create regulatory and compliance issues (i.e. consideration as advertising), financial consultants should first check with their affiliate company to determine guidelines/permission for use.*

Web search engines enable consumers to seek out insurance quotes and obtain referrals to local agents by zip code. An advisor can sign up with these vendors and obtain referrals from prospects who have initiated interest in insurance. Although the leads are expensive, they tend to be good ones.

Identifying and selecting a target audience requires both self-assessment and market research. As with any business-related planning process, financial advisors need to reflect first on the current state of their business and the environment in which they operate. The focus then shifts to researching market opportunities in the marketplace that may represent a good fit.

The Internet is a good place to research marketing opportunities. By going through your client and data base, you may already have identified possible groups or categories of prospects to research. Fortunately, the internet and its vast research capabilities have vastly improved the ease and speed for researching and identifying prospects. As an example, if you wished to focus on women business owners, categories of women's organizations as classified by the Gale Directory, a global leader in cataloguing companies and associations include:

1. Athletic and sports
2. Chambers of commerce, trade, and tourism
3. Cultural interests
4. Educational pursuits
5. Engineering, technological, natural and social sciences
6. Environment and agricultural
7. Fraternal, nationality, and ethnic
8. Greek and non-Greek letter societies, associations, and federations

9. Health and medical organizations
10. Hobbies and avocations
11. Labor unions, associations, and federations
12. Legal, governmental, public administration, military
13. Public affairs
14. Religious
15. Social welfare
16. Trade, business, and commercial
17. Veterans, hereditary, and patriotic

Source: Gale Directory Library, Cengage Learning.

From this point you could continue your search to identify prospects by drilling down to more specific names, businesses and organizations within a category of interest. Search key words on Google, Yahoo, etc. for leads you are looking for in your target market. This becomes your "call list" for daily prospecting. Many companies sell lead lists based on demographics, industry type, size of company, and other numerous criteria. Do your homework to ensure that the company you choose specializes in the types of leads you are looking for, and that their databases are updated frequently.

Your company may have an internet prospecting program or resources that can help you identify prospects. Relationship selling, or using your relationships within your client base, natural market, and target markets can help you find out about problems or opportunities where you can assist. Using professional relationships can help you do this through networking.

Networking is the process of continual communication and sharing of ideas and prospect names with others whose work does not compete with yours, but whose clients might also be eligible to become your clients. Conversely, your clients may need their products too. It's a two-way street. Networking involves the following:

- sharing knowledge, resources, and contacts
- receiving advice and assistance from people you know
- giving advice and assistance to people who know you
- leveraging your time to increase productivity
- seeking out and building long-term, prosperous relationships

Effective networking requires a commitment of resources (time, energy, money) to cultivate and nurture relationships. Building relationships requires more than passing and collecting business cards. It isn't the occasional phone call, the holiday greeting card, or remembering names of individuals you met at last week's soccer game. It is getting to know people and becoming their friend.

Lists, Reference Books, Directories, and Public Records

Several successful advisors in the business market recommend the use of directories and reference books as sources of quality prospects.

One advisor has devised a novel method of obtaining business directories. While sitting in an office waiting for a prospect, this advisor asks the receptionist, "Does your firm or your boss belong to a trade or professional association?" If the receptionist says yes, the advisor responds by asking if he or she has a directory handy, and if so, asks to look at it.

This method achieves several key goals. The advisor immediately learns if there is a published directory. If a directory is provided for review, the advisor learns what kind of data is included in the directory and how a copy may be obtained. Later, using that directory, the advisors can develop a list of prospects to review with clients in the specific association when seeking referrals.

Another successful advisor recommends the local library or the Internet as a source of prospects or of lists to assist centers of influence in providing referrals. At least once a month he visits the reference and business periodical sections of the library to review local papers, magazines, and reference directories. He searches for names of persons who have been promoted recently or who have been elected to positions of leadership in business associations or local civic or social organizations. Local newsletters are especially helpful because they provide names of local business people who have won honors and the names of business that are advertising their products or services.

While reviewing each publication or directory, he dictates appropriate names into a small portable recorder for later transcription by his administrative assistant. On a typical 3- to 4-hour visit to the library, this advisor gathers almost 100 names. The names are typed or written on cards and then are organized geographically for use in preplanned canvassing of business people.

Among the directories and related sources of prospect information that have been used effectively by successful advisors are the following:

- Notices in newspapers and legal publications giving new business firms, changes of ownership, additions to plants, and so forth
- Classified section of telephone directories where you can match this year's yellow pages with last year's to determine new businesses
- City business directories
- Membership lists for local civic, sales, or social organizations
- Chamber of Commerce and/or local Better Business Bureau membership lists
- State industrial directories
- Public records in local courthouses or halls of records
- *Standard and Poor's Register of Directors and Executives*
- *Moody's Investor Service*
- Dun and Bradstreet Reports
- *The Corporate 1000*—The Washington Monitor (directory of who runs the top corporations in the United States which includes the names and addresses of all officers)
- Library's business section
- Company list of employees' names, addresses, and phone numbers
- Real estate tax appraisal records
- Trade association journals and directories
- Professional journals and directories
- *Research Centers Directory* (the organizations listed in this book are generally not-for-profits, eligible for tax deferred annuities)
- Criss-cross or reverse directories like phone books, but listings are by street address, with another section listed numerically by phone numbers
- The Thomas Register of American Manufacturers lists companies by product
- The Encyclopedia of Associations (11 volumes) has over 70,000 listings with names of key officers, addresses, and size, listed by broad fields such as science, business, and law.
- Polk Company publishes a number of business directories, including local ones
- State medical directories

• State law directories

Prospecting by Promoting Yourself

This section will examine some of the ways you can project a very positive public image and thus improve your success in approaching qualified prospects for business insurance. Your image as a competent professional is very important to your success.

Community Involvement

Strong participation in community activities usually leads to a positive public image. There are no real secrets to creating a positive community image. It is a matter of determining where your community interests lie and then committing yourself to them. Committing yourself to an organization or cause in which you believe is always easier—and more effective—than undertaking a task for the sole purpose of local exposure. By participating actively in community organizations, you increase your visibility as others notice your involvement and realize that you are working hard to accomplish a worthwhile goal. But community involvement does much more than simply provide exposure to key community and business leaders.

As you make new acquaintances through frequent interaction in various civic, charitable, and political activities, you will become more relaxed when you eventually approach these people about business insurance. They will no longer be strangers!

The leaders of these and many other groups are constantly looking for new members who are willing to perform the many tasks that organizations undertake. Your hard work in handling these initial tasks will help you earn a reputation as a "doer" and result in increased credibility.

Public Speaking

Whether you work in a big city or a small town, there are many officers of social, civic, and fraternal organizations in your community who need a speaker for next week's or next month's meeting. Here again is an opportunity for you! As an advisor with a growing knowledge of financial and business insurance matters, you may be a natural to speak before local organizations. You may already have developed a basic speech in conjunction with a seminar you are preparing. If not, you can pick a topic with broad appeal such as business continuation, group insurance, pensions, wills, or estate planning.

Resource Person

James E. Rogers, CLU, is a Canadian life insurance professional who has successfully used newspaper articles to increase his public exposure. The following comments come from a presentation made by Mr. Rogers at a Million Dollar Round Table annual meeting.

An article ran in a local metropolitan newspaper. The article, by the newspaper's well-known consumer writer, was on the subject of life insurance. The piece contained what I thought were some errors of fact, as well as certain common biases that often characterize articles written by somewhat indifferent, uninformed or negative noninsurance people.

I phoned the newspaper to speak to the writer and chatted with him in specific terms about the article, thanking him first of all for giving the subject exposure, but suggesting, in the most polite way that I could, that the story contained some factual errors. I can remember vividly his comment to me, "Do you think you could write a better article on the subject?" I answered, "Yes, I do."

The chemistry between the writer and myself was, fortunately, quite positive. We agreed to meet for lunch, at which time I promised to lay out for him in writing what I thought was a more balanced approach to the subject of life insurance. When we met, I reviewed my notes with him and convinced him that there was another side to his story.

This writer had a great need for material to fill out his column requirements and was seeking a number of sources from various business and economic disciplines. Following our luncheon meeting, I became his "life insurance resource person."

On numerous occasions he would telephone me when he was doing a piece related to insurance. I was building up credibility with this man. When he did insurance-related pieces, he started to quote me by name in the articles.

I began to enclose these articles with letters that I would send to prospective clients. As often as not, I made no comment about the accompanying article, but the article would bear a relationship to the idea that I was discussing in the letter. I feel that the letter (and the follow-up phone call particularly) was better received because of the "third-party influence" that the attached article represented.

I have continued to build up a book of articles in which my name as been mentioned. I now have an article on nearly every subject with which we deal in our business because over time this writer has done pieces on most of the common areas of consumer interest in our business. Naturally, when I think of an idea that I feel might have broad consumer appeal, I let him know. Quite often, he does a piece on the subject.

I should add here if you feel that all you'll need to do is get in touch with a key business writer in your area and have that person quote you in a series of articles, I don't believe you will be successful. Subsequent to my initial contact with this writer, a great number of advisors have contacted him in the hopes of being quoted or interviewed for publication.

> In the interest of editorial integrity, on occasion he has quoted certain competitors of mine because of his and the newspaper's need for balance in his articles. However, I have found that most advisors are more interested in being quoted and promoted and less interested in really doing some work in order to obtain the publicity.
>
> Specifically, I have taken time to actually write out in detail articles that I think his readers would find of interest. He then edits these articles and employs his particular writing style in rewriting them for publication. But I have saved him many hours of research work by writing the outline of the articles for him. I would suggest that if you attempt this approach, you go the extra mile and do the same thing.

Design a catchy title for your speech to arouse the interest of program chairpersons or committees, such as "Creative Retirement Planning," "Putting the New Tax Laws to Work for You," or "The Best Insurance Policy Varies with the Individual."

Even though you may not feel ready to make speeches, you can begin building files or writing speech outlines. As you become more confident in your abilities in the business insurance area you can turn this material into actual presentations.

Developing a Personal Brochure

An important marketing device you can use for self-promotion is a personal brochure or resume. You may have seen these from other successful businesses or advisors, or from professional marketing sources. If you want to create a favorable impression with a prospect, there is no better way to do it. Some companies offer advisors a template to create a compliance-approved sales promotion piece.

A personal resume or brochure should include your business information, such as company, address, phone, e-mail, and so on. You may want to include your picture or even a photo of your family. Your experience and achievements, products offered, personal and business planning services can be highlighted. Additional information about yourself and your company can also be included. Of course your finished product should be company-compliant.

PREAPPROACH AND APPROACH

preapproach

approach

After identifying prospects, your next step in the sales process is to contact them to arrange an appointment. No matter what method you choose for contacting prospects, you are seeking to achieve one primary goal: getting an appointment. This may involve awakening your prospect's interest in you and your services.

The keys to successful implementation of preapproach and approach systems lie as much in your attitude, preparation, creativity, and commitment to action as they do in technique. In this section you will study how to secure interviews with your prospects.

Keys to a Preapproach

The purpose of preapproach is to *arouse curiosity, create concern, or upset complacency* in order to make your prospect want to meet with you to hear what you have to say. Success in the area of preapproach usually depends on three things:

- prospecting
- attitude
- creating trust and prestige

Prospecting

Prospecting and preapproach are generally intermingled. Both are part of "getting in front of people." Prospecting can also involve gathering information about a prospect as a means of helping to open the door. For every piece of information gained before making the preapproach, you gain an insight into that person that might be a "hot button" to the prospect's granting an interview. Everything you do at this step is aimed at getting to meet the prospect on a favorable basis.

Attitude

Attitude is of essential importance in every phase of sales work, and the preapproach is no exception. You are looking for a way to help the business prospect—knowing full well that the prospect may be in need of advice and counsel but may not be unaware of this fact. This lack of awareness or concern about potential risk exposures by the prospect may lead him or her to be indifferent or even negative toward your approach. This is where a positive attitude and belief in what you do come through.

If the prospect does indeed need help, you can make a sale as well as perform a valuable service for this new client. Keep a positive attitude. You are, after all, providing something the business owner needs. You can provide a valuable service because of your knowledge of and belief in your products. Follow the golden rule. Help others as you would have them help you if they had special knowledge that would benefit you.

Creating Trust and Prestige

Your ability to build trust and prestige with a prospect is often the key to obtaining a fact-finding interview and a closing interview. To prime the first call and reduce the prospect's reluctance to talk, use preapproach techniques that will create some personal prestige and build a preliminary base of trust and respect.

What's Different between Personal and Business Markets?

Most advisors are hard-pressed to explain how the business insurance preapproach differs from the personal insurance preapproach. Everyone agrees that the purpose is the same, namely, to obtain an appointment. In addition, most experienced advisors agree that the particular style and process you already use in obtaining personal insurance appointments should also work in obtaining business insurance appointments.

Following are differences you can expect.

Time and Timing

Business people are likely to guard their time more jealously than are personal insurance prospects. Even if time is not really more important to them, they may think it is more important or they may want others to think it's more important.

You can overcome the time "problem" by honoring it in fact and appearance. Let business owners and key employees know that you realize their time is important and that time is important to you too. One way you can accomplish this is by being specific about how much time you will require in your first face-to-face meeting.

For example, you might say:

> "Prospect, if we can set aside a time to visit that is convenient to both of our schedules, our initial visit should last no longer than 30 minutes," or "Prospect, if our initial visit lasts longer than 30 minutes

it will be because you have asked me to stay beyond this time."

Another time factor with business people involves when you call on the telephone or in person. Different businesses have different busy times. Of course, there is no way for you to get an unfailing handle on the best and worst time to call on every business prospect, but you can develop a helpful awareness of this concern. At the very least, you can avoid making calls at times when you know your prospect is likely to be busy. The more you are involved with a particular market, the better you will know the time peculiarities of that market.

Focus on Maximizing Profits and Solving Problems

The overriding concern of business owners generally is to maximize profits. In your preapproaches, try to incorporate an idea that touches this motivation. Any idea that can reduce taxes is always welcome. So too are ideas that can reduce employee turnover, increase employee loyalty, or help in attracting or keeping key employees. Another hot button is the use of corporate dollars to provide personal benefits for the owners.

Offering to solve a potentially disastrous business problem is another motivational hot button. Included among these business concerns are such things as problems caused by the death of an owner or loss of profits caused by the death or disability of a key employee.

Two other motivations—although not commonly thought of as hot buttons—are referrals from or references to people in the same line of business as your prospect.

Accessibility—Getting Through the Gatekeeper

Sometimes you will find it relatively easy to get to speak with the key decision maker of a business. This may or may not be an owner of the business. Many key decision makers accept all calls directed to them because they never know when it may mean good business to answer the phone or to see a person who is visiting. Of course, this is not always the case.

Thus, you will want to be prepared to work with a receptionist and/or administrative assistant whose job it is to "protect" the boss. Sometimes this is only a mild screening process. At other times, though, the screening process is very thorough, and you will find it difficult or impossible to talk directly to your prospect.

Don't let this disturb you, but do be prepared for it. Your best preparation is to develop a specific mental attitude. Tell yourself that you are calling on a matter that is personal and which therefore is not something to be shared with the receptionist or administrative assistant.

"Hot Button" Ideas
• Ideas that reduce employee turnover, increase employee loyalty, or help in attracting or keeping key employees
• Use of corporate dollars to provide personal benefits for owners
• Solutions to potentially disastrous business problems such as the death of an owner or loss of profits due to the death or disability of a key employee
• Referrals from others in the same line of business as the prospect

If you have mailed the prospect a letter with an enclosure such as the "Areas of Possible Interest" sheet, proceed as follows:

After introducing yourself to the owner's administrative assistant, asking to see the owner, and being asked what you want to see the owner about, say this to the administrative assistant (as you give him or her a copy of the "Areas of Possible Interest" sheet): *"I sent (Business Owner) a letter 3 days ago. This is what I want to talk to (Business Owner) about."* Have your name and business address imprinted on the sheet. Be pleasant throughout your conversation with the receptionist or administrative assistant. Being pushy or belligerent will decrease your chances.

Depending on your personality, here are a few unconventional approaches to consider:

- With a hole puncher, punch holes in your business card and send it to a business owner. When you later call or visit the business owner, tell him/her (or the administrative assistant), that you're the one who sent the business card with holes in it; and could you see the owner. If asked, say that you'd like to tell him about the holes in the card. *"I work in the fringe benefits area, and I try to help business owners spot holes in their insurance and fringe benefit coverages."*

- Write something enticing on the back of your card. For example, "Save money on your payroll taxes with IRC Section 125 plans." Either give the card to the administrative assistant (to give to the boss), or mail it to the owner beforehand.

- Attach your business card to a dollar bill. Send it to a business owner with a letter of your choice. On the envelope write: real dollar bill enclosed. As a PS to your letter, tell the business owner that the dollar bill was sent just so he/she would remember you when you called. Suggest that he/she might want to give the dollar bill to a needy person.
- Develop an "Introduction Book" binder with references from local business owners.
- Keep a list of a few businesses you will try to develop over a long period of time. Stop by occasionally. Introduce yourself. Pay a compliment. Don't talk insurance. Build rapport. Develop trust. Eventually sales will come as a relationship develops.

Your Attitude

You have expertise! You have solutions to serious problems! Your work will help your prospect! As a result, you should not be intimidated by business owners or key executives any more than you would be by personal insurance prospects.

Remember that you are not approaching an awesome, impersonal business. You are approaching a person who has a sincere and deep-seated concern for the success of his or her business. Don't think for a moment that your business is unrelated to the prospect's business. Insurance is very much a part of every business—or it should be.

Believe in the value of your products and your knowledge of them and how they work. You in most all cases will know more than the prospect about insurance and related topics. He or she is an expert in their area of specialty, not yours.

Recognize that you may have a fear of rejection, which is natural. Counterbalance this with your belief in what you and your products can do to help business owners and their families.

Specialized Approaches

If you have expertise, background, or experience in a particular industry or line of business, be sure to use this to your advantage to establish rapport and credibility in situations where you are calling on prospects in those lines of endeavor.

This is what target marketing is all about. You use your knowledge, expertise, and contacts to your advantage in selecting and calling on prospects. For example, if you have particular knowledge of accounting or if you have several accountants as clients you might say something like this to a prospect who is a CPA:

> *"Prospect, for several years I have been helping local CPA firms with employee benefit plans. David Michaels recently found our specialized services to be very valuable to his firm, and he recommended that I call on you. May we visit at a mutually convenient time?"*

Preapproach Techniques

The purpose of the preapproach is to precondition your prospects to expect your request for an appointment and be receptive to it. The preapproach usually occurs after you have a prospect's name but before you ask for an appointment. There is often a fine line separating prospecting and the preapproach. Sometimes, as in a cold call, they occur simultaneously.

There are various prospecting and prestige-building tools such as involvement in civic and community organizations, conducting seminars, and submitting articles to local papers. These activities help build your prestige, thereby preconditioning your prospects to be receptive to your request for an interview. This section will review the traditional preapproach techniques: preapproach letters and telephoning.

Preapproach Mail

Properly used, preapproach letters can be a powerful aid to your approach. The purpose of the letter is to help prepare your way by arousing the prospect's interest, establishing prestige, and helping put the first personal contact on as favorable a basis as possible.

Before embarking on a preapproach mail plan of your own devising, see what direct mail programs may be available through your company. Choose the letters best tailored to your target market from among several standard letters offered by your company. The company prepares and mails these letters to those prospects whom you select.

Obtain company approval whenever you develop mailing lists and draft preapproach letters. A well-written preapproach letter will arouse your prospect's curiosity, suggest that there is a problem that needs to be solved, and build goodwill for you by offering service.

Effective use of preapproach mail will bring some other advantages to your operations:

- It helps develop good work habits. By sending a definite number of letters on a regular basis, you commit yourself to calling on prospects every week. This gives you a measure of outside discipline—discipline that requires a regular schedule of prompt follow-up calls. When you use direct mail regularly, you let the law of averages work in your favor.

- It relieves some of the pressure on the first call. The prospect has seen your name at least once.

- It improves the ratio of interviews to calls. All things being equal, a previous contact with the prospect, however slight it was, means you have a better chance of obtaining a fact-finding interview than if the call were completely cold.

- The very fact that you can start by saying "I wrote to you last week saying I would call on you..." creates common ground with the prospect.

- It tends to make some prospects more receptive. There may be at least some curiosity about what you have to offer.

These ideas can help you use direct mail more effectively.

- Carefully select the mailing list rather than mailing on a random basis. Complete lists of names about which you know nothing are generally not worth the investment of time and postage.

- You certainly do not need a full picture of the prospect before sending a preapproach letter. Most advisors would be satisfied, for instance, to mail to a list of business prospects who are all members of the same trade association.

- Ensure that the letter conveys an image of professionalism by using quality stationery and type.

- Individually address each letter by hand, typewriter, or letter quality printer. Many advisors have experienced poorer results when they have used address labels.

- Affix postage with an individual stamp rather than a postage meter. Some advisors highly recommend the use of commemorative stamps.

- Consider including an attention-getter in the envelope. One advisor includes a dollar bill to pay the prospect for reading the letter. One advisor includes a Band-Aid with a health insurance preapproach letter.

- Attention to the wording, grammar, spelling, and punctuation of any letter is crucial.

- Generally, the shorter the better.

- Send preapproach letters—perhaps a few a year—to your best prospects. Nurture them. In target markets, use wave mailings.

- No letter is good enough to do a selling job by itself. An efficient and effective system of follow through is crucial to the success of any mail program. Do not send letters to more prospects than you can visit the following week.

- If you live in a rural area, and know most of the people, direct mail is less important.

sales ratios

- Regular use of preapproach mail allows the law of averages to work in your favor. By keeping records, you will develop confidence in your preapproach and sharpen your awareness of the dollar value of preapproach letters and follow-up calls by calculating *sales ratios* as follows. For example:

  - 25 letters per week
  - 20 follow-up attempts, in person
  - 10 face-to-face visits, owner seen
  - 6 fact-finding interviews
  - 2 sales

Commissions earned: $ _____

Commissions:

25 = dollar value of each preapproach letter

Commissions

Visit Tries = dollar value of each attempted visit

Commissions

Owner Seen = dollar value of each owner seen

Commissions

Interviews = dollar value of each fact-finding interview

Sample Letters

The following examples have been used successfully in preapproaches to business prospects. Your company may provide similar material. Be sure to have your company's preapproval with any material you use with the public. As you study the samples provided here, keep in mind that they can also be adapted to a preapproach in person.

The prospect may not be as aware of losses from forced liquidation as the first paragraph of this letter suggests. If not, he or she may be more curious because of this lack of information. The letter then moves closer to home. When a business owner dies, these losses can occur. Has the prospect given thought to the effect of this on the family? If not, perhaps this will start the prospect thinking along these lines. The prospect learns that there are various "insurance ideas" that other business owners are using. Most of us have an interest in what others do to solve problems similar to ours. Then there is a promise to call.

Dear (Prospect):

As you know, a distress sale is a costly proposition. When an entire business is put up in a forced sale, especially on a piecemeal basis, the losses are often 50 percent or more.

Yet this is precisely what does happen, in many cases, when a business owner dies. You may have already given some thought to this problem and its possible effects on your family.

I would like to show you some of the insurance ideas that other business owners are using to solve this problem. I plan to call on you in a few days to see if we can arrange an appointment.

Sincerely,

Marie Advisor

Like the first letter, the next sample letter focuses on a single problem that can occur at the death of a business owner.

Dear (Prospect):

Have you considered that if adequate legal provisions are not made while you and your associates are all living, then, in the event of the death of an associate, that person's business interest might be sold to a competitor?

There is a time-tested alternative to this potential problem, and I would like to discuss it with you. I will call on you within a few days to see if we can get together soon.

Sincerely,

Jane Advisor

The following letter broadens the scope. Because this letter mentions transfer of ownership as well as piecemeal, it probably has wider appeal than the samples given earlier. On the other hand, it does not present a specific problem as forcibly as do the earlier examples.

Dear (Prospect):

My purpose in writing is twofold. First, I wish to introduce myself. Second, I want to let you know that I would like to arrange to talk with you concerning a problem that many business owners have thought about, but relatively few have taken action to solve.

The problem I am referring to is transfer of ownership or other disposition of a business interest after the death of an owner. As you may know, transfer of ownership or piecemeal sale of a decedent's business can be potentially disastrous—from a financial point of view—unless formal arrangements have been made in advance.

I would like to show you an insured arrangement that other business owners are using to resolve this problem.

I would like to call or drop by in a few days to meet you.

Sincerely,

John Advisor

---

third-party influence

The next sample letter makes use of a third-party influence in motivating the business owner to recognize a potential problem. This letter can be adapted to sole proprietors or partners.

> Dear (Prospect):
>
> Do you know why so many closely held corporations end in failure when a stockholder dies?
>
> Milo J. Warner, a prominent corporation attorney and the former national commander of the American Legion, has said that one of the major reasons is "the common failure to make provisions in advance for the purchase, by the surviving stockholders, of the stock of the deceased."
>
> I plan to call on you in a few days to arrange an appointment so that I can outline an insured buy-sell plan, which has saved many companies from forced sale or liquidation.
>
> Cordially yours,
>
> Chris Advisor

Some preapproach letters rely on a total-needs approach. Consider, for example, the following letter.

This letter has the advantage of being very direct and professional. Its directness also makes it very businesslike. On the other hand, this letter does not present any specific problem for the recipient to think over.

> Dear (Prospect):
>
> Every business owner knows the value of having expert legal, accounting, and tax advice.
>
> Yet many business owners neglect to seek out the same kind of professional advisors when it comes to analyzing fringe benefits, ownership transfer plans, key person protection, and other life and health insurance needs.
>
> The enclosed brochure describes some ideas you might want to talk about. I plan to call on you soon to see if an appointment might be to our mutual advantage.
>
> Cordially,
>
> Lee Advisor

Note that a brochure is designed to be included with this letter. Such a pamphlet might give a brief description of the advisor, including time in the community, local involvements, education, insurance and related background, and other confidence-building information such as the name of the local agency and company affiliation.

If you are sending a letter to a referred lead, you might wish to send a message that reads like the following:

Third-Party Influence

Many advisors have found that material from their own companies or commercial services can be valuable in establishing prestige for an approach.

Dear (Prospect):

Our mutual friend, Doug Watson, suggested that my services might be of value to you.

My work involves the use of insurance to solve risk-related business problems.

Various publishing houses have available such items as series of tax letters, legal bulletins, and other mailing pieces that are of interest and value to business owners and executives. Obviously it would help to establish prestige if your name appears as the source of such publications. Articles of this sort also could be enclosed with a preapproach letter.

Those who receive third-party material from an advisor will probably come to know that the advisor has an appreciation of tax and business matters. They may remember the advisor's name, especially if they receive material from the advisor on a regular basis (every month or every quarter, for example). Thus they are more likely to be willing to listen to what the advisor has to say.

Whenever possible, a preapproach letter should contain something special that puts the prospect at ease regarding the advisor's qualifications or professionalism. A mutual friend's reference is excellent, as is a letter of introduction from the referrer. A "Here's Who I Am" brochure is very helpful. A statement of the advisor's business philosophy can also prove a useful enclosure. One example of the latter is shown under the heading "Here Is How I Conduct My Business."

Here Is How I Conduct My Business

Here is what you should expect from me if you select me to serve as your insurance advisor:

1. It will be my responsibility to provide you with advice based on an analysis of information about your financial situation, including your goals for your family and business.

2. To carry out this responsibility, I will work hard to earn the full cooperation of every person in your organization with whom I deal.

3. From time to time, I will ask you to provide the information I need to make accurate and personalized recommendations. Any information provided to me for review will be held in strictest confidence. I realize that my business career is in jeopardy if any item of confidence ever escapes from my office.

4, If you judge that my services and recommendations have been worthwhile to you, and if new life insurance is needed, and if you decide to purchase any such insurance, I expect to have earned the right to assist you in placing that coverage.

5. I will work hard to help you plan ahead financially for the ultimate fact of death. Since very few of my clients are likely to die soon, my commitment to service and updating extends many years ahead.

The Telephone

Consider how you use the telephone. For many purposes, such as keeping in touch with clients, there is little or no disagreement about its usefulness and value. For other purposes, however, such as a follow-up to non-referral business insurance preapproach letters, there is disagreement about the usefulness and value of the phone.

The telephone's chief advantages for the advisor are that it's a quick, convenient, and inexpensive way to talk to people. Its chief disadvantage to the advisor is that people find it easier to say no on the phone than they do in person. New technology and legal restrictions also complicate the use of the phone for business uses.

Making appointments by telephone means to prepare a telephone track carefully and in detail, learn it, practice it, and then use it with regularity, determination, and as much confidence as you can convey. It is just as important to be completely organized and prepared for a telephone preapproach as it is for a contact in person. A well-mastered or personalized approach will help you overcome apprehension.

Do Not Call (DNC) Regulations

The Federal Communications Commission (FCC), the Federal Trade Commission (FTC), and the majority of states have adopted rules regarding unsolicited telemarketing calls without the consumer's prior consent, or sales calls to persons with whom the caller does not have an established business relationship.

These restrictions are seen as less of an obstacle in the business market, since business-to-business calls fall within the exceptions to the do-not-call regulations. These exceptions apply when there is

- *an established business relationship.* A business relationship exists when there is a product or service in place, and it continues for 18 months after that product or service is no longer in effect or active. Several states have stricter requirements. If a consumer contacts an advisor, whether by phone, mail, or in person, to inquire about a product or service, an existing business relationship exists for 3 months after that inquiry. (Referrals do not satisfy the established business relationship exceptions and are not a basis to call someone on the list.)

- *prior express permission.* Advisors may make calls to a person on the DNC lists if they have a signed, written agreement from the consumer in which he or she agrees to be contacted by telephone. Written permission if it is received prior to the call is valid indefinitely unless revoked by the consumer.

- *a business-to-business relationship.* The DNC regulations do not apply to business-to-business calls.

- *a personal relationship.* Calls may be made to people with whom an advisor has a personal relationship, including family members, friends, and acquaintances

Following are some telephone procedures advocated by leading advisors.

- Telephone on a consistent basis. Using the telephone to make appointments is typically most effective if you set aside regular periods of time for phoning. Make an appointment with yourself. Write it down in your calendar.

- Have everything you need available and ready to use. Items needed include your list of names to be called (with full address and telephone number), pad for notes, pencil or pen, and your written telephone approach (if needed).

- Know what to say. Write out exactly what you are going to say to the prospect, master it, and then practice it until it sounds natural. Practice on your spouse or a friend. Use audio or video recorders to critique yourself.

- The objective of the telephone call is to get an appointment. That's all! Once you have scheduled an appointment, politely end the phone conversation. Do not try to sell insurance over the telephone.

- Try to be natural and relaxed. Taking a few minutes to prepare will help you be relaxed and thus more effective. You may also find it helpful to consider the individual on the other end of the line as a nearby and cordial person, rather than a distant, hostile voice. Speak clearly, neither rushing nor dragging your words. You want to sound friendly, intelligent, and confident.

- If you sense that a business associate, advisor, or family member will play a vital role in the decision-making process, you might wish to make the appointment at a time when this person can also be available. If you choose to meet with your prospect alone for an initial interview, remember to involve the other person as soon as possible thereafter.

- Try not to be discouraged. It takes endless practice to perfect any sales technique, especially one with as many variables as telephoning for appointments. The longer you work at it, the more you keep improving and getting more interviews.

- Do not argue on the phone. "Let's meet" is the idea on which to focus. "I want to meet you."

Time Bandits

Have you ever thought about your greatest time bandit? This time bandit is bigger than all of the others combined. It is the fear of rejection!

The fear of rejection can immobilize you for hours, days, weeks, and even months. When you are not approaching prospects on a daily basis, you are not selling.

The fear of rejection is always with us. You can deal better with your fear of rejection if you recognize and understand it. Then you can counter this time bandit with its enemy-good habits learned and sustained by mental toughness. Indeed, try to turn rejection around by making prospecting a search for acceptance. Let yourself feel especially good when you get an appointment.

Sample Telephone Approaches

Advisors who use the telephone regularly usually call the prospect within two or three days after the probable receipt of the preapproach letter. The telephone follow-up might resemble one of the samples below. (Note that each telephone preapproach could also be used in person and that the concepts are much the same as with personal insurance sales.)

Prospect, my name is _____ *of* _____ . *I sent you a letter a few days ago concerning the impact of disability on business ownership. Do you recall receiving it? (Wait for a response. Whatever the response, continue.)*

In my letter I promised to contact you to see if we could get together to discuss this.

Would you have any objection to discussing your insurance with me sometime?"

If the advisor is fortunate and the prospect immediately designates a time that is convenient, then the advisor should end the call by saying something like:

> *"Thank you, (Prospect). You're located at 7650 Shannon Avenue, aren't you? I will be in your office promptly at 9:00 a.m. on Tuesday. Good-bye."*

Prospect, my name is _____ of the _____ Company. Do you have a moment to speak on the phone? (Wait for response.)

A few days ago I sent you a letter regarding the continuance of your business in the event of the occurrence of various risks. I'm involved in risk management and insurance planning. I'd like to arrange an appointment with you and tell you more about the kind of work I do. Will it be convenient to meet at ...?

In trying to obtain an initial interview, many successful advisors promise that they will take only, say, 20 minutes of their prospect's time, unless their prospect invites them to stay longer. If you make a promise like this, be sure to keep it. That is, after 20 minutes, remind your prospect of your promise, and start to leave.

(Prospect), my name is_____ of the _____Company. A few days ago my agency sent you a letter concerning insured ownership transfer plans.

I'm calling this morning to request the courtesy of your time to explain this idea to you in person. With my promise that this will take no more than 15 minutes of your time, will it be convenient for you to see me...

(Prospect)? Good morning. This is _____ with _____ Life. Do you have a moment to speak on the phone? (Wait for a response.)

I wrote you last week to see when we could arrange a convenient time for us to get together. Do you recall my letter? How's your schedule for early next week, perhaps Monday or Tuesday morning?

As you know from experience in your practice, prospects don't always agree to your request for an interview. There are literally hundreds of objections prospects can—and do—raise. When you realize that objections are a normal and natural part of the sales process, you will see that you needn't be put off when a prospect begins finding reasons to avoid meeting with you.

Perhaps the best response with all of these objections is to repeat the essence of the objection in a matter-of-fact way, and then say:

> *"I understand. In fact, I think it is fair to say that most of my clients felt that way initially. I'd like to meet with you anyway. Could we do*

that?"

Most new prospects will not listen to you respond in detail to their telephone objections.

Your Office or Theirs?

Where is the most appropriate location for this initial interview? Is your office best, or should you suggest meeting at your prospect's place of business? Should later meetings be held in the same location as the first one?

More and more advisors today are conducting the bulk of their interviews in their own offices. They report that their business prospects and clients are accustomed to meeting in the offices of their various business advisors and exhibit much less resistance to this idea than anticipated. In fact, these advisors say that the key to getting prospects to come to your office is simply to ask them to do so.

On the other hand, many advisors prefer to conduct business in the offices of their clients and prospects. Some choose to conduct all of their initial and/or fact-finding interviews at their prospects' offices, moving to their own facilities for subsequent interviews. The same decision will result if your prospect expresses genuine resistance to coming to your office. But, assuming that you have a suitable office and your prospects are willing to meet with you there, what factors should you consider in selecting an interview site?

Meeting at your prospect's office permits quicker access to some of the fact-finding data you and your prospect will need. It affords you an opportunity to observe your prospect's business operation and to meet your prospect's business associates and/or key employees. Furthermore, many advisors contend that prospects and clients are more relaxed when meeting in their own environments.

However, conducting interviews in a prospect's office can have some disadvantages. Meeting at a prospect's office means that the advisor generally will not be able to control the environment. The interview is subject to interruptions that can have a disastrous effect on the sales process. To get around this problem you can politely ask your prospects if it would be possible for the switchboard operator to hold their calls for the time needed for the meeting.

Many advisors make extensive use of computers as sales aids. If a computer is to be used, you must either meet at your office or have a laptop computer.

Your office is generally better, because you have more control over interruptions, and you have reference materials and supplies on hand.

Experienced advisors cite several advantages for conducting their interviews in their own offices. An obvious plus is the reduction of travel time. Perhaps even more important is that they can be more effective in their own environment than in the client's often hectic office.

Having prospects and clients come to your office conveys an attitude of professionalism and subtly establishes the premise that they are coming to you to seek advice. A client who agrees to meet you at your office has indicated that he or she is interested. Using your office for interviews allows you to have everything you need on hand, including reference materials, sales aids, and computer hardware and software. You can arrange all of your sales aids (overhead projector, flip charts, and chalkboard) prior to a prospect's arrival.

Instruct the office staff appropriately regarding greeting clients, offering coffee, handling potential interruptions, and so forth. Controlling the environment in this fashion permits you to devote your full attention to the needs of your prospects and clients.

The Approach

When you have secured an appointment, you have gotten an important commitment from the prospect. Whether your initial interview will be under favorable circumstances is determined in part when you make your approach. The deciding factors will be appearance, manners, what is said, and how it is said.

When you meet a prospect in person for the first time, it is a meeting of two strangers—despite any previous telephone conversation. This is the time to demonstrate your credibility and desire to be of service. The prospect sizes you up and forms an impression that might be lasting. You want to convey a verbal and physical image that will build a bond of trust with the prospect.

The Rule of Eight

Some advisors have a creed that goes by the name of the Rule of Eight. They believe that a sale may be won or lost in the first 8 seconds of the approach, by the first eight words the advisor speaks, and by the 8 feet of floor space crossed to shake hands with the prospect.

There is some truth in this rule, even if it exaggerates the point. What is the first impression you create? It is visual, of course. Does this mean that a sale was made or lost on the day the advisor was born? Of course not! But every advisor can have well-groomed hair, clean shoes, clean hands and nails, and well-kept clothes.

This reaction on the prospect's part is not usually a conscious one—but it happens nevertheless. Few people react to others with complete indifference. You cannot afford to gamble. Appearance is far too important to indulge in carelessness or eccentric dress. Style and the right colors for you are also important.

The second impression is then given by the advisor's opening words. If the advisor's speech is pleasant and confident, if his or her opening remarks are clear, well organized, and interesting, the advisor has made another important step in building confidence in the prospect.

Confidence

Common sense will keep you from outlandish mistakes of appearance, dress, and manners. Careful preparation can save you from the more subtle errors than can be equally costly. What you do and say should be calculated to establish professional prestige and personal respect. The process begins in the preapproach, and it is carried to near-fulfillment in the approach.

Whatever serves to establish the prospect's confidence in you will help open the door to a favorable interview. Whatever serves to restrict confidence or tear it down will tend to close the door. Prospects listen to and buy from those they trust and respect. Thus a major purpose of the approach is to establish rapport and begin a business friendship. The prospect must be willing to become an acquaintance of yours and then a business "friend" if a sale is to be made. This is the meaning behind the saying that "no one sells life insurance to a stranger." It is also implied in the shrewd observation that "people do not buy from us only because they believe what we say. They buy also because they believe that we believe in what we say."

Confidence on both sides (advisor and prospect) is vitally important. The first sale you make is to yourself. It is important to believe that you have something to offer this prospect. This is the essence of confidence in yourself.

The second sale is to sell the interview. Why should the prospect interrupt work or leisure to talk with you? How are you qualified to help the prospect? These are the unspoken questions in the prospect's mind. The answers come from you.

Preparation

Good approaches share one thing in common: they bridge the gap between the first moments of a meeting and your next objective, starting the fact-finding interview.

Sales Psychology

Breakout: Read the following and think about how Harry presents himself and relates to his prospect

Harry would probably be late for his 11 a.m. appointment with George Robertson, a successful businessman who owned a dry cleaning franchise, a lawn-care company, and three printing/photocopy shops. Traffic was slow because of the heavy rain. It hadn't been a good day... and it wasn't half over. Harry was tired and somewhat irritable from too little sleep after watching last night's late show; the rejection notice at the office hadn't helped; and a just-completed telephone conversation with a frustrating prospect had left him exasperated and short on time. He was 10 minutes late and wet when he hurriedly approached his prospect's administrative assistant and introduced himself.

"Yes," she said, "please follow me. Mr. Robertson has been expecting you."

"Good morning, Mr. Robinson. I'm Harry Culver, and I'm sorry to be late. Traffic is unreal with this rain."

"That's perfectly all right. Please have a seat. And feel free to take off your coat. As wet as it is, you'll probably need to have it cleaned and pressed."

Harry thanked Mr. Robertson and carefully started to hang his coat on the back of the chair. "You're right about the suit, and cleaning prices are sky high these days."

The remaining 8 minutes of the interview went down hill very quickly, and Harry left not knowing why.

There are many Harrys who make and lose sales without having a clear insight as to why. There are many who could substantially improve their chances for success if they were more fully aware of the factors that underlie a sale—if they were more fully aware of the seen and unseen, spoken and unspoken forms of communication that pass back and forth between advisor and prospect.

Such awareness covers a wide range of factors. If Harry asks you for advice, what would you tell him?

In each case, the approach is designed to unsettle the prospect's complacency. When you come in, the business prospect is not thinking about the problem of what would happen to the business in the event of death or disability. The business owner may have been thinking about how to pay the sales taxes due on merchandise sold after having neglected to put enough aside to settle up with the government. Or the prospect may be thinking about an order that was just cancelled by an old customer, or about a piece of equipment that broke down two hours ago and stopped production cold. These immediate concerns don't leave a business prospect with time to focus on what might happen someday.

You want your prospect open and receptive to your perspective and way of thinking. This generally means asking questions that have an unsettling, disturbing or provocative effect. It means having the prospect become aware that there are serious problems that need to be addressed and resolved.

People are usually motivated when they see the light or feel the heat. Fear is a powerful motivator. When a prospect is unsettled by the realization that everything is not as well arranged as had been assumed, he or she begins to fear the possible loss of something important.

All of this presupposes that the advisor is knowledgeable enough. This means having a working knowledge sufficient to pursue an intelligent discussion with a business prospect and to recognize problems your products can help solve.

Much of your success in the approach is a matter of preparation. Don't rely on spur-of-the-moment inspiration. You will be far more effective if you have carefully prepared an initial approach, memorized it, and practiced it. (A series of disturbing questions appears later in this chapter.)

More Questions

To sell, you must get prospects to talk. *The skillful use of questions is the most effective way to keep the focus of the discussion on your prospect.*

There is no real difference between this technique in business insurance and personal selling. You will find that business prospects welcome an invitation to tell about their business and its problems—if you ask.

Design direct, non-apologetic questions. Questions that imply a negative response will probably get one. Consider, for example, the response that a prospect is most likely to give to the question, "Do you mind if I ask you a very personal question about your income from the business?" Compare this with, "Business Owner, to properly evaluate your needs we must review your business financial situation. Can you provide your financial statements for the past few years, or would it be more convenient for me to get them from your accountant?"

The Service Approach

As with personal sales procedures, no one approach is best. Your choice will probably be determined largely by your comfort and success with approaches you are already using. Basically, there are two categories of approaches; they are opposite sides of the same idea:

- the service approach
- the idea approach

The main purpose of the service approach is to help you gather enough information from the prospect to identify problem areas. Once you have identified the problem areas, you will be in a position to provide meaningful solutions.

You will find it helpful to select and memorize a number of "idea-hooks" which can be used following a preapproach letter, with or without a telephone appointment, on a referred lead, or on a cold-canvass call.

Idea hooks are short statements that contain the basic concepts of an idea that could be beneficial to the prospect. The purpose of an idea hook is not to educate your prospect about some technical matter but rather to stimulate your prospect's interest in learning more about the idea and about you.

> *"Prospect, several of my clients have been able to protect their companies against the risks associated with the death of a key employee with only minimum initial impact on their firms' financial statements."*

> *"Prospect, I would like to explain in more detail some ideas on how to pass on your business to your son or daughter but still provide your spouse with financial security."* (These concepts are described in detail later in the text.)

When approaching a prospect, it's natural to begin with courteous introductory remarks. For example:

> *"Business Owner, I am John Advisor of the _____ Company. I asked Chris Doakes for an introduction to you because I have some ideas that I think will be valuable to you—ideas that could affect the future of your business."*

Note that there is no great emphasis on the mutual friend, Chris Doakes. This prevents an interruption for small talk about Chris and avoids a challenge about Chris's "presumption" in sending you. You don't say, "Chris sent me" or "Chris says you will be interested." You say only that "I asked Chris for an introduction because..."

The third-party influence, and the prestige it lends, is gained without risk of "overplaying your hand." Common ground has been established without specific reference to the relationship between you and Chris.

If Chris is your friend, you could say, "my friend, Chris Doakes." If Chris is a policy owner, the reference would be to "my client, Chris Doakes." Where there is no referral, you might say, "I have asked you for an interview because..." or "I called you because..." or "We wrote to you because..."

Assume you've said that you have some ideas that may be valuable for the prospect and the prospect's business. This sets the stage for the beginning of the interview. People are more willing to listen if they know you are going to talk about things in which they have an interest.

The word "ideas" doesn't confine you to any set track, but it does arouse some curiosity. This is not a speech or a canned sales talk. It's only "some ideas" that your prospect can take or leave.

You might continue in this manner:

> *"It's been our experience, (Business Owner), that most business people are very busy with all the responsibilities of running a profitable business... that they have taken little time to devote to some extremely important contingencies that are simply not part of the everyday routine—contingencies that touch on the very heart of their business, but which are often not apparent until it's too late to solve them by the best means. To explain what I mean, may I ask you a question or two?"*

Note that you've asked your prospect only to agree to "a question or two"—no third degree, only a few questions. What harm could there be in answering a few questions? Besides (thinks the prospect) this will show me what the advisor has in mind. This also implies a quick meeting—a few questions and it's all over because then the prospect will be in a position to call a halt to the meeting—then the prospect has something to which he or she can say no.

The Questions

At this point, you should have some thought-provoking questions ready. Every one of the following transitional questions has been used successfully for this purpose. Brief, powerful questions followed by your silence can be a very effective way to get your prospects to talk about their real concerns.

- *Did you know that your business might live only as long as you do, unless special arrangements are made before your death? How do you feel about that?*
- *Have you made provision in your will for disposition of this valuable business when you die?*
- *Does your will authorize anyone to open the doors of your business tomorrow if you should die tonight?*
- *Who would you want to take over your business if you should die tonight? (Wait for a response.) Why this person? Is there anyone else? Have you made any plans?*
- *Have you ever considered the possibility that your business might die with you? (Wait for a response.) What would that mean to your family and your business partner?*
- *Would you be interested in a way to make your business worth as much after your death as it is today?*
- *If you wanted to buy out your competitor, Jack Smith, do you have an idea what it would cost? Are you aware that his business could be available at half that price if Jack Smith were to die tonight?*
- *Do you want your family to keep your business going after you die? Why do you feel that way?*
- *If you had to collect all your receivables within 30 days, what percentage would you expect to lose?*
- *Is any member of your family completely willing and as capable as you to run this business?*
- *If you had died last night, would it make more sense for a member of your family to run this business or for your family to sell it to your employees or competitors?*
- *If your health required you to move to another climate, would you want to keep this business or sell it?*

- *Do you think your employees would look for other jobs if you had died last night, or would they wait to see what would happen to your business?*

- *If one of your associates should die, would you and your surviving costockholders be certain of future control of the company?*

- *If one of your associates should die, would you want the surviving spouse to have a voice in the management of your business?*

- *If one of your associates should die, what would you want to do about the surviving spouse—take that person into the business or buy them out?*

- *If one of the stockholders of your company had died last night, what financial headaches would there be for the surviving stockholders today?*

Initial Time Confirmation

Sometimes, in seeking an appointment, you will commit yourself to a specified time limit. Early in the interview or approach, you should seek to confirm the time available for the visit.

You may say, *"Business Owner, when we set this appointment, I indicated that I would need only 20 minutes (or whatever period was indicated) of your time. I plan on taking no more than 20 minutes, and then I will leave. With this in mind, is your schedule okay for the next 20 minutes?"*

Asking a question of this kind achieves two goals. First, it confirms the fact that you respect your prospect's time. Second, when the prospect confirms that the requested period is available for the interview, he or she is more likely to allow the period to go by without interruptions.

- *If you had to take in a new associate, would you rather pick that person yourself or have a deceased associate's executor pick the person for you?*

- *In the event of your death, would you want the financial security and happiness of your family to be dependent on the continued success of this business—without you around to help run it?*

- *Do you have any assurance that your heirs will get a fair price for your stock when you die?*

- *If you became sick or disabled for a lengthy period, how would you pay yourself?*

- *Do you plan on having any of your children enter your business? Will your associates consent to this?*

- *If only one of your children enters your business, how will you provide for your spouse and other children in the event of your death?*
- *Will the laws of this state determine the disposition of your business?*
- *Will your business last only as long as you do?*
- *If anything happens to you, could your spouse devote full time to the business?*
- *Is there a market for your business if you were not part of the package?*
- *How much will your company's goodwill be worth after your death or disability?*
- *Whom have you trained to run the company after your death, disability, or retirement?*
- *Would you like to have a stranger run the business for you? Would you want your spouse to turn the business over to a stranger and trust that person to run the company?*
- *Do you have a will? Do you have a will for your business?*
- *When did you last have a complete audit of your business insurance?*
- *Would you like to know what your competitors and other business owners are doing about the problems we've been discussing?*
- *How much of a liability would this business create for your estate?*

By asking questions such as these, you invite your prospect to share his or her feelings and wants. The rapport that develops at this stage will help the prospect to view the ultimate sale as a mutual agreement.

The Idea Approach

In contrast to the service approach, the idea approach involves presenting one or more specific ideas that may be of value to your prospect.

Arouse Curiosity

Sometimes you present a particular idea in the belief that this idea will help solve a specific problem your prospect faces. More frequently the presentation is intended to stimulate your prospect's curiosity.

Another variation is to use the idea approach initially, because it permits you to focus on a specific concept that may fit into the prospect's planning.

Then, if the prospect does not find the idea particularly appealing, you can change gears to a broader-based needs approach such as the "Areas of Possible Interest" sheet or some other fact-finding process.

Communication

On the platform of the Million Dollar Round Table, many speakers have indicated that the difference between achievers and non-achievers in the life insurance business is that although both sets of advisors may use similar words, the message they communicate is often different.

One life underwriter may appear to prospects to be saying, "I've got a problem. I've got to make a sale." Another advisor may use almost the same words, but this advisor may appear to the prospect to be saying, "You've got a problem, and when I walk out that door I'm going to take your problem with me."

Tax Ideas as Approaches

Certain tax-favored ideas have great appeal and are helpful in the approach. Here are a few of them.

- Life insurance death proceeds usually carry the same advantages in a business situation as in personal insurance. In general, this means no income tax on death proceeds. However, C corporations with 3-year average annual gross receipts in excess of $7.5 million are subject to the alternative minimum tax (AMT). (For corporations in existence less than 3 years, the initial qualification for exemption from the AMT involves having average annual gross receipts of no more than $5 million, with the respective number of years the corporation was in existence to be substituted for the 3 years). Consequently, life insurance cash values and death proceeds will enter the AMT calculations of larger corporations.

- Cash values accumulate free of federal income taxation. (See above regarding corporations.)

- Premiums paid to insure the lives of key people receive no favored tax treatment, but the death proceeds of key person life insurance are received by the business free of federal income tax.

- The same is true of premiums and proceeds of policies that fund a business-owned buy-sell agreement.

- In both situations (key person and buy-sell), life insurance offers a low-cost way to be certain that enough money will be available when death creates the need for money. Without life insurance, the business owners' alternatives would be much more expensive and much less certain.

- Life insurance often is purchased by business owners as a low-cost method of providing liquid funds to pay the federal estate tax that is levied against the estate of a deceased person. Many estates contain nonliquid assets that the heirs don't wish to sell, so the ready cash provided by life insurance is an effective, sure, and inexpensive solution for the heirs.

- Life insurance is used by many corporations to buy back (redeem) part of a deceased shareholder's stock in conformance with Section 303 of the Internal Revenue Code. This allows the deceased's heirs to sell part of the stock back to the corporation for cash. It's a way to get money out of the business on a tax-free basis, while still retaining an interest in the business.

Non-interviews

One successful business insurance advisor has suggested that your first contact with any prospect should be what this advisor describes as a "non-interview." A non-interview is any initial contact—whether at a Kiwanis meeting, while standing in line at the supermarket counter, or at a first formal sales interview. Many life underwriters hold planned, informal non-interviews with a prospect over a cup of coffee.

As described by this advisor, the non-interview serves three purposes.

First, the advisor wants to find out if he even wants to proceed to do business with a given prospect. Is this an individual who fits the advisor's target? Is this prospect the advisor's "kind of person?"

Second, the advisor wants the prospect to like him and to appreciate his skill. He wants both himself and the prospect to be comfortable enough so that the chemistry is right to proceed.

Third, the advisor wants to learn enough about the prospect's needs and desires to assess what to do next.

The key to the non-interview is to get the other person talking by asking questions. The advisor gets his prospects to tell him about their spouse, kids, business, and hobbies.

His favorite opening line is, "Do I know you from somewhere?"

Prospects often respond, "I don't know, but you look familiar, too."

The advisor continues with questions such as, "What clubs do you belong to? Where do you work?"

Before the advisor finishes, he knows what he needs to know in order to proceed.

SUMMARY

Prospecting techniques in the business market are essentially the same as in the personal market. Build your prospects for business needs through your current clients and contacts and expand from there. Base approaches on the problems that business owners face in the event of death or disability of an owner or key employee. Persistent prospecting and good record keeping are essential keys to success. Building prestige and a trustworthy reputation is important, as is an understanding that the time frame on business insurance markets is longer than in personal markets.

CASE HISTORY: THE VALUE OF A COLD CALL AND FREQUENT CONTACT

Agent

This case was written by Ray Kahn and Frank Bits. Ray is a former engineer with a large steel company and sells mostly in the business market. Frank is a little older than Ray, and has been in life insurance work a few years longer. They are both active in civic and community activities.

Prospects

Our prospects were three business owners, ages 28, 33, and 55. They were engaged in a "short run" stamping business.

Approach

The first visit was a cold call. We knew only the type of business and the approximate ages of the partners. Our opener was one we have found effective in almost all cold canvass situations: "Do you have a business will?"

The owners did not understand the question. When they asked for clarification we followed with a discussion of problems and solutions. We found that their business was suffering from growing pains—their space was limited and orders were increasing. However, although they were interested in our initial comments, they felt their lack of operating capital prevented any action at that time.

They agreed to have us keep in touch with them and to receive literature pertaining to their business and its problems. We sent birthday cards, educational materials, and other prestige-building mailings at periodic intervals.

Fact-Finding

When we returned later in the year, we were well received. This call was made at a new location. The fortunes of the business were on the rise.

The problems of death disturbed the two younger owners. They wanted to proceed if the arrangement wouldn't hamper the current finances of their operation. However, the older owner was decidedly unsold on the proposal—an attitude he hadn't revealed at the first meeting. He felt that the problems of today were worse than the problems that death would cause; he was willing to accept a "calculated risk."

We did not hesitate to point out to the younger owners that the risk was also theirs. The older owner's attitude endangered their families in the event of either's death. There would be no money to buy out the deceased's interest; the family might be forced to demand liquidation. Everyone would suffer losses as a consequence.

Realizing their predicament, the younger owners persuaded the older associate to reconsider and listen to our presentation in full. He finally agreed reluctantly.

There was a temporary obstacle in that they could not agree on the true worth of the business. This, we believe, was the turning point of the sale. A thorough examination of the financial statements yielded an agreed-upon going-concern valuation of $600,000. We obtained agreement on the probable liquidation value, a value significantly below the going-concern value. At this point the eldest owner was convinced that neither survivors nor the family of a deceased could afford the liquidation risk. They asked us to return the following week with a detailed proposal and a sample agreement.

Planning

I drafted a proposal, designed around the prospect's specific needs and current financial resources as determined in the fact-finding interview. We designed a cross-purchase plan funded with interest-sensitive permanent life insurance policies: six policies of $100,000 each.

Close

I phoned to set a time for the interview. The appointment was made but the owners also insisted on being told, over the phone, the cost of the insurance.

The first thing we did at the interview was to review a sample agreement. This made them all the more interested in solving the problem. Next we showed them an illustration of the life insurance funding arrangements, emphasizing the values that would build up in the policies.

At this point, about 20 minutes after starting the interview, we asked, "What do you think about it?" One of the owners reached into a desk drawer and pulled out a check. It had been made out for the full annual premium before our arrival at the plant.

Post Sales

The attorney prepared a rough draft of the agreement. We suggested that the final draft should be prepared and signatures obtained as soon as possible. The attorney agreed. It was also agreed that new wills would be completed to conform to the agreement.

Before the meeting ended, we also suggested that the owners allow us to complete our services by evaluating their personal insurance and business insurance for the benefit of their families. The attorney agreed. Eventually we were able to complete a full review of the insurance needs and coverage of the two younger owners.

Following this review, each of these clients purchased additional insurance (total additional was $265,000). The eldest owner procrastinated, stating that he would like to consult with his brother to whom he went for advice in such matters. His brother advised against the purchase of further insurance! Because we could not persuade the brother to meet with us, we dropped the matter temporarily, hoping that time would change the attitude.

We had created such a good relationship with the younger owners that they referred us to several members of their families, leading to additional coverage of $442,000 on five lives. In addition, two business insurance leads were secured, one of which was closed for $250,000. The other never went anywhere.

Since our first sale, we have made it a practice to see the owners regularly. A rich friendship has developed from these calls.

Postscript

During our calls, we repeatedly asked if the agreement had been signed. We were told that the attorney had as yet not drawn up the finished copy. We took it upon ourselves to call the attorney to hasten delivery of the document for signature.

After we had practically made "pests" of ourselves, the attorney finished the document. We took for granted that the owners would sign the agreement upon receipt. This was a mistake!

Ten months after our original sale we were notified that the eldest owner had died suddenly of a heart attack. In checking, we found that all the owners had not signed the agreement.

Furthermore, in the preceding month the business location had once again been changed, with considerable expenditure involved in the moving of heavy equipment. Coupled with the loss of business necessitated by a retooling program for a new contract, the value of the business had declined slightly from the value specified in the unsigned contract. The attorney and the accountant were of the opinion that the younger surviving owners should settle for only the reduced value of the deceased's interest.

A further facet of this case was the fact that the deceased only had $50,000 of personal insurance and other property in the amount of $25,000. Since we had been unable to set up an adequate insurance program for him, as a result of his brother's advice, his wife was counting heavily on the business insurance. She was in a precarious financial position.

Happily for all concerned, the younger owners of their own volition agreed that the spouse should receive the full $200,000 for her husband's share of the business. They believed that if one of them had been the deceased, they would have wanted their families to receive the full amount of the insurance proceeds just as if the agreement had been signed.

Proper legal steps were taken and the case was brought to a successful conclusion. Thus, for one annual premium, the two younger owners purchased a $200,000 interest between them.

Because they now owned a $600,000 business, and because it was anticipated that the business value would increase in the near future, an additional $150,000 was placed on the lives of each of the survivors.

This case showed that:

1. Cold canvass calls can prove lucrative.

2. Use of comparison of going-concern value and liquidating value will encourage the prospect to seriously consider business continuation insurance.

3. Unsigned agreements do not solve the problems of business owners at death. The agent should be persistent in insisting that the agreement be signed. Fortunately in the above case, the outcome was a happy one, but it would not have been if the two surviving owners had not been so generous.

4. New business can result from good service.

CHAPTER REVIEW

Key terms and concepts are explained in the Glossary. Answers to the Review Questions and Self-Test Questions are found in the back of the book following the Glossary.

Key Terms and Concepts

selling/planning process	approach
center of influence	sales ratios
preapproach	third-party influence

Review Questions

1. List eight categories of sources of business insurance prospects.

2. Name three attributes of centers of influence.

3. Endless chain prospecting is a natural outgrowth of _____.

4. Name three lists or directories that could be helpful to you as an aid in prospecting for business insurance.

5. Name five ways in which your preapproach to a business insurance prospect might be different from your preapproach to a personal insurance prospect.

6. What is the purpose of the preapproach?

7. Name two preapproach methods.

8.
   A. Name three advantages of the telephone as an approach/prospecting tool.
   B. Name three disadvantages of the telephone as an approach/prospecting tool.

9.   When you first meet your prospect face to face, what four factors generally influence how well you are received?

10. In the space below, write out one thought-provoking question you could use to encourage your business prospect to talk about her or her concerns. The following questions concern the case study, "Value of a Cold Call and Frequent Contact."

11. The agents' approach was "Do you have a business will?" What did they mean by that?

12. Do you think cold canvassing is a good prospecting method for business insurance? Explain the pros and cons.

13. Should the buy-sell agreement be completed before the life insurance is placed? Explain.

Self-Test Questions

Instructions: Read the chapter first, then answer the following questions to test your knowledge. There are 10 questions. Circle the correct answer, then check your answers with the answer key in the back of the book.

14. Which of the following does the text suggest as the best source to start prospecting in the business markets?

(A) tip clubs
(B) current clients
(C) centers of influence
(D) businesses that you and/or your family patronize

15. Which of the following statements about prospecting and the preapproach is true?

(A) Third-party influence refers to your social status.
(B) The advantages of conducting the initial interview in the prospect's office far outweigh the disadvantages.
(C) Most agents agree that direct mail is the most effective follow-up to preapproach letters.
(D) Having prospects and clients come to your office conveys an attitude of professionalism and establishes the premise that they are coming to you for advice.

16. Preapproach mail can be helpful to a business insurance practice because it

   (A) eliminates the need for a scheduled appointment
   (B) preconditions the prospect to expect a request for an appointment and to be more receptive to that request
   (C) does an effective job of selling by itself and prospects will call you
   (D) makes your work easier because you do not have to follow up on the mailing

17. The "rule of eight" states that

   (A) The first eight seconds of the approach or eight words of the agent may win or lose the sale.
   (B) Prospecting results improve if you have just eaten before making calls.
   (C) It is best to stand at least eight feet from the prospect in the approach.
   (D) Your phone approach creates a first impression and your first meeting a second.

18. A major purpose of the approach in business insurance is to

   (A) prepare for an appointment
   (B) establish rapport and start a business relationship
   (C) begin a fact-finding interview
   (D) recommend types of policies the prospect could purchase

19. Third-party influence refers to

   (A) your social connections
   (B) those centers of influence who refer you to others
   (C) reference material that establishes prestige and credibility
   (D) endless chain prospecting

20. The business purpose of becoming involved in community activities is to

   (A) make sales in the business community as soon as possible
   (B) increase your visibility and become known
   (C) further your personal interests and motivate yourself
   (D) seek ways to gain additional business tax deductions

READ THE FOLLOWING DIRECTIONS BEFORE CONTINUING

The questions below differ from the preceding questions in that they all contain the word EXCEPT. So you understand fully the basis used in selecting each answer, be sure to read each question carefully.

21.   All of the following are criteria for a person to be a center of influence for business insurance sales EXCEPT

   (A)   a person who is a former policyowner
   (B)   a person who has high prestige in the community
   (C)   a person who has more than a passing interest in your business success
   (D)   a person who has access to or knowledge of a wide circle of successful people on a regular basis

22.   All of the following statements about prospecting are true EXCEPT

   (A)   Cold calls are seldom successful in the business insurance markets and should not be used for prospecting in this field.
   (B)   The local library often contains reference books and directories that can be effective tools for identifying prospects.
   (C)   Tips clubs are composed of local salespersons from a diverse group of industries and are formed for the exchange of information on business prospects.
   (D)   Active participation in community organizations is a way to gain valuable contacts because the more successful business owners are often among the leaders of these organizations.

23.   All of the following are keys to an effective preapproach EXCEPT

   (A)   your attitude
   (B)   your prospecting ability
   (C)   your knowledge of taxes
   (D)   your ability to build trust and prestige

Learning Objectives

By reading this chapter and answering the questions, you should be able to

1. Explain how the selling cycle and buying cycle interact in the sales process.

2. Explain the fact-finding process and how to use fact-finding forms in data gathering.

3. Identify information that should be gathered in this step of the selling process.

4. Explain concepts that can be used in approaching business owners to generate interest in continuing the sales process.

5. Describe types of decision-making and social styles that impact advisor-client relations.

6. Describe the problems facing a business when a business owner dies.

7. Describe the options available to the different forms of business when an owner dies

This chapter examines the fact-finding process: gathering information from the prospect, establishing rapport, credibility and trust, and qualifying the prospect. Several sample fact finders are provided in the Appendix. Concepts designed to generate the prospect's interest in continuing the advisor/client relationship are discussed.

The chapter also reviews decision-making and social styles that can aid the advisor in understanding how the prospect's personality may affect his or her behavior and the advisor-prospect relationship.

The problems faced by a business at the death of the owner and options available to the different types of business organizations are examined. This serves as a preparation for the discussion of buy-sell agreements in the next chapter.

THE FACT-FINDING PROCESS

The fact-finding process lays the foundation for any recommendations to be made or implemented by the financial advisor, or any buying decision by the prospect. Granted, each step in the sales process is important, but the fact-finding interview is the primary tool an advisor uses to demonstrate the need for the prospect to act. This is the heart of the selling process.

This section will focus on the importance of the fact-finding/feeling-finding interview, on the significance of the questions you ask, and on ways and means to conduct these interviews.

There are several objectives to accomplish during this phase of the sales process.

- First, build on the trust and credibility that was established during your initial meeting. Sell yourself. Be professional.
- Second, gather the data that will allow you to construct a proposal based on the prospect's needs and wants.
- Finally, get agreement from your prospect to continue with the next step of the process.

The Buying Cycle and the Selling Cycle

selling cycle   Too frequently, concern about technical knowledge in business insurance cases can lead to the fatal trap of forgetting about the importance of relationship building. There is no difference between the basic selling "rules" of business insurance and personal insurance. The underlying process is the same. The one difference you may find is that business insurance is almost always a multiple interview process. Let's briefly review the buying and selling cycle.

From the Buyers Viewpoint

buying cycle   Buying is the decision people make when they want a service or a product more than the cash in their pocket. In reaching this decision, people go through a process called the buying cycle, which has four basic steps:

1. Recognize a problem.
2. Desire a solution.
3. Decide on a solution.
4. Make the purchase.

This process applies equally to a decision to visit the family doctor as it does to buy a new pair of shoes or a business continuation plan. Understanding the buying cycle is crucial because to help a prospect buy, you must guide that prospect through the steps of the buying cycle.

From the Seller's Viewpoint

The selling cycle is simply the opposite side of the same coin from the buying cycle. Depicted side by side with the buying cycle, the basic steps of the selling cycle are as follows:

Buying Cycle	Selling Cycle
1. Recognize a problem.	1. Help prospect discover a problem.
2. Desire a solution.	2. Show the consequences of the problem.
3. Decide on a solution.	3. Offer solutions, emphasizing the best solution.
4. Make the purchase.	4. Help the prospect to buy now.

Developing a strong advisor/client relationship with your prospects will help you avoid offering solutions before fully developing the problem and before gaining the prospect's acknowledgment of the problem's existence and importance. The advisor must understand the buying process from the prospect's side and assist the prospect through it in conducting the selling process.

Building Prestige and Confidence

Any discussion of selling would be incomplete without stressing the importance of prestige and confidence. Underlying every purchase is confidence on the part of the buyer. One of the goals of the fact-finding interview is to build prestige and confidence. A person who lacks confidence in you, your products, your company, or your service is unlikely to become a buyer.

Your challenge is to create prestige and develop the prospect's confidence in you. Some factors you can use to create prestige and instill confidence include your time in the business and knowledge of insurance and related financial subjects. In addition, designations such as CLU, ChFC, CFP or LUTCF, community involvement, personal and professional achievements, and knowledge of the client's business and its problems can help. Prestige by association can result from the positive perception of your prospect regarding the quality of your centers of influences, referrers, and clients.

The Transition to Fact-finding

Business life insurance is bought when your prospects understand and acknowledge their needs and want solutions. Fact-finding interviews help prospects make these discoveries. Your fact-finding interview is generally held as a continuing part of your initial meeting, but it may be a separate meeting, held later. Either way, you will need to make at least a brief transition to fact-finding. The main idea is to explain to your prospect the next step in the process and tell why it's important. You may also explain the process you will follow in taking this step.

You might say something like this:

> *"Business Owner, my main goal is to help you find ways to accomplish your business objectives. To do this, I need information about you and your business—not only factual information, but also your attitudes and feelings about your business and its future. This fact-finding process will be the foundation of any and all planning we do. It's a crucial step, and it's also our next step. To put it in a time frame, we should plan to set aside (duration) for it. I am ready to proceed right now with that next step. Would you like to proceed now, or would you rather set another appointment?*

If you or your prospect cannot continue immediately with the fact-finding interview, you might say,

> *"I would like to get together with you soon. Can we check our calendars now and schedule a meeting one week from today?"*

Your words and your tone through all of this should reflect your personal style of doing business. For example, if you are more assertive, you may want to convey a sense of urgency and try to exercise more influence over the situation. The approach might sound like this:

> *"It's very important that we meet again, as soon as possible, to proceed with the information-gathering process. We cannot do any planning until it is done. Is next week at this time good, or would the following afternoon be better?"*

Part of your transition will depend on how extensive and formal your fact-finding will be with this prospect. As you know, fact-finding forms involve endless varieties of sizes, details, and approaches. If you will be using a long and detailed fact-finding process, stress the advantages of thoroughness and completeness. However, if your fact-finding with this prospect involves a short form that addresses the bottom line almost from the start, you should stress to your prospect that your fact-finding will be simple and direct.

In this chapter, you will find a few examples of fact-finding forms. Your company may have others. Some fact-finding forms are tied directly to computer software, so your form selection may depend on your software selection. Ask your associates what forms they use. Talk with the appropriate people at your company about your need to adopt one or more fact-finding forms for business insurance purposes.

The Fact-Finding Process

Regardless of the fact-finding process you choose, you will probably start with some notion of what the prospect's problems might be. *However, during the fact-finding interview, do not pass judgments and do not make specific recommendations.* Reserve them for your sales presentation, when you present what you advocate as solutions. Two problems can result if you make specific recommendations prematurely. First, prospects will tend to view you as unprofessional, as someone only interested in making a sale. Second, your immediate conclusions about your prospect's needs could well be wrong. It is far better for you to take the time to review the data carefully and present a solution later.

Listening

All of us were created with two ears and only one mouth. We need to learn to listen at least twice as much as we talk. Experts say that the prospect should do 80 percent of the talking in the fact-finding interview. If not, you are not asking enough questions or not waiting for answers.

Because there are many concerns that the financial advisor may need to address, the advisor will have to gather considerable information from the prospect. Defining the prospect's current situation, determining future goals and time frames, and establishing what the client is willing to do to get there requires information. This information must be complete, accurate, up-to-date, relevant and well organized. Otherwise any recommendations and plans based on the information will be deficient, possibly erroneous, inappropriate, inconsistent or even dangerous to the prospect's financial well being. The only way for the financial advisor to accomplish this successfully is to listen carefully and ask questions that clarify the prospect's viewpoint.

Using Fact-Finding Forms

Be sure to use some type of fact-finding form—this is essential. Fact-finding forms help you cover all your points. Nothing is left to chance or memory because you have a list of questions in hand, and you write down information as it is given.

Certain other advantages may be less obvious. For example, most advisors turn to the fact-finding questionnaire when they feel that the prospect is ready to discuss his or her own situation seriously, frankly, and in depth. At this point, you will get feedback about your prospect's willingness to continue by saying, *"Business Owner, to do a thorough and professional job for you I need certain information about you and your business."*

Then, with pen and questionnaire in hand, you begin to ask the questions. The prospect's intentions will soon become obvious. Either the prospect will give the information requested, will express disinterest, or will balk for some expressed reason. Whatever happens, you soon become more aware of the prospect's intentions and feelings than before.

Some business owners are sensitive about releasing financial data and may therefore be reluctant to give you everything you want to know. On these occasions, be prepared to accept only partial information initially. When you sense this attitude in a prospect, you can change your style of questioning somewhat. For example, you can use questions such as, *"Are you earning in excess of . . .?"*

In the fact-finding process condition yourself mentally. Adopt the attitude that this prospect has a problem you can help solve! You are a financial physician. The fact-finding/feeling-finding form will help diagnose the problems and interests.

It is impossible to say what will really trigger the prospect's interest. It may be some small point you could pass over quickly, without realizing its significance. Hence, you should touch on all the points that reflect problems of business prospects in general. Using a fact-finding questionnaire will help you avoid skipping a point that could prove important, even vital to the sale.

Condensed and Limited-Purpose Fact-finding

Sometimes you might conduct only a condensed fact-finding session in the first interview. This can give you essential facts to pinpoint a definite need but not enough to make a thorough analysis of the prospect's overall situation.

If the prospect responds favorably to a particular need, you should know what to do next. In many cases this means asking pertinent questions of the prospect or showing the prospect some point-of-sale material regarding that specific need. Assume, for example, that you have made an approach involving the future of a business at the death of its owner. If the owner expresses interest, you could turn to the list of questions contained on the accompanying limited-purpose fact finder titled "Disposition of Business at Death."

In large measure, the "best" form depends on the type and extent of fact-finding necessary in a specific interview. For example, if you soon determine that your prospect's only pressing concern is about group health insurance, complete an employee census form and ask about desired coverage levels.

Adaptable Fact Finders

Some advisors prefer to select just one comprehensive fact-finding form and then use some or all of its parts as each interview dictates. One example is provided in the Appendix. This fact finder is basically for estate planning and total needs financial planning. It uses many of the questions that are asked on Treasury Form 706, the federal estate tax booklet/form. A tax attorney might use a fact finder this long.

Notice that questions relating specifically to business interests do not begin until question 72! The first 71 questions apply to all prospects, whether or not they are business owners. Questions 72, 73, and 74 apply respectively to sole proprietors, partners, and corporate stockholders. Questions 75 through 79 apply to all business owners. As you can see, many of the 79 questions have sub questions, so there are really many more than 79 questions. It is more accurate to say that the form has 79 question categories.

Brief Fact Finder/Feeling Finder Regarding Disposition of a Business at Death

These questions are designed to help you get quickly into a discussion with your prospect concerning a possible need for a buy-sell agreement funded with life insurance. Here is a suggested initial question for this single-need approach to a business owner:

"Business Owner, what do you want to happen to your business when you die or retire?"

There are only three alternatives available to business owners regarding disposition of a business at the death of an owner:

- Keep it—Keep the business in the family.
- Sell it—Sell the business, probably to the other owners.
- Liquidate it—Sell the assets after stopping the business.

There are a number of follow-up questions you can ask the business owner, depending on his or her answer. If the business owner does not know what to do with the business—maybe does not even know or understand the options—then you will have to spell them out.

Intertwined with the buy-sell questions are questions that attempt to place a key-person value on the owner. You do not have to memorize these questions. You can just read them from a photocopy of these two pages. Depending on answers you receive to some previous questions, you may be able to skip some subsequent questions.

Keep—If a business owner's goal is for family members to retain the business, ask questions such as:

- Which family members would you like to own your share of the business?
- Who will run the business on a day-to-day basis in your place?
- What age is he or she? Have you talked to that person about this? What was the person's reaction? Does that person want to run the business?
- How realistic is it for that person to run the business?
- What is the person currently doing to earn a living?
- How compatible are your heirs and the surviving owner(s)?
- What do you think will happen to profits under new management?
- Assuming no one dies or becomes disabled over the next 5 years, how much annual profit or loss do you estimate over the next 5 years?
- Should you die, would you want to guarantee these profits for your family for a number of years? How many?
- Are there other financial needs that would be caused by your death?
- What arrangements have you made to see that your objectives are carried out?

Brief Fact Finder/Feeling Finder Regarding Disposition of a Business at Death

Sell—If the prospect wants to sell the business (typically, it would be sold to other existing owners), ask the following questions.

- To whom would you sell your share of the business?
- For how much would you sell the business?
- What would be the method and the terms of payment?
- Are the method and terms of payment legally enforceable?
- Does the purchaser have all of the needed money to buy out the business?
- How much will be needed?
- Can the purchaser get the money? Where? At what price?
- What impact will the key owner's death have on the certainty of getting money and of getting enough money?
- Would you like to see a way to discount the purchase price?
- How will your death, or the death of any other owner, impact the financial strength of the business? Would you like to offset that loss?
- What arrangements have you made to see that your objectives are carried out?

Liquidate—If a prospect indicates a desire to liquidate the buisness, ask these questions. (In this context, liquidate means to sell the assets after shutting down the business. in contrast to selling the business as a going concern.

- What is the going-concern value of the business today? That is, if there were a willing buyer, what would be the sale price of the business?
- Have you calculated the likely amount of the dollar loss if the business were sold in a forced liquidated instead of as a going concern? (If yes, what amount? If no, offer to make that calculation as part of your planning process.)
- Do you have any other business-related debts? Do you want to pass them along to your heirs, or would you want to eliminate them at your death?
- What arrangements have you made to see that your objectives are carried out?

In addition to questions such as these, you will need "hard" information such as names, ages, and addresses of all the owners.

Short-Length. This "Estate Analysis" can be made into a short-length business fact finder by using only selected questions. For example, you could make a short-length business fact finder by using those questions following question 71, along with questions 1, 2, 7, 18, 19, 20, 21, and 22.

Medium-Length. To have this "Estate Analysis" serve as a medium-length fact finder for business purposes, you could use the questions just mentioned, plus others that help round out the picture. For example, you could pick up questions 27, 28, 29, 32, 34, 37, 39, 42, 45, and 47. To convert this all-purpose long form into a usable medium or short business one, just make a list on a separate sheet handy as a guide for which questions to ask.

The longer you use any fact finder, the more you will become comfortable with it. Eventually you will want to drop, add, and modify some questions. Feel free to use the "Estate Analysis" in a way to make it your own. Later in this text you will learn more about the rationale and significance of many of the questions used in this fact finder.

When properly completed, this fact finder should help an accountant determine what state inheritance and federal estate taxes would be due in the event of death. It should also help an attorney draw the most appropriate will to fulfill the distribution wishes of the client. It should also help the financial advisor plan life insurance and other financial products that can provide cash when needed for taxes, income, debts, and retirement.

Appendixes. You may prefer to use customized fact-finding forms. A short form of this variety for buy-sell fact finding is included in Appendix B. Appendix A includes questions that explore current coverages. Appendix C is the long fact finder. These forms are found at the end of this textbook.

In addition to information obtained through a fact-finding form, remember to ask your prospects for copies of the firm's

1. balance sheet
2. income statement
3. flow of funds statements
4. existing business agreements (buy-sell, deferred compensation, key person)
5. in-force insurance contracts
6. federal income tax returns for the business for the last 3 years

It is not crucial to get these forms and statements. However, they do provide useful insights into the structure and direction of the business.

"Areas of Possible Interest" Fact Finder

"Areas of Possible Interest" Not all fact finders fit the typical mental image of dozens of questions on dozens of pages. The accompanying "Areas of Possible Interest" list does not look like a fact finder, but it most certainly is one.

This one-pager doesn't waste any time. It gets right to the bottom line, namely: What interests the business owner? You can use this "Areas of Possible Interest" list as a focal point and/or giveaway piece of literature on cold calls, or as a preapproach mailer with a cover letter saying that you plan to stop by, or as an abbreviated fact finder on your initial interview. You can also use it to show your prospects the kind of work you do.

One way to use the "Areas of Possible Interest" list is to say:

> *"Business Owner, this list shows the areas where my business clients took action during the past year. Which of these items are most important to you?" or "Have you looked into any of these items recently? Which ones? Have you adopted any of them? Which of these items are you most interested in exploring further?"* Another variation is to say, *"Business Owner, the insurance needs of most business owners fall into one of the following categories." (Show the "Areas of Possible Interest" list to the business owner.) "I would like to ask you about this first one."* You then explain each item partly by telling, partly by asking questions.

Following a process of placing a priority rating on each item, there are several ways for you to proceed at this point:

Option 1, Come back later— If you need to learn more about these business areas, you might make an appointment to call back on the prospect. Later, research the area(s) carefully and come back with an associate who has agreed to work with you and split the business.

Option 2, Describe and come back later—Give a brief description of each idea on the list. Tell your prospect briefly about the concept of each. Then come back, as above.

Option 3, Describe, conduct a brief fact finder, and come back later—This method is step (2) plus a fact finder. After briefly describing the concept of each item, ask questions. Thank the prospect and set another appointment. Come back after some intensive research and/or bring someone to help you. As you become better acquainted with business insurance, you will be able to handle the "Areas of Possible Interest" list without assistance.

Option 4, One-pagers and concept presentation books—Another way to respond is to use a business insurance presentation book when prospects express interest in an item on the list. A presentation book consists of simple one-page tables or diagrams depicting the key aspects of each business insurance concept, tool, or problem. For example, the diagram on key person insurance contained elsewhere in the text is a one-pager that could be used to explain the basics of this concept. Be sure your one-pagers are approved by your company.

Prospects generally like one-page summaries of the key aspects of various ideas. You can use the presentation book during the initial interview (fact-finding) or in the presentation interview. The choice will depend on the nature of the fact-finding and feeling-finding process you ultimately use.

Future chapters cover specific business insurance tools and some contain one-pagers. Consider building your own business insurance presentation book with the graphs, tables, and diagrams that you can use to explain complex or technical subjects in a simple yet powerful way. Your company may provide such illustrations and sales material to put in your presentation book.

Areas of Possible Interest

The list below can be used as a fact finder in any one of several ways. The best and most basic use is simple, however. Just show your prospect the list and ask which of the items he/she is most interested in.

- Group Medical
- Buy-Sell Funding
- Key Person Indemnification
- Split Dollar
- Disability Income
- Disability Buyout
- Tax-Deductible Retirement Planning
- Personal Estate Planning with Corporate Dollars
- Salary Continuation
- Business Debt Liquidation
- Personal Life Insurance
- Business Mortgage Insurance
- IRC Section 162 Bonus
- Group Long-Term Care Insurance
- Business Overhead Expense Insurance

Open-Ended Fact/Feeling Questions

open-ended questions

Ask your prospects open-ended questions—questions that tend to get subjective and emotional responses. When your prospects tell how they feel and what they want, they are telling you the most important things.

Questions that elicit such personal responses include the following:

- *What do you want to happen to your business when you retire? (Or when you die? Or if you are totally and permanently disabled?)*

- *What do you see happening to your business over the next several years?*

- *What will your business be like 5 years from now? What would you like it to be 5 years from now?*

- *I'm very interested in knowing about you and this business. How and when did it begin? Or how did it get started? Or were others in it from the start besides you?*

Memo

TO: The Business Owner

SUBJECT: If you had died last night, how would these questions be answered today?

- Who is running the business?
- To whom do the employees report?
- How does your spouse get income?
- Who will pay the creditors?
- Does the bank have your personal guarantees on loans?
- Are there co-owners?
- Who will the co-owners want regarding ownership and control of the business?
- Should your shares be sold?
- Will your co-owner(s) buy?
- At what price?
- Where will they get the cash?
- Is that what you want?

If interview time is limited, be careful about asking the prospect an open-ended question such as "How did you get started in this business?" The prospect may be anxious to cover as much "meaty" discussion as possible in the short time available. Asked too early, this question may cause impatience. You can help change the prospect's attitude somewhat by first telling the prospect good things you know about his or her business. Then ask the open-ended question.

Summary of Fact-Finding

With work, study, and exposure, you will gain new insights into the fact-finding process for business insurance. Information that might seem unimportant or insignificant now may prove to be helpful when encountered in the future. The rationale that underlies some questions on a fact finder may escape your notice now but you will gain a deeper understanding of their purpose with more experience.

Even little bits of knowledge can go a long way in knowing how to proceed—or what to avoid—in certain situations. With this in mind, the following items are presented in hopes that they may be helpful as you uncover new situations in your fact-finding interviews.

- If a business has two or more owners, the advisor's automatic reaction should be to ask about a buy-sell agreement. Each owner will probably want to buy out the other when one dies. In such cases, making a written agreement is extremely important. Otherwise, an owner's wishes could be unfulfilled. Life insurance is most important here because it provides money at death to fund a buy-sell agreement.

- If the business has only one owner, the most common need is not a buy-sell agreement but rather such areas as debt coverage, money to offset losses if the business will be sold piecemeal, insurance to pay estate taxes, tax-favored retirement plans, and certain other fringe benefits. That does not mean a buy-sell plan is not appropriate. Sometimes a sole owner may find it possible to enter into a buy-sell agreement with a competitor or key employee.

- If the business has only one owner, ask the owner to consider the purchase of life insurance on his/her own life equal to the value of the business. *"Picture it this way. It's as though my insurance company were to enter into a buy-sell agreement with you to buy your business when you die. Not only would my company give your family the cash for the value of the business but they will also let your family keep the business or decide the future of the business without the pressure of needing money to pay estate taxes, creditors and so forth."*

- Is this a professional corporation (called a professional association in some states)? If so, ownership is restricted to licensed practitioners of that profession. A funded buy-sell agreement is vital if the business is to continue and if the decedent's heirs are to get full value.

- Is this a "big business?" Life insurance sales to large businesses usually require specialized knowledge and technical backup. Big business can be thought of—in the extreme—as public corporations whose stock is bought and sold by the general public. These will not likely be your markets at present.

- Is this a nonprofit establishment? In general, nonprofit groups include hospitals, educational and charitable establishments, foundations, and certain literary and scientific organizations. Nonprofit groups generally are exempt from federal income taxation. They are nonprofit in the sense that profits cannot be distributed to the people who control such organizations. Nonprofits can be good prospects, but they are different and need to be approached from a different perspective. For example, a buy-sell agreement would be impossible because there are no owners of such organizations, just members, officers, founders, and/or staff. However nonprofits do frequently present an opportunity for fringe benefits such as qualified retirement plans, deferred compensation, and split dollar plans.

- It is helpful to know whose money is being used by the business. Who provided the start-up money? The money put into the business was either a loan or an investment. If it was an investment, that person owns and controls some (or all) of the business. If it was a loan, the lender probably is not one of the owners. Much like "mortgage insurance," life insurance is often bought to cover business debts. Lenders often require life insurance collateral.

- Farms are businesses with special problems. Some farms are owned by large agri-corporations, but the advisor's best market generally is the family-owned farm. Family-owned farms can have high value (because of the land value) but modest profit. A major problem that can be solved with insurance is how to pay the estate tax at the farm owner's death without selling land or incurring high debt. Life insurance is perfect here. It provides cash to pay the taxes, thus letting the family keep the land and avoid liquidation or debt. Also, farmers are big borrowers, mostly for seed and living expenses until harvest. Key person insurance here can give the family money to pay off the debt and even provide an extra year's income to go without borrowing; the bank might not lend to the new "head of the family farm."

- In regular corporations, any owners who work for the business are considered by the IRS to be employees. Therefore such corporate owner-employees can cover themselves and any other employees with group insurance (and certain other fringe benefits) and deduct 100 percent of the premiums for federal income tax purposes. Selective fringe benefits for corporate owners and other key people can be arranged. Sole proprietors and partners can deduct such premiums for coverage on the lives of their employees. Starting in 2003 sole proprietors, partners, and S corporation owners can deduct 100 percent of the cost of health care on their own lives, their spouses and dependents.

- Provisions of the Internal Revenue Code generally encourage businesses to adopt rather uniform levels of fringe benefits for their employees. That is, a business's fringe benefits will generally treat all employees of that business to similar levels of benefits in order to avoid taxation that accompanies discrimination in favor of highly compensated employees. This opens the way for you to talk with business owners about supplementing their fringe benefit programs with individual insurance such as Section 162 bonus plans or split dollar plans.

- Every business has at least one key employee. Key person life insurance provides money to offset profits lost when a key employee dies. The smaller the business, the more likely it is that there is no satisfactory backup person to replace a key employee who dies. Key person life insurance provides cash to hire a replacement for a year or two. Or it can be used to pay off some immediate debt, thereby preventing insolvency and allowing the business to continue.

- Although business owners do some things for altruistic reasons, when it comes to business dealings the motivation usually centers on the question, "What's in it for me?" Don't overlook this fact in learning about and selling business insurance. Look for the less-than-altruistic appeal of what you're selling. Some business insurance sales are little more than personal insurance paid for with corporate dollars.

RELATIONSHIP PROCESSES

In interacting with business prospects, it is important to keep in mind that decision-making may involve more than one person and style of decision making, and that behavior is often affected by personal psychological patterns referred to as social style. We will review highlights of these concepts in this section.

Decision-Making

decision making styles

Accessibility to the decision maker is a critical factor in the sales process. In every sales situation, try to assess how decisions are made and which persons hold the real power to say yes to insurance services and products.

A person's title does not always indicate that an individual has real decision-making authority. You may be referred to a corporate treasurer or chief financial officer. This person may claim to have full responsibility for all decisions on insurance and financial proposals. Without offending this individual, you need to determine if real authority rests with this person or if the final decision will in fact be made elsewhere.

For example, sometimes your initial contact person may be responsible for reviewing all proposals, but may lack ultimate decision-making authority. In many businesses, the formal management decision structure is really subordinate to an informal decision-making process. The owner of a company may have one or two trusted confidants who have a critical influence on decisions. These confidants may be officers within the company or outside advisors such as a CPA, attorney, or banker.

By identifying and understanding these relationships, you can make efforts to earn the respect and trust of the real decision makers. Often your referrer or center of influence can provide information on a firm's informal decision processes. You can discretely ask your initial contacts within the company about any informal decision processes and about the key players involved.

Not all businesses use the same style in arriving at decisions. Styles of management decision making range from authoritative to consultative to fully participative. The box below summarizes some common decision styles you may encounter. This information comes from the work of two well-known management researchers, Victor Vroom and Phillip Yetton. Knowing the type of decision processes your prospect is likely to follow allows you to respond in a more effective manner.

Decision Styles
Authoritarian The owner/executive resolves problems or makes decisions using information available at a given point in time with no outside participation.   OR The owner/executive obtains information that he or she deems important from others and then makes the decision. Other employees or advisors may not know why information is requested or how it will be used. They only provide information requested and are not part of the process to evaluate alternative solutions to problems. The most readily accepted sales approach here would be deferred compensation, pension benefits, and estate planning, with all benefits skewed toward the owner(s).
Consultative The owner/executive shares problems or concerns individually with some other employees or advisors and asks for input. After receiving input, the owner/executive makes a decision that may or may not agree with suggestions of other employees or advisors.   OR The owner/executive shares problem or concern with other employees or advisors as a group and asks for group input. After group input is obtained, the owner/executive makes a decision that may or may not agree with group suggestions. Your best sales approach here would be benefits skewed toward the consultative group members: key person insurance, group insurance, and split dollar.
Participative The owner/executive shares problems or concerns with many other employees and advisors, both as individuals and as a group. The owner/executive works with involved parties to generate and evaluate alternative solutions. The owner/executive stresses the need to generate a group consensus on how best to solve the problem. After the group reaches consensus, the owner/executive accepts the decision and works to implement it. Your best reception in this setting will be to employee-oriented fringe benefits, and lots of them.

Social Style

social style   The creation of rapport with your prospect is your responsibility. You should try to detect what each prospect wants in a sales relationship, and use your versatility to adapt your responses to his or her respective needs. Everyone seeks a "magical" solution to the complexity of human behavior, citing birth order, various personality traits and a myriad of other components of behavior that will help us understand and interact effectively with others. One such behavioral characteristic which many have found help them work with others is referred to as social style.

Responding to the Prospect's Social Style

drive

expressive

amiable

analytical

Psychologist Dr. David Merrill described the characteristics of individuals with four different social styles:

- Driver
- Expressive
- Amiable
- Analytical

When you adapt to the prospect's social style, you make the person feel at home and less threatened. By listening and observing carefully during the first few minutes of the interview, you get an idea of how to treat the prospect.

The chart titled "Responding to Prospects' Social Styles" summarizes the characteristics of each social style and indicates how you can best respond to establish rapport with a person who has that style. Listen carefully and observe your prospect to determine which set of characteristics most closely describes the person you are talking with and then build rapport by responding in the appropriate way throughout the interview.

Responding To Prospects' Social Styles		
Social Style	**Prospect's Style Characteristics**	**Your Best Response**
Driver	Forceful, direct	Focus on objectives
	Will not waste time on small talk	Move right along
	Wants to be in control	Get to a decision, provide options
Expressive	Outgoing, enthusiastic	Focus on dreams
	Enjoys telling about personal projects and dreams	Take time to listen
	Wants to be recognized	To get decisions, provide incentives
Amiable	Easygoing, dependent	Focus on relationships
	Enjoys telling about personal relationships	Be personal
	Wants to be accepted	To get decisions, provide personal assurances
Analytical	Logical, quiet	Focus on principles and thinking
	Is uncomfortable with small talk	To get decisions, provide evidence
	Wants to be respected	Be accurate

EXAMPLE 1
If your prospect, Jane Weston, enthusiastically talks at length about the plans she has for the new business she is starting, you would classify her as *expressive*. To establish rapport, take time to listen and ask about her plans.
EXAMPLE 2

If your prospect, Ben Hammer, tells you where to sit when you go into his office and looks at his watch when you ask about the photograph of the sailboat on his wall, you would classify him as a *driver*. To establish rapport, respond by getting down to business and explaining the purpose, process, and payoff of the appointment.
 	
    What would happen if you responded to Jane Weston by going directly into an outline of the agenda for your meeting? What would happen if you tried to share a sailing story with Ben Hammer?
 	
    Let's look at two more examples.

EXAMPLE 3
If your prospect, Bob Hinds, greets you with a worried smile, apologizes for being 15 minutes late, and says that he could not get away from his last meeting, where they were planning a retirement party for his administrative assistant, a wonderful woman who has been with him since he started the company, you would classify him as *amiable*. To establish rapport, respond by taking time to ask about the retiring administrative assistant.

EXAMPLE 4
If your prospect, Dr. Patricia Gibbons, stands to greet you from behind her desk when you are ushered into her office, waits for you to take a seat, and immediately asks if you can tell her what the maximum gift she can give tax-free to each grandchild, you would classify her as *analytical*. To establish rapport, respond by taking the time to answer her question with a detailed and documented reply describing how she can give up to $11,000 to each grandchild, and with her husband can give up to $22,000 using gift-splitting techniques.

What would happen if you responded to Bob Hinds this way by launching into a discussion of gift taxes? How would Bob Hinds respond if you took a few moments to tell him about seeing old friends at your reunion?

What would happen if you tried to tell Patricia Gibbons about your high school class reunion that you attended last weekend?

Summary

By paying attention to how decisions are made and the social style of the prospects you meet, you can improve your ability to relate to others and build rapport more effectively. By building rapport you are building trust. People buy from those they like and trust. Paying attention to relationship issues will improve your ability to understand the why behind what is taking place. This should improve your ability to communicate with the prospect.

BUSINESS CONTINUATION: THE PROBLEM

The owners of closely held businesses have strong emotional ties to their companies. They are justifiably proud of the company's accomplishments and want their families to continue to benefit from this success. But despite these hopes and dreams, few business owners have given a great deal of thought to what will happen to the business when they retire or die. While many business owners have some vaguely defined notions about passing on their business to a family member or perhaps selling it, they typically have not explored all of the available legal and financial options. Nor have they become familiar with the necessary legal and financial decisions that must be made.

Few business owners have implemented formal and financially sound business continuation or liquidation plans designed to control the values in the business before or after their death.

This section and the next two chapters focus on business continuation and liquidation planning (a major source of business insurance sales). Regardless of whether your prospect wants to retain the business in the family, liquidate it, or sell it, careful planning and adequate funding are crucial.

This section examines the options available to the business and involved parties at the death of an owner. As you explore each option, you will become increasingly aware of the pitfalls that can beset a business that fails to adopt and fund a business continuation or liquidation plan. The next chapter will explore the major aspects of buy-sell agreements and funding options.

Working with Business Continuity Needs

Business continuation/liquidation arrangements are sound and prudent measures, and are widely accepted by the financial, accounting, business, and legal communities. Funding them with life insurance is customary and good business practice.

In addition to the fact-finding skills discussed in the previous section, a few concepts for working successfully in business continuity situations need to be stressed.

Develop a team approach

Buy-sell agreements will require you to work with other advisors. For example, an attorney will be needed to draw up the buy-sell agreement. In addition, you will probably work with the firm's accountant. The situation may also require the expertise of an appraiser. Thus your ability to work with other professionals is critical. You should establish working relationships with these types of advisors whenever possible.

Focus Prospects on the Need to Act Now

Remember that your role is to focus prospects on the need to act now to protect the future of their business and their families, by presenting ideas that are solutions to real problems. The temptation with business continuity needs is to delve into discussions of abstract legal agreements. Such discussions will only confuse prospects. The prospects need first to recognize there is an urgent problem that can be solved with proper planning.

Explore the Prospect's Goals

Proper planning begins with understanding prospects' goals and dreams. Where do they envision the business being in 10 years? What do they want to happen to the business when they retire, if they are disabled, or if they die? Clearly defined goals are the foundation for planning.

Consider Goals within Context of Interpersonal Relationships

Often your prospects have not thought through their goals for the business within the context of the interpersonal relationships between the important people in their business and personal lives. Prospects have not considered how these relationships will affect the realization of their goals. Thus, it is important for you to ask questions to help prospects think through their goals and dreams within the context of these relationships. Here are some questions you might ask.

- **Client and Co-Owner.** *What roles do you and your co-owner(s) play in the business? Are your roles interchangeable? Could one co-owner operate the business at the death of the other?*

- **Client and Spouse.** *Does your spouse own any part of the company? How does your spouse feel about business continuation/liquidation planning? Does your spouse have any strong feelings about taking part in the management of the company now or in the future?*

- **Client and Children.** *Are any of your children currently active in the business? Do you expect that your children will enter the business? How do your associates feel about this?*

- **Client and Key Persons.** *Do you have any key employees other than the owners? What role would you like them to play in the business when you die?*

Build your presentation around a clear understanding of your prospect's goals and interpersonal relationships. In this way you will increase your chances for a business continuation/liquidation sale. You will also avoid any tendency to confuse your client by discussing complex legal concepts early in the interview process.

With this background in mind, let us look now at the options that business owners face in planning for the future of their business. There are some basic differences in the options available to sole proprietors, partners, and stockholders.

Options for Sole Proprietorships

There are basically four things that can happen to a sole proprietorship when its owner dies:

1. The business may be liquidated by the estate executor.
2. The business may be continued by the estate executor until it can be sold as a "going concern."
3. The business may be transferred by will to a specified individual, usually a family member.
4. The business may be sold to an individual or group under the terms of a pre-death agreement.

Liquidation

In the absence of a sole proprietor's specific instructions included in a Will or business agreement, the final disposal of his or her estate (including any business interests) rests with the estate's executor.

Although state law usually allows the executor to run the business until it can be sold as a going concern at a fair price, the executor is personally liable for any losses the firm may suffer during this time. This liability exposure is usually sufficient to prompt the executor to dispose of the business as quickly as possible.

This generally means liquidation of the business. Liquidation means selling the assets for cash and bringing business activity to a halt. Such a forced piecemeal liquidation typically is a tragedy for everyone concerned—an unnecessary event that no sole proprietor would willingly permit to happen if he or she realized the consequences of a forced liquidation.

"Piecemeal" means selling the assets a piece at a time, as contrasted with selling all the assets as a group. A "forced" liquidation is when the executor has virtually no other options for the future of the business. That is, he is virtually forced to sell the assets piecemeal. See the accompanying chart titled: "Comparative Results of Forced Versus Planned Liquidation."

Planned Liquidation. Although forced liquidation generally can and should be avoided, orderly and planned liquidation may be a viable option for some sole proprietors.

With a planned liquidation, the executor is given the time, flexibility, and authority to dispose of the assets of the business at their optimum value. This option may be appropriate when there is no one in the sole proprietor's family or in the business who is willing and able to continue the business.

Even if there are willing family members or employees, the success of the business may be completely and irrevocably tied to the personality, skills, or goodwill of the sole proprietor in such a way that the value in the business will effectively die with this person.

A Will and Life Insurance. A properly prepared will and sufficient life insurance on the sole proprietor's life are essential to the success of an orderly, planned liquidation of business assets.

The will should be drafted by an attorney to give the executor broad powers to dispose of the proprietor's assets in accordance with a plan designed by the owner prior to death. Furthermore, the will must relieve the executor of personal liability for appropriate actions taken during the orderly liquidation of assets.

Without such relief from liability, no executor would be willing to participate in an orderly liquidation but would instead sell assets at any price and as quickly as possible.

Key Functions of Life Insurance. Adequate life insurance on the sole proprietor provides four key things:

- money to pay estate taxes and other obligations, thus reducing pressures for a quick sale of assets
- immediate income for the family, thus reducing the need to sell assets immediately to generate cash for the family
- funds to offset for the difference in the value of the business as a going concern and its liquidation value
- continuing income for the family independent of the business

Comparative Results of Forced Versus Planned Liquidation	
FORCED	**PLANNED**
Many accounts receivable are almost impossible to collect. They may lose 70 to 80 percent of the pre-death value if sold to a specialized financial institution that purchases accounts receivable	Executor can afford to wait for orderly collection of most accounts receivable. If necessary, executor has time to force legal action for collection
Inventory, fixtures, and equipment will be sold at auction for a fraction of their value.	Executor in a better position to negotiate sale of inventory, fixtures, and equipment with potential buyers. Especially important if assets are seasonal in nature or very specialized.
Any goodwill is totally gone—a significant loss for many small companies	Cooperative venture with other businesses or individuals is arranged prior to the death may facilitate transfer or sale of some goodwill value.
Immediate push by creditors for full and immediate payment of all claims against the business. May impair credit record of surviving family members.	Provides a method of paying claims of creditors. No injury occurs to creditworthiness of surviving family members.
Proceeds of the sale of assets will first go to satisfy the claims of creditors and the IRS, and may leave nothing for the family.	The family will receive the income it needs, creditors will be paid, and so will IRS.

Problems with a Sale as a Going Concern

Sometimes your prospect will want the executor to continue the business until it can be sold as a going concern.

While the value of a business as a going concern typically far exceeds the value of its assets, this option is fraught with the following special problems:

- The executor is usually not familiar with the day-to-day operations of the company and is not likely to be able to give full time to the business. Instead, the executor typically relies on the support and loyalty of key employees to continue the firm. Since these employees may perceive that they have no vested interest in the firm beyond their own jobs, they may not be as diligent in conducting the affairs of the business as the family would like. In fact, they are not at all sure that they will retain their jobs when the business is sold.

- Creditors may push for escalated payments on any outstanding debts and may refuse to issue the additional credit the business needs for working capital.

- Goodwill does not transfer to the executor.
- The sale of the business may result in lesser value than if the assets had been liquidated.
- The courts may delay approval of any sale, thus impairing the executor's ability to realize an optimum value for the business.
- Legal problems may delay the sale of the business.

Planning Is Essential. State laws hold the executor responsible for any losses the business may suffer while the executor runs the business after the sole proprietor's death. Pre-death planning is needed if a going-concern sale is to prove successful. The sole proprietor's will should give the executor the power to continue business operations while attempting to find a buyer. It should also relieve the executor of the liability exposure.

The executor will need flexibility to wait for the best purchaser. The executor may need authority to borrow money for working capital and inventory. The executor may also need the right to restructure the business into a corporation if such action will facilitate a sale.

Funding is Critical. Adequate funding through life insurance is also critical to the success of this option. The business often will be more attractive to potential purchasers if life insurance dollars have helped reduce or eliminate the firm's debts and/or provide working capital or inventory.

By enhancing the liquidity and financial solidity of the business, life insurance benefits can increase the value of the business by an amount that often exceeds the actual insurance proceeds.

The family also needs proceeds from life insurance to meet estate obligations and living expenses. With these needs met, the family will be able to wait while the executor sells the business as a going concern. Alternatively, the family may be willing to retain some equity in the business, possibly maximizing the long-term value that can be obtained from the sale.

Transfers by Will

Like other assets, sole proprietorships often are bequeathed to family members. Although many business owners talk of the time when their children will run the business, the decision to give the business to an adult child (or to a spouse) is often a difficult one. It requires the owner to step back and realistically assess the potential owner's management skills.

Factors That Make a Successful Transition Likely. Even assuming that the sole proprietor can identify a competent and willing successor from within the family, the transition to a new generation cannot be left to chance. A smooth transition is likely only if the following conditions are met:

- The sole proprietor's will clearly transfers control of the business.
- The business is financially sound.
- The returns realized from business operations are higher than those that might be earned if the company was sold and the family lived on the invested proceeds from the sale.
- The family has an alternative source of cash funds to pay estate obligations and taxes, and to provide continuing income without selling business assets.
- The firm's suppliers and customers are likely to continue doing business with the company.
- Banks and other creditors are supportive of the successor management.
- A mechanism exists for fairly compensating those family members who do not inherit and/or participate in the business. For example, a sole proprietor who wills the business to one child might leave the spouse and the other children life insurance proceeds equal to the value of the business.

Sometimes a business owner wants to leave the business to a child, and in the process, ends up shortchanging the spouse. That is, the child might get more than the spouse. This is risky because state laws allow the decedent's spouse to "elect against the will." This means that the spouse can go to court and demand at least as much as would have been received if the deceased had died without a will. (The law applies equally to men and women.)

It is much easier to resolve this kind of issue before it occurs. One way to handle it is to establish a buy-sell agreement between owner and child. Another is to place more insurance on the business owner's life, payable to the family member (or to his estate, if necessary) who would not otherwise be compensated fairly.

Keep In the Family. A sole proprietor who wishes to keep the business in family hands may lack a family member who is capable of running the business. Perhaps the sole proprietor wants a child to someday own the business, but that child is currently only a teenager.

In such a case, one or more key employees may be able to run the company until the heir is capable of assuming control. Remember, though, that the key employee will need sufficient motivation to assume this role. The incentive could come from increased salary or from an opportunity to gain partial ownership in the company.

Seasoned Manager. Alternatively, the family may need to bring in a seasoned manager to run the company at the death of the sole proprietor. This individual is likely to eventually demand an ownership position—perhaps even an option to purchase the family's interest in the business. While this may run counter to the sole proprietor's original intentions, selling the business to a seasoned manager at a fair price is certainly better for the family than a forced liquidation.

One way to help retain the loyalty of the seasoned manager is to establish a "golden handcuff" deferred compensation plan, funded informally with life insurance. "Golden handcuffs" are any contingent financial (golden) benefits that tend to keep or retain (handcuff) a key employee in the employ of the firm.

Avoid Pitfalls in Passing the Business On to Family. As seen from the preceding paragraphs, planning and liquidity for both the business and the family are critical in avoiding the potential pitfalls associated with passing the business on to a family member. Even under the best of conditions, the transition of ownership to a successor family member can be a painful process—one that often ends in failure.

Buy Time. Funds from life insurance can buy time while the family member decides whether the normal transition problems can be resolved or whether he or she should try to sell the company as a going concern.

Sale under a Pre-death Agreement

Some sole proprietors enter into agreements that bind their heirs to sell the business interest to an outside party, most often a key employee. This option is often attractive to sole proprietors who lack a viable family successor. While less common, the possibility of a buy-sell agreement with a competitor should not be overlooked.

Favorable Conditions. The following conditions would favor the use of this business continuation option of a sole proprietorship:

- the existence of a qualified employee who is capable of retaining the support of bankers, trade creditors, suppliers, and customers
- liquidity in the company that is sufficient to meet any transition problems
- a written and funded agreement between the owner and the employee that details such aspects of the transaction as price, method of payment, and funding mechanism

Advantages of a Sale to a Key Employee

A funded buy-sell agreement with a key employee can be advantageous to a sole proprietor. The sole proprietor need no longer fear that the business will crumble into disarray at his or her death. In addition, the family is assured of receiving an optimum value from the business instead of experiencing the problems of liquidating the business or searching for professional managers.

Knowing that he or she may one day own the business, the key employee now has a strong interest in the growth and prosperity of the company. The other employees benefit from the agreement, too, because they have greater opportunity for long-term employment with the firm.

There is one often overlooked advantage of a buy-sell agreement between a sole proprietor and a key employee: the role it plays in strengthening the firm's position with creditors and customers. Creditors and potential customers may be leery of doing business with a sole proprietor who is advancing in years unless they know that a viable plan for succession is in place. Funding the buy-sell agreement is covered in the next chapter.

Options for Partnerships and Corporations

One way in which a corporation with only one stockholder differs from a sole proprietorship is that it does not dissolve automatically when the sole stockholder dies. The two are similar in that both are likely to suffer forced liquidation unless a funded business continuation/liquidation plan is in place. The options facing a sole stockholder are like those facing the sole proprietor.

Two or More Owners

The introduction of a second stockholder makes the business continuation/liquidation problems of a corporation similar to those of a partnership, despite the legal differences between the two forms of business organization. The discussion that follows covers both partnerships and corporations, with the co-owners referred to as business associates.

The need for a buy-sell agreement in most closely held corporations and most partnerships generally arises from the fact that there is no ready market for the business. That is, typically, there are no outside buyers ready to buy the business interest.

Effects of an Owner's Death

The death of a partner or a stockholder in a multi-owner corporation has an immediate and vital effect on the company itself, the surviving owners, and the heirs of the deceased.

Effects on the Company. The death of a business associate typically means a significant change in company management because management and ownership are virtually synonymous in a closely held business. The management team is usually a tightly knit one, and the death of one of its members can prove very disruptive.

The extent of the impact depends on how valuable the deceased was to the company's profitability. The death of an associate may also trigger disagreements between the surviving associates, other key employees, and possibly the heirs as they struggle to fill the management void left by the untimely death. The company's smooth operation is likely to be impaired until this issue is resolved.

Effects on Surviving Business Associates. In a partnership or a multi-owner corporation, the surviving owners have a significant interest in the continued survival of the company—an interest that could be in conflict with the estate executor and the heirs. The executor will likely be harried by the need to pay settlement costs and estate taxes; the heirs may be pressed for present income. As a result, both may demand cash from the business. The surviving business associates, on the other hand, are likely to favor reinvesting the profits.

These opposing interests can make it almost impossible to operate the business profitably. The actions of the executor and the heirs may be due to ignorance of business management and to their divergent interests rather than by a deliberate intent to injure the company. Nevertheless, the results might be the same. If the business is a corporation, the problems of the surviving business associates will depend on whether the deceased held a majority or minority interest.

Majority Shareholder. If the deceased was a majority stockholder, the executor (or the family) now controls the company. The executor could elect a new board of directors, appoint new officers, and reorganize the company to the advantage of the heirs. The surviving stockholders would be forced either to follow these dictates or to give up their jobs.

Having taken control, one of the first actions of the executor might be to have the new board of directors declare a dividend, maybe even financed in part by a reduction in the salaries paid to the surviving business associates as officers of the corporation.

If the wishes of the heirs are not satisfied, they may offer to sell their stock to the surviving business associates. If the intended purchasers find the price exorbitant, the heirs might threaten to offer their controlling interest to an outsider. Obviously, the death of a majority stockholder in a closely held corporation can create a serious situation for the surviving business associates.

Minority Stockholder. What would happen if the deceased were a minority stockholder? In this case, the surviving business associates would still control the corporation and would not be in much danger of losing their jobs. But although the executor and the heirs of the deceased stockholder could not control the firm, their "nuisance value" could be substantial.

Minority stockholders have certain legal rights, such as the right to vote at corporate meetings and the right to demand information about the management and financial affairs of the company, which can be used to harass and frustrate the majority stockholders.

These problems arise from the fact that the courts generally consider majority stockholders to have a fiduciary (trustee) relationship to the minority stockholders. The majority stockholders must exercise more than ordinary care not to take any action that would be harmful to the minority, upon penalty of being held personally liable for damages.

Although the majority would not be held responsible for errors in judgment, the distinction between errors in judgment and breach of trust or neglect of duty might not always be clear-especially to a jury sympathetic to the heirs.

Effects on Heirs. The immediate and most urgent problem of the heirs usually is the need for current income to replace the deceased's salary. In most cases, the family has been dependent on this salary for support. When the partner or stockholder dies, this salary ceases unless the heirs become active in the firm.

Directors of a corporation have no right to vote salaries to one another as mere incidents of their office. They are not prevented from becoming employees of the corporation, and as such they are entitled to a reasonable compensation for their services.

However, as trustees fixing their own compensation, their action is subject to question by the stockholders or to review by the court of equity at the suit of a stockholder. (Fitchett v. Murphy, 46 App. Div. 181, 283.)

No Salary. Thus, at the very time of greatest need, the family's principal source of income is removed. Unless the heirs are employees of the corporation, salary cannot be paid. This may be the case, but not necessarily, as discussed throughout this section. They would be entitled to dividends, if any are paid.

No Dividends. Of course, if the business is a corporation, the heirs are now part owners and are entitled to their share of any dividends paid. But closely held corporations hardly ever pay dividends. Instead, the stockholders vote themselves salary increases for their capacity as employees.

The absence of dividends places the heirs in an untenable financial position. As owners they receive none of the monetary rewards of ownership. Because they are not employees, they receive no salary. In essence, they may own worthless stock. It will not do them any good unless they can sell it.

Even on the outside chance that the corporation had been paying dividends, they are likely to be stopped quickly if the surviving stockholders need additional cash flow during the readjustment period.

Another reason for stopping any payment of dividends is that the surviving stockholders will probably resent doing all the work and carrying all the management responsibilities while paying out dividends to persons who make no contribution to the operation.

It is clear, then, that the death of a partner or stockholder in a multi-owner corporation is a real and serious problem to all concerned—to the company itself, to the surviving business associates, and to the heirs.

Impairment of the Business. Any one of the threats to the continuance of the business as a successful enterprise—the divergent interests of the surviving business associates and the heirs, the loss of a key person in management, or the shock to credit stability and business momentum—could seriously impair the business. When they all occur at the same time, there is little wonder that the very existence of the business is seriously threatened.

Available Alternatives Upon Death

There are at least five possible outcomes when a partner or stockholder dies. These alternatives are discussed here briefly, and then more completely on the following pages:

1. *Liquidate*—Working with the estate executor, the surviving associate(s) may sell off all of the assets, pay off creditors, dissolve the company, and then split any remaining funds among themselves and the heirs.

2. ***Heirs and Surviving Associates Sell All as Going Concern to Outsiders***—The surviving business associate(s) and the heirs may sell the entire business to an outside party as a going concern.

3. ***Heirs Become Active Employees***—The company may be reorganized or restructured to allow the heir(s) to enter the business or to receive a regular income from the business without becoming active in its management.

4. ***Heirs Sell Their Share to Outsider***—Heirs of a corporate owner may sell their share of the business to an outsider, while the surviving business associates retain their ownership interest. (If this is a partnership, the other partners must agree to the new partner.)

5. ***Heirs Sell Their Share to Surviving Business Associates***—The heir(s) can sell the business interest to the surviving business associate(s) and/or to a key employee. This sale could be arranged either after the death or under the terms of a buy-sell agreement.

Liquidation. Partnerships and multi-owner corporations are rarely liquidated at the death of one of the owners because the survivors have a significant vested interest in continuing the business. The heirs, too, stand to benefit if the business can be continued profitably and/or sold as a going concern.

However, liquidation may be the most attractive option for a few partnerships or multi-owner corporations. This is especially true in companies where the following conditions exist:

• The deceased owner had personal skills or contacts that were the real and only source of value in the company.

- The surviving business associates are not interested in purchasing the deceased's ownership interest.
- There is no viable successor management.

For reasons discussed earlier, a planned liquidation is far preferable to a forced one. Once again, life insurance is important as a source of liquidity for the business and income for the family.

Heirs and Surviving Associates Sell All as a Going Concern.

Sometimes the heirs and surviving owners can avoid liquidation by selling the entire business as a going concern. Assuming a buyer can be found, selling the business in this fashion normally would generate greater value for both the heirs and the surviving owners than could be obtained from a liquidation.

The most likely buyer often is a competitor. If the purchase is arranged after the business owner has died, the executor and surviving owners will be unlikely to have a strong bargaining position. Negotiating the details of the sale prior to the death would be far more advantageous.

The details of buy-sell agreements are covered in the next chapter.

Heirs Become Active Employees in the Company.

As you might imagine, many prospects prefer to pass on their ownership interest to a spouse, child, or other family member. This option is especially attractive to prospects that believe that the company is going to grow substantially in value in the future.

Retaining family ownership may require a reorganization of the financial or management structure of the company. For example, a partnership technically ceases when one partner dies. Therefore, the business would need to be reorganized as a new partnership in order to include the heirs as active members of the firm.

If the heirs wish to retain an ownership interest but are unable or unwilling to assume an active role in the management of the company, the partnership could be restructured as a corporation. This means that the heirs would become stockholders and receive dividends as declared by the board of directors. But they would receive no salaries.

Whether or not the heirs hold a controlling interest, the surviving owners might decide to accept them graciously as new members of the management team. Conceivably, the heirs might possess a great deal of talent for management. Perhaps the spouse or a child of the deceased could step in and become a worthwhile member of the firm.

Unfortunately, this is frequently not the case. The heirs may be inexperienced and incapable of contributing anything to the good of the business. Where this is true, the surviving business associates would then be working for both their own families and the deceased's family. They would be doing all the work and carrying all the management responsibilities, yet sharing the profits through salaries or dividends with the heirs. This situation could soon bring disagreement and ill will.

Of course, if the heirs hold a majority interest, the surviving business associates may have no choice. The survivors could find themselves in an awkward and intolerable situation because the heirs could oust them from company management. Even if the heirs hold only a minority interest, they could so harass and frustrate their new associates that successful operation of the business would be impossible.

If the heirs remain inactive, assuming no management responsibilities, it is obvious that the active owners will have to carry the full burden. Although this may seem attractive to the survivors because the business would remain in their control, there would still be the same basic divergence of interest.

- How long would the heirs remain silent and inactive while the active owners are drawing generous salaries?
- How satisfied will they be with any dividends that might be paid after those salaries and after reinvestment of large amounts of profit for business expansion and growth?
- What if there are no dividends or no method of compensating inactive owners?

Of course, if the heirs have a majority interest they can force a distribution of profits, whether or not it is in the best interest of the business. On the other hand, heirs who are minority owners have no assurance of any income whatsoever because they have no control over the business.

In either case, the heirs would not have a dependable source of income since they would be dependent on the uncertainties of a business in whose active management they have little voice, whether or not the arrangement is of their own choosing.

Heirs Sell Their Share to Outsiders. Faced with the alternatives the heirs of a corporate owner may try to sell their business interest. In fact, they may have to try this whether they like or dislike their inferior position. The executor's need for cash to settle the estate and the family's need for cash to meet living expenses may force the heirs to look for a buyer. If the surviving business associates do not have adequate cash or if agreement cannot be reached on price, the heirs will naturally look for a willing and able outsider—maybe a competitor.

If the deceased had been a majority owner, the sale of his or her interest would pass control of the firm to a stranger and the position of the surviving business associates might very well become intolerable. They might even be ousted eventually.

On the other hand, the purchaser of a minority interest is likely to become a disrupting and frustrating influence. Eventually it would become difficult, if not impossible, for the surviving business owners to function successfully.

Price. Another problem inherent in selling to an outsider is the difficulty in reaching agreement on a fair cash price. A purchaser with adequate cash who is willing to pay a fair price is seldom found in a reasonable period of time.

Possibly an eager buyer could be found if the heirs could accept a small down payment and installment payments for balance. Unless they have sufficient funds from other sources such as life insurance, few heirs are in a financial position to gamble on the future of the business and on the ability of the purchaser to repay the debt.

Heirs Sell Their Share to Surviving Business Associates. Some of the same problems exist in a sale to survivors as in a sale to outsiders.

Price. The first problem is reaching agreement on price. Naturally, the heirs will be inclined to value the business on the basis of the income the family had been receiving from it, without considering that this income consisted mostly or entirely of salary. The asking price is usually more than the surviving business associates are willing to pay.

When the heirs hold a majority interest in the firm, they are in a strong position to demand a higher price. Should the surviving business associates refuse, they could very well lose their jobs.

On the other hand, heirs who have a minority interest are somewhat at the mercy of the survivors. If they wish, the survivors could refuse to pay even a reasonable price for the heirs' interest. Ultimately they could force a bargain price by such actions as increasing their own salaries and cutting off any profit distributions to the heirs.

Financing the Sale. The second problem in selling to the surviving business associates is financing the sale. Even assuming that the price is right, where will the survivors get the money? Most closely held businesses have their capital tied up in the business. Even if the firm has other substantial assets, the survivors may be unable to convert these assets quickly into cash.

Assuming that the survivors do not have the purchase price in cash, they must borrow the money at the bank or, in effect, borrow it from the heirs by getting them to agree to an installment payment plan.

In either case, repayment of a loan or buying on installments would heap a severe burden on the survivors, especially during the adjustment period following the death of a key owner. The burden of the payments may put pressure on the survivors to bleed the business of its profits beyond the dictates of good management.

Not all heirs will be willing or able to accept an installment purchase plan, especially since such a plan makes the heirs dependent on the future success of the business and on the skill and continued life of the surviving business associates.

Example A—Installment Sale. Example A will help illustrate the strain that the purchase of the deceased's business interest can put on the survivors. Consider the case of the stockholder in a two-person C corporation who buys the stock of a deceased co-owner.

Assume that the survivor is a woman who had been earning $80,000 gross annual income, had taxable income of $70,000 (after deductions), and filed a joint return. After $21,700 of income taxes, the take-home pay was $48,300.

Assume further that the deceased co-owner had also been earning the same amount. The survivor is now grossing $160,000 (her own $80,000 plus the deceased's $80,000).

If the buy-sell agreement calls for an installment buyout of $300,000 to be paid in five equal annual installments of $60,000 a year plus 12 percent interest, the annual installments would amount to approximately $83,223.

Assume also that the surviving owner decides to take care of some of the deceased co-owner's more routine duties by hiring a middle management replacement at $30,000 per year. Assuming a 30 percent combined federal and state corporate tax bracket, the $30,000 salary costs the corporation only $21,000. This means that the survivor's $160,000 gross income is now reduced to $139,000.

Assume that the survivor's gross income will be further reduced by tax-deductible expenses of $10,000 (as before). This leaves $129,000 of taxable income. If the income taxes on this amount are $39,990 then $89,010 will remain. Finally, the $60,000 installment payment itself must be made, along with $23,223 of interest, leaving the owner with $5,787 of take-home pay.

Example A, Illustration of Installment Sale. The accompanying illustration summarizes what has happened. The owner was looking at $160,000 of annual income. Now her $160,000 nets $5,787. Even last year, when the survivor's gross income was $80,000, she took home $48,300!

Imagine how the surviving owner must feel. Not only is there much more work to do with the co-owner out of the picture and more time required to do it, but her spendable income has been cut sharply. On top of this, it is very likely that efficiency will suffer and profits from the business will decrease because one of the two key people has just died.

Imagine, too, how the surviving owner's family must feel. They seldom see her any more. When they do, she is tired and perhaps irritable from long hours of hard work. The family might understand if their income had just doubled. But it has not even stayed the same; it has been cut by over 85 percent for 5 years until the debt is paid.

Another way of looking at this example is in terms of how much additional gross income would be needed to meet the $83,223 annual installments. Working with the same income assumptions, the surviving owner would need to gross about $120,000 in additional income to net $83,223. Over a 5-year period, this would require additional gross earnings of $600,000 to fund a $300,000 obligation! In addition, the $21,000 cost of hiring a replacement would still have to be met. Life insurance is obviously a more cost-efficient funding mechanism.

The two business owners had been wise to enter into a buy-sell agreement. If only they had carried their business continuation planning one step further and funded their agreement with life insurance, it could have provided the entire $300,000 purchase price and eliminated the payment of interest. It could even have provided additional income to pay the replacement's salary for a few years.

Example A—Installment Sale			
Before Death of Co-Owner		**After Death of Co-Owner**	
$80,000	gross income	$160,000	gross income
−10,000	deductible items	21,000	cost of $30,000 salary*
70,000	taxable income	−10,000	deductible items
−21,700	taxes (31% bracket)	$129,000	taxable income
$48,300	net income	−39,990	taxes (31% bracket)
		89,010	net income
		−83,223	$60,000 installment plus
		$5,787	interest net after installment

The survivor's net income has been reduced by over 85 percent!

*Assuming a combined 30 percent federal plus state tax bracket for the corporation, the $30,000 salary for hiring a replacement for the deceased co-owner will cost the corporation $21,000 after taxes.

Example B—Corporation Purchases Stock. Assume now that the corporation itself—rather than the survivor—purchased the dead owner's stock.

In this case, the dead owner's $80,000 salary remains as corporate income. Corporate taxes at 34 percent would take about $27,200 of the $80,000, leaving $52,800. Hiring a $30,000 replacement at an after-tax cost of $21,700 (as in Example A) would leave $31,100. Finally, deducting the $60,000 annual installment payment and interest of $23,223 on the $300,000 principal amount would leave the corporation $52,123 in the red each year for 5 years.

For the corporation to break even, it would have to net an additional $52,123 each year after taxes. This might be the equivalent of about $787,000 in additional sales. Yet the chances are that sales, income, and profit will decrease—not increase. It cannot be emphasized enough that it was not "just anybody" that died. It was 50 percent of the most vital key people who died! One of the two most valuable assets of the business is gone!

It should be obvious that installment buyouts are expensive and inconvenient at best. At worst, they can bankrupt a business or an owner. This doesn't mean that it cannot be done. It can. But using credit to buy out the heirs would be an expensive drain on corporate earnings, just as it would be prohibitive for most individuals.

The problem facing the surviving business associate in the example above could have been reduced significantly by stretching the installments out from 5 years to 10 years or 20 years. While this would have helped the surviving business associate, it would expose the heirs to a significant long-term risk—a risk they should not be asked to assume!

The cost does not begin to answer all the remaining questions. There is still the question of what happens if one or more of the surviving business associates dies after the installment payments have begun.

Example B—Corporation Purchases Stock **Impact of Owner's Death on Corporation's Income and Expenses**	
Deceased owner's salary is now corporate income	$80,000
Less corporate taxes at 34%	−27,200
	52,800
Less after-tax cost of $30,000 salary of replacement	−21,700
Less $60,000 annual installment and interest of $23,223 on $300,000 buyout principal	−83,223
Annual loss	$(52,123)

The money may simply not be available to continue the payments. Then what do the heirs of the first to die do? And what about the heirs of the second to die? The situation could become almost hopeless for all concerned if this gamble is risked.

THE SALES PROCESS: ESTABLISHING AND FUNDING THE BUY-SELL AGREEMENT

The framework for making sales in the business continuation/liquidation area follows a familiar pattern:

- Ask what the prospect wants to happen to the business when he or she dies. *Then stop talking and listen carefully.*

- Help your prospect to explore the implications and/or pitfalls of his or her goals. Emphasize what will happen if careful planning is not done to achieve the goals.
- Communicate clearly the alternative plans/programs that should be implemented now if your prospect is to accomplish the desired goals.
- Help your prospect understand the importance of funding these plans.
- Help your prospect select the best funding mechanism.

Questioning and Listening—A Sample Advisor-Client Dialogue

Listen in as Don, an experienced business insurance advisor, talks with his client, Arthur.

Arthur has been telling Don about a conversation he had with another advisor. Arthur says this advisor confused him because the advisor had spent over an hour "lecturing" Arthur on the details of a proposal to implement what the advisor had called a funded buy-sell agreement.

Without commenting on the other advisor's approach, Don begins to help Arthur to share his dreams for his business and to determine the business continuation/liquidation option best for him.

Arthur: Don, this guy said I need a buy-sell agreement and some life insurance. Is he right?

Don: Arthur, do you want the business to continue after your death?

Arthur: Of course I do.

Don: Who will own it then?

Arthur: My wife, Alice. At least, that's what my will says.

Don: Have you discussed this with Alice? Who will run it for her?

Arthur: My key people: Tom, Dick, and Mary.

Don: Why should they do this? (Arthur has never considered this question before. He may need some clarification.)

Arthur: What do you mean?

Don: Can Alice run the business without Tom, Dick, and Mary?

Arthur: Not a chance. She's rarely been inside the shop.

Don: Can Tom, Dick, and Mary run the business without Alice?

Arthur: Sure. In fact, they even run it pretty well without me.

Don: So why should they run the business for Alice, who knows nothing about the business but will expect to take the same income out of it that you've been drawing?

Arthur: Because she owns it. She will be their new boss.

Don: Have you discussed this with Tom, Dick and Mary? How will they like having Alice in this role?

Arthur: They'll probably hate it, but they'll have to learn to like it if they want to keep their jobs.

Don: Would it be hard for them to find new jobs?

Arthur: Are you kidding? My competitor down the street would jump at the chance of getting any one of them. If he could get all three, he'd be overjoyed.

Don: Would he approach them if Alice took over?

Arthur: He'd be pretty dumb if he didn't. And he's not dumb.

Don: And what would happen to the business without you, or Tom, or Dick, or Mary to run it?

Arthur: It would fold within 6 months.

Don: Is that what you want?

Arthur: Certainly not! I want the business to continue, and I want Alice to be guaranteed a decent income.

Don: Would owning the business guarantee Alice a decent income?

Arthur: I guess not. We've just figured out that the mere fact that Alice owns the business doesn't mean she will have a good income from it.

Don: What would guarantee her a decent income?

Arthur: Cash. I guess she needs enough cash to invest.

Don: How could she get enough cash to invest?

Arthur: She could sell the business.

Don: Who would want to buy it?

Arthur: Tom, Dick, and Mary.

Don: Where would they find the cash?

Arthur: That might be a real problem. I pay them well, but I doubt they have enough saved to buy my company for the price I'd want.

Don: Could they take out some insurance on you and use the money to buy the business?

Arthur: Yes, maybe that's what that other advisor was trying to tell me.

Don: How could you be sure they'd use the insurance money to buy the business?

Arthur: Well, we would probably need to sit down with my attorney and draft some kind of agreement.

Don: So, do you need life insurance?

Arthur: It sure looks like Tom, Dick, and Mary will need a policy on me.

Don: And do you need a buy-sell agreement?

Arthur: Yes. That's an important part of the answer. Thanks, Don, for explaining it so well. I guess that's why you're my advisor!

Don's question-oriented selling style helped Arthur understand that he really has a problem. Don asked a series of questions that gave Arthur an opportunity to express his desire for the business in the event of his death.

The main point is this: we develop the need with prospects by asking questions rather than immediately giving answers to problems our prospects may not feel or accept yet. If you initially tell a business owner about the "best" way to set up a business continuation/liquidation plan, that plan is yours, not his or hers.

Remember: in the area of business continuation or liquidation you are talking with persons who have poured heart and soul into building a business. They are likely to have some strong feelings and desires for the business. Rather than ignoring these feelings, you will want to learn all about them so that you can build your sales presentations around them. If you can show your prospect how to do what he or she already wants to do, you are much more likely to make a sale.

BUSINESS CONTINUATION/LIQUIDATION FLOW CHARTS (SALES TRACKS)

Successful tracks for business continuation/liquidation sales for sole proprietorships, partnerships, and closely held corporations are found in the charts in the appendix at the end of this chapter. Each chart shows the various options available to the business if the owner dies. It then shows the problems or pitfalls associated with each option. Finally, each chart shows the steps that should be undertaken to implement each option. The charts for partnerships and corporations use the perspective of a survivor because prospects are more likely to assume that they will outlive their co-owners.

Using the Flowchart with Prospects

Depending on whether your prospect is a sole proprietor, partner, or stockowner of a closely held corporation, select the appropriate chart of business continuation/liquidation choices.

Placing the chart in front of your prospect, say: "This chart shows the choices that confront a business when an owner dies. As you can see, the options fall into a few broad categories. Basically, the company can be liquidated, or it can be sold as a going concern, or it can be kept. Which of these options would you want to see happen for your business?"

Some prospects will immediately respond. Others may show some hesitancy. If you sense that your prospect needs some guidance, you might ask, "Would you like me to briefly explain each option?"

Using the material from this chapter, describe each option clearly and simply. Following this brief discussion, ask your prospect again to express his or her goals by saying something like this: "Following your death, will this business continue to be a valuable income-producing asset that should be continued by your family or an associate, or is it a potential albatross for them that should be liquidated or sold to outsiders?"

Plan to Avoid Potential Pitfalls

Having discovered what your prospect wants to happen to the business, next help your prospect to recognize the need for planning to avoid potential pitfalls. Ask your prospects more questions about the desired option or goal. Your purpose for now is to give your prospect plenty of time to respond—to talk about the problems in an open, free manner.

The more your prospect talks about these pitfalls or problems, the more likely he or she is to realize the importance of good planning. By raising questions, you are helping your prospect to come to his or her own conclusions.

Bear in mind that there is no "right" option for every business. Instead, any of the options can be designed to meet your prospect's goals of ensuring the financial security of the family and business if proper planning, including life insurance, is undertaken.

Planning for Solutions

You can close this introductory portion of the sales interview by using the chart to highlight ways in which planning will permit your prospect to achieve his or her goals. Once again, note the role that life insurance plays regardless of whether your prospect wants to liquidate the business, sell it, or keep it in family hands.

Reviewing An Existing Buy-Sell Agreement

In closing this introductory portion of the sales interview, it is usually helpful to tell your prospects that you would like to review a copy of their buy-sell agreement. If the prospects cooperate with you in this regard, they are expressing confidence in you.

Editing or changing the agreement is solely the job of an attorney, but you can gain helpful information from reviewing it. In addition, you may be able to raise some important questions when you next see the prospect. Information you can learn from reviewing the buy-sell agreement includes:

- The names of all the owners and their percentage of ownership
- The date of the original agreement
- The dates of any subsequent changes or amendments
- The form of business (corporation, partnership, and so on)
- Whether it is a cross-purchase, entity, or wait-and-see agreement
- Whether life insurance was used to fund the agreement

- How much life insurance was purchased initially
- Who pays the premium
- How any balance of the sale price is to be funded
- How the value of the business is calculated
- How and when the value is to be recalculated
- What event(s) can trigger the agreement (death, disability, retirement)
- Whether the agreement has the other provisions usually found in buy-sell agreements (see below)

Some of the other provisions usually found in buy-sell agreements include:

- Promise by the deceased's heirs to sell the deceased's shares
- Promise by the business or the surviving owners to buy the deceased's shares
- Price or formula to determine the value of the business
- Funding method(s)
- Authorization to purchase additional insurance on existing owners
- Authorization to purchase insurance on any new owners
- Disposition of the life insurance on the life of the survivors
- Restrictions on sale of the business during life (first-offer provision, also known as first-right-of refusal provision)
- Right of a withdrawing owner to purchase the insurance on his/her life
- How the contract can be amended

Why Finance With Life Insurance?

- The annual premiums are comparatively small amounts (1 to 4 percent of face amount).
- Life insurance guarantees that the amount required to finance the purchase under a buy-sell agreement will be available, even if only one premium has been paid.
- Safety is virtually assured.
- The survivors could receive a financial windfall if an associate should die during the early years of the agreement.
- Life insurance provides the necessary money at the very moment it is needed: when a business associate dies.

Business Continuation Sales Track Flow Charts

- One for use with sole proprietors
- One for use in partnership situations
- One for use in corporate situations

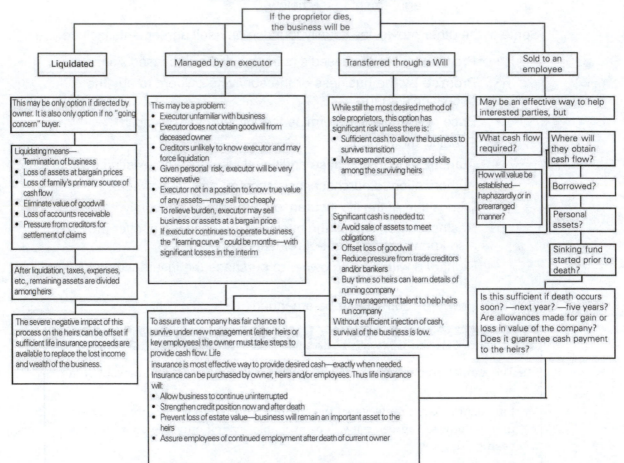

Sole Proprietor Chart

Choices Confronting the Sole Proprietor

If the proprietor dies, the business will be

Liquidated

This may be only option if directed by owner. It is also only option if no "going concern" buyer.

Liquidating means—
- Termination of business
- Loss of assets at bargain prices
- Loss of family's primary source of cash flow
- Eliminate value of goodwill
- Loss of accounts receivable
- Pressure from creditors for settlement of claims

After liquidation, taxes, expenses, etc., remaining assets are divided among heirs

The severe negative impact of this process on the heirs can be offset if sufficient life insurance proceeds are available to replace the lost income and wealth of the business.

Managed by an executor

This may be a problem:
- Executor unfamiliar with business
- Executor does not obtain goodwill from deceased owner
- Creditors unlikely to know executor and may force liquidation
- Given personal risk, executor will be very conservative
- Executor not in a position to know true value of any assets—may sell too cheaply
- To relieve burden, executor may sell business or assets at a bargain price
- If executor continues to operate business, the "learning curve" could be months—with significant losses in the interim

To assure that company has fair chance to survive under new management (either heirs or key employees) the owner must take steps to provide cash flow. Life insurance is most effective way to provide desired cash—exactly when needed. Insurance can be purchased by owner, heirs and/or employees. Thus life insurance will:
- Allow business to continue uninterrupted
- Strengthen credit position now and after death
- Prevent loss of estate value—business will remain an important asset to the heirs
- Assure employees of continued employment after death of current owner

Transferred through a Will

While still the most desired method of sole proprietors, this option has significant risk unless there is:
- Sufficient cash to allow the business to survive transition
- Management experience and skills among the surviving heirs

Significant cash is needed to:
- Avoid sale of assets to meet obligations
- Offset loss of goodwill
- Reduce pressure from trade creditors and/or bankers
- Buy time so heirs can learn details of running company
- Buy management talent to help heirs run company

Without sufficient injection of cash, survival of the business is low.

Sold to an employee

May be an effective way to help interested parties, but

What cash flow required?

How will value be established—haphazardly or in prearranged manner?

Where will they obtain cash flow?

Borrowed?

Personal assets?

Sinking fund started prior to death?

Is this sufficient if death occurs soon? —next year? —five years? Are allowances made for gain or loss in value of the company? Does it guarantee cash payment to the heirs?

Partnership Chart

The Choice for Surviving Partners

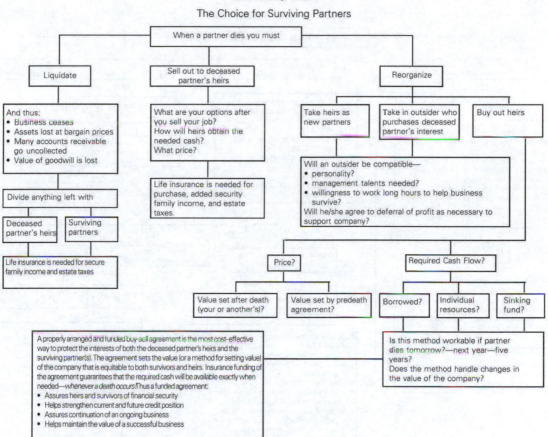

A properly arranged and funded buy-sell agreement is the most cost-effective way to protect the interests of both the deceased partner's heirs and the surviving partner(s). The agreement sets the value (or a method for setting value) of the company that is equitable to both survivors and heirs. Insurance funding of the agreement guarantees that the required cash will be available exactly when needed—*whenever a death occurs!* Thus a funded agreement:

- Assures heirs and survivors of financial security
- Helps strengthen current and future credit position
- Assures continuation of an ongoing business
- Helps maintain the value of a successful business

Corporation Chart

Choice for Surviving Stockholders

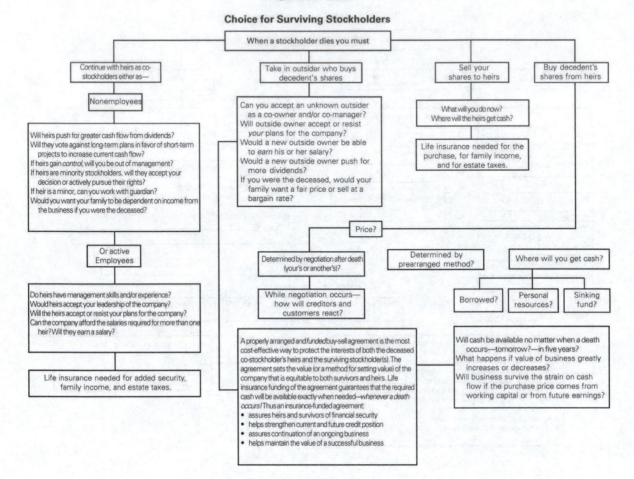

When a stockholder dies you must

Continue with heirs as co-stockholders either as—

Nonemployees

Will heirs push for greater cash flow from dividends?
Will they vote against long-term plans in favor of short-term projects to increase current cash flow?
If heirs gain *control*, will you be out of management?
If heirs are minority stockholders, will they accept your decision or actively pursue their rights?
If heir is a minor, can you work with guardian?
Would you want your family to be dependent on income from the business if you were the deceased?

Or active Employees

Do heirs have management skills and/or experience?
Would heirs accept your leadership of the company?
Will the heirs accept or resist your plans for the company?
Can the company afford the salaries required for more than one heir? Will they earn a salary?

Life insurance needed for added security, family income, and estate taxes.

Take in outsider who buys decedent's shares

Can you accept an unknown outsider as a co-owner and/or co-manager?
Will outside owner accept or resist *your* plans for the company?
Would a new outside owner be able to *earn* his or her salary?
Would a new outside owner push for more dividends?
If you were the deceased, would your family want a fair price or sell at a bargain rate?

Price?

Determined by negotiation after death (your's or another's)?

Determined by prearranged method?

While negotiation occurs— how will creditors and customers react?

A properly arranged and *funded* buy-sell agreement is the most cost-effective way to protect the interests of both the deceased co-stockholder's heirs and the surviving stockholder(s). The agreement sets the value (or a method for setting value) of the company that is equitable to both survivors and heirs. Life insurance funding of the agreement guarantees that the required cash will be available exactly when needed—*whenever a death occurs!* Thus an insurance-funded agreement:
* assures heirs and survivors of financial security
* helps strengthen current and future credit position
* assures continuation of an ongoing business
* helps maintain the value of a successful business

Sell your shares to heirs

What will you do now?
Where will the heirs get cash?

Life insurance needed for the purchase, for family income, and for estate taxes.

Buy decedent's shares from heirs

Where will you get cash?

Borrowed?

Personal resources?

Sinking fund?

Will cash be available no matter when a death occurs—tomorrow?—in five years?
What happens if value of business greatly increases or decreases?
Will business survive the strain on cash flow if the purchase price comes from working capital or from future earnings?

CASE HISTORY: THE RIGHT FIT

Agent

Vic Thomas has been a leader in his company since he entered the financial services business. He is active in community and civic organizations.

Prospecting

Getting acquainted with successful business owners can often be just as easy as getting acquainted with anyone else. It is daytime activity, the rewards are great, and the referrals seem to carry more prestige.

Joan Snow was the successful owner of the best orthopedic shoe stores in the eastern part of my state. I first met her a few months ago at a regular meeting of the Kiwanis.

When I ran into Joan at a recent meeting, her first question was, "What's this idea that Matt Gaines says you cooked up for him?"

"Would you like me to come by the store tomorrow and explain the whole deal?" I asked.

She agreed. I had just sold Matt Gaines $250,000 of insurance to finance a buy-sell agreement. Before I visited Joan, I called Matt, told him of Joan's interest, and asked if he minded my telling her the facts. He had no objection. He and Joan were good friends, and Matt was proud of his new plan.

Fact-Finding Interview

Joan Snow's chain of orthopedic stores had been well established before I settled in town. Her five stores did a marvelous business, keeping 25 employees very busy. Joan was the sole owner.

After the usual greetings, the interview went something like this:

"Joan, you own this business, lock, stock, and barrel, right?"

"Right."

"How long have you had it?"

Twelve years."

"Did you buy it from someone, or did you start it up yourself?"

"I started from scratch—and believe me, the going was plenty tough."

"How old are you, Joan?"

"Fifty, next July."

"Is anyone else dependent on the income from this business?"

"My husband is...to a large extent. And I have a son who has 3 years remaining to finish his college education."

"How old is your husband?"

"George is 51."

"Have you made out a will, Joan?"

"Yes, about 3 years ago."

"Does it provide for your business to be continued or sold?"

"I never thought about that. I guess I just assumed that George would become the new owner."

"Joan, that's just what Matt said when I asked him that question. He was simply assuming that his son would continue to operate the business. In fact, Paul would be a logical successor since he's been working with his dad for over 2 years now. Has George ever helped you out in the stores? Would he want to take over the business?"

"No! He doesn't know the first thing about the orthopedic business."

"Joan, if you went on a trip which would keep you away for 3 months or more, who would you leave in charge of your company? It wouldn't be George, would it?"

"No, of course not. I guess I'd ask Frank Bell and Gordon Hall to take over. They're both expert orthopedists and knowledgeable business people."

"Suppose, Joan, that you went on a trip from which you never came back. Do you think Bell and Hall would go on working for George indefinitely, continuing to produce for him just as they do for you today?"

"That's a tough question, Vic. On second thought, I guess they'd do just what I did when my old boss died. The widow tried to run the show, and I finally decided to start out on my own. You know, Vic, its funny how you expect other people to do things you would never expect yourself to do. What can I do to guarantee that I'll be leaving George something besides a hope that he can carry on if I'm not here?"

At this point, I asked Joan how much her business was worth as a going concern. She indicated that successful retail orthopedic shoe businesses typically were worth about seven times earnings. This was an industry standard, with some businesses selling for more or less depending on the quality of their operations. In the last 3 years, Snow's had generated an average profit of $60,000. Based on this, Joan valued her company at about $420,000.

As I questioned Joan further, she indicated that if no buyer could be found and the assets of the business had to be liquidated the company would realistically net just under $75,000 ($100,000 liquidation value of the assets less $25,000 in debts).

The more she talked, the more anxious Joan grew to find a way to prevent a $345,000 loss (going-concern value of $420,000 versus liquidation value of $75,000) in the value her family would realize from her business.

Closing Interview

Having worked out similar solutions before, I was able to take Joan through the possible solutions to straighten things out. Everything added up to getting out of the business when Joan died and selling it to the logical buyers, Frank Bell and Gordon Hall.

"But they would never be able to raise the money!?" Joan lamented. Further discussion revealed that Hall and Bell were both married, had children, and each was earning in the high thirties in salary and bonus.

"Joan, could you afford to give these fellows a special raise?"

"I guess I could—but why?"

"Just this: If you were to sell the business to them, and they could pay for it, what would be the rock bottom price you would accept?"

"Well, it might be worth more than that, but if I could be sure to pass on to George at least $400,000, I would sell it for that."

"Fine. Now getting back to the raises, would you agree to give Hall and Bell each a special $3,000 raise if they agreed to do three things: First, promise to work for you for the next few years without any special additional increases.

Second, put the net increase aside each year, along with about $100 a month of their present after tax income. And third, pledge to use this fund to buy out the business if you die. Would you agree to these conditions, Joan?"

"Will that give George the $400,000?"

"It sure will, Joan, if you're healthy right now?"

(What I had in mind was for Bell and Hall to each own a $200,000 policy on Joan's life. The $3,600 annual premium for each policy would come from the $3,000 bonus ($2,400 net after taxes) and the $1,200 each would contribute. The buy-sell agreement would require Bell and Hall to use the insurance proceeds to each purchase one-half of the company at Joan's death.)

No further sales talk was needed at this point. Joan agreed to proceed with an insurance exam and to have a buy-sell agreement drawn by her attorney. She called Hall and Bell into her office to review the program. They looked at each other somewhat mystified, and their mouths almost literally dropped open in surprise when Joan explained the proposal. They were obviously delighted about the chance to own Snow's Orthopedic Shoe Company.

The Sale

When I left, no one could have doubted Joan's happiness. She had solved a problem that would have plagued her husband had she died earlier. She had also given a golden opportunity to her two key employees. Frank Bell and Gordon Hall were no longer merely employees, plodding along day by day. They were potential owners of a thriving business.

And I had in my pocket an application for $400,000 and a semiannual binder. Everybody was happy!

Post-Sales Service

This is the kind of case you often read about but seldom experience yourself. Within 5 years after the buy-sell agreement had been signed and the insurance policies put into the hands of a trustee, it was my sorrowful duty to carry out the plan. Joan had gone into the hospital for what was supposed to be a simple operation. Complications set in, causing her death.

I'd never been so glad I'm in the insurance business. Everything went like clockwork in carrying out Joan's desires for her business. In exchange for the rights to the business, Bell and Hall turned over the proceeds of the policies.

Mr. Snow will receive an income from the policy proceeds for as long as he lives. Together with other property Joan had, including some personal insurance, this left him fairly well off and able to handle the obligations they had accumulated on their double income.

The two ex-key employees are now co-owners in a business with which they had been associated for years. They are on their way to a grand future. Thanks to life insurance, a calamity has been avoided.

CHAPTER REVIEW

Key terms and concepts are explained in the Glossary. Answers to the Review Questions and Self-Test Questions are found in the back of the book following the Glossary.

Key Terms and Concepts

selling cycle	social style
buying cycle	drive
"Areas of Possible Interest"	expressive
open-ended questions	amiable
decision making styles	analytical

Review Questions

1. Explain how the selling and buying cycle intersect in the sales process.

2. Explain why the fact-finding process is so important.

3. Name five fact finders found in this textbook and briefly tell the general purpose of each one.

4. How can the knowledge of the decision-making and social styles improve the relationship of the advisor with the prospect?

5. When an owner of a closely held C corporation dies, one of five possible outcomes will result. Briefly describe these five alternative outcomes.

6. Are the five <u>corporate</u> alternatives (described above) largely the same in <u>partnership</u> situations?

7. When a sole proprietor dies, one of four possible outcomes will result. Briefly describe these four alternative outcomes.

8. What problems may confront a sole proprietorship when the sole proprietor dies?

9.   What effects would the death of an owner have on a partnership or a closely held corporation?

10.   How does a majority or minority shareholder position of a deceased owner affect the surviving shareholders and heirs?

11.   What general effects may the death of a business owner have on heirs? The following question pertain to the case study.

12.   How did the agent establish the need in the fact-finding interview? What questions did he/she ask?

13.   How was the value of the business determined?

14.   What solution is proposed in the closing interview?

Self-Test Questions

Instructions: Read chapter four first, then answer the following questions to test your knowledge. There are 10 questions. Circle the correct answer, then check your answers with the answer key in the back of the book.

15.   Which of the following characteristics of a sole proprietorship does not point directly to a need for life insurance?

   (A) The sole owner is usually the manager of the business and the only person completely familiar with its operation.
   (B) A sole proprietorship expires with the death of the owner.
   (C) There are no associates who must be consulted on major decisions.
   (D) The owner does not usually have the full range of fringe benefits available to an owner of a corporation who serves as an employee

16.   Select the life situation below which must urgently calls for life insurance coverage.

   (A) Mr. Braunschweiger becomes a stockholder of General Motors.
   (B) A stockholder personally guarantees his corporation's note for a $100,000 loan.
   (C) A business executive signs a will leaving his Kodak stock to his son and government bonds of equal market value to his daughter.
   (D) Smith purchases 5 percent of the stock in a small corporation but continues to work for General Motors as a line foreman.

17. On the death of a partner, the surviving partner is charged with the specific duty of

    (A) continuing the business to help support the widow
    (B) buying out the heirs within 6 months
    (C) notifying the newspapers of the firm's new status
    (D) winding up the firm's business and accounting for the remaining assets

18. Select the most important reason why close-corporation stock is usually an unsuitable investment for a deceased stockholder's family.

    (A) It is usually too expensive for the average investor.
    (B) Ordinarily the other stockholders comprise the only market for the stock, and there isn't likely to be much return except through a sale.
    (C) Stock ownership and management of a close corporation are separate.
    (D) Dividends are subject to income tax at surcharge rates.

19. Which of the following is a goal of the fact-finding interview?

    (A) obtain referrals
    (B) build prestige and confidence
    (C) make tentative recommendations
    (D) get agreement on a solution to the need

20. The immediate and most urgent problem of heirs to a closely held business is typically

    (A) to liquidate the business interest without probate
    (B) payment of federal estate taxes within 3 months of death
    (C) a need for current income to replace the salary of the deceased
    (D) a need for current income to replace the dividends paid on the deceased's stock

21. In the transition to fact-finding, the advisor should

    (A) move ahead without any explanation
    (B) explain the next step and tell the prospect why it is important
    (C) explain the importance of the fact-finding and then immediately leave
    (D) insist that the fact-finding interview be a continuing part of the initial meeting

22. Which of the following statements concerning liquidation of a business in the event of the owner's death is (are) correct?

    I. Even in a forced liquidation, any value in goodwill is retained and passed on to the heirs.
    II. With a planned liquidation, the estate executor generally has no time to wait for an orderly collection of accounts receivable.

    (A) I only
    (B) II only
    (C) Both I and II
    (D) Neither I nor II

23. Which of the following statements concerning the use of fact-finding forms is (are) correct?

    I. Fact-finding forms help you cover all points and leave nothing to chance and memory.
    II. After you have chosen a fact-finding form, use it the same way in all situations regardless of the prospect's personal needs.

    (A) I only
    (B) II only
    (C) Both I and II
    (D) Neither I nor II

READ THE FOLLOWING DIRECTIONS BEFORE CONTINUING

The questions below differ from the preceding questions in that they all contain the word EXCEPT. So you understand fully the basis used in selecting each answer, be sure to read each question carefully.

---

24. All of the following are goals of the fact-finding interview EXCEPT

    (A) Build trust and credibility with the prospect.
    (B) Obtain at least three referrals.
    (C) Gather information that will be needed for a proposal.
    (D) Obtain agreement to proceed to the next step in the sales process.

Learning Objectives

An understanding of the material in this chapter should enable the student to

1. Name two benefits of a funded buy-sell agreement to the deceased owner's heirs, and two benefits to the surviving owners.

2. Name and describe the three kinds of buy-sell agreements.

3. Identify four sources of funding a buy-sell agreement.

4. Explain what should be included in a buy-sell agreement.

5. Describe six benefits of using life insurance to fund a buy-sell agreement.

6. Explain the federal income tax status of premiums and proceeds of life insurance used to fund a buy-sell agreement.

7. Explain the solutions to providing a buy-sell plan where one owner is uninsurable.

This chapter provides a detailed discussion of buy-sell agreements. It reviews their purpose, the types of agreements, their benefits and tax implications. The types of buy-sell agreements discussed include the cross purchase, entity, stock redemption and wait-and-see methods. Consideration is given for solutions to situations where there is a disparity of age or disproportionate business interests, or where a business owner is uninsurable. The alternative methods of funding are identified and the advantages and disadvantages of each are discussed. The sales process section focuses on client concerns and objections that may stall the process, and how an advisor may resolve these issues.

BUSINESS CONTINUATION: THE SOLUTION

The preceding chapter discussed the various business continuation/liquidation options available to sole proprietors, partners and owners of closely held businesses. This chapter will explore the one business continuation tool that

has proven over the years to be most effective for business owners: the
funded buy-sell agreement.

Purpose of a Buy-Sell Agreement

The death of a business owner has an immediate and drastic impact on a
business owner's heirs, the surviving business owners, the business itself,
and the employees. Without a well-thought-out business continuation plan,
all of these interested parties will face significant uncertainties and problems.
Furthermore, they must face these uncertainties and problems without the
guidance of the now deceased business owner.

Here is a summary of the problems and alternatives previously discussed.
You can use something like this to conduct a fact-finding/feeling-finding
interview.

Problems and Alternatives Facing Heirs

1. **Sell to surviving business owners.** At what price? Where do the
   surviving business owners get the cash to buy out the heirs?

2. **Retain the decedent's business interest and participate in
   management of company.** Are the heirs qualified? Will their
   desire for current (and continuing) income be in conflict with the
   surviving business owners who might want to reinvest much of the
   firm's income back into the business? If the business provides little
   or no income, how can the heirs obtain the income they need? Can
   the business afford to pay the heirs significant salaries?

3. **Sell the business to an outsider.** At what price? Where is a buyer
   to be found? How can heirs who are unfamiliar with the business
   determine the true value of the company?

Problems and Alternatives Facing the Surviving Owners

1. **Continue the business with the heirs as new co-owners.**
   Are the heirs knowledgeable about the business? Are they
   experienced? Are their hearts in it? Will they push for immediate
   sale of the business? Can the surviving owners get along with the
   heirs? Are business goals and philosophies of the surviving owners
   compatible with those of the heirs? If the surviving owner is a
   minority stockholder, he or she may have no real control over his or
   her future even if heirs bring him in.

2. **Try to buy out the heirs.** At what price? Where will surviving
   owners get the funds?

3. **Sell out to an outsider.** At what price? Where will the surviving owners find a buyer?

Problems Facing the Business

1. The death of a business owner means that the company also suffers the loss of key management talent. How will this management talent be replaced, from where, and at what cost?

2. Banks and other creditors may restrict credit lines until the heirs and/or the surviving business owners can demonstrate their ability to run the company successfully. Can the business survive such a liquidity crunch?

3. Employee morale may be impaired. How can the firm assure its employees that this will continue to be an excellent place to work, or even if it will continue to exist as an employer?

4. Customers may turn to competitors. How can the company assure its clients and customers that it will continue to provide necessary service and products?

Accompanying this discussion below is an illustration to use in talking with your prospects about these problems. One part is titled "Conflicting Interests;" the other is "Conflicting Goals."

The best way to avoid these conflicts is through a buy-sell agreement that (1) gives cash to the decedent's heirs for the business, and (2) gives the surviving owners complete ownership and control of the company. A buy-sell agreement has several key characteristics that make it an attractive and realistic solution to the problems of business continuation.

- A buy-sell agreement facilitates the orderly transfer of the deceased's ownership interest in the business.

- A buy-sell agreement helps assure continuous management and control by the surviving business owners(s).

- With appropriate funding, a buy-sell agreement provides the cash needed to purchase the business interest from the heirs at the exact time that the sale must be completed.

You may want to use an illustration when discussing this topic with prospects. The following example outlines the unique benefits of a buy-sell agreement for all interested parties ("Benefits of a Funded Buy-Sell Agreement"). It mentions funding, but does not specify any particular funding vehicle.

Conflicting Interests	
At the death of a business owner, the interests of the surviving owners and the heirs may be in conflict:	
Interests of the Surviving Owners Who Are Also Employees:	Interests of the Heirs Who Are Non-employees:
Receive competitive tax-deductible salary	Obtain ongoing income!
Build business for future growth	Realize funds from business to pay estate costs
Establish cash reserves	Oust non-family surviving shareholder employees who are not "cooperating" with the heirs
Take long-term perspective in most decisions relating to the business	
Dividends ARE NOT relevant	Dividends ARE relevant

AND

Conflicting Goals

In addition to different interests, the surviving owners and the heirs may have different goals:

Goals of the Surviving Owners Who Are Also Employee	Goals of the Heirs Who Are Non-employees
Retain control	Reduce risks and fluctuations in business income and business value
Realize long-term growth in value of business	Obtain cash for personal needs
Invest both business earnings and borrowed funds in new products and services in order to fuel long-term business growth	Get a "fair" price for all or part of the inherited business interest

Funded Buy-Sell Agreements

After you have helped your prospects explore various possible courses of action and their attendant problems, you will find that most prospects want two things to happen following an owner's death:

1. The surviving owners receive full ownership of the business.
2. The heirs receive full value in cash for the business interest.

Benefits of a Funded Agreement

The most practical and certain way to assure these objectives following the death of an owner is through a funded buy-sell agreement. The funded, properly drafted buy-sell agreement produces the following benefits:

- It establishes a fair price for the business interest or it clearly specifies a method or formula for determining a fair price.
- It guarantees the heirs that they will receive cash for the inherited business interest.
- It assures the surviving business owners that they will have uninterrupted control and full ownership of the company.
- It helps creditors and suppliers to know today that the company is more likely to survive the problems associated with a future death of a key employee-owner.
- If properly funded, it provides cash at the exact time needed and in a predetermined, specified amount.
- Establishes a value for estate evaluation acceptable to the IRS.

Funded buy-sell agreements may be fully funded or partially funded, fully insured or partially insured. Sometimes they begin as fully funded and fully insured agreements, but as time passes and the formula value of the business increases, the funding doesn't keep pace, and the agreement becomes under funded and underinsured. In any event, the agreement should include a provision stating how any unfunded portion of the sale price is to be handled. Typically this is done by taking the balance in installment payments, even though it is a more costly and more speculative method than fully funding it with life insurance.

When your prospect decides that a funded buy-sell agreement is a good idea, the next step is to discuss how to fund the agreement. Later, the prospect's attorney will draw up a written buy-sell agreement. You need to be knowledgeable about the types of agreements. The following pages discuss these topics:

- Types of buy-sell agreements
- Funding the buy-sell agreement
- Contents of the buy-sell agreement

Benefits of a Funded Buy-Sell Agreement

Benefits to Heirs

- Creates a qualified purchaser for the inherited business interest.
- Establishes a fair price for the business interest.
- Helps set the value of the business interest for the purpose of estate tax filings, thereby helping the planning process and possibly reducing the estate tax obligation.
- Provides cash in exchange for the business interest-a risky asset for heirs to hold.
- Reduces the time needed to administer the estate, thereby reducing estate administration costs.
- Provides the estate with the cash needed to meet estate taxes and estate administration costs.

Benefits to Business

- Increases likelihood that banks and suppliers will continue to extend credit lines.
- Helps to assure employees that the business will continue despite the death of a key owner-employee.
- Lessens the probability that customers or clients will seek other suppliers following death of an owner.

Benefits to Surviving Owners

- Assures the surviving owners control of the company because the heirs must sell to the firm and not to outsiders.
- Provides funds to purchase the business interest held by the heirs.
- Guarantees full management control by eliminating the possibility that the heirs will assume management positions for which they are not qualified.
- Eliminates potential emotional conflicts between the heirs and the surviving business owners—conflicts that could impair the harmonious operation of the company.
- Eliminates pressures on the surviving owners to help the heirs financially because they are also family friends, even though such aid might exacerbate the problems of a business struggling to adjust to the recent loss of a key owner-employee.

Types of Buy-Sell Contracts

cross-purchase plan

stock redemption plan

entity plan

wait-and-see plan

Two traditional buy-sell agreements are the *cross-purchase plan* and the *stock redemption plan (or entity plan)*. The main difference between the two is who will be the buyer. With stock redemption plans, the buyer will be the business itself. In cross-purchase plans, each owner will be the buyer. While this section refers to corporations, the basic concepts are applicable to other forms of business.

Table 5-1 Buy-Sell Insurance—Chances of Death

Here are the statistical chances of death prior to age 65 of a business owner. Column one shows the chances that a sole owner will die. Column two shows the chances of death when there are two owners, and column three shows chances of one death when there are three owners. As you can see, the odds are high that a buy-sell agreement would be used!

If the owner's age is:	Then the chance of death by age 65 is:	If ages of the two owners are:		Then the chance that one of them will die prior to age 65 is:	With three owners, here are the chances:							
					Ages			Chance	Ages			Chance
30	28%	30	30	48%	30	30	30	63%	35	45	60	51%
35	27	30	35	48	30	30	35	62	35	50	50	56
40	26	30	40	47	30	30	40	62	35	50	55	54
45	24	30	45	46	30	30	45	61	35	50	60	50
50	22	30	50	44	30	30	50	60	35	55	55	51
55	18	30	55	41	30	30	55	58	35	55	60	47
60	17	30	60	36	30	30	60	54	35	60	60	43
		35	35	47	30	35	35	62	40	40	40	60
		35	40	46	30	35	40	61	40	40	45	59
		35	45	45	30	35	45	60	40	40	50	58
		35	50	43	30	35	50	59	40	40	55	55
		35	55	40	30	35	55	57	40	40	60	52
		35	60	35	30	35	60	54	40	45	45	58
		40	40	45	30	40	40	61	40	45	50	57
		40	45	44	30	40	45	60	40	45	55	54
		40	50	42	30	40	50	59	40	45	60	51
		40	55	39	30	40	55	56	40	50	50	55
		40	60	35	30	40	60	53	40	50	55	53
		45	45	43	30	45	45	59	40	50	60	49
		45	50	41	30	45	50	58	40	55	55	51
		45	55	38	30	45	55	56	40	55	60	46
		45	60	33	30	45	60	52	40	60	60	42
		50	50	39	30	50	50	56	45	45	45	57
		50	55	36	30	50	55	54	45	45	50	56
		50	60	31	30	50	60	50	45	45	55	53
		55	55	33	30	55	55	52	45	45	60	50
		55	60	27	30	55	60	48	45	50	50	54
		60	60	22	30	60	60	44	45	50	55	32
					35	35	35	61	45	50	60	48
					35	35	40	61	45	55	55	49
					35	35	45	60	45	55	60	45
					35	35	50	59	45	60	60	41
					35	35	55	57	50	50	50	53
					35	35	60	53	50	50	55	50
					35	40	40	60	50	50	60	46
					35	40	45	59	50	55	55	48
					35	40	50	58	50	55	60	44
					35	40	55	56	50	60	60	39
					35	40	60	52	55	55	55	45
					35	45	45	59	55	55	60	41
					35	45	50	57	55	60	60	36
					35	45	55	55	60	60	60	31

Source: Commissioners Standard Mortality Table

A more recent and flexible approach is called the "wait-and-see" buy-sell plan. The wait-and-see plan allows the interested parties to wait until after a death to select between cross-purchase and entity. All three plans are discussed on the following pages.

The Cross-Purchase Plan

The cross-purchase plan is an agreement between individual stockholders. Under this plan the executor of the deceased stockholder's estate sells the deceased owner's stock to the surviving stockholders, and the surviving owners buy the stock of the deceased stockholder at a price stipulated in the contract. This may be a specified dollar amount or a price determined by a formula included in the agreement.

The agreement also provides for funding of the agreement. When insurance is used for funding, each stockholder is the applicant, premium payer, beneficiary, and owner of insurance on the life of each other stockholder in an amount equal to his or her share of the purchase price.

Cross Purchase Example

For example, assume a three-owner corporation valued at $1,500,000, with equal ownership valued at $500,000 each. Under a cross-purchase plan:

- stockholder A owns $250,000 of life insurance on stockholder B and 250,000 on stockholder C
- stockholder B owns $250,000 on A and $250,000 on C
- stockholder C owns $250,000 on A and $250,000 on B

Assume that stockholder A dies. Then stockholders B and C will each receive $250,000 in life insurance proceeds. In accordance with terms of the agreement, they will turn this over to the executor of A's estate in exchange for A's stock. Thus B and C become equal $750,000 stockholders in the business.

Most agreements also allow the surviving stockholders to purchase the policies on their own lives from A's estate by paying an amount equal to the cash value. B and C each now own equal $750,000 interests in the business. They should each buy an additional $500,000 on the other to fund the continuing agreement.

trustee plan   ***Trustee.*** Sometimes a trusteed plan is used-one that employs a trustee to be the middleman in carrying out the agreement. Trustees make sure that the agreement is carried out completely, impartially, fairly, and quickly. (See the illustration titled "How Plan Works" in the appendix of this chapter.)

Number of Policies. One drawback of a cross-purchase agreement where there are multiple owners and each owner purchases a policy on every other owner is that there may be many policies needed. A simple way to calculate the number of policies needed for a cross-purchase buy-sell agreement is to use a formula $N \times (N - 1)$. N equals to number of owners, which is multiplied by the number of owners minus one, since each owner does not buy a policy on him or herself. For example, if there were four owners, the number of policies needed to complete the agreement would be twelve: $4 \times (4 - 1) = 12$.

The Corporate Stock Redemption Plan or Entity Plan

The stock redemption plan is an agreement between the corporation and its stockholders. This plan calls for the executor of the deceased stockholder's estate to sell the deceased stockholder's interest to the corporation and for the corporation to buy the stock of the deceased stockholder at a price stipulated in the contract. Although the price may be a specified dollar amount, it is generally best for the price to be determined by a formula spelled out in the agreement.

Funding. The agreement also provides for funding. When insurance is used for funding, the corporation is applicant, premium payer, beneficiary, and owner of insurance on the life of each stockholder. The amount is equal to the value of each stockholder's interest in the company.

Stock Redemption Example. For example, assume a five-owner corporation valued at $1 million, with each stockholder owning a $200,000 interest. The company buys $200,000 of life insurance on each stockholder.

Upon the death of one of the stockholders, the company receives $200,000 cash from the life insurance company and turns that over to the executor of the deceased stockholder's estate. In exchange, the executor transfers the deceased's ownership interest to the corporation.

The interest of each of the four surviving stockholders increases in value from $200,000 to $250,000. The company then insures each surviving stockholder for an additional $50,000 of life insurance to fully cover the contractual obligations of the insured buy-sell agreement.

In a partnership or other non-corporate forms of business, such a plan would not be called a stock redemption plan because there is stock only in corporations. In other forms of business the plan would usually be called an entity plan.

Choosing Between Cross-Purchase and Entity Plans

There are a number of factors that enter into the choice between these two plans-the choice, of course, is to be made by the owners of the business.

Validity of the Entity Plan. Before an entity plan is adopted, the corporation's attorney will determine if the corporation has the legal power to buy its own stock. Such purchases can generally be made if

1. the purchase price is determined in good faith
2. the purchase will not endanger the solvency of the corporation
3. the transaction will not be harmful to the rights of creditors and stockholders

These are extremely important conditions. What (2) and (3) mean, in effect, is that the corporation may buy its own stock only from retained earnings. If the corporation doesn't have enough retained earnings, then it cannot buy its own stock. This is another reason why proper financing is vital; the retained earnings account must be sufficient to allow the purchase. There is no better way to guarantee this than through life insurance.

Number of Stockholders. In the case of a large number of stockholders, the sheer number of policies involved would, from a practical standpoint, favor the entity plan.

Under a cross-purchase plan, if there were, say, eight stockholders, 56 policies would be required. (Each stockholder owns seven policies, one on each associate.)

An entity plan would require a total of only eight policies. Cost factors such as policy fees or volume discounts are also considerations in deciding between an entity and cross-purchase plan. To reduce the number of policies in certain situations, some companies will issue a first-to-die policy, although this is rare.

Insured Stock Redemption Plan

What Is It?

Under an insured stock redemption plan, the corporation purchases a deceased shareholder's shares from the estate.

How Does It Work?

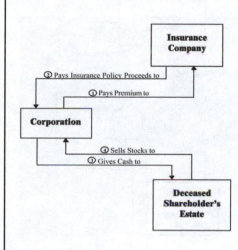

The corporation

- applies for insurance on eac h stockholder's life
- pays premium
- is owner and beneficiary
- receives policy's death proceeds
- pays agreed upon price to estate
- receives deceased's shares

How Do You Do It?

In a written buy-sell agreement, the corporation agrees to purchase the shares of a deceased stockholder.

What Are the Considerations?

- Surviving shareholders do not receive stock that carries a stepped-up basis.
- Stock redemption plans are subject to the alternative minimum tax, while cross-purchase plans are not.
- If the individual's income tax bracket is less than the corporation's tax bracket, then nondeductible expenses such as premiums for funding an insured buy-sell plan are generally less costly when paid at the individual shareholder level (cross-purchase plan) than at the corporate level (stock redemption plan).

What Are the Advantages of a Stock Redemption Plan to the Corporation?

- Simplicity—Only one policy is needed for each shareholder.
- The corporation pays the premiums, thus not directly affecting personal income.
- Disparity of ages is not a problem because the corporation pays the premium.
- Premiums paid on policies are not reportable as income by the owners/insureds.

Insured Cross-Purchase Plan

What Is It?

Under an insured cross-purchase plan, surviving stockholders individually buy a deceased stockholder's shares from the decedent's estate.

How Does It Work?

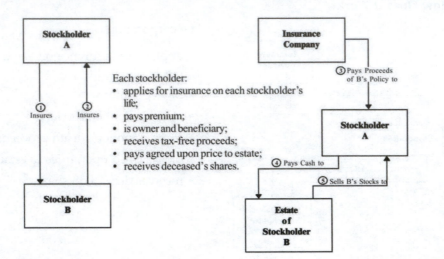

Each stockholder:
- applies for insurance on each stockholder's life;
- pays premium;
- is owner and beneficiary;
- receives tax-free proceeds;
- pays agreed upon price to estate;
- receives deceased's shares.

How Do You Do It?

In a written buy-sell agreement, eac h stockholder agrees to purchase the shares of a deceased stockholder. Each stockholder's estate is obligated to sell the shares to the surviving stockholders at a price established in the agreement and insured by policies issued to each stockholder.

What Are the Considerations?

- Many separate policies are needed if there are more than two stockholders.

- Disparity in ages of stockholders might cause an imbalance of premium payments.

- If there are more than two stockholders, transfer-for-value problems could arise after the first death. (This problem does not arise in partnership situations.)

- Premiums are paid from personal income.

What Are the Advantages of a Cross-Purchase Plan?

- Surviving stockholders receive shares with a stepped-up cost basis. This means less reportable gain if the shares are later sold by the owenr.

- Proceeds are not subject to the claims of corporate creditors.

- No corporate alternative minimum tax is involved with cross-purchase plans.

Premium Distribution under Cross Purchase Plan. Under the cross-purchase plan each stockholder pays the premiums on the policies he or she owns. If there is a substantial difference in ages this sometimes creates a problem.

For example, if one owner were 20 years younger than the other owner, the younger stockholder would pay a much higher premium per thousand. In return, however, he or she has a better chance of surviving and acquiring the interests of the other stockholder. As a practical matter, the younger stockholder may find it difficult to pay the higher premium on the older stockholder.

The older stockholder might be willing and able to help by sharing some of the premium. If this seems workable, you might suggest that an extra amount of insurance be purchased. Then, if the older owner dies first, the extra insurance could be used to reimburse the older owner's estate for the extra premiums paid. This may produce income tax consequences.

Other variations might be suggested along the lines of a split dollar plan. In effect, split dollar would produce approximately the same results as the preceding idea. For example, the older owner advances an amount of premium equal to the cash value increase each year. The "investment" is protected, since the cash value amount would be assigned to the older owner in the event of death or if the plan is canceled.

Another plan to help a younger stockholder afford the premium outlay is to finance the agreement with term insurance, or part permanent and part term. There are definite drawbacks, however—no cash reserves for emergencies, no extended term or paid-up life insurance during possible business reverses, and a premium that may be too high when it is needed most and all the owners are much older (these problems are reviewed in some detail later in this chapter).

Premium Distribution under Entity Plan. Under the entity plan each stockholder indirectly pays a share of the total premiums of all policies.

If the premiums are $3,000, for example, and there are three equal owners, each in effect pays $1,000 when the corporation writes the check. If there are wide differences in ages, the older stockholder is paying not only one-third of the premium on each associate, but also part of the premium on his or her own life.

Unless all stockholders are insurable at the same rate and all own an equal interest in the business, there may be questions raised about fairness or equity of payments made in proportion to percentage of ownership.

Someone Else

"Partner, would you want your spouse's future security to depend on someone else's generosity or ability? Let me explain what I mean. Unless there is a written agreement, your spouse can't be certain of getting a fair price for your business. Instead, your spouse will be dependent on the generosity and ability of your surviving business associates."

Nevertheless, other agreements may be made separately to balance the scales (as discussed above). And it may be that the older stockholders will disregard the apparent inequity in view of the probability that the younger owners would outlive them. The advantages to their own families, in other words, may outweigh the extra costs to them.

Psychological Factor. The entity plan is sometimes selected because shareholders are more willing to use corporate funds rather than personal funds, for any purpose.

Wait-and-See Buy-Sell Agreement (Also Known as Optional Buy-Sell Agreement). Choosing between a cross-purchase and an entity approach is not easy. When a choice of methods is not clear to the client and the client's attorney, you might suggest a wait-and-see buy-sell agreement. Under this method, no decision is made until after a death occurs. At that time, all interested parties examine the relevant facts and make an informed decision.

How The Wait-and-See Buy-Sell Works. The wait-and-see buy-sell agreement is basically a series of options to buy.

right of first refusal

First Option. It gives the business a first option to acquire the interest of the deceased business owners. This is also known as a *right of first refusal*. The company must exercise this option within a time period specified in the agreement. It would be exercised only if the interested parties (owners, heirs, etc.) and their tax advisors agreed that an entity approach was most appropriate given the facts at the time of death.

Second Option. If the business does not exercise its initial option to buy, the surviving business owners then have an option to purchase the deceased owner's business interest.

(It is important to note that the surviving owners hold only an option. They are not legally bound to purchase the stock. If stockholders were legally bound under the agreement to purchase stock and failed to do so, then at a later time when the corporation purchases the stock, the surviving owners may be considered to have received a taxable dividend equal to the purchase price paid by the corporation.)

The second option held by the surviving owners would be exercised if it were concluded by all interested parties that a cross-purchase approach was most advantageous. The agreement would, of course, clearly specify the details of the purchase (valuation method, payment method, and so on).

Contingent Final Option. If the first and second options are not exercised, the business would then be required to purchase the interest of the deceased owner. By having this contingent mandatory final step, the owners are assured that their heirs/estate will be able to sell the ownership interest at a guaranteed and funded price.

Given the uncertainty as to which party would ultimately purchase the ownership interest, you may be wondering who should purchase the insurance necessary to fund a wait-and-see buy-sell agreement. There is flexibility in this important decision too-the insurance can be owned initially by either the company or the individual owners.

Who Owns the Insurance. Assume the company is owner, beneficiary, and premium payor on the policies. If it is decided that the company should exercise its initial option and redeem the business interest, it would obviously use the insurance dollars to complete its purchase option.

Where Will the Money Come From?
1.　CASH—100 cents on the dollar.
2.　EARNINGS—100-plus cents on the dollar.
3.　BORROWED FUNDS—100 cents plus interest on the dollar.
4.　LIFE INSURANCE—pennies each year on the dollar for premiums.

But what if the cross-purchase method is best? Under this scenario the business would lend the insurance proceeds to the surviving owners with the loan fully secured by the purchased business interest. Over time the loan would be repaid from funds generated in the business—either through higher salaries or occasional bonuses.

Many experts believe that with a wait-and-see agreement it is better to have the individual owners purchase the necessary insurance contracts. If a cross-purchase approach is desirable (if option 2 is exercised), then the surviving owners are in a position to use their insurance proceeds. If an entity approach is deemed most desirable (exercise option 1), the surviving owners could provide the insurance proceeds to the business in one of two methods—either loan the funds to the business or make an additional capital contribution to the company. The capital contribution would have the added benefit of increasing the owners' cost basis in the company and could reduce taxes in the event of a later lifetime sale of their business interest.

FEDERAL INCOME TAXES AFFECTING CHOICE OF AGREEMENTS

The tax aspects of buy-sell transactions can influence the choice between a cross-purchase plan and an entity plan. Although the choice should be made on the advice of a competent tax attorney, you must be knowledgeable about the tax implications to discuss them intelligently with the client and the client's advisors.

There are three income tax aspects to consider in deciding whether to use a cross-purchase plan or an entity plan in corporate situations:

First is the question of whether the IRS will view the transaction as a sale of stock or as a dividend. Cross-purchase plans are always treated as a sale of stock. This means favorable tax treatment because in the sale of anything only the gain (profit) is taxable. However, the full amount of a dividend is taxable.

Entity plans can go either way. In general, if the corporation buys a person's entire interest, it will be treated favorably as a sale of stock. Even with partial redemptions, if certain conditions are met, the same favorable results can apply. However, the IRS views most partial redemptions as dividends. This is a highly undesirable result because it means that every dollar of the purchase price will be taxable income to the seller.

Partial redemptions are stock redemptions in which a corporation buys only part of an owner's stock. When all of an owner's stock is purchased, it is called a complete redemption. More will be said later about taxation of entity plans.

Second, if there are more than two stockowners, there can be a transfer-for-value income tax problem after the first death. The transfer-for-value rule is discussed later in this chapter. As noted there, the tax does not apply in partnership situations.

The third income tax consideration in deciding between an entity and a cross-purchase plan is one that can arise months or years after an owner dies. It arises when the stock is later sold again during the owner's lifetime and it has to do with whether the stepped-up basis is available to reduce taxes at the time of the subsequent sale. The bottom line is this: If a cross-purchase plan had been used initially, the federal income tax results of a later-lifetime sale will be more favorable. Conversely, an entity plan means less-favorable tax results with later lifetime sales. Explaining how this happens means explaining

- gain
- cost basis
- the stepped-up cost basis on inherited property

cost basis   The cost basis of a share of stock is, essentially, what you paid for it.

Gain is the profit you make when you sell it (gain equals selling price minus cost basis). For example, if you paid $100 for a stock, your cost basis is $100. If you later sell it for, say $300, your gain is $200.

stepped-up basis   Stepped-up basis for inherited property: When a stockowner dies and an heir inherits the stock, the stock takes on a new and higher cost basis. It is referred to as a stepped-up basis or stepped-up cost basis. This new basis will be the stock's market value at the time of the owner's death (or 6 months after death).

For example, assume you initially paid $100 for a stock. On the day you die, the stock has a market value of $500. Your spouse inherits your stock. Your basis in the stock was $100. Your spouse's basis is $500. For tax purchases, the stepped-up basis stock is very important because-and this is the key point-higher basis means less gain; less gain means less tax.

To illustrate, continuing the example above: If you had sold your $100 stock during your lifetime for $650, your taxable gain would have been $550. But if instead, your widow or widower eventually sells the stock for $650, his or her taxable gain is only $150. The one and only factor that causes this difference is the fact that the law gives a stepped-up basis to inherited property. In our example at death, the basis was stepped up from $100 to $500.

Now that these three terms have been described, here's how they affect the decision to go with a cross-purchase plan rather than an entity plan. The key factor is that all of the stock stays in circulation with cross-purchase plans. Under entity plans, however, some of the advantageous stepped-up basis stock is taken out of circulation. It is retired, unusable. The new, higher-basis stock will not help anyone once it's out of circulation.

Tax under Cross-Purchase

To illustrate the difference, assume that Able and Baker initially put $100,000 into their new corporation ($50,000 each). Several years later, when the business was worth $340,000, they entered into a cross-purchase agreement. Able died. Able's stock went into Able's estate, carrying with it a stepped-up basis of $170,000 (its fair market value). In selling it for $170,000 to Baker, the estate pays no tax because there is no gain in selling $170,000-cost-basis stock for $170,000.

Baker now owns 100 percent of the $340,000 corporation. Half of Baker's stock has a basis of $50,000. (This is the half that Baker has owned from the time the corporation was first started.) The half that Baker bought from Able's estate has a basis of $170,000 because that's how much Baker just paid Able's estate. Baker's basis now totals $220,000 ($50,000 plus $170,000) on a business with a value of $340,000.

A few months later Baker decides to sell out completely. He finds a buyer and receives $340,000. His gain is $120,000 ($340,000 selling price less $220,000 basis). Tax on this gain for a 28 percent bracket taxpayer would be $33,600.

Tax under Entity Plan

Now, using the same basic facts, assume that the death buyout plan had been an entity plan instead of a cross-purchase plan.

At Able's death the corporation buys Able's stock for $170,000. Baker is now 100 percent owner of this $340,000 corporation. Total outstanding stock all belongs to Baker and has a basis of $50,000. (Able's old stock is no longer outstanding stock. It now belongs to the corporation, and for our purposes it can be forgotten. It is treasury stock not personally owned by Baker.)

After a few months Baker decides to sell out completely. He finds a buyer and receives $340,000. His gain is $290,000 ($340,000 selling price less $50,000 basis). Tax on this capital gain would be $81,200 for a 28 percent bracket taxpayer.

Compare this with the $33,600 tax when a cross-purchase plan was used. It becomes clear that a cross-purchase plan is financially advantageous when a later lifetime sale by the surviving owner is anticipated.

Remember, this comes about only when a lifetime sale follows (anytime after) the death buyout. You will find that many lawyers and accountants are not aware of this significant tax difference. Your knowledge can help increase the accountant's and attorney's confidence in you.

Notice that with subsequent death buyouts (versus subsequent lifetime buyouts), there is no difference between the plans. For example, if Baker died and his estate sold the business for $340,000, there would have been no taxable gain because the basis would have been automatically stepped up to the $340,000 current market value.

Under the cross-purchase plan it would have been stepped up from $220,000 to $340,000; under the stock redemption (entity) plan it would have been stepped up from $50,000 to $340,000. In both cases, there is no reportable gain and no tax.

Accumulated Earnings Tax

accumulated earnings tax

The tax advantage of the corporate tax rates on earnings accumulated by the corporation is limited somewhat by the accumulated earnings tax. The accumulated earnings tax provides an incentive to distribute income as dividends. The accumulated earnings tax is a penalty tax designed to prevent tax avoidance through the accumulation of earnings within the corporation beyond the expected needs of the business. For years 2002 through 2010, the IRS imposes an additional "accumulated earnings" tax of 15 percent (set at the highest individual tax rate for all other tax years) on earnings a corporation accumulates above $250,000 ($150,000 for a personal service corporation). If the corporation can show that the accumulations above $250,000 are for definite and reasonable business purposes, the tax can be avoided.

The question to be addressed in the following few paragraphs is whether the tax applies to money accumulated to fund a buy-sell agreement. That is, do the courts and the IRS consider buy-sell funding a reasonable or unreasonable business need?

First, the accumulated earnings tax applies only to C corporations. Sole proprietorships, partnerships, LLCs, and S corporations are exempt. Because the latter are pass-through forms of business, the owners report all earnings each year on their individual Form 1040 tax returns.

Second, if the buy-sell plan is a cross-purchase plan (versus a corporate stock redemption plan), there will be no corporate accumulated earnings tax. This is because cash values of a cross-purchase plan are by definition personally owned, not corporately owned.

Do the courts (and the IRS) consider buy-sell funding a reasonable business need? The courts have decided differently in different situations. In reaching their decisions, the courts examine the main purpose of the stock redemption agreement, and two viewpoints emerge.

The tax on accumulated corporate earnings is likely to apply only when the buy-sell agreement is designed primarily to serve the estate planning needs of the shareholders, and not so much to serve the needs of the business. For example, the tax is likely to apply to buy-sell cash values when these earnings are being accumulated to fund a *partial* redemption of the majority shareholder's stock.

On the other hand, cash values will generally be safe from the accumulated earnings tax if the stock redemption seems designed to do such things as promote corporate harmony or efficiency of management, or enables the corporation to continue its accustomed practices or policies. Put differently, a reasonable business purpose seems to include providing for the orderly continuation of a business, keeping stock out of unfriendly hands, and increasing the equity interest of key employees.

If a buy-sell agreement has a purpose that might not hold up under scrutiny of the courts, the owners might be wise to consider using a cross-purchase agreement, thereby clearly and definitely avoiding the possibility of an accumulated earnings tax.

One final point: *Professional corporations* are probably free from the accumulated earnings tax when it comes to earnings set aside to fund buy-sell agreements. This is so because the law in many states *requires* the corporation to buy the stock of a deceased shareholder.

Transfer-for-Value Rule

transfer-for-value   There will generally be no transfer-for-value tax problems if a cross-purchase plan is later changed to a stock-redemption plan. But this tax trap is almost always encountered if a stock-redemption plan is later changed to a cross-purchase plan. Transfer-for-value problems will be discussed in more detail later in this chapter

The Uninsurable Owner

The discussion of the insured buy-sell or business continuation plan is based on circumstances found in a simple, hypothetical firm composed of two or more owners, all of whom are insurable and whose respective interests are equal. Of course, these circumstances do not always occur and different circumstances will call for modifications of the standard sale and purchase arrangement.

When you realize that approximately one person in every 20 who applies for life insurance is uninsurable, we can expect that some business owners who wish to set up an insured buy-sell plan will occasionally find that one of their associates is uninsurable. There are several possible solutions to this unfortunate scenario. The problem is solved immediately if the uninsurable individual has sufficient personal life insurance that he or she is willing to sell and assign to the business or the other owners. Where this is not possible, there may be a reaction of the parties to abandon their plan to execute the continuation agreement. This should not be the course of action since it may and probably will result in considerable hardship and financial loss to the survivors. The insurable owners could establish a sinking fund for the uninsurable owner, with a series of notes (IOUs) for the remainder of the purchase price, should the uninsurable owner die before the purchase price has been accumulated. The agreement must allow that the remainder of the purchase price will be paid in installments spread over an agreed upon period of time. The business may also consider purchasing key person insurance on the insurable owners, in order to augment the sinking fund should any of the insurable partners predecease the uninsurable owner. It should not be assumed that because one of the owners is uninsurable that he or she will die first. If the uninsurable owner does die first, however, the additional cash value created by the key person insurance will be available to make partial payment for the deceased owner's interest.

FEDERAL TAX CONSIDERATIONS WITH THE BUY-SELL

Specific tax matters pertaining to the individual needs and goals of each client should be delegated to attorneys and accountants who are retained by the clients. However, your knowledge of tax-related matters will allow you to be known by prospects and their tax advisors as a competent professional advisor.

Federal Income Taxes

Premiums

The premiums paid for individual life insurance policies are generally not tax deductible, whether paid by the business owners or by the business itself. This is true of life insurance purchased to fund a buy-sell agreement, as well as key person insurance and most other individual coverages. If split-dollar coverage is used to fund the buy-sell agreement there can be a taxable economic benefit. If a bonus is used to help fund the buy-sell agreement, there will be a taxable economic benefit to the employee.

Proceeds

With two notable exceptions, death proceeds of a life insurance policy are received by the beneficiary free of federal income taxation. This is true for all beneficiaries including individual business owners or businesses.

Naturally this is a great advantage in business situations. It means that a business can receive from a life insurance policy all the cash it needs to purchase the interest of a deceased owner, yet pay no income tax on the sudden increase in its retained earnings account.

The Exceptions

The two exceptions, described below, are

1. the federal income taxation corporate alternative minimum tax (AMT)
2. the transfer-for-value tax

Corporate Alternative Minimum Tax (AMT)

corporate
alternative
minimum tax

alternative
minimum tax

In response to the popular perception that corporations do not pay a fair share of federal income taxes, Congress enacted the alternative minimum tax provisions. Corporations must pay the alternative minimum tax if it is greater than the regular corporate income tax for the year. To the extent that the AMT paid exceeds the regular income tax for the year, the corporation may use this excess to offset regular tax liability in future years. C corporations with 3-year average annual gross receipts in excess of $7.5 million are subject to the alternative minimum tax (AMT). For corporations in existence less than 3 years, the initial qualification for exemption from the AMT involves having average annual gross receipts of no more than $5 million, with the respective number of years the corporation was in existence to be substituted for the 3 years. Generally, a corporation will be exempt from the AMT in its first year of existence.

The tax is calculated under special rules that add 75 percent of certain "tax preferences" into the tax base of a corporation to determine its alternative minimum taxable income (AMTI). The corporation's tax for the year is the greater of its regular tax or its alternative minimum tax. For AMT purposes, the tax rate is a flat 20 percent (IRC Sec. 55 (b)(1)(B).

The tax preferences mentioned above include the net inside buildup in cash value life insurance policies owned by the corporation.

In addition, net life insurance death proceeds increase current earnings for purposes of calculating the corporate alternative minimum tax. Another way to think of it is that, in corporate situations, net death protection may be reduced by as much as 15 percent (75% of 20% = 15%), because of the alternative minimum tax.

The upside of this tax is that it generally means larger sales and additional sales when a corporation is beneficiary of a policy. For example, a corporation owned $20 million of life insurance on one of its owners. A young financial advisor told one of the firm's accountants about the potential tax liability of life insurance proceeds in corporate situations. Within a month the corporation had increased the insurance, though this advisor, by about $3,000,000 so that after the tax, the remaining amount would still be $20 million.

Pennies on the Dollar

"Prospect, who will pay the federal estate taxes due at your death or your spouse's death? Your estate can pay them at 100 cents on the dollar—or even more if the estate needs to borrow the money. Or, my company will pay the taxes if you put aside only pennies a year on each one dollar due then. Let me show you how this would work out for your estate."

Transfer-for-Value Rule

If you work in the business market, it is essential that you are mindful of the transfer-for-value rule, perhaps the most prominent exception to the general rule that life insurance death proceeds are income-tax exempt. Where a policy transferred by assignment or otherwise for a valuable consideration matures by reason of death, the transferee will be liable for income tax on the amount of death proceeds in excess of the actual value of the consideration paid for the contract, plus the total of net premiums and other amounts subsequently paid by the new owner. This rule is designed to prevent a tax-free windfall that might come about from speculation in life insurance policies.

However, certain transfers of life insurance for consideration are not motivated by a desire for profit but for valid business reasons. Therefore Congress included five exceptions in the Code to the transfer-for-value rule. When any one of these transfer-for-value rule exceptions applies, the full death proceeds will be income tax free in the hands of the beneficiary, even though the policy was transferred for a valuable consideration.

The five specified exceptions are (1) transfers to the insured, (2) transfers to a partner of the insured, (3) transfers to a partnership in which the insured is a partner, (4) transfers to a corporation in which the insured is a shareholder or an officer, and (5) transfers in which the transferee's basis in the transferred policy is determined in whole or in part by reference to the transferor's basis. This latter exception (referred to as the carryover-basis exception) would apply in a tax-free exchange, where, for example, one corporation transfers a corporate-owned key person policy to another corporation in a tax-free reorganization.

One significant omission is the transfer of a policy from an insured who is a shareholder in a closely held corporation to a fellow shareholder. As in the transfer of a policy from a partner-insured to a fellow partner, there may be sound business reasons for such a transfer, yet the rule excludes the latter but not the former. Conscientious advisors need to be especially mindful of these nonexceptions.

The tax results of a transfer-for-value problem can be onerous. The amount of death proceeds exposed to ordinary income in one year can be substantial. Thus careful attention must be paid to every transfer of a life insurance policy in order to avoid the tax pitfall of the transfer-for-value rule. Examples of transfers that are not uncommon but that violate the rule include the following:

- A policyowner sells a policy on his or her life to a corporation in which he or she is an employee and/or member of the board of directors. (The insured must be a shareholder or officer.)
- Alice and Bruce own all the stock of a corporation and enter into a buy-sell agreement on a cross-purchase basis. Instead of buying new life insurance on each other's lives to fund the agreement, Alice and Bruce each transfer to the other an existing policy on their lives. (Coshareholders are not exempt transferees.)
- The Alice-Bruce Corporation has a stock redemption agreement with Alice and Bruce funded with corporate-owned insurance on Alice and Bruce. The parties wish to change the stock retirement arrangement to a cross-purchase plan. The corporation transfers Alice's policy to Bruce and Bruce's policy to Alice.

In some instances the parties may be unaware that a transfer is being made or of the consideration involved. They may not be aware they are transferring anything to each other, and an actual act or physical transfer is not required, only a transfer for a valuable consideration. Consideration may be simply an agreement of reciprocal promises to fund their business agreement with cross-beneficiary designations.

A case example will demonstrate this problem. Two shareholders (Bob and Dave) of a new corporation purchase $400,000 life insurance policies on themselves, naming each other as beneficiaries. Two years later, Dave dies, and the insurer pays the proceeds to Bob, the policy's beneficiary. Bob's tax professional advised him that due to the manner in which the policies were issued, the proceeds for the most part were taxable to him under the transfer-for-value rule, and Bob paid $135,000 of income taxes on the proceeds.

There was an obvious agreement between the shareholders in the way these policies were set up. When Bob named Dave beneficiary in exchange for Dave naming Bob beneficiary, there was the requisite consideration. A quid pro quo ("I will do this for you, if you will do that for me") is consideration just as if there was an exchange of money. There need be nothing in writing or anything specifically stated by the parties involved for there to be consideration. The IRS will assume that there is consideration where it is reasonable to believe that, without it, the transfer would not have occurred.

One other exception to the transfer-for-value rule applies to divorce situations. If an existing policy is transferred as part of a divorce or separation settlement, the policy proceeds will not be taxable as a transfer for value.

With business insurance, the most likely situation to cause a transfer-for-value problem is where an existing life insurance policy has been sold to a corporate stockholder who is not the insured person. This can happen when an entity plan is later changed to a cross-purchase plan.

It can also happen under a corporate cross-purchase plan when, following the death of one owner, the other owners buy the policies that the now-deceased owner had owned on the other stockholders. The transfer-for-value problem can also happen when an existing personally owned policy is used to fund a corporate cross-purchase plan. This method is sometimes used where the stockholder is uninsurable and therefore uses an existing policy to fund the buy-sell.

Using an entity plan, rather than a cross-purchase plan, generally avoids these practical problems. The transfer-for-value rule is another of those not-too-well-known tax laws that can cause serious problems. By knowing about it, you can get lots of well-deserved kudos from attorneys, accountants, and clients.

Federal Estate Tax

Proceeds

When a life insurance policy on the life of an owner is owned by and payable to the business or another owner, and the insured has no incidents of ownership in the policy, the proceeds are not subject to federal estate tax. The value of the owner's business interest is included in his/her estate for federal estate tax purposes.

Tax Role of an Agreement

As discussed in the previous chapter, the Internal Revenue Service will generally accept the value of the business stated in a buy-sell agreement if the agreement meets several criteria, including these:

- The price must have been fair and reasonable price when established.
- It must have been an arm's-length transaction.
- It must contain a first-offer provision.

If the buy-sell involves family members, other rules apply. They are covered in Chapter 6.

IRC Section 6166

Section 6166 of the Internal Revenue Code is an extended payment plan for business-related federal estate taxes. Details of this installment plan are discussed later in Chapter 8.

What if the policy is a modified endowment contract (MEC)? A MEC is a MEC whether it is a business or an individual situation. Policy loans or withdrawals will be taxable to the extent of any gain in the policy, on an income-first basis. This means that a distribution from a MEC in a gain situation will be subject to current income taxation. A 10 percent penalty will be imposed on withdrawn gains prior to the insured's age 59 1/2.

Summary of Federal Income Taxation

Life Insurance that Funds a Buy-Sell Agreement

Buy-sell insurance is life insurance that provides the cash to buy the deceased person's share of the business, as set forth in the written buy-sell agreement. In some cases the insurance is owned by the business itself, and the business is also the beneficiary. In other cases, the insurance is owned individually by the other owners, and the other owners are also the beneficiaries of the policies.

Premiums—The premiums paid for buy-sell insurance are not income tax deductible. This is true for all kinds of businesses. It is true whether the insurance is owned by the business itself or by the other owners individually.

Proceeds—In general, proceeds paid to the business at the insured's death are free from federal income taxation. There are two main exceptions to this general rule. One happens when a C corporation is subject to the corporate alternative minimum tax, in which case it may have to pay some tax on the gain in the policy at death. Another is if there has been a "transfer for value," in which case part of the death proceeds may be subject to federal income tax.

Cash Value—In general, the policy's cash values accumulate free from federal income taxation. One exception to this happens if the insurance is owned by a corporation that is subject to the corporate alternative minimum tax, in which case it may have to pay some tax on the gain in the policy.

You and the IRS?

"When you die, the value of your stock will be determined by the IRS. Do you know there's a way for you to establish its value instead? This could save your heirs tens of thousands of dollars of federal estate tax. May I explain?"

FUNDING THE BUY-SELL AGREEMENT

When the decision has been made to establish a buy-sell agreement, you need to help your client in answering a critical question: "Where will the money come from to facilitate the required purchase?" There are five alternative sources of funding for the client to consider:

1. Accumulated capital or a sinking fund
2. Borrowed funds
3. Installment payments by surviving owners from their personal income or assets
4. Installment payments by the business from future profits
5. Insurance

An illustration in the appendix summarizes the salient points of each funding alternative. (See illustration titled "Funding the Purchase of a Business Interest.")

By reviewing each approach with your prospects, you can let them see for themselves that the insurance alternative is not only the most effective funding vehicle but is also the most cost effective.

1. Use of Cash, Accumulated Assets, or a Sinking Fund

sinking fund   Any accumulated company assets (cash or other business assets) have likely been set aside for a specific business purpose. For example, existing cash reserves are probably for current working capital used to handle the ongoing daily needs for cash. It is fairly rare to find a company with extra cash reserves.

Extra Cash?

To highlight this characteristic, try asking your prospect: "How much extra cash do you normally have in the business, beyond what you maintain either to meet the current needs of the company or to meet unforeseen cash emergencies?" Most prospects will respond that cash is one of their very precious rare assets and seldom is there such a thing as "extra cash."

Not Good Business Sense

To use hard-earned cash reserves to fund a buy-sell agreement could add a burden to the company just when it faces unusual business pressures. A key executive just died and business problems are likely to result. Is it reasonable to drain company cash reserves at this time of dramatic change in the company? It just doesn't make good business sense.

As an alternative to relying on normal cash reserves, some prospects (or their advisors) might think about creating a special sinking fund. This entails making periodic deposits to a separate asset account to gradually build up the necessary funds.

This ties up a lot of cash so it won't be too popular. In addition, it has a major flaw—does the business or its owner know when a death will occur? Obviously not! Because the date of death is unknown, the amount to be set aside each year is also unknown.

Further, if an owner dies in the early years, there will not be enough money to handle the purchase. The only way to reduce the significant risk associated with an early death is to make very substantial, periodic contributions to the sinking fund—that is, build the necessary fund in a very short period. However, this would likely be too severe a drain on the business and would likely be rejected as a viable alternative.

2. Borrow Funds

This approach is very similar in actual results to the use of an installment purchase (see the next segment). If funds are borrowed, a significant amount of the future earnings of the company will be committed to paying the debt—both interest and principal.

Illustration

The accompanying illustration demonstrates the relative costs of borrowing money to fund a buy-sell agreement. It shows the heavy drain created by the required loan payments. While extending the loan amortization schedule from 5 years to 20 years reduces the monthly cash flow pressure, it nearly doubles the total cost.

The Cost of Borrowing to Fund a Buy-Sell			

Assume:

- a $1,000,000 buy-sell
- 10% interest required on borrowed funds
- 5-year, 10-year, and 20-year amortization of the required $1,000,000 loan.

	5-Year Loan Schedule	**10-Year Loan Schedule**	**20-Year Loan Schedule**
Monthly Payment	$21,250	$13,220	$9,650
Total Cost	$1,275,000	$1,586,400	$2,316,000
Total Interest	$275,000	$586,400	$1,316,000
Cost Per $1.00 Borrowed	$1.28	$1.59	$2.32

Use insurance rather than borrowing. Insurance costs only pennies a year per dollar, or, in this example, $30,000 a year for $1,000,000. The cost of insurance is even less than just the interest on borrowed funds.

Before using this illustration, get approval from your company's compliance department.

Expense aside, it may be very difficult, or even impossible, to obtain a loan. The loan application will be filed at the very time that the company has lost a key owner-employee. The company will likely face a risky and uncertain period following the loss of the deceased's valuable skills and contacts.

From the banker's perspective, this factor will increase the risk of the loan and could either lead to a rejection of the application or to a higher interest rate to offset the added risk.

3. Surviving Owners Make Installment Purchase

A cross-purchase agreement could specify that the surviving owners will purchase the interest of the deceased owner through an installment plan.

This has the same problems for the business as does a bank loan. The pressure on the owner to generate cash from the business to make the installment payments can seriously hamper the operations of the company. However, the greatest peril with an installment sale lies with the insecurity it creates for the heirs.

With a loan arrangement, the heirs get cash and the surviving owners have a loan obligation to a bank. With an installment sale, however, the heirs receive periodic payments directly from the surviving owners. The heirs are in the position of creditors to the surviving owners!

The heirs are therefore dependent on the ability of the surviving owners to generate sufficient cash flow to fulfill the obligations of the installment sale. If the business fails, the heirs probably will not be paid. It is unlikely that the surviving owners will have enough personal wealth outside the business that would allow them to meet their installment obligations. The future financial security of the heirs is tied to the success or failure of the business.

If your prospect likes the idea of installments, try asking one of the following questions:

- Do you want your heirs to gamble their futures on the future of the business?"
- "Would you advise your heirs to invest their inheritance in the debt of a closely held business in which they have no say in management—a business which has just lost a key profit maker?"

4. Business Makes Installment Purchase

If an entity buy-sell is used, the funding vehicle could conceivably be an installment purchase contract between the company and the heirs. This has virtually the same problems for the business as a bank loan or an installment sale by the individual owners. The cash drain on the company at the exact time it has lost a key profit maker could be a catastrophe.

However, the greatest peril lies with the heirs whose very future will be dependent on the success of a business over which they have no business control. This alternative may be even more risky for the heirs than an installment sale with the individual surviving owners. If the business is a corporation and the company fails to make the required installment payments, the heirs will have a claim only on the assets of the company. Unless there is a separate collateral agreement, the personal assets of the surviving owners could not be reached by the heirs if the business failed.

5. Insurance Funding

In contrast with the uncertainty of the foregoing funding methods, life insurance funding provides guarantees and certainty for owners and heirs. With life insurance, the liability is immediately removed and both groups get exactly what they want: The heirs get a prearranged amount of cash and the surviving owners get total control of the business. Neither owners nor heirs are burdened with a long-term buyout.

Benefits of Insured Funding

There are several reasons why insurance is a most practical solution for a buy-sell agreement:

- The event (death) causing the need for cash creates the cash exactly when it is needed.

- The annual outlay for insurance is relatively small compared to the potential benefits. For example, at most ages, the annual premium for life insurance may be only 2 to 4 percent of the insurance amount.

- If an owner dies shortly after the insurance is purchased, the full amount needed is available, not just the amount set aside up to that time.

- Cash value products available today have competitive interest earnings.

- If the insured lives until retirement and wishes to sell at that time, the cash value of the insurance may be used as a down payment (or possibly total payment) for the business interest.

- Because the insured agreement determines the value and disposition of this asset in advance, each owner can incorporate this value into an overall estate plan.

- Existing assets remain intact for distribution to heirs.

- The buyout occurs as predetermined, with no lingering disputes or further incurrence of debt.

- All parties can get on with their lives without a "cloud" hanging over them.

Funding does not have to be limited to just one method. For example, business owners might do partial life insurance funding and partial installment funding. For example, this could include life insurance to cover, say, half of the purchase price, and perhaps a 5-year installment purchase for the other half.

Which Comes First—the Agreement or the Insurance?

If insurance is to be used, a critical question results: Which comes first, drafting the agreement or buying the insurance? The written agreement is an important document. It not only tells what the intentions are, but it can be viewed as creating the insurable interest. In fact, some companies require a written buy-sell before issuing the policies.

Ideally, they will both become effective at the same time. Unfortunately, it usually doesn't work that way. As a general rule, the insurance application should be submitted even if the legal documents have not been completed. If one of the owners is uninsurable, or insurable but at an unacceptable rate, the agreement needs to reflect an alternate funding technique.

In the meantime, all owners sign a letter of intent specifying the purpose of the insurance. In a corporate situation, the corporate minutes will reflect this. Thus if an owner dies or becomes disabled before the agreement is completed, the desires of the owners can still be carried out. If, on the other hand, the agreement is executed before insurance is purchased, and an owner dies or becomes uninsurable, the surviving business owners can find themselves in a disastrous financial situation.

What happens if the insured commits suicide within a year or two? The death proceeds would not be payable and the other owners might not be able to carry out their financial commitment. For this reason, the buy-sell agreement should address the issue of suicide within two years. One way to handle it is to state that the buyout is not mandatory if the death proceeds are not payable.

Sales Aids in Appendix—You will find some helpful one-page sales materials in the appendix immediately following this chapter. Be sure to get approval from your home office before using this material.

Contents of the Buy-Sell Agreement

The properly designed buy-sell agreement has several typical provisions regardless of the type of agreement. Failure to draft the buy-sell agreement properly may result in the inability of the plan to meet some of its goals or, in the extreme, its failure to be carried out at all. For this reason it is advisable to obtain the services of a competent attorney in drafting the agreement. Typical provisions of buy-sell agreements include the following:

- *parties to the agreement.* This provision identifies the parties to the agreement (who will be the buyer and who will be the seller under the terms of the agreement).
- *purpose of the agreement.* This provision gives a brief statement of the purpose of the arrangement. For example, the provision may state that the agreement is being formed to provide for the orderly transfer of the business ownership when triggered by its operative event—the death of the owner (the disability of the owner could also trigger a buy-sell agreement). Should disagreement result

over the terms of the agreement, the statement of purpose should clarify the debated issues by providing evidence of the parties' intentions when forming the agreement.

- *commitment of the parties.* This provision indicates the obligations of the parties—that the estate will sell the business interest and that the purchaser will buy it according to the terms of the agreement.

- *description of the interest subject to the agreement.* This provision describes the property that will be sold by the estate. This is particularly important in the unincorporated business where operations tend to be informal and it is difficult to differentiate between the assets of the business and the personal assets of the owner.

- *lifetime transfer restrictions.* This provision, also known as a *first-offer provision* (or *right of first refusal*) prevents the business owner from making a lifetime transfer of the business to anyone without first offering to sell the business to the buyers under the agreement at the agreed-upon price. This provision serves two purposes. First, the expectation of the buyer cannot be frustrated without the buyer's consent. Second, the provision is necessary to establish the estate value of the business interest at the price established in the agreement.

- *method of determining the purchase price.* This provision either stipulates a price or provides a method of determining the purchase price for the business interest. This is extremely important since the adequacy of the purchase price is necessary both for (1) the satisfaction of all parties to the agreement and (2) the acceptance by the IRS of the purchase price for estate tax purposes.

- *funding.* Unless the purchaser has substantial wealth, it may be impractical or impossible to carry out the buy-sell agreement without arrangements for adequate funding. The contents of this provision will depend on the actual funding mechanism chosen. For example, if life insurance will be purchased to fund the buy-sell agreement, this provision should specify such things as the ownership of the policies, premium payment, and beneficiary designations. If the agreement will be financed with installment payments, this provision should include the size of each payment, the duration of the installment period, and the interest rate that the buyer will pay.

- *transfer of the business.* This provision describes the details of the actual transfer of the business interest at the owner's death. The provision should indicate how the proceeds will be transferred to the purchaser. For example, a trust is often established to carry out the buy-sell agreement. In this case it is usually the trustee who will hold the insurance policies, collect the proceeds at the death of the owner, and transfer the proceeds to the estate in exchange for the business interest.

- *modification or termination of the agreement.* This provision is included to provide flexibility for contingencies. For example, it may be necessary to add new parties to the agreement if the business grows. The bankruptcy of either party or the failure of the business may make it unnecessary to continue the agreement. There may be a need to amend the purchase price or the formula to determine the purchase price. This provision may be drafted to operate automatically in the event of some future contingency, or by joint content of the parties to the contract.

Objections and Concerns

Following are several objections common to the buy-sell process along with some suggested responses.

Objection: *"My business associate and I, and our families, are very close. If something happened to me I know that my associate would do right by my family, and I would certainly do the same by my associate's family. We trust each other.*

Response:

- "Prospect, your feeling for each other is fine, but no matter how close you are, is it really fair to expect the surviving owner to shoulder the double burden of preserving the business and assuming the financial responsibilities of caring for the family of the deceased?"
- "Isn't it better for everyone concerned for you and your associate to enter into a mutual agreement that would guarantee business security for the surviving owner and financial security for the deceased's family?"
- "Over the years a few people have mentioned that to me as a possible alternative. So I developed a list of potential problems with an unwritten mutual understanding. Let me review these with you:

  1. A verbal agreement is not legally binding on anyone.
  2. Agreement on the price—or a formula for determining the price—is not likely to be very objective after death occurs. Before death, because no one knows who will

die first, the agreement on price will almost certainly be fair and objective.

3. Financing the purchase remains a problem.

4. If anyone decides not to buy (or sell), a forced liquidation of the business could result.

5. When an owner dies without a formal business continuation agreement, the creditors, suppliers, and employees may feel that the future of the business is not secure. This can cause problems with credit, suppliers, and employee loyalty."

Objection: *"We don't need a plan like that. Our business is very stable. It has been producing big profits for years—better than our families could get from any alternative investment."*

Response:

• "Yes, Prospect, you have a very prosperous business, but isn't that the very reason you need a formal business continuation plan?"

• "Are you aware that, when an associate dies and no legal arrangements have been made beforehand, the deceased's heirs may demand immediate cash for their share of the business?"

• "Do you know what can happen then if you don't have the cash to buy them out, or if you don't agree to their price? They can try to force the business into liquidation. This almost always means heavy financial loss and it also would mean no more business. One other alternative that might be open to you would be to take your associate's spouse in as a 'partner.' This might cause irresolvable conflicts because you may be doing all the important work and have all the responsibility and yet be forced to indefinitely share the profits with your new 'partner'."

Objection: *"I don't need your plan. I have some money, and if I should need more cash I think I could borrow it from my bank, or from friends and relatives."*

Response: "You are very fortunate to have substantial assets, and of course your credit is excellent. Even though you have adequate assets, why spend them to buy the deceased owner's interest—especially at a time when you may need cash for business purposes? Wouldn't you rather get all of the business without being forced to commit significant capital? That's what this plan will do for you. Isn't it good business to pay while you can most readily afford to? Wouldn't you rather pay only a few cents annually on the purchase price, which will automatically be delivered to you at the exact time you will need it? For only pennies per dollar each year, you can stop worrying about having to repay a future loan plus substantial interest."

Objection: *"Wouldn't it be better to carry more personal insurance, and then let the business go for whatever it will bring? Then my widow would have more personal insurance proceeds, plus the value of the business."*

Response: "Yes, adequate personal life insurance for your family is of prime importance. There is really nothing wrong with your idea. But there are two important questions to answer before you decide to let the business go into a forced liquidation with the resultant low dollar value it will bring. First, does your co-owner want to keep the business going after your death? And if so, do you want to accommodate his/her wishes? If so, you will want to readjust your plans. Second, what do you want to happen to the business if your co-owner is the one who dies first? Do you want to keep the business going? If so, don't you really need to set up a plan for the transfer of ownership?

Objection: *"If my co-owner dies, I would have no difficulty in getting a new associate."*

Response: "What you say might be true, and it would certainly be a fortunate thing for the right person. But when you get right down to it, can you count on your prospective co-owner to be able to get the needed cash at that particular time? And isn't the estate of the deceased likely to demand a price that seems unreasonable to your prospective new co-owner? And could a new co-owner be found within the time available? Wouldn't it be better to guarantee that immediately upon death of your associate, you would automatically become the sole owner of the business? That would give you time to find a new associate if you decide that you really need or want one."

Objection: *"Why use life insurance to finance the plan? Why not build my own reserve fund to purchase my associate's interest if he should die?"*

Response: "What if you or your associate should die within the year?"

(Wait for response.)

"Even if both you and your associate live long enough to complete the fund, wouldn't it be more financially prudent to retain your profits for working capital, and instead buy the interest with income-tax-free dollars that have been bought at only pennies per dollar each year?"

Objection: *"We just simply cannot afford it."*

Response:

- "Prospect, thanks for your frankness. Your comment shows how important this plan is. If you can't afford to pay $____ per year for insurance premiums now while both you and your co-owner are active in the management of the business, what will happen financially to your family at your death?"

- (If the objection is valid:) "Then I would suggest a plan that you can afford. By using term insurance the annual premium can be reduced substantially without reducing the amount of the insurance. That will give you the full insurance protection you need without the build up of cash values. Then, as your business prospers you can consider gradually converting your term insurance to permanent insurance which will have a level premium and a decreasing net cost."

- "If you can't afford to cover the entire purchase price now, then I would suggest that we cover part of it now—enough to provide a satisfactory down-payment on the purchase price. Then the balance can be covered with a series of notes payable over a reasonable number of years. A half loaf of security is better than no security at all!"

Objection: *"The plan sounds wonderful, but unfortunately my associate is uninsurable."*

Response: "I'm sorry to hear that. However, if your associate is still uninsurable, then a modified plan can be worked out which will be to the advantage of both of you. But before we go any further, let's make sure of the facts by having our medical department pass on your associate's present insurability. It has happened so often that a person who was uninsurable at some time in the past is insurable today."

Buy-Sell and the One-Owner Business

The sole owner of a business has a unique set of business continuation concerns. These concerns may be further complicated if the owner has no heirs to whom he or she can ultimately transfer control of the business.

Even if heirs exist, they may lack the training and/or the desire to take over the business. Planned and orderly liquidation is an alternative to be considered. However, the use of a one-way buy-sell agreement should also be carefully considered.

Key Employee

The most logical candidate for a buy-sell agreement with the sole owner is a young key employee who is a member of the family.

It's also possible that a group of key employees may want to buy the business. Key employees have a financial interest in the profitable continuation of the business. They may, thus, be willing to make current financial sacrifices in order to have assurance of owning the company when the current owner dies, is disabled, or retires.

How It Works

The owner and the key employee(s) enter into a funded buy-sell agreement specifying that at the owner's death, the estate must sell the business interest to the key employee and the key employee must purchase the business for a stipulated price.

The key employee purchases insurance on the owner's life in an amount sufficient to fund the stipulated price. The insurance guarantees that the key employee will have the necessary funds to complete the buy-sell transaction.

The use of a funded buy-sell agreement with a key employee will typically generate a higher cash price for the business than other business continuation options available to the sole owner (liquidation, negotiate sale after death, and so on). With an insured buy-sell in place, the heirs of a sole owner are assured of obtaining the full going-concern value of the business in cash!

Funding the Key-Employee Buy-Sell Plan

With the typical key-employee buy-sell plan, the key employee acquires insurance on the life of the current owner. For some key employees the required premiums may be a true burden. The key employee could genuinely lack the assets and/or the current income (after meeting personal obligations) to pay the premium.

There are some solutions to this common problem that you may suggest to prospects/clients:

- employee purchases term insurance
- employer increases employee's salary
- employer pays premium as a bonus to the key employee
- employee purchases insurance under a split dollar arrangement

Purchase Term Insurance

The use of term life insurance can significantly reduce the current cash requirements needed to obtain the proper amount of insurance. This may be a viable initial funding alternative. However, you need to help your prospect understand that the use of term insurance to fund a buy-sell agreement can create at least three potential long-term concerns.

- A buy-sell agreement is typically not intended to be a short-term contract—the event implementing the contract (death) may occur next week, next year, or not for 20 years. As the owner gets older and the probability of death gets higher, the burden of the term insurance cost will significantly increase.

- Term insurance has no cash value and, thus, no loan or withdrawal options. Any temporary reversal in the employee's financial position can create a serious problem in maintaining the insurance (preventing a lapse).

- Term insurance does not build cash reserves that can assist in completing a lifetime sale of the business. If it is assumed that the current owner may survive to a point in time when he or she decides to "sell out" and retire, the key employee will need accumulated funds sufficient to provide at least a down payment on the purchase price.

The IRS is Your Partner

Your sole proprietor says, "I don't need a buy-sell agreement. I'll just leave this business to my family."

You respond, "But someone other than you already owns half your business."

He says, "What? What are you talking about? Who do you mean?"

You: "The IRS has a claim on half your business. What I'm referring to is the fact that when you and your spouse die, the IRS will take half the value of your business. I'm talking about death taxes—the federal estate tax. The death tax rates are that high. In fact, they go up to 45 percent."

You continue: "Look at these estate tax death rates. And let me also show you how life insurance can be used to pay off the IRS and let your family keep the business."

Purchase Permanent Insurance

The acquisition of a permanent form of life insurance deals with these needs and concerns. The following three approaches to purchasing insurance are designed to facilitate the employee's purchasing a permanent form of life insurance to fund the buy-sell agreement.

Employer Increases Employee's Salary—One solution to a key employee's inability to pay premiums is for the owner to increase the key employee's salary. The size of the increase could range from a portion of the premium to the full premium plus any added tax on the salary increase.

Assuming the total salary received by the key employee is "reasonable compensation," the IRS will allow the salary increase to be fully deductible by the business. The owner is using tax-deductible dollars to fund the buy-sell agreement.

However, your business owner-prospect might ask, "Why should my business directly pay the full cost incurred by the employee to fund the buy-sell agreement? Why not use the same dollars to purchase added personal insurance on my life that will be paid directly to my heirs?"

This is, of course, a good buying signal. Your response can be to tell the prospect that buying more personal life insurance is indeed a good solution. Then move more toward a sale by asking other questions, such as what amount of insurance to start with.

Most business owners want the business to continue. Try saying, "Unless you make plans, your competitors will figuratively steal your business when you die. It will be like money taken from your family."

Following are some beneficial results that accompany a key person buyout:

- It clearly helps tie the key employee to the company as he or she can see a high financial future—the successful growth of the company.

- By assuring some continuity in management, the owner will likely obtain an improved current position with all employees, creditors, suppliers, and customers—they can better rely on the long-term continuity of the company. Thus, there is a significant current gain to the owner by facilitating the establishment of a viable funded buy-sell agreement.

- The cash values building for the employee in the permanent insurance could one day be used to help finance a living sale of a portion or all of the business to the key employee.

- The sole owner's family does not have to concern itself with continuing to run the business. It has the full purchase price in cash without facing daily aggravation or worry in running or selling the business.

Employer Pays Premium with a Bonus—As an alternative to increasing the employee's salary, the owner may prefer to pay the premium directly from the business and charge it to the employee's compensation account as a bonus. The only cost to the employee would be tax on the annual bonus. As compensation, the bonus would also be tax deductible to the company. While the net effect is the same as increasing the key employee's salary, the owner has the added assurance of knowing that the annual premium will in fact be paid each year.

Employee Split-Dollar Arrangement—While the salary or bonus approach can help the key employee finance the required buyout premium, these methods provide little or no security to the business owners if the key employee decides to cancel the agreement and/or to leave the company.

A split-dollar plan meets the needs of the employee and the corporation. It helps the employee pay the premiums. It assures the corporation that it will eventually recover its outlay. Any split-dollar plan can be used.

The policy is taken out on the life of the owner. Premiums can be split in any way agreeable to both parties. The employee is the beneficiary of most of the death benefit. The owner's estate is beneficiary of a portion of the death benefit, possibly an amount equal to the owner's contribution to the plan. This way, the owner's outlay is eventually recovered.

Whenever a corporation owns split-dollar insurance on the life of a sole or controlling stockholder, the proceeds may go to the controlling stockholder's estate. This happens because incidents of ownership by the corporation are attributed to the owner. Careful planning is required if this result is to be avoided. It generally requires that the corporation have no incidents of ownership in the policy.

Benefits of an Insured Buy-Sell Agreement

Benefits to Heirs

- *Provides a market*—often the only market—for the deceased's interest, at a fair price, in cash, and without delay-at a price previously fixed by agreement.
- *Expedites settlement of estate.* The business interest, which is usually the major asset of the estate, is immediately converted into cash. The executor has the liquidity necessary to pay final expenses, debts, taxes, bills, and all probate costs—promptly and economically.
- *Creates cash.* The deceased's interest, instead of remaining in a speculative business, is converted into cash, which may, when the estate has been closed, be invested by the heirs in gilt-edged,

Benefits of an Insured Buy-Sell Agreement

non-speculative assets, thus providing a stable income for the family. The family of the deceased is not dependent upon the surviving owners for an adequate income.

- *Eliminate emotional conflicts.* The danger of friction and bickering between the heirs and the surviving stockholders has been reduced or eliminated.

- *Controls value of stock for estate taxes.* It does this in the absence of any evidence of fraud or collusion; and provided the agreed-upon price was fair and reasonable at the time the agreement was made; and provided that any sale, while living, requires a first-offer to the other stockholders, at a price specified in the agreement.

Benefits to Owners (While Living)

- *Guaranteed market at fair price.* In the event of the death of a stockholder, the heirs of the deceased will receive the full value of the business interest in cash at once, and without delay. This makes it possible for an owner to plan intelligently for the financial security of heirs.

- *Stabilizes the business.* In the event of the death of an owner the survivors will own the company and control of the business is assured.

- *Creates peace of mind.* Owners have a positive attitude knowing that if an owner dies, heirs will receive the full value of interest in cash, and the survivors will be the sole owners of the business.

- *Insurance values provide increasing cash reserve.* This can be used, if necessary, for a down payment in the event an owner wishes to sell and retire, or as a cash reserve account for emergencies or special business opportunities.

- It strengthens credit by increasing cash reserves and facilitating automatic payment of cash to buy the interest of an owner at death.

- *Promotes peace of mind.* It will create goodwill among employees and creditors, by insuring the preservation and continuance of the business.

Benefits to Surviving Business owners

- *Guaranteed fair price.* It guarantees full ownership at an agreed price. The courts have held that a buy-sell agreement must be specifically performed. The purchase price or valuation formula, and all other terms of transfer, are fixed in the agreement, and the business can go on unimpaired. No negotiations are necessary.

- *Reliable funding.* Life insurance provides the full purchase price in cash, or a down payment, when it is needed, at the death of an owner.

- *Implementation assured.* It helps eliminate friction and disagreements with the heirs of the deceased. Practically everything has been settled by contract.

- *Strengthens credit.* It strengthens their credit, and enhances their business and family prestige in the community—they are the sole owners of the business. It is not necessary for them to use their business' capital or credit, with resultant jeopardy to their own estates.

- *Control retained.* It prevents the entrance of outsiders into business ownership.

Characteristics of an Optimum Funding Mechanism

Benefits of an Insured Buy-Sell Agreement
• Relatively low or modest cost
• Easy for all interested parties to understand/communicate
• Simple to administer
• No negative impact on financial/credit position of business

APPENDIX: SALES AIDS

An Insured Buy-Sell Agreement (Entity Plan)

A written contract between the business and its owners providing that upon the death of one of the owners the estate of the deceased shall sell, and the business shall buy, the interest of the deceased stockholder.

The agreement stipulates:

- the price to be paid for the interest of the deceased,
- the value shall be kept up-to-date by regular semiannual or annual reappraisals, or by a formula included in the agreement.

LIFE INSURANCE TO FINANCE THE AGREEMENT

The business shall be the:

- applicant
- premium payor
- beneficiary
- owner of sufficient life insurance on each of its stockholders to provide the cash purchase price of the deceased's interest.

Upon the death of a stockholder:

- the life insurance shall be paid to the business, the business shall pay this money to the deceased's estate, which
- then shall sell the deceased's interest to the business.

SUMMARY OF RESULTS

- The surviving stockholders become the sole owners of the business.
- The heirs of the deceased stockholder receive the full value of their interest in cash.

The Ideal Solution An Insured Buy-Sell Agreement (Cross-Purchase Plan)

A written contract between the owners providing that upon the death of an associate the estate of the deceased shall sell and the surviving owners shall buy the interest of the deceased.

The agreement stipulates:

- the price to be paid for the interest of a deceased stockholder
- the value shall be determined by a stipulated formula (or possibly by a designated dollar amount, updated annually)

LIFE INSURANCE TO FINANCE THE AGREEMENT

Each stockholder shall be the applicant, premium payer, beneficiary, and owner of sufficient life insurance on his associates to provide the cash purchase price of the deceased's interest.

Upon the death of a stockholder:

- the life insurance shall be paid to the surviving stockholders
- the stockholders shall pay this money to the deceased's estate
- the estate shall sell the deceased's interest to the surviving stockholders

SUMMARY OF RESULTS

- The surviving stockholders become the sole owners of the business.
- The heirs of the deceased stockholder receive the full value of their interest in cash.

Number of Years to Associate's Death	If You Borrow The Money or Use an Installment Buyout (10% Interest)*	If You Pay Cash**From Sinking Fund	If You Use Permanent Life Insurance (Approximations)
	Sinking Fund versus Borrowing versus Insurance		
1	$1.10	$1.00	2 cents
2	$1.10	$1.00	4 cents
3	$1.10	$1.00	6 cents
4	$1.10	$1.00	8 cents
5	$1.10	$1.00	10 cents
6	$1.10	$1.00	12 cents
7	$1.10	$1.00	14 cents
8	$1.10	$1.00	16 cents
9	$1.10	$1.00	18 cents
10	$1.10	$1.00	20 cents
15	$1.10	$1.00	30 cents
20	$1.10	$1.00	40 cents

HOW DO YOU PROPOSE TO BUY OUT YOUR BUSINESS ASSOCIATE?

*This assumes the loan is repaid in one year. The amount would be greater with longer repayment period. Interest rates will vary of course; 10% is used only as an example.

**This assumes the availability of cash when it is needed.

Funding the Purchase of a Business Interest			
Once the purchase price of a decedent's stock has been determined—either in a buy-sell agreement or through negotiations with the estate's representative—the buyer faces the problem of providing cash.			
WHAT ARE THE ALTERNATIVES?	AT WHAT COST?	WHAT CASH FACTORS?	POSSIBLE OBSTACLES?
There are five basic options:	For each $1 of purchase price:	Items which add to the cost of buying the business	Each alternative is viable
1. Liquidating existing cash/capital	100 cents, +	-principal -lost future earnings on principal	IF the buyer has sufficient cash or other assets at the time of purchase
2. Borrowing from a bank and paying a lump sum to the estate	100 cents, +	-principal -interest paid to the estate	IF loan can be made IF interest rates are reasonable IF after-tax, disposable income can absorb interest and principal payments
3. Making installment payments to the estate out of personal income	100 cents, +	-principal -interest paid to the estate	IF the estate is willing to accept installment payments IF the buyer and estate agree on the duration and interest rate of installments
4. Company makes installment purchase out of future profits	100 cents, +	-principal -interest paid to the estate	IF sales and income don't drop IF profit margins remain the same IF corporate income taxes remain the same
5. Insuring the purchase price in advance	Discounted $ (less than 100 cents)	-premium payments	IF the stockholder is insurable

Summary of Advantages of an Insured Buy-Sell Agreement

TO THE SURVIVING BUSINESS OWNER

- Complete ownership and control of the business is assured.
- Haggling, hard feelings, and misunderstandings with the deceased's heirs are eliminated.
- Financial strain resulting from long-term installments is eliminated.

TO YOUR SPOUSE AND FAMILY

- Your family is free from any business reverses.
- A fair price is assured in advance to your spouse.
- Your family will receive the money without red tape of long delays
- Cash proceeds can be used by your family to pay death duties on your estate.
- The family is free from risks and uncertainty which accompany a long-term installment buyout.

TO THE BUSINESS

- Policy cash values accumulate free of current income tax.
- Loyalty of employees is strengthened by insuring the stability and continuity of the corporation.
- Credit is improved because the cash values appear as a corporate asset.
- Death will not interfere with the smooth continuation of the corporation and its business.

HOW PLAN WORKS

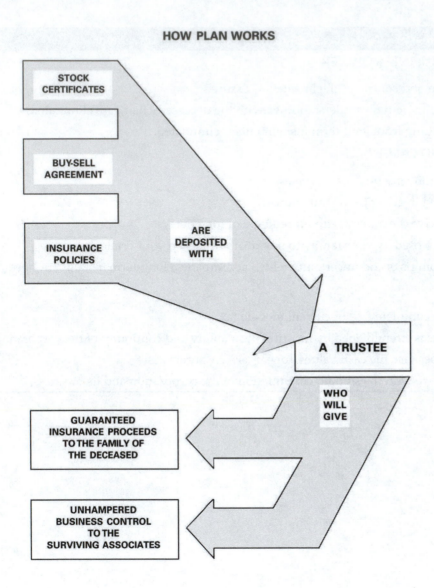

STOCK
CERTIFICATES

BUY-SELL
AGREEMENT

INSURANCE
POLICIES

ARE
DEPOSITED
WITH

A TRUSTEE

WHO
WILL
GIVE

GUARANTEED
INSURANCE PROCEEDS
TO THE FAMILY OF
THE DECEASED

UNHAMPERED
BUSINESS CONTROL
TO THE
SURVIVING ASSOCIATES

Cost of Funding a Buy-Sell Agreement Using Borrowed Money		

METHOD 1: Assumes paying 10% interest and liquidating the principal over a 10-year period.

To pay interest and liquidate principal on a note of $250,000 will require corporate gross sales of $734,000 per year, computed as follows:*

	Yearly	Total for 10 Years
Average Principal Payment	$25,000	$250,000
Average Interest Payment	15,600	156,000
Tax Credit on Interest**	3,900	39,000
After-Tax Earnings Required	36,700	367,000
Gross Sales Required	$734,000	$7,340,000

METHOD 2: Assumes paying 10% interest only, with principal to be repaid at end of the 10-year period.

To pay only the interest on a note of $250,000 will require corporate gross sales of $375,000 per year.*

	Yearly	Total for 10 years
Average Interest Payment	$25,000	$250,000
Tax Credit on Interest**	6,250	62,500
After-Tax Earnings Required	18,750	187,500
Gross Sales Required	375,000	3,750,000

*Based on assumed net profit on sales of 5%.

**The tax bracket of the corporation is assumed to be 25%. Before using this illustration, get approval from your company's compliance department.

Tax Impact of Life Insurance Funding for Buy-Sell		
	<u>Cross Purchase</u>	<u>Entity</u>
Are life insurance premiums deductible for income tax?	No	No
Are life insurance proceeds taxed as income?	No	No*
What is the effect of the policy premiums on corporate profits?	No effect	Premium will reduce in early years. Cash values offset this reduction. Ultimately, death proceeds significantly increase earnings—exactly when needed.
What is the impact of life insurance policy values on corporate financial position?	No effect	Annual increases in cash values is an increase in earnings and corporate assets.
Accumulated earnings tax	No effect	A potential problem can arise if the accumulated earnings account exceeds $250,000.
What are the estate tax consequences of life insurance proceeds?	Proceeds not in taxable estate-only stock value in estate.	Proceeds not in taxable estate-only stock value in estate.

*If a corporation is subject to the alternative minimum tax (AMT), life insurance proceeds and cash values will enter the corporation's calculations of taxable income. Corporations with average annual gross receipts under $5 million are exempt from the tax.

Before using this page, get approval from your company's compliance department.

CASE HISTORY A BUY-SELL SALE

Agent

Narrator Chris Nash is a veteran of 14 years in the life insurance business. Over the last several years, Chris has specialized in the sale of business life and health insurance.

Prospects

Bob Miller and John Wilson are equal partners in a small manufacturing business. Eight years ago, the company was worth only the $25,000 they had invested in it. Today it is worth about $500,000. Both of my prospects are married and have dependent children.

Approach

I had a very strong referred lead to John Wilson. My center of influence gave me a good bit of information about John and the business conducted by the partners. I didn't know anything about Bob Miller.

I found it rather easy to obtain a daytime appointment with John Wilson because of the strength of my referred lead. I toyed with the idea of asking John to come to my office, but I had second thoughts and made the appointment at his place of business.

I made the appointment only with John. I didn't suggest that Bob Miller join us. I had decided that this would be simply an introductory meeting. I would tell John something about myself and the kind of work I do. I then would try to arrange a fact-finding interview with him. If possible, Bob Miller would be present at the fact-finding interview as well.

First Interview

After introducing myself to John and explaining the kind of work I do, I said something like this:

"I see myself as a problem solver. Therefore, one of my most important jobs is gathering sufficient information about you, your associates, and your business so that I develop well-founded recommendations:

"Most business owners have their own attorneys and accountants, but quite often they overlook the importance of having a financial advisor as a member of their support team. This usually means that only passing thought is given to such important planning areas as

- employee fringe benefits
- business continuation in the event of death or disability
- using the business as a means of helping to strengthen the family's financial position and standard of living"

"In essence, I'm seeking to be your advisor in insurance and related financial matters. If you like my recommendations, all I ask is that if you buy insurance, you buy it from me. If you like my work but you don't choose to take advantage of my recommendations, all I ask is that you refer me to other business owners who could benefit from my work. If this is agreeable to you, I would like to work with you. How do you feel about this?"

John asked what kinds of fees and charges were involved. I told him that I work strictly on a commission basis and those commissions were built into the products I sell.

As we talked, I reminded myself that I didn't know whether John and Bob were equal partners. I also didn't know what responsibilities each of them had for making decisions in the area of insurance and fringe benefits. With this in mind, I asked some questions. I learned that they were equal partners but that John handled most of the financial matters.

I told John that I would be anxious to meet Bob Miller. I felt that it would be in everyone's best interest if Bob could be present at our next interview so that I could get a good understanding of the feelings and attitudes of both partners. John said "Come on. I'll introduce you to Bob right now." John's willingness to introduce me to Bob made me feel certain that I had just been "hired."

If I needed further assurance, I got it. When John introduced me to Bob, John referred to me not only as a friend of a good friend but also as an expert in business insurance and fringe benefits. John said that I had been asked to look over their insurance coverages and to make recommendations.

When John sounded out Bob about this idea, Bob expressed agreement. He felt that they were long overdue for such a review. We set a date for the following week for the fact-finding interview at their place of business.

In thinking back over just this early part of the case, I found myself wondering why everything had gone so well. I pinpointed two factors:

1. A strong referral secured the initial interview. This referral established prestige for me even before I met my prospects.

2. I did a good job of presenting myself as a competent and dedicated professional working in the area of business insurance.

Fact-Finding Interview

The fact-finding interview lasted about an hour and a half. Although I called it a fact-finding interview, one of my main objectives was to determine the attitudes and feelings of my prospects about the future of their business.

Specifically I wanted to find out what they wished to happen to the business in the event that one of them were to die or become disabled. In addition, I wanted to learn about their plans for continued ownership of the business when they reached retirement age.

I am constantly surprised at how little thought most business owners have given to plans for these contingencies. Often the fact-finding interview is a real eye-opener. I would characterize it as a planning session for many prospects—a session in which they make tentative plans about the future of the business in the event of death, disability, and retirement. Most of them don't know what options are available.

From my point of view, fact-finding sessions are much more like counseling sessions. During this session I find out a great deal about the families of business owners. This includes discovering how much family participation there is in the business.

If no other problem presents itself as the highest priority problem and if there is no formal plan already in place for transfer of ownership at the death of one of the owners, I automatically give ownership transfer top priority. I find myself focusing on the need for a written buy-sell agreement.

The interview with John and Bob was very similar to many of the discussions I have had with business partners. Both Bob and John indicated that in the event of the death of the other partner the survivor would like to become sole owner of the business. I asked:

- Have you made any formal plans for the transfer of ownership at one partner's death?
- How much would you want your family to receive for your share of the business?

- Have you made any plans regarding financing of such an ownership transfer, such as the method and terms of payment?
- Do you currently have the money to buy out the business?
- Where would you get the money?
- What would be the cost of the money if you were to borrow it or buy out the other on an installment basis?

(I previously had written out these and the other questions which I planned to use.)

I obviously had hit a hot button with John and Bob. They began to ask me questions about buy-sell agreements.

Based on their estimate of $500,000 as the value of the business, I asked how long it would take them to accumulate the necessary $250,000 to buy out the other partner. That is, if they were to establish a sinking fund today, how long would it take to build up one or two funds with $250,000 in each?

As they hesitated, I asked if they could do it in 10 years by setting aside about $20,000 apiece over each of the next 10 years. They said there was no way they could each set aside that kind of money every year.

I responded, "If setting aside that kind of money would be a problem now, while you're both healthy and working, wouldn't it be even more difficult if one of you weren't living?"

"Coming up with the money after the fact is not only an expensive way to do it, it's also a risky way for the family and the business. The family can never be sure of receiving the money because it must come from business profits over many years after the death of one partner. The business itself is likely to be put into a shaky financial condition, too, with such large chunks of money coming out of business profits over a long number of years. The best buy-sell agreement ever written isn't worth much if the money is not there to buy the deceased's share from the family."

I had the feeling that I could easily have closed on an insured buy-sell plan during this fact-finding interview. However, I made a conscious decision not to do so at this time. I had promised a complete and thorough review of the situation based on the facts that I obtained. Therefore, I finished the balance of the fact-finding interview and set a date for a subsequent meeting to present my recommendations.

Where the Sale Is Really Made

Although the primary purpose of the fact-finding interview is to gain necessary information about the financial situation and future plans of prospective clients, I have found that the fact-finding interview is much more than that for me. It offers me the opportunity to pinpoint various problems, find the prospective clients' hot button, and to disturb prospects about these problems! *This is where the sale is really made.*

This was the case with Bob Miller and John Wilson. In retrospect, it's obvious to me that they had been concerned for some time about the financial disposition of their business in the event of the death of one of them. My line of questioning brought the problems to prominence and made them realize that both time and money were important factors in preparing a solution.

Planning

With assistance from the home office, my agency is well equipped to assist me in the planning process for business insurance situations. Although I always bring along computer-generated printouts and various other proposal forms, I strive for simplicity. I use a one-page illustration that shows how a buy-sell agreement works, how the funding works, and what the end results are for both the surviving partner and the deceased's family. If additional printed information is needed, I have printouts with me regarding the policy, its benefits, and its options.

Generally I have a specific recommendation regarding the type of insurance, but I also have a backup plan ready as well. In this case, I really hadn't done as good a job as I should have.

I always talk about both permanent insurance and term insurance, because if I don't, my competitor might. I want to be sure to tell the whole story. I let my prospects know that I favored the permanent policy because it could provide funding for a lifetime buyout at retirement or disability as well as funding in the event of death.

In addition to my recommendation of implementing a buy-sell agreement funded with life insurance, I also prepared broad recommendations in the areas of retirement planning, fringe benefits, and key person insurance.

These recommendations were not specific in that they did not include any dollar amounts. I simply was setting up these other areas as concerns that needed to be addressed in the future. First and foremost, it is important to make the prospect a policyowner. More will come later.

Closing Interview

Things had gone so well up to this point that I began to worry about what might go wrong. I imagined all kinds of things:

- Would they change their minds?
- Would another agent get the business instead of me? (I should have discussed this earlier with my prospect.)
- Were they sincerely interested?
- Were they in a position to pay $8,000 a year?
- What would their accountant say?
- Would their lawyer advise them to proceed?
- Would they want to postpone the whole thing?

Before going to the closing interview, I did my usual job of reviewing their situation carefully and asking myself what I would do if I were they. What would happen to the business if they didn't implement my ideas and one of them subsequently died? In general, I was psyching myself into a positive frame of mind, knowing that I was helping John and Bob solve a potentially disastrous problem with the best solution they could find anywhere.

My fears were baseless. The interview went just as smoothly as had the fact-finding interview. They already had spoken with their attorney, and she had indicated strong approval of the idea.

Their only serious decision was between the term and permanent. They decided on cash value insurance and decided to handle the premiums through a monthly automatic check plan. The physical examinations went well, and the policies were issued standard. A buy-sell agreement was drafted by their attorney with some input from my office.

Commentary

As you would guess, not all of my cases go this smoothly. I was especially fortunate in this situation. Not only was the initial sale very nice, but also more sales ensued as the business really blossomed over the years.

The attorney has since become a client and an excellent center of influence for me. In addition, a few of the suppliers for Bob Miller and John Wilson have become clients of mine. I would love to have a case like this every month!

Over the years, I have since learned that a good bit of mental trepidation is removed if I involve the CPA and the attorney along with the principals before the closing interview. I can get agreement on my figures and suggestions. I needn't worry that the principals will not present their case to the CPA and/or attorney as well as I, or that the CPA and/or attorney will become an adversary if I'm not present.

CHAPTER REVIEW

Key Terms and Concepts

cross-purchase plan   stepped-up basis
stock redemption plan   accumulated earnings tax
entity plan   transfer-for-value
wait-and-see plan   corporate alternative minimum tax
trustee plan   alternative minimum tax
right of first refusal   sinking fund
cost basis

Review Questions

1. Name two benefits of a funded buy-sell agreement to the deceased owner's heirs, and two benefits to the surviving owners.

2. Name and briefly describe the three types of buy-sell agreements.

3. Name five sources of funding a buy-sell agreement.

4. Explain what should be included in a buy-sell agreement.

5. Describe six benefits of using life insurance to fund a buy-sell agreement.

6. Briefly describe the federal income tax status of premiums and proceeds of life insurance used to fund a buy-sell agreement.

7. Explain the solutions to providing a buy-sell plan when an owner is uninsurable.

Note

The following questions pertain to the case study.

8. How did the agent present himself in the initial interview? Describe what he said.

9. What issues did the advisor focus on in the fact-finding interview?

10. According to this advisor, where and how is the sale made?

Self Test Questions

Instructions: Read chapter five first, then answer the following questions to test your knowledge. There are 10 questions. Circle the correct answer, then check your answers with the answer key in the back of the book.

11.   Some portion of a life insurance death benefit may be subject to federal income tax if

    (A) the insured had any incidents of ownership

    (B) the death benefit exceeds the value of a business interest as established in the buy-sell agreement

    (C) the transfer-for-value rule is applicable

    (D) all of the above

12.   Which of the following is a characteristic of a wait-and-see buy-sell agreement?

    (A) It is the same as a cross-purchase plan.

    (B) All surviving stockholders are required to buy the stock of the deceased stockholder.

    (C) Purchase options must be exercised at least 30 days before the death of a stockholder or the agreement is void.

    (D) If options to purchase are not exercised, the corporation is required to purchase the interest of the deceased owner.

13.   Under an insurance-funded cross-purchase buy-sell plan:

    (A) Death proceeds are taxable to the corporation.

    (B) The agreement is between an owner and the corporation.

    (C) The surviving stockholders are not allowed to purchase policies on their own lives.

    (D) Each stockholder is typically the owner and beneficiary of insurance on the life of each other stockholder.

14.   When life insurance is used to fund a partnership buy-sell agreement, what is the federal income tax result?

    (A) Premiums are not deductible and proceeds are received income tax free.

    (B) The life insurance proceeds may be subject to the corporate alternative minimum tax.

    (C) Premiums are tax deductible to each partner, but proceeds are taxable when received.

    (D) Any annual increase in policy cash value must be reported by each partner as taxable income.

15. Smith, Jones and Carey enter into a cross-purchase buy-sell agreement funded by life insurance. How many policies must be purchased?

    (A) 3
    (B) 6
    (C) 9
    (D) 12

16. The price at which property would exchange hands between a willing buyer and a willing seller, neither being under any compulsion to buy or sell describes:

    (A) net worth
    (B) goodwill value
    (C) fair market value
    (D) fair return on investment

17. In a two-owner corporation, who normally owns the life insurance policies that fund a cross-purchase buy-sell agreement?

    (A) Each policy is jointly owned.
    (B) Each owns a policy on him or herself.
    (C) Each owns a policy on the other.
    (D) The corporation owns a policy on both owners.

18. Which of the following statements is (are) correct regarding the federal income tax treatment when life insurance is used to fund a buy-sell agreement under an entity plan?

    I. Premiums are tax deductible by the firm and the proceeds are received tax free.
    II. Premiums are deductible and the proceeds are fully reportable as taxable income.

    (A) I only
    (B) II only
    (C) Both I and II
    (D) Neither I nor II

19. Which of the following statements regarding a funded buy-sell agreement
     is (are) correct?

     I. It can provide assurance that heirs will not be forced to sell to outsiders.
     II. It provides assurance that a bank will lend the funds needed to buy
         the heirs' interest in the company.

     (A) I only
     (B) II only
     (C) Both I and II
     (D) Neither I nor II

READ THE FOLLOWING DIRECTIONS BEFORE CONTINUING

The questions below differ from the preceding questions in that they all
contain the word EXCEPT. So you understand fully the basis used in
selecting each answer, be sure to read each question carefully.

20. A buy-sell agreement is appropriate in all of the following business forms
     EXCEPT

     (A) S corporation
     (B) Sole proprietor
     (C) Limited liability company
     (D) Large publicly held corporation

THE FAMILY-OWNED BUSINESS, VALUATION AND DISABILITY CONSIDERATIONS

6

Learning Objectives

An understanding of the material in this chapter should enable the student to

1. Name and describe factors that distinguish family-owned businesses from other closely held businesses.

2. Describe the main purpose of Internal Revenue Code Chapter 14 regarding buy-sell agreements.

3. Explain the purpose of Section 303 of the Internal Revenue Code.

4. Discuss the function of business valuation and the different methods used to value a closely-held business.

5. Describe three problems that can occur when a business owner becomes seriously disabled.

6. Name three issues that must be resolved in order to draft a disability buyout agreement.

7. Explain answers that can be used for commonly given objections to business insurance.

This chapter examines the special problems that are associated with a family-owned business, both in terms of the intrafamily issues that must be dealt with and resolved, and the special taxation issues posed by IRS. These tax issues relating to the family-owned business are known as the family attribution rules, which can complicate the buy-sell solution in family-owned businesses. A special IRC section known as Section 303 Stock Redemption is an alternative tax solution involving the family-owned business.

Another important area of insurance planning for the business owner involves disability income insurance. We will look at the Disability Buy-Out and Business Overhead Expense plans and end with some techniques for closing the sale and servicing the client after the sale.

THE FAMILY-OWNED BUSINESS

Although family-owned businesses share most of the characteristics of all closely held businesses, there are enough differences to warrant this separate discussion. Following this section on family-owned businesses is a discussion of business valuation and disability buyout agreements.

Family-owned businesses are those where all or most of the ownership and day-to-day management of the business involves individuals who are related by blood or marriage. Quite often, other family members are also regular workers in the business.

Differences from Other Types of Businesses

The following factors distinguish family-owned businesses from other types of businesses.

Future Ownership

Family business owners do not generally plan to sell the business, nor do they plan to transfer ownership outside the family. At death or retirement, the family business owner often will transfer the business (by gift or by inheritance) to a son, daughter or other family member. This is in contrast to non-family businesses, where the owners are generally inclined to sell their share to the other owners.

Another aspect of future ownership is trying to determine who should own the business and why. Ideally, the owner would like to have ownership pass to a family member who is already active in managing the business. In non-family businesses, kinship is not a critical factor.

Treating Heirs Fairly

In a nutshell, the "fairness" question is this: If a father gives the business to his daughter, will he be shortchanging his son? Will there be enough other assets in the father's estate to provide fairly for the son? Or, to compound the problem: What if there are four sons, none of whom wants to run the business? The daughter does, so the father gives daughter the million-dollar business. How likely is it that the father will have $4 million estate so that he can give each son an inheritance of $1 million? Where will the extra $4 million come from?

Giving stock to the sons would not solve the problem because the stock of any closely held business is useless until the business is sold. One practical answer is to insure the father's life for $4 million, with each son as beneficiary of $1 million.

Another point to remember concerning fair treatment of heirs is that the law will not generally allow a testator to completely disinherit a spouse, without consent of the spouse. Moreover, the spouse of a deceased testator usually has the right to "elect against the will" of the deceased spouse. This means that if the share of the estate left to the spouse does not equal the minimum portion established by state law, the spouse can claim the minimum amount the tax law provides. For example, if the testator leaves most of the estate to a child, the spouse can demand—and get—the legal minimum portion, which is often one third or a half of the estate.

The business owner should not try to reduce the value of the business (for estate tax purposes) to such an extent that the widow or widower would not get enough buyout money to meet her income needs.

Spouse's Income

Assuming again that the father is the owner of the business, the mother's income may be derived solely from the business. If the business is given to heirs via gift or inheritance, the mother will need an independent replacement source of income.

In fact, she should not have to rely on income from the business. Otherwise, what would she do for income if the business failed? This is a terrible situation for the widow. She should not be forced to take such a risk.

Here again, life insurance on the father can provide a reliable source of income for the mother. It is guaranteed, risk free, and it is available just when it's needed.

Fact Finding/Feeling Finding

Fact finding in family corporations requires extra focus on feelings. Your fact-finding should put more emphasis on exploring the prospect's fears, dreams, and family relationships. In non-family businesses, much of your work is logical and analytical. In family businesses, however, there is increased emphasis on feelings, personal values, and family interaction.

Life Insurance Needs in a Family-Owned Business

Life insurance needs in a family owned business are like most business needs, with some variations. Life insurance can be used to

- provide income to the surviving spouse
- pay estate and income taxes, including Section 303 funding
- fund a buy-sell between generations
- provide fairness to the children in the size of their inheritances
- pay off bank debts
- provide key person insurance
- provide funds for retirement

Valuation and Taxation of Family-Owned Businesses

Valuation of family businesses is different in a couple of ways from valuation of non-family businesses.

Distorted Profit

Profit plays an important role in valuation of any business, but in family businesses, the level of profit is often distorted because of high salaries and costly perks given to family members.

To get an accurate picture of value, profits must be recast. An accountant would recalculate the company's profit by subtracting the owners' and key family employees' salaries and perks, and then adding back in a reasonable (market value) amount for those expenses.

Intrafamily Transfers, IRC Chapter 14

IRC Chapter 14   Late in 1990, Congress enacted legislation establishing new gift-tax rules for valuation of interests in family-controlled businesses (corporations and partnerships) that are transferred to family members of the owner, wherein the owner retains certain types of interest in the transferred property.

The main targets of the legislation are owners of family corporations (or family partnerships) who transfer some ownership (stock) that is expected to appreciate in value, while the owner nonetheless retains control of the business.

The legislation goes on to say that the IRS will accept the value stated in a buy-sell agreement if the agreement meets four criteria:

1. The buy-sell agreement must be a bona fide business arrangement.
2. The buy-sell agreement cannot simply be a device to transfer the business to other family members for less than full value.
3. The terms of the agreement must be comparable to similar arrangements entered into by persons in arm's-length transactions.
4. The valuation formula must be one that is acceptable to the IRS.

These gift and estate tax valuation rules are contained in Chapter 14 of the Internal Revenue Code, in Sections 2701, 2702, 2703 and 2704.

Attribution-of-Ownership Rules

attribution of ownership rules Another factor affecting the valuation of a family-owned corporation is the attribution-of-ownership rules of Section 318 of the Internal Revenue Code. Attribution of ownership means that the corporate stock owned by one family member is considered to be owned by another family member (spouse, children, grandparents, and parents) for purposes of determining how a stock redemption is taxed. The rules are also known as constructive ownership rules. The rationale for these rules is that a shareholder may effectively control a corporation owned by related individuals as well as through shares he or she actually owns. Although this may or may not be true, redemptions should always be structured to comply with the attribution rules when these rules are applicable.

These rules cause a problem for family businesses who redeem stock in a stock redemption agreement. Even though an owner sells some of his or her stock to a family member and would be entitled to favorable capital gains tax treatment, the law presumes he/she still owns the stock and refuses to grant favorable capital gains treatment on the transaction. Instead the payment by the corporation to the shareholder is considered to be a dividend and taxed as ordinary income. There will be no deduction for basis, no capital gains treatment at lower tax rates, and profits will be reduced by the distribution.

IRC Section 302 provides that if the corporation redeems all of a shareholder's remaining shares (so that the shareholder's interest in the corporation is terminated), the amount paid by the corporation will be treated, not as a dividend, but as payment in exchange (sale) for the stock. In other words, the redemption will be treated as a capital transaction with capital gains tax treatment. The difference of taxation between a sale (capital gains) and dividend (ordinary income) can be significant because of the higher marginal tax rate for ordinary income and because with a dividend, the entire transaction is taxable, whereas in a sale only the gain (proceeds minus basis) is taxable.

However, unfortunately this is not easily accomplished in a typical family-owned business where all the stock is owned by the parents and their children. The sale of stock back to the corporation, even all the stock that seller actually owns personally, may not be a complete termination of their interest in the corporation because the seller is deemed to own (constructively owns) stock actually owned by others. The constructive ownership rules are complicated, thus their application and interpretation require expert legal advice.

The risk of dividend treatment of the redemption proceeds is an unnecessarily high price to pay since a redemption that does qualify as a sale or exchange will probably be nontaxable due to the basis step-up available to an estate. In any event the redemption of stock in a family corporation is quite complex and should be planned carefully if this is the method selected to transfer the family corporation.

These adverse effects of the family attribution rules can be overcome (waived) if the shareholder from whom stock is redeemed

1. retains no interest in the corporation, except as a creditor, immediately after redemption

2. does not acquire any such interest, other than stock acquired by bequest or inheritance, within 10 years after the redemption; and

3. files an agreement (called a waiver agreement) to notify the IRS of redeeming shareholder's acquisition of a forbidden interest within the 10-year period.

Section 303

Section 303 Stock Redemption

Valuation is also affected by Section 303 of the Internal Revenue Code dealing with the income taxation of stock redemptions in closely held corporations. Section 303 has a particularly favorable appeal to family corporations because it offers partial relief from the family attribution rules just mentioned.

SECTION 303 STOCK REDEMPTIONS

Whenever stockholder and death are mentioned in the same breath, many of us automatically think of a buy-sell agreement that would transfer ownership to the remaining stockholders. But sometimes—especially when a majority interest is involved—the stockholder wants the family to keep and operate the business, and the family wants it that way too.

This is seldom true with minority interests because there is little incentive to keep the stock since it pays no dividends and the minority owners have no control, not even authority to hire themselves.

However, keeping ownership in the family means getting cash to settle the decedent's estate without selling the business. Over the years many small family-run businesses have had to be sold—often to former competitors—for this very reason. Estates comprised largely of close corporation stock generally have a liquidity problem.

Recognizing the frequency of this kind of occurrence and fully aware of its unfavorable impact, the Senate Finance Committee reported that "remedial action is desirable in order to prevent the enforced sale of family businesses which are vital and desirable elements of our system of private enterprise." This "remedial action" was enacted into law and is now Section 303 of the Internal Revenue Code.

Section 303 of the Internal Revenue Code is a tax relief measure for the benefit of estates of corporate shareholders. It allows the estate or heirs of a deceased shareholder to convert stock into cash on an income-tax-free basis. More specifically, it permits a corporation to make an income tax-free partial stock redemption from the estate of a deceased shareholder in sufficient quantity to cover funeral expenses, administration costs, federal estate taxes, and any state death taxes imposed because of the shareholder's death. This special treatment is available only after a stockholder's death.

In contrast, a similar partial-stock redemption prior to death would be considered a dividend and would therefore be taxable in full to the shareholder as ordinary income.

The decision to use (or not use) Section 303 is an after-death decision. But it is important to sell key person life insurance before death so that the business will have the cash to fund the Section 303 portion of cash needs. Even if Section 303 is not used, the extra cash from the key person policy will help the business survive.

Life Insurance Funding for Section 303

Many closely held corporations will not have sufficient cash on hand at the death of a shareholder to redeem the necessary stock. Others may have the cash, but realize that it would not be wise to drain the cash reserves this way.

To take advantage of Section 303, the prudent shareholder will arrange to have the corporation own, pay for, and be the beneficiary of life insurance equal to the projected liquidity need. Basically this is key person life insurance that will be used at death for this special purpose.

Here's an example. Assume that Tom is the insured stockholder. As with any key person policy, the corporation is the owner and beneficiary of the policy. When Tom dies, his stock passes to his estate. Also at Tom's death, the insurance company pays the corporation the face amount of the key person insurance proceeds covering Tom. The corporation uses the life insurance proceeds to pay Tom's estate for the stock that qualifies for the Section 303 stock redemption. Assume that $200,000 qualifies. The estate transfers $200,000 worth of stock to the corporation. Tom's estate uses $200,000 to pay federal and state death taxes, plus administrative and funeral expenses.

Qualifying for Section 303 is sometimes uncertain until the person dies and the estate is valued. (See the "Section 303 Conditions," especially the 35 percent rule.) Regardless of the availability of Section 303, it's wise and prudent to fund payment of the taxes and expenses with life insurance. Then, if Section 303 can be used, the personal insurance will provide extra money to the family. If the estate does not qualify for Section 303, the family will still have cash from the personal insurance to pay these costs.

Most often, personal insurance used to pay these costs should be kept out of the estate. This means having it owned by someone other than the insured, possibly the spouse or an irrevocable trust.

Inner Workings of Section 303

For tax purposes, what actually happens under Section 303 is that a stipulated portion of a stock redemption is treated as a sale of stock (capital gain) rather than as a dividend. This is a nice tax break in itself because all of a dividend would be taxable, but only the "profit" portion of a sale is counted as gain—not the entire redemption price.

Next, because the stock takes a stepped-up basis at death to its fair market value, there is usually no gain to tax. When a stockholder dies, his or her stock receives a new basis equal to its fair market value at he date of death (or alternative valuation date). Because the stock would normally be redeemed at its fair market value, there is no gain. In fact, the corporate resolution authorizing a Section 303 redemption would generally stipulate that the redemption price shall be the value of such stock as finally determined for federal estate tax purposes.

Section 303 Conditions

A tax-free partial redemption can be made under Section 303 if the following conditions are met.

1. *The 35 percent rule:* The value of the stock the decedent owned in the redeeming corporation must be 35 percent or more of the adjusted gross estate, and must be includable in the gross estate for federal estate tax purposes.

2. *Time limit:* Redemption must be made within 3 years of death and 90 days after filing the estate tax return or within 60 days after a Tax court decision on any tax deficiency becomes final. An alternate of up to 14 years is available if an eligible estate elects to defer tax payments under the stretch-out provisions of Section 6166.

3. *Multi-corporation 20 percent rule:* If the decedent owned stock in two or more corporations, the stock can be combined and treated as the stock of a single corporation, so long as 20 percent or more of the value of the outstanding stock in each corporation is included in determining the value of the decedent's gross estate.

4. *Combine all classes of stock to meet the 35 percent test:* All classes of stock in a corporation may be taken into account in determining whether the stock constitutes a sufficient percentage of the adjusted gross estate. If the estate consists of both common and preferred stock, the value of both can be aggregated to meet the percentage requirements.

5. *Redemption tied to the person who is liable for the payment of the expenses/costs/taxes:* The shareholder from whom the stock is redeemed must be one whose interest is reduced by the payment of funeral expenses, administration costs, and death taxes. In other words, the party whose shares are redeemed must be liable for these costs. (More detail follows.)

The following items can be included in determining the amount of stock that can be redeemed via a Section 303 redemption:

- Funeral expenses

- Administration expenses
- Federal estate taxes
- State death taxes

Section 303 Approach Letter
Dear Corporation Owner:
In 1954, Congress passed legislation that dealt with problems encountered by families of owners of closely held corporations at the death of a stockholder. The Senate Finance Committee reported that "remedial action is desirable in order to prevent the forced sale of family businesses which are vital and desirable elements of our system of private enterprise."
That legislation is still on the books as Section 303 of the Internal Revenue Code. In essence, it gives eligible shareholders a one-time chance to get money out of the corporation income tax free for the benefit of their heirs.
May I ask you to consider your own plans? Is your preference that your family keeps its corporate ownership interest at your death? Would you rather they dispose of it? In either event, insurance can play a part. I'd like to talk with you about your options, and what can happen if no plans are made. I can help you determine whether you are eligible, and how this opportunity applies specifically in your case.
I plan to contact you within the week to arrange a meeting.
Sincerely,
Advisor

Burden of Paying Death Taxes and Costs Must Fall on Stock

A Section 303 redemption is allowed only to the extent that the burden of paying the expenses and taxes (for which Section 303 is available) actually falls on the stock to be redeemed, either directly or through a binding obligation to contribute, by law or under a contract [IRC §Section 303(b)(3)].

In most cases this will mean that the redemption must be made from the estate itself or from the beneficiaries of the residuary estate. The recipient of a specific bequest, or a surviving joint owner or appointee, who is usually exempted from the estate tax burden, generally cannot take advantage of Section 303.

Control of the Corporation

In planning a Section 303 redemption, the shareholder should know that ownership percentages, and thus corporate control, may shift as a result of the redemption. For example, if there are two equal shareholders and one dies, and his or her executor submits one-half of the decedent's stock for redemption, the ownership percentages shift from 50-50 to 33-67. Sometimes the family finds it impossible to both make the redemption and keep control of the corporation.

How an Insurance-Funded Agreement Can Assure a Section 303 Redemption

When it is contemplated that a majority shareholder's stock will be redeemed under Section 303, there should be a written agreement between the shareholder and the corporation.

A written agreement guarantees that the shareholder's estate will be able to sell what may otherwise be a non-liquid asset. Also, it assures the surviving stockholders that outside, inactive interests will not come into the business at the death of an owner.

When a minority shareholder's shares are to be redeemed under Section 303, or if the shareholders are unrelated, an agreement lends certainty to the arrangement. In addition, if antagonism exists between majority and minority interests in a particular corporation, a preexisting agreement to redeem a majority shareholder's shares under Section 303 could have the desirable effect of deflecting criticism by the surviving minority interests.

The Advantages of Life Insurance Funding

The shareholder should seek assurance that the corporation is financially able to carry out its purchase obligation under the agreement.

Retained Earnings

In virtually all states, a corporation may purchase its own shares only out of retained earnings. Without enough retained earnings, the redemption will not be allowed by law. Even if these capital-impairment statutes are not violated, the corporation could harm its financial soundness by paying for a Section 303 redemption, especially at such a critical time when a key person has just died. This would be doubly harmful if the corporation's working capital were already low or committed to other purposes.

Borrowing

Borrowing money for the redemption may sometimes be possible, but it generally is not an attractive funding alternative to rely on. For one thing, it is an uncertain option because no one knows what the company's financial standing will be when the need to borrow arises. Second, it is a more costly option than life insurance. Finally, it is a generally unwise option because one of the guiding hands of the business will have died just as the new burden of a loan is placed on the business.

Life Insurance

Therefore, to assure that there will be retained earnings at any given moment, the corporation should own life insurance on the primary stockholder, and on any other who desires Section 303 treatment. The policy should be payable to the corporation and equal to at least the amount eligible for a Section 303 redemption.

Life insurance funding for a Section 303 redemption agreement offers the following advantages:

- Life insurance places in the corporate treasury at the time of the shareholder's death the funds necessary to purchase the maximum amount of stock permitted by Section 303.

- Life insurance provides the corporation with the cash to redeem stock quickly, long before the Section 303 redemption time limit expires.

- Income taxes: While the corporation cannot deduct the premium, since it is the beneficiary of the policy [IRC §264(a)(1)], it receives the death proceeds income tax free [IRC §101(a)(1)]. Even if the corporation has purchased an existing policy to fund the redemption, this will fall under an exception to the transfer-for-value rule, and the proceeds will remain income tax exempt [IRC §101(a)(2)(b)]. (Note: If the corporation is subject to the alternative minimum tax, there can be a tax of up to 15 percent of the policy's net death proceeds.)

- Life insurance can prevent depletion of a corporation's cash account and other current assets, avoid possible violation of state capital impairment laws, and eliminate the need for borrowing by the corporation.

- Life insurance helps prevent accumulated earnings tax problems by accumulating funds on a discounted, installment basis. With life insurance, the business does not have to keep the total purchase price on hand.

- Life insurance proceeds increase the book value of the stock, and thus may enable a marginal estate to qualify under the 35 percent test.
- To the extent a premium purchases cash value, it is an expenditure for the purchase of a corporate asset, rather than an expense.

Life insurance is, by far, the best and least expensive asset an individual can purchase to create liquidity. For a fraction of its ultimate value, life insurance can be bought to create enough cash to satisfy all of a stockholder's cash needs at death, whenever that death occurs. No other liquid asset can promise the same thing at such a low cost.

Casual Conversation

In casual conversations with business owners, whether they are clients or not, listen carefully for clues that point to possible insurance needs.

For example, is a new owner coming into the firm? If so, there may be need for additional business continuation planning or key person insurance.

If the owner talks about an increased line of credit at the bank, there may be a need for more key person insurance. Expansion plans can also mean a need for more key person debt coverage.

Even a conversation about vacations can be an entree for you to ask about who will be running the business in the owner's absence. Is the replacement a key person who should be insured?

How long could the business operate profitably if the owner were on an extended vacation?

Every time the owner talks about a competitor, a supplier, or a customer, you may be on to a new prospect if you listen carefully and ask questions.

Double-Duty Section 303. Another way to structure the insurance ownership—and solve the problem of income for the surviving spouse at the same time—is called the double-duty-dollar approach. Here's how it works. The stockholder is insured and is the owner of the policy. At death,

- the proceeds are paid to the surviving spouse
- the spouse lends an amount to the business sufficient to redeem stock from the estate
- the estate then pays appropriate expenses

- the corporation then repays the spouse, usually in installments which include tax-deductible interest

This arrangement has a number of advantages. If, at death, the stock does not qualify for Section 303, the surviving spouse has the insurance proceeds rather than the corporation.

Furthermore, there is no possibility of the proceeds "ballooning" the stock's value. If the redemption takes place as planned, the spouse will receive all proceeds back, plus interest from the business. For the corporation, paying interest is preferable to paying dividends because dividend payments are not deductible; interest is.

Section 303 Eligibility Worksheet

For

    Shareholder: _____

    Corporation: _____

(Use a separate worksheet for each stockholder who would like to see if he or she is eligible for Section 303. This is an estimate only. Coordinate with a CPA or tax attorney.)

1. Birth date: _____

2. Total value of corporation: _____

3. Your percent of ownership: _____

4. Value of your ownership (line 2 times line 3): _____

5. Size of your gross estate: $_____

6. Your debts (including mortgages): $_____

7. Estimated funeral and administrative expenses: $_____

8. Adjusted Gross Estate (line 5 less the sum of lines 6 and 7): $_____

9. 35% of line 8: _____

10. Does line 4 exceed line 9? If "no," stop here because the shareholder does not qualify for Section 303. If "yes," proceed to line 11. (Yes) (No)

11. Estimated federal estate taxes: _____

12. State death taxes (estate and/or inheritance taxes): $_____

13. Sum of lines 7, 11 and 12. This is the maximum amount of stock that may be redeemed under Section 303: $ _____

A serious potential problem is that the business must continue to be profitable for this arrangement to work. For example, if the business becomes insolvent or goes bankrupt, it would likely default on the balance of its payments to the spouse. Even if it "only" comes on hard times financially, it might decide that payments to the spouse don't have a high priority and can therefore be postponed or skipped entirely until the business recovers.

VALUATION OF A BUSINESS INTEREST

For financial advisors, the subject of valuation of a business comes into play in several business situations. One example is in discussing the estate and related issues of the business owner or for buy-sell situations, where an agreement is being made to sell part or all of a business at the death or disability of an owner. Some value or valuation formula must be established because the buy-sell agreement will require it.

Having a familiarity with the factors and methods used in valuing a business will let you be more comfortable and speak more intelligently with business owners and their other advisers. They will come to accept you as a peer. This also means they are generally more willing to do business with you.

Valuation is a complex and inexact process. In the case of smaller business units, valuation is usually the function of the accountant. Computer software designed for this purpose is playing an increasing role.

Larger business units often use valuation experts. Firms specializing in this field have become quite numerous in recent years in response to increased needs for valuation for such purposes as taxation, reorganizations, recapitalizations, mergers, credit, and expansion.

Fair Market Value

The purpose of a valuation is usually to determine the fair market value of a business. Fair market value is the price at which the business interest would exchange hands between a willing buyer and a willing seller, each having knowledge of all the pertinent facts, and each having equal negotiating ability, with neither being under compulsion to buy or sell.

Valuation Factors

The fair market value of a stock traded actively on a stock exchange or over the counter is easy to establish from newspaper quotations. The value is the average between the highest and lowest prices paid on the valuation date. Closely held business interests are not listed on the stock exchanges.

Hence, the valuation of such interests often is challenged by the Treasury Department.

Continue or Sell?
Reasons to sell:
• The future of the business does not look good.
• No one from the family or the firm itself is willing or able to take over company.
• There is an offer too good to refuse.
• Selling the business would help to avoid conflicts in the family.
• Selling the business for cash would give surviving family members increased financial security.
Reasons to continue:
• It is not a good time to sell.
• The business is prosperous and providing family members with an excellent income, exceeding what might be realized on the investment of sales proceeds.
• Profits are growing now and are likely to continue to grow in the near future.
• There is proven successor management available in the family or the business.
• There is sufficient liquidity to meet cash needs at the death of the owner.

The IRS issued Revenue Ruling 59-60 to provide guidance to the appraisers of closely held stock. This Ruling does not delineate a procedure or formula for valuing closely held stock. Instead, it gives detailed explanations of basic (though not exhaustive) factors requiring careful analysis in each case, including

- the nature of the business and the history of the enterprise from its inception
- the economic outlook in general and the condition of the business
- the earning capacity of the company
- the dividend-paying capacity
- whether or not the enterprise has goodwill or other intangible value
- sales of the stock and the size of the block of stock to be valued
- the market price of the stock of corporations engaged in the same or a similar line of business having their stocks actively traded in a free and open market, either on an exchange or over -the counter

Two Factors Considered by Government

The U.S. government considers two factors in valuing a business: earning power and owner's equity.

Earning Power

An important factor in estimating the value of a business interest is how much profit has been earned by the firm each year and at what rate of growth (if any) such earnings can be expected to continue. A fair selection of past earnings for the past 5 or more years is averaged to derive an estimate of future earnings.

Weighted Earnings. The recent earnings of a business generally are more meaningful than earnings of, say, 4 or 5 years ago. Therefore, it is logical to give more weight to recent earnings and less to earnings of prior years. There are various ways of doing this. In sophisticated weighting procedures, profits may also be adjusted by a cost-of-living index factor to compensate for the effects of inflation.

> "Prospect, your balance sheet might look fine today, but what will your family's balance sheet look like soon after your death?"

Going-Concern Value. The moment a business opens its doors, a value is created over and above the assembled assets. This value is known as the going-concern value.

When customers are coming in and out, the business has a going concern value well above the total value of separate assets. Although part of the profit may be attributed to the tangible assets, only a going concern earns a profit. Therefore, in determining the value of a business, a clear distinction is made between value as a going concern and the value of the tangible assets.

Management. To run successfully, a business must be headed by efficient management. Such management is definitely a profit-producing asset to any firm.

In a corporation, salaries and bonuses are paid to the key executives over and above any dividend paid to them as stockholders. Thus, in computing its profits, the corporation already has deducted the proper share attributable to the management provided by its owner-employees. The same sort of deduction should be made in analyzing profits of proprietorships and partnerships.

Goodwill. Goodwill is an intangible quality that attaches itself to an established business. Goodwill represents the possibility of future business from established customers who will continue to patronize the firm because of its location and/or because of the prestige and reputation built up through the years. Many people will return automatically to an establishment even though its management has changed.

Carryover goodwill refers to how long and how much a new owner benefits from the established customers and business reputation of the previous owner. With time, this old influence diminishes. Eventually, carryover goodwill disappears.

In a professional firm where a confidential relationship exists with clients, it is usually difficult to separate goodwill from the personality of the practitioner. For example, the goodwill of a physician who has built up a successful practice usually cannot be entirely transferred to a successor, even though many patients will continue to come to the same office.

Owner's Equity

The second element we will examine in valuation is owner's equity. This is often referred to as book value and represents the excess of assets over liabilities. Sometimes, the book value of a corporation is stated on a per-share-of-stock basis.

As a result of the imprecise values underlying the owner's equity figure, few business owners would be willing to sell their interests for book value. At best, owner's equity can be viewed as the rock-bottom minimum value for a business—a base from which to start.

Some valuation experts give additional weight to book value but only after adjusting the historical asset values to reflect current market values. The result is "adjusted book value."

Miscellaneous Factors

Other factors considered in valuing a business are any prior sales of the business, economic conditions affecting the business, and expert opinions.

Methods of Computation

business valuation methods

Although there are several traditional methods of valuation, the government often tends to use a combination of whichever methods produce the most taxes. Some of the traditional methods are:

1. book value
2. capitalization
3. sales method
4. price/earnings comparative analysis

Book Value Method

book value

Book value is calculated by subtracting liabilities from assets. Book value is also known as owner's equity. For reasons already discussed, book value is only a starting point. However, an adjusted book value that reflects the current values for assets may be given additional weight in the overall valuation process.

Straight Capitalization Method

Another method uses a capitalization formula of average earnings divided by a certain percentage. This method is called capitalization because it assumes that the net income of the business comes from the equivalent of a piece of property, or capital. If you know what a reasonable rate of return would be on that type of property and if you know the actual return (or net income), you can compute the value of the property itself.

A comparison will help make this method clear. Suppose you are discussing personal life insurance needs with a husband and wife. They tell you that they have accumulated "some" money in a savings and loan association. If they tell you how much interest they receive each year and if you have a reasonably good idea of the current interest rates being paid by savings and loan associations, you can figure out roughly how much they have in savings.

For example, assume that your prospects tell you they receive about $600 of interest each year from the local bank. If the current interest rate on savings is 6 percent, you can easily determine that their amount of savings is about $10,000 ($600 divided by .06). If the current interest rates were 8 percent instead of 6 percent, their savings total would be approximately $7,500 ($600 divided by .08).

> "Business Owner, how much would you want for your interest in this business if you were retiring or moving away today?"

capitalization method   The straight capitalization method uses the same idea but applies it to estimate the value of a business whose earnings are known. The percentage used is determined by considering the average rate of return for the industry and the kind of business.

For example, if earnings over 5 years or more averaged $20,000 and if 10 percent is judged to be a reasonable rate of return for that type of business, the company might be said to be worth $200,000 ($20,000 divided by .10). This would be a going-concern estimate. It includes book value (or tangible net worth) and all intangible items (such as goodwill and patents).

Auction
"Prospect, am I correct in assuming if you were going to sell your business today, you would rather sell it as a going concern than to see it go up for auction piecemeal?"
(Wait for a response.)
"Have you made plans to see that this in fact will happen eventually?"
(Wait.)
"Would you have any objection to discussing it with me sometime?"

Sales Method

sales method   In valuing stock of closely held corporations, the taxing authorities will consider prior sales as a fair valuation basis. However, such sales must have been consummated in an arm's-length transaction wherein the selling price must have been what a willing buyer would have paid a willing seller. For example, sales between close relatives are not often considered arm's length transactions.

Price/Earnings Comparative Analysis

price/earnings method   A business cannot be appraised without reference to the world around it. Therefore, comparisons with publicly owned corporations that have stock traded on active security markets can provide helpful valuation information.

Lack of Marketability. The value of a business, like that of any asset, is higher if a ready market for its sale already exists. The converse is also true; the value of a business is less if the ownership interest is not easily marketable.

Minority Ownership Interest Discount. A minority ownership interest in a closely held corporation is generally worth less per share than a majority interest. This lower value is appropriate because of the difficulties a minority stockholder encounters in trying to control corporate management and/or convert company assets into cash or dividends.

Oddly enough, the most difficult part of your job will not be persuading the owners to fund a buy-sell agreement with insurance. It will be getting them to see that a buy-sell agreement is important enough to implement.

The next step, that of funding the agreement, cries out so logically for an insurance solution that it is most often a less difficult case of persuasion.

Setting a Tentative Value

At some point, you will be in sales situations where insurance funding is the point of discussion. You and your prospects will want to settle on a specific dollar amount to use for insurance illustrations and later for the insurance application. This dollar amount will be an estimate of the value of the business—a working figure or tentative value.

It's important for the business owner (and you) to focus on some value for the business. Then you can talk specific dollar amounts, and the problem seems much more real. So, do something regarding value, even if it needs to be changed later. Here is an example of what to say:

"Prospect, for working purposes right now we need to settle in on some tentative value of your business. How much would you say it's worth?"

(As necessary, assure the prospect that this amount will ultimately be determined based on the accountant's advice. This is only a tentative amount to use for now.)

Usually your prospects will say they don't know. If that is the case, proceed as follows:

"If you had died last night, how much would you want for your share of the business?"

The prospect will probably come up with an amount at this point. If not, ask the question again in different ways to help elicit an answer.

For example, *"How much would you want your family to receive?"*

Or, *"What would you be willing to sell your business for today, assuming you could never work again?"*

Or, *"What's the minimum you'd expect? What's the maximum?"*

Or, *"How much would your family expect?"*

When you get an answer, proceed as follows:

"Suppose your partner died last night. How much would you be willing to pay for his (her) share of the business?"

The prospect will usually come up with an amount. If not, ask additional questions, as previously, to encourage a response: *"What's the most you would pay? What's the least you would expect to have to pay?"*

Or, *"Would you be willing to buy your associate's share for the same proportionate amount for which you're willing to sell yours?"*

After getting the two basic amounts (selling price, buying price), get the prospect to decide on an in-between amount to be the tentative value. Sometimes the two amounts are the same so no midpoint needs to be decided. You can use this tentative value to determine the amounts of insurance.

"Before we go to your accountant to get a figure for the value of the business, we need to see if you can qualify medically for the insurance. If you can't get the insurance, you will still have a problem. It's just that we won't be able to solve it with insurance."

"After we're sure you can get the insurance, we can adjust the dollar amount, if necessary, based on your accountant's recommendation. In this way, you can get the insurance process started. It's best to get the coverage in force and then adjust the dollar amount later if necessary. Most companies are more than willing to do this."

Valuation and Estate Taxation

As will be discussed in chapter 8, the federal estate tax is a transfer tax based on the value of the property owned by a person who dies. A business is part of that value and is subject to the tax.

For example, if a person owns one third of a $6 million dollar business, and dies, then $2 million will be included in the estate and will be subject to the federal estate tax. To give you an idea of the amount of the tax, if the owner's other personal assets (house, and so on) bring the estate's overall net value to, for example, $2,500,000, the tax might be $800,000 or so, depending primarily on the amount of various credits and the marital deduction.

Estate Tax Role of a Buy-Sell Agreement

The IRS can, and frequently does, step in at death to make its own judgment on the value of a decedent's business interest.

The IRS valuation, done for estate tax purposes, generally arrives at a substantially higher value for the business than that placed on it by the owners. Although legal appeals can be made by the decedent's estate, they are costly in time and money. Besides, the court's decision may only reinforce the IRS position or reach a compromise value.

High valuations of this sort mean higher and unexpected estate taxes. Planning becomes a futile exercise because everything is thrown drastically out of kilter when the value of this major estate asset can't be pegged in advance.

The result is often a hurried sale or liquidation of the business at a small fraction of its fair value. Heirs cannot only lose control of the business by having to sell off large parts of it for low prices, but then they must pay heavy estate taxes from the already diminished sale price.

The good news, however, is that there is a way for owners of a business to be reasonably certain that IRS will accept the value placed on it by the owners. If the owners are *not related* to one another, here are the three tests that must be met if the IRS is to accept the value specified by the owners. A similar set of rules, discussed earlier in this chapter, applies in situations where the owners *are* related:

Value of Knowledge

This is a thumbnail sketch of an actual sale made by an advisor who knew and understood a few salient points about valuation. It is a combination of the capitalization and book value methods of valuation.

The XYZ Company showed a year-end book value of $65,930, or $68.68 per share for 960 shares.

I know that most companies are worth far more than their book value. I called this fact to the attention of my prospects.

"Dollars are worth only what it costs to borrow them. Your book value of almost $66,000 could be borrowed (or lent) at a rate no higher than 12 percent. The difference between what it would cost to borrow your book value and what your business actually earned on it last year probably reflects a truer value of this business.

Corporate earnings	$31,297
$65,930 at 12%	−7,912
"Excess earnings"	$23,385

"The 'excess earnings' were a product of management skill and many other factors which add up to the going-concern value of this business.

"To put a price tag on your corporation, let me ask this: Is an 18 percent return reasonable for the degree of risk in this business?"

My prospects agreed. I then capitalized the "excess earnings" at 18 percent. Adding the book value to the capitalized earnings resulted in a reasonable estimate of the going concern value.

$23,385 capitalized at 18%	$129,917
Book value	65,930
Going-concern value	$195,847

The value per share on this basis was not $68.68 but $204 ($195,847 divided by 960).

This business had a classic need for a buy-sell agreement. It also had a pressing need for protection against the loss of its key management talent.

When my prospects saw the "new" estimated value of the business, they felt it more important to implement a buy-sell agreement and key person insurance. I sold the insurance—with a $7,100 premium—because I knew how to dramatize the problem and show my prospects that their business was much more valuable than they had previously realized.

Second, they realized that it was their own expertise that gave the business such a high value—that they were valuable assets.

> Third, they realized that a lack of planning for the certainty of death could mean loss of value and loss of control of the business—and possibly loss of the business itself.

- First, the formula used to establish the price must have been fair and reasonable at the time the agreement was made.
- Second, there must have been no fraud or collusion in setting the pricing formula. It must be an arm's-length transaction among the participants, not some kind of a subterfuge to save estate taxes.
- Third, the sale of the business while all the parties were living must have required a first-offer provision, allowing the other parties to buy the business at a price not higher than the price stipulated in the agreement.

The *first-offer provision,* sometimes called the *first right of refusal*, or the lifetime sale provision, stipulates that if an owner desires to sell his interest during his life, he shall give the remaining owners written notice of such desire, and the remaining owners shall have the right to buy that interest at the price established in the agreement's formula.

DISABILITY BUYOUT

disability buyout
Talking with business owners about the need to include disability in buy-sell agreements can be a powerful door opener to those businesses that already have agreements covering death but not disability. For the numerous firms that do not have a buy-sell agreement of any sort, the disability approach is an excellent way to open substantial life insurance sales as well as disability sales.

Three Choices
"Business owner, if you were to be disabled, one of three things would happen to your business:
1. It would continue in operation.
2. It would shut down.
3. It would be sold.
"Which of these three outcomes would you like to occur?" (Wait for a response.)
"What plans have you made to ensure that this will be the outcome in your case?"

The market for disability income insurance to fund buy-sell agreements is fairly substantial. The chart that follows comes from a study by LIMRA. As can be seen, only a very small percentage of the businesses that were surveyed had any form of disability insurance to handle a buy-sell situation.

A word of encouragement is in order. Some advisors who enter the business insurance market are reluctant to get involved with disability buy-sell agreements. They fear that the legal complexities and technical nature of appropriate insurance products and contract provisions will be overwhelming.

Remember, you don't have to know all the answers. Focus attention on problems caused by long-term disability. Learn the questions to ask to arouse your prospect's attention, the issues which must be resolved, and where you can get help.

As is often the case, planning is the essential ingredient in resolving the problems accompanying the disability of a business owner. You make the "sale" when you encourage your prospect to recognize that he or she has a problem and that a solution is available.

Buyout Needs in Sole Proprietorships

The sole proprietor and his or her business are closely intertwined. The continued success of the business depends on the owner's ability to be active at work.

Probability of at Least One Long-Term Disability* Prior to Age 65						
Number of Owners						
Age	1	2	3	4	5	6
35	50.30	%75.30%	87.70%	93.90%	97.00%	98.50%
40	47.7	72.7	85.7	92.5	96.1	98
45	44.3	69	82.7	90.4	94.6	97
50	39.4	63.2	77.7	86.5	91.8	95
55	32.1	53.8	68.6	78.7	85.5	90.2
*Disability lasting at least 90 days						
Source: Commissioners Disability Table						

In most sole proprietorships, the owner is typically also a key employee (often the only key employee). Most sole proprietorships lack management depth. If the owner becomes disabled, a new manager would have to take over his or her duties. Yet, finding a replacement for the disabled owner is difficult-to-impossible because potential replacements know that the job will likely disappear as soon as the owner recovers. Even if the firm could attract a suitable replacement, the double salary requirements (the proprietor and the substitute manager) would likely be a severe drain, especially on a business that has just lost the services of its key person.

Suitable Replacement?

Here is a way to begin a conversation on disability needs with a sole proprietor: "Business owner, assume for a few minutes that you were disabled yesterday. If you didn't know when (or if) you would be returning to work, who would step in to handle your business until you came back?"

If No One. If your prospect responds that there is no one capable of continuing the business, you have a candidate for a salary continuation sale.

If Someone. On the other hand, your prospect may name someone who could serve as a replacement. This person may be a family member, a key employee, or a competitor.

Ask a few probing questions about the background, capabilities, and desires of the potential replacement. If the business owner remains confident of the replacement's ability to operate the business alone, ask your prospect, *"Should your replacement have to continue paying your salary indefinitely? Should there be some point at which your replacement should be allowed to buy out your interest in the business for a fair price?"*

Encourage your prospect to do everything necessary to help the plan succeed. A properly arranged buy-sell agreement will give the replacement legal authorization to assume ownership of the firm.

In general terms, the agreement obligates the replacement to buy and the sole proprietor to sell the business upon the disability of the business owner. To avoid controversy, the agreement clearly defines the conditions under which the buyout is to occur and stipulates a price to be paid or a formula by which the value is to be determined.

Most importantly, cash will be needed to fund any buyout and to help the business cope with the financial losses that are almost certain to occur while the replacement struggles to master the job of being a sole proprietor.

Funding the Buyout

Almost always, disability insurance is the best source of cash. So long as there is insurance, the sole proprietor can be assured that the money will be there. The security of the proprietor's family will not depend on the continued profitability of the business. The cost of the insurance is almost always less than alternative funding methods such as borrowing.

Buyout Needs in Partnerships

Understanding the disability need in a partnership requires an awareness of some points of partnership law.

- A partnership is not automatically dissolved if one of the partners becomes disabled.
- The rights of a disabled partner are basically the same as before the disability. The disabled partner has a continued right to an equal voice in management and to an equal share of any profits.
- If the active partners wish to "remove" a disabled partner, they must dissolve the partnership by declaring it to be at an end or by obtaining a dissolution decree from a court.

The assets of the partnership will be converted into cash to first satisfy the claims of the firm's creditors. Any remaining cash will then be divided among the partners in proportion to their interest in the partnership.

When a partner becomes disabled, the business loses that partner's special talents. Generally, the partner becomes a financial drain on the business. The healthy partners must often take on increased responsibilities, usually without additional compensation.

As much as they want to continue financial support to their disabled colleague and his or her family, the active partners may not earn enough profit to do so. When they can no longer shoulder the total functions of the disabled partner without help, they must hire a replacement. This means even more expense for the active partners.

After a period of time, the active partners are likely to want to resolve this trying situation. But what can they do? Dissolving the business in accordance with partnership law is highly undesirable and often totally impractical. If this occurs, none of the partners is likely to realize the full value of the business.

Furthermore, the active partners will have liquidated their own jobs. While they could form a new partnership and start anew, this is a major undertaking, especially if the old partnership has gone through the liquidation process. Such a dissolution and liquidation is not likely to inspire the confidence of customers or potential lenders.

Two Sales Possibilities

Obviously, then, the partners need a written agreement that addresses the possibility that one of them will become disabled.

Maintaining Dignity

In this era of change... we still mustn't forget the fundamental concepts of our business. This point was brought home to me a few years ago when I suggested to a 58-year-old client that he purchase disability income insurance. He owned a small business that was doing very well, but he had no key people. I recommended a program that would provide him $2,500 disability income per month. "If something happens to you," I argued, "there would be no one to run the business. "

He laughed and told me that the business could run itself... "Anyway" he said, "I can't afford to insure against every contingency. It would be money down the drain, just to provide you another commission." Despite this rebuff, I persisted in showing him how vulnerable he was. "The worse you could lose is the premium," I said, "and that wouldn't be enough to restrict your lifestyle at all." Finally, he allowed himself to be persuaded into applying for the insurance.

For the next three years, his business continued to grow. As a meat supplier to a fast-food chain, his business was bringing in $250,000 a week. When the chain decided to process its own food, however, my client's business suddenly fell to $30,000 a week. The profit margin in this type of business is limited. Consequently, huge losses began piling up almost immediately.

It was barely a week after he lost the account that my client suffered a heart attack. The next day creditors began swarming in trying to seize the assets. The company's collapse was imminent, Meanwhile, he lay helpless in the hospital. Fortunately, he was able to survive bypass surgery, but by the time he recovered there was little left of his business. When I visited him, he spoke of the $5,000 he would be receiving each month, free of taxation. "I've thought a lot about that policy," he said. "A man's dignity is his most precious gift. And you've let me keep mine."

That was one of the most emotional moments of my life. The man was my father.

Source: Richard M. Kagan, CLU, "Evolution of a Life Insurance Career," Life Association News (now Advisor Today), Vol. 79, No. 1, the official publication of the National Association of Insurance and Financial Advisors (NAIFA). All rights reserved.

This need creates two sales opportunities. The disabled partner needs an individual policy to continue his or her salary for a specified period of time (an income replacement sale), and the healthy partners need cash to purchase the disabled partner's business interest if he or she cannot resume active employment (a buy-sell sale).

Buyout Needs in Corporations

Unlike a partner, a disabled corporate owner has no inherent or legal right to receive a salary. Stockholders in closely held corporations typically are employees as well and therefore are paid a salary by the firm—a salary that is no longer deductible if the stockholder-employee is not actively at work and if there is no formal plan in effect. This presents a ready-made opportunity for an insured salary continuation plan.

In addition, the disabled corporate owner needs a mechanism for recapturing his or her investment in the business. Remember that closely held corporations rarely pay dividends. A majority stockholder who becomes disabled could, of course, force the board of directors to declare dividends, but the corporation would be restricted as to the dividend amount because dividends can be paid only from current profits or accumulated profits.

Remember, too, that stock in a closely held corporation is not very marketable. It is not traded on a stock exchange. Furthermore, it is often not attractive to potential investors because it represents only a minority interest in the business. Few investors would want to purchase a minority interest in a closely held corporation unless they could also obtain a management position in the company.

This leaves a disabled stockholder in an unenviable position. A disabled stockholder who cannot rely on dividend income and who cannot find an outside buyer for his or her stock may be forced to accept an otherwise unattractive offer made by the firm's healthy owners.

Alternatively, a competitor may offer to buy a disabled owner's minority interest, hoping thereby to gain some control over the firm. Obviously the firm's remaining stockholders would not welcome such an outcome. However, they might not be in a financial position to match the offer of a competitor.

A disability buy-sell agreement can solve these potential problems by creating a ready market for the stock of a disabled corporate owner.

The Buyout Agreement

Like other legal documents, a buy-sell agreement must be prepared by an attorney. Nonetheless, you should be familiar with the issues that must be resolved before the document is drafted:

- What is the definition of disability for this purpose?
- When will disability payments begin?
- How long must an owner be disabled to trigger a buyout under the agreement?
- Will the buyout be mandatory?
- How will the disabled owner's interest be valued? By whom? Will valuation occur at the time of disability or at the time the buyout is triggered?
- What will be the source of the money?
- Will the disabled owner be paid in a lump sum or over a period of time?
- If installment payments are to be made, what happens if death occurs before payments have been completed?
- What happens if the disabled owner recovers after the buyout has been put into motion, but before payments have been completed?
- What happens if the disabled owner recovers after payments have been completed?
- What is to be done about life insurance policies on the disabled owner?

Defining Disability

In order to avoid potential legal disputes, the buy-sell agreement must define disability in the same manner as does the disability policy used to fund the agreement.

In this way, the insurance company becomes the party that determines if a disability has in fact occurred. The impartiality of an insurance company in deciding this potentially divisive issue is a definite advantage to an insured plan—an advantage that you can use in selling disability income insurance.

Timing the Buyout

Most disability buyouts provide for a waiting period of 12, 18, 24 or 36 months. When this waiting period expires, implementation of the disability buyout is generally mandatory.

Salary continuation coverage from another policy should provide income as salary (if the business is a corporation) or "draw" (if it's a partnership) to be paid to the disabled owner during the waiting period and beyond. These payments are best funded with disability income insurance. A funded salary continuation agreement can be used if the business is incorporated. In partnerships, each partner generally purchases a disability policy on himself or herself, with the premiums being a nondeductible personal expense.

It is important not to let your prospect confuse buyout insurance with salary continuation (disability income) coverage. Both are needed to maintain a business owner's security, but each need is insured under completely different policies.

Disability policies generally have a waiting period of 3 or 6 months before benefits begin at about two-thirds of the disabled owner's normal salary. It is important to make the waiting time the same for both the policy and the agreement.

Valuing the Business Interest

The buy-sell agreement must resolve several valuation issues. First is a decision as to the date of valuation. One of two dates is typically used: (1) the date of disability or (2) the date on which the buyout is to occur.

A valuation method must also be selected. Again, there are basically two choices: (1) stipulate a fixed value in the buy-sell agreement and review it annually, or (2) include a formula by which the business is to be valued that adjusts the value automatically, depending on the firm's changing financial status.

Funding

The issue of funding a buyout is a crucial one. Without adequate funding, there is no guarantee that the buy-sell obligations can be met. In addition to using disability income insurance, there are several other funding alternatives.

- **Use Current Income:** The active owners could use business income to pay for the disabled owner's interest on an installment basis, but the company's continued profitability is typically unreliable, so this is a high-risk funding method.
- **Use an Uninsured Sinking Fund:** Using an uninsured sinking fund to build the needed cash has drawbacks as well. Disability could strike before there is sufficient cash in the sinking fund to affect a buyout.

- **Borrow:** Another possible source of funds would be through loans. However, this is an unreliable solution because banks are generally unwilling to extend credit to a business that has lost a key owner. Even if a loan were obtained, this is a high-cost solution that might eventually become an impossible burden on the firm.

It should be evident that disability insurance is the only guaranteed funding source. A few insurance companies write policies specially tailored for buy-sell situations. These disability contracts have underwriting limits based on the value of the business interest owned by the insured rather than on his or her income.

Some disability contracts designed for buy-sell situations pay a lump-sum benefit rather than monthly payments. These policies typically have elimination periods of 2 years or more.

Lump Sum Versus Installment Payments

The buy-sell agreement specifies whether the purchase price is to be paid in a lump sum or in a series of installments.

If the installment method is used, the sale is generally considered to be final once payments begin. In some buy-sell agreements, however, a seller who recovers from his or her disability has a right to buy into the company.

Selling a business interest under a disability buy-sell agreement may create significant tax obligations for the disabled seller. If the business has been successful, capital gains taxes will be due on the appreciation realized from the business. Taxes need to be considered when planning because they can substantially reduce realized gains.

If the buyers do not have the cash needed for a lump-sum transaction, installment payments are the only alternative. The buy-sell agreement should address the possibility that the disabled owner might die before all the installments have been made. If the disabled owner was covered by life insurance to fund a buyout at death, this policy should be kept in force until the installment payments have been completed. The disability waiver of premium provision can keep the life insurance policy in effect during this time.

Your Role

While you need to understand the advantages and disadvantages of various provisions in a buy-sell contract, avoid becoming a champion of any one approach or contract provision.

Your job is to make your prospects aware of the problems they face, help them understand their options, and show them that the cash they need is best provided through disability insurance.

One approach is to ask prospective clients if their existing buy-sell document says that disability is one reason to trigger a buy-sell. Whatever the answer, a significant discussion has begun.

"Where's the Other Half"

Selling only the life insurance portion of a buy-sell agreement is completing only half of the job. The need for disability buyout insurance is as great as the need for life insurance, and in some cases greater. Consider that the probability of at least *one* long-term disability prior to age 65 increases as the number of business partners increases (see chart).

As you meet with business owners to discuss insurance and financial products, remember your disability products. Don't let anyone follow up behind you and ask, "Where's the other half?"

Where's the Other Half?

Financial Advisor Joel Goodhart feels that reviewing buy-sell agreements is a good opportunity to sell a disability buyout policy. He encounters many situations where the buy-sell agreement will have a list of the associated life insurance policies but will not list a single disability policy.

Should you encounter a situation like that, Joel recommends: "Act stupid. Shuffle the papers around as if you were looking for something that should be there and then ask, 'Where's the other half?' The business owner will probably ask you, 'What do you mean?' Then you can explain, 'I see the life insurance policies to handle the transfer of the business in the event of death but I see nothing that corresponds with the transfer of the business in the event of disability.'"

This vignette demonstrates two things: the sharing of sales ideas and knowledge by seasoned professionals in the insurance and financial services industry; and one of the many opportunities you will find in the disability income market.

BUSINESS OVERHEAD EXPENSE INSURANCE

business overhead expense
We have discussed the ways that disability income insurance purchased by an individual or business can provide money to buy out a disabled owner's interest in the business. Regardless of the kind of business—sole proprietorship, partnership, LLC, or corporation—the business owner must be concerned

with continuing business expenses during a disability before a buy-out situation would arise.

Expenses Will Continue

In order to continue to produce earnings, the business must stay open even when the owner is too sick or injured to work. Many business expenses will continue—salaries, interest on loans, utilities and so on. Without the owner's input, business is likely to decrease and income drops. Many businesses can be crippled or shut down by the disability of the owner, faltering under the weight of business expenses. For a single-owner business or practice, a lengthy period of disability leaves very few options.

Closing Down

Closing the business can avoid some business expenses until the owner recovers. Other expenses, however, may continue. Office rent, for example, may be on a long-term lease not easily broken.

The savings realized from closing down may be at the cost of the success of the business. Earnings are lost while the business is closed. Customers and clients will be forced to go elsewhere. When the business finally reopens, they may not come back.

Employees may leave to find other jobs. They cannot wait without pay until the business reopens. When the business finally reopens, the owner may be faced with the expensive procedure of recruiting, hiring and training new employees. Rebuilding a staff can be an expensive process for a business.

Hire a Replacement

Another solution is to hire a replacement. This keeps the business going and the income flowing at the same level, but replacements can be difficult to find. A substitute may not know the business and the market like the owner.

Income from the business is likely to decline. Goodwill with customers and suppliers can be lost. If the owner continues to take income from the business while paying a replacement, the business's cash flow will be significantly reduced.

Personal Funding

Some owners feel they can use benefits from individual disability income coverage or other assets to keep the business going. This might work for a while, but it is likely to have a disastrous impact on both personal and business cash flow.

With the added financial burden of a sickness or injury, the owner may need all his or her resources for personal expenses. Even if the owner has individual disability coverage, using these funds to pay for business expenses may create a hardship for the family.

Trying to split limited funds between personal and business expenses can also damage the business. A money shortage may mean cutting corners. The resulting poor service can mean lost customers. The business may fall behind in payments to creditors and a good credit record can be lost. Although the business may limp along for a while, a lack of operating funds can seriously jeopardize its chances of survival.

Disability Risk Is Not Understood

A recent study by ACLI (American Council of Life Insurers) finds that small companies do not give enough consideration to the matter of disability insurance. The life insurance association says almost 50 percent of employers polled for the study "Disability Income Insurance: Penetrating the Small-Employer Market" believe the odds of their workers becoming disabled are one in 50, when the actual likelihood is one in three. ACLI Senior Counsel Terri Sorota says: "small employers, much like the population at large, are woefully ill informed about the possibility of becoming disabled." The study also found that respondents agreed that reasons for adding coverage would be if it improved employee performance and attitude, aided in retention and recruiting, and protected the business.

Source: "Small Employers Grossly Miscalculate Disability Risk, ACLI Survey Finds", February 11, 2003, 2002 American Council of Life Insurers, 101 Constitution Avenue, Washington, DC 20001

Selling the Business

Business owners may plan to sell the business if they are too sick or injured to run it. This has many drawbacks. For example, the owner is likely to receive much less than the true value of the business in a forced sale.

The Insurance Alternative

The alternative is a policy covering business overhead expenses, commonly known as BOE. This coverage pays operating expenses when the owner is unable to work because of a disabling illness or injury. It is a common-sense product, and business owners can readily appreciate the need for it because it is an excellent way to help insure the continuation of a business. BOE insurance reimburses the business owner for ongoing business expenses so employees' income can continue.

An important distinction must be made between BOE coverage and regular disability income policies. Business overhead plans are "reimbursement" policies. The business is reimbursed for actual expenses while regular disability plans are considered "indemnity" contracts, paying a specified monthly benefit.

Determining Need

Not all business owners need, or qualify for, business overhead expense insurance. Some businesses may be large or established enough to maintain a consistent level of income even if the owner cannot work. If a normal level of business income can be maintained during the owner's disability, coverage is not needed. Most insurance companies set limits on the number of principals and employees eligible for this coverage because businesses with a number of principals are better able to distribute and handle the disabled owner's share of the business.

THE BUSINESS OVERHEAD PRODUCT

The business overhead expense policy covers the ongoing expenses of a business, including

- utilities
- rent or mortgage interest
- accounting, billing, and collection fees
- premiums for business and professional insurance, including malpractice insurance
- interest on business indebtedness
- employee salaries, fringe benefits, and payroll taxes
- lease payments
- depreciation

- other expenses normally deducted by the business

What Is Not Covered

There are several business expenses that are usually excluded. They are categorized as expenses that are not affected by the owner's inability to work. In other words, they are expenses that would not continue if the owner was not working. They often include

- salaries, fees or other remuneration for the owner or persons in the same occupation
- salaries, fees or other remuneration for the owner's replacement, although this expense is covered in come policies or may be covered by riders
- the cost of equipment or merchandise, supplies to inventory, or capital expenses

A few companies now offer a business overhead rider or policy specifically designed for professional practices. This coverage is known as professional overhead coverage. It is similar to standard business overhead protection except that it provides benefits to help pay for the temporary replacement of the insured professional. By hiring a replacement, the insured has greater control over the continuity of service provided to his or her patients or clients. Check with your carriers to see if the extra level of protection is available as a separate policy or as a rider to your basic overhead policy.

Benefits

The benefit amount available for business overhead expense insurance can be quite large. However, monthly benefits must be geared at underwriting to actual expenses.

How Coverage Works

The business overhead expense policy does not have a fixed benefit like the individual disability income policy. Payment is made for the reimbursement for actual expense only.

For instance, a business owner has a policy with a monthly benefit of $6,000. The owner is injured in a skiing accident and cannot work for several months. Actual business overhead expenses are $4,000 per month, and that amount is paid, even though a total of $6,000 monthly benefit is available. The policy reimburses the insured for the actual cost of the covered expenses.

Some companies offer a "carryover" feature, wherein the excess benefit not used in a given month can be "carried over" if needed in later months.

Working With Expenses

Covering business expenses can be complicated because some expenses, like utilities, vary from month to month. Other expenses, such as malpractice insurance premiums, may be due quarterly, semiannually, or annually. These varying expense payments need to be taken into consideration at the initial underwriting.

Most policies today offer extended benefits, but some policies are designed to pay up to the full monthly benefit throughout the benefit period only. For example, the insured has a monthly benefit of $5,000 for 15 months. This means that a total of $75,000 in benefit is available. The insured has a heart attack and cannot work for a year and a half. During the first 15 months of the disability, overhead expenses are $3,000 per month, so a total of $45,000 of expenses is paid.

During the next 3 months, before the owner returns to work, an additional $20,000 of expenses are generated. Even though more than $20,000 of benefits remain, the expenses would not be covered because they occurred after the benefit period expired. Many companies extend the benefit period in a case like this until the full amount available has been used.

Qualifying for Insurance

Business overhead insurance is not needed in all cases. Applicants must qualify for coverage, meeting many of the same requirements needed for other types of disability income insurance.

Applicants must qualify in both the type of business and the occupational class. For instance, a doctor or lawyer usually has a close relationship with patients or clients and provides services that cannot be delegated to or performed by employees. These professionals may qualify for substantial coverage of business overhead expenses if their ongoing business expenses are high.

On the other hand, a shop owner may have delegated many of the duties involved with his or her business. The employees may have developed the experience and expertise to allow the business to continue without the owner's direct involvement. In this case, the owner may not qualify for business overhead expense coverage.

Definition of Disability

The coverage is designed to protect the business and its continuation, so disability is defined in relationship to the business. Disability is generally defined as the inability to perform the duties of the insured's occupation in the business.

Elimination Period

Policies generally offer an elimination period of 30 or 90 days. The most common elimination period is 30 days, since most businesses cannot cover overhead expenses from reserves or out-of-pocket for very long.

In the policies offered by several companies, there is also a presumptive disability clause that looks much like that contained in personal disability income coverage. Under this clause, an insured will be deemed totally disabled if a sickness or injury results in the loss of one of the following:

- sight of both eyes
- hearing in both ears
- power of speech
- use of any two limbs

Benefits begin immediately. Any unexpired portion of the policy's elimination period is waived.

Duration of Coverage

Coverage is generally available for periods of 12, 15, 18 or 24 months. The coverage is designed to keep the business going until the owner returns to work. If the owner is disabled for more than 2 years, his or her return to the business is unlikely. However, if the owner is permanently disabled, business overhead coverage will help keep the business going so that it can be sold for full value as a going concern.

Conversion Privilege

In many business overhead policies there is a conversion privilege. If, before a certain age, the insured is no longer responsible for overhead expenses, the business overhead policy can be converted to a regular disability income policy subject to the usual issue and participation limits then in effect.

This makes it possible, for example, for a sole proprietor to move to a salaried position, converting the policy to individual coverage without additional evidence of physical insurability and often at premiums corresponding to the original issue age.

Benefit periods on converted policies are usually limited to the period of the business overhead coverage up to a maximum of 24 or 36, and may also be limited as to the amount of coverage available.

Future Increase Option

If available, this option is usually issued with a stated maximum dollar amount. Options to increase coverage may be based on specific years or the policy anniversary date.

Benefit amounts can be issued on proof of increase of business overhead expenses, but no additional evidence of physical insurability is required. If the insured is disabled on an option date, some companies issue the additional amount, but it is effective only at the inception of a new disability.

Survivor Benefit

Under some policies, if the insured dies while benefits are being paid, the insurance company will continue the reimbursements of eligible expenses to the insured's estate for a period of time, such as 2 months.

Indexing of Benefits

This provision automatically increases the available benefit amount each year, either by a stated percentage or according to a formula defined in the benefit clause in the policy. Indexing of benefits provides a method of increasing available coverage to meet the increasing costs of overhead expenses during periods of inflation.

Tax Treatment

The tax consequences of business overhead expense coverage are quite favorable. Premiums are usually tax deductible as a business expense to all forms of ownership (Rev. Rul. 55-264, 1955-1 C.B. 11).

Since the premiums are deductible, the benefits are taxable. However, the benefits reimburse deductible business expenses, so the tax impact is erased.

KEY EMPLOYEE DISABILITY INCOME INSURANCE

key employee disability
If an employer feels that key employee coverage is warranted in the event of a death, then it is logical that the loss of a key person's contribution to the business should be considered in the case of sickness or accident.

The disability of a key employee presents problems to the business similar to those posed by the key employee's death. The loss of one or a few talented individuals could be crucial to the success of the business. The business will need to pay the disabled employee's replacement, fund training costs that may occur to prepare the replacement to carry out the disabled employee's duties, and have funds to cover reduced earnings and profits. It will also incur an additional expense when salary continuation payments are made to the disabled key employee. To cover this risk exposure, the business could purchase a key employee disability income policy. The benefits are paid directly to the firm, therefore premium payments are not deductible for federal income tax, as is the case with key employee life insurance. These benefits are received by the business free of federal income tax.

This coverage is difficult to obtain. There are only a few companies writing key person disability coverage today. The employee may suffer from psychological or stress-related causes that are difficult to precisely diagnose. Insurers will also want clear evidence that the employee is essential to the business and clearly a direct contributor to profits. Because it is a difficult task to estimate lost revenue, the possibility of adverse selection always exists for the disability insurer.

CLOSING AND SERVICING

The time between the fact-finding interview and the presentation/closing interview closing interview is a very important time for you. It is the time when you review your fact finder and your notes and recall your impressions of what's important to the client. It is when you decide what need is primary and what solution you will present. It is when you try to put yourself in the prospect's position and determine what you would want to happen.

Implementing the Solution and Supporting the Decision to Buy

During this time you decide what strategy to use in presenting the problems and solutions to your prospective client. You decide also on a backup strategy, again constantly asking yourself what you would want for yourself if you were the client.

Presenting the Problem and the Solution: Selling Benefits

Business owners do not purchase life insurance; they purchase solutions to problems. Big problems lead to big sales. While this may seem trite, it is true.

Your primary goal in the closing interview is to help the prospect see and acknowledge the problem, its size, and its urgency. The ultimate goal is to have the prospect take action to solve the problem.

Presenting the Problem

Begin the presentation by outlining the prospect's current situation. As you go through this review, be sure to ask feedback questions if the prospect is not already giving you positive feedback with words or gestures. It is important not only to hear what prospects say, but also to listen to their concerns.

Ask the prospect: "Does this analysis (or conclusion) fit your perception of the situation?" or "Are we in agreement about the nature of the potential problem?"

If there is a lack of consensus, ask clarifying questions. It may be that your analysis (or conclusion) is correct but the prospect does not readily wish to admit to a problem. Until there is agreement on the problem, it is not productive to discuss solutions.

After obtaining agreement that there is a problem, use probing questions to let the prospect know that there are serious consequences that go with inaction.

If there are no serious consequences to the prospect, then he or she should not and generally will not buy. If the prospect does not know and feel the serious consequences, the prospect will not likely act.

If the prospect has an important objective, and if something can prevent achievement of this objective, then you have cause to disturb the prospect about inaction. You may find it effective to use visual aids that highlight the nature of the problem.

Presenting Solutions and Selling Benefits

Once you have some agreement that a problem exists but the degree of agreement is still too feeble for a close, enlarge upon the problem until it becomes uppermost in the prospect's mind. Then close. Sometimes, before closing, you may need to explain the alternative solutions to the problem. Communicate clearly that inaction will not solve the problem.

At this stage of the presentation, help the prospect to see the costs, benefits, and risks of each alternative solution—even those that may not involve the purchase of insurance. As each alternative solution is reviewed, be sure to obtain feedback to confirm that the prospect understands the costs and risks. This is critical because the insurance solution will usually have the lowest cost and lowest risk. The risk we are discussing here relates to the possibility that a proposed solution may not work. Remind the prospect that doing nothing may have the highest long-term cost as well as the greatest risk.

After your prospect acknowledges that a serious problem exists, and that it must be solved, you can focus the prospect's thinking through this process:

Knowledge ⇒ Attitude ⇒ Desire ⇒ Beliefs ⇒ Conviction ⇒ Close

Design your presentation to communicate knowledge concerning the advantages and benefits of the recommended solution and your services in providing the solution. If the benefits are truly understood and felt by the prospect, then he or she should begin to develop a positive attitude toward you and your products. This positive attitude should help stimulate a desire for your services and products.

When there is a positive attitude and a clear desire, it is much easier to help the prospect to believe that the proposed solution (services and/or products) is the best approach to solving the problem. At this point the prospect is nearly ready to purchase. The close simply helps the prospect to finalize a conviction that the proposal is the best choice for solving his or her problem. This is when the prospect decides to take action and does so.

Closing

The close is often called "the moment of truth." As noted, a decision to buy involves a change in attitude. This change can be painful, as it requires the prospect to acknowledge that there is a problem that needs to be solved.

Prospects generally need help to make a go-ahead decision. Closing is, thus, the process of helping prospects make a decision that will benefit them or their business or both.

Not surprisingly, the prospect is aware that you are making a sales presentation. The prospect knows that you are there to make a sale, and he or she has likely had time to think about a problem or need. At some point in the sales presentation prior to your planned close, the prospect may be ready to buy. It is important that you be aware of any buying signals that the prospect gives during the presentation. Simply make the sale when the prospect is ready.

Trial Close. Before going to a close, it may be helpful to use a trial close to gauge the prospect's buying attitude. A trial close will reveal answers to the following questions:

Buying Signals

- *Prospect asks question.* The more specific the question, the stronger the buying signal. For example, the prospect may ask:

  - How much will it cost?
  - How long would it take to put the plan in effect?
  - Will this plan require a lawyer?

- *Prospect needs to seek an opinion.* This especially is a buying signal if an outsider is sought during the presentation (for example, if the prospect stops the presentation to call a key executive or partner into the room) .

- *Prospect becomes very friendly and relaxed.* If the prospect moves from an initial state of concern or anxiety to one of relaxation, trust has been established. It generally means too that the prospect sees a clear solution to a genuine problem.

- Does the prospect understand the problem?
- Does the prospect comprehend the benefits and advantages of the proposed product or services?
- Is the prospect ready to buy?
- If not ready to buy, what are the prospect's objections?

If you move to close the sale without getting clarification on the foregoing questions, you might prematurely force the prospect to take a negative stance. By first using a trial close and determining the prospect's buying position, you can avoid forcing the prospect to make a negative commitment.

In a trial close, you ask for a response to questions. Specifically, ask for the prospect's opinion about either the problem or an alternative solution. A trial close does not directly ask a prospect to buy. The best trial close is a very brief question that stimulates an opinion response. Here are some examples.

- How does this concept sound to you?
- Do you think this is important?
- This benefit is especially good—isn't it?
- This feature seems to fit your needs—do you agree?

Asking Questions

Direct Questions. These are questions that only require a very brief response—typically "yes" or "no." Direct questions are best used as a transition to a key sales point. For example, you might say, "Mr. Prospect, reducing your group insurance cost is important, isn't it?" Because they generate very brief responses, direct questions are not designed to provide feedback.

Open-Ended Questions. These are direct questions that serve the primary purpose of getting the prospect to talk. The old reliables (who, what, where, when, how, and why) are your most powerful allies in designing open-ended questions.

In addition, you will find one-word questions to be very powerful. For example, assume your prospect makes a statement that is either negative or confusing to the issue at hand. Try responding with "Oh?" or "Really?" Such a question often gets the prospect to rethink the comment and to keep talking—both actions that will help you.

Clarification Questions. The prospect's response to a direct or open-ended question may be inconsistent with the direction of the sales presentation, and/or the prospect's meaning may not be clear. Move past this awkward situation by rephrasing the prospect's response into a powerful question.

For example, assume the prospect avoids your question and goes into a complaint about the high cost of insurance. Try asking, "Prospect, do I hear you saying that if we can implement a solution to your problem with little or no impact on your corporate balance sheet, you would be interested in learning more?" Another response: "Prospect, are you saying that cost is the most important factor we need to review today?"

If you receive a negative response, do not try to close the sale. Rather, ask additional questions to determine objections or points of uncertainty. If you receive a positive response to the trial close, you can move to close the sale. Trial closes can be used several times until you receive buying signals or other positive feedback.

It is helpful to know these time-tested categories of closes:

- *Choice*—The prospect is given a choice between two desirable outcomes. Both involve buying: "Would you prefer to purchase the full $1,000,000 of permanent life insurance or $500,000 of permanent insurance with a $500,000 term rider?"

- *Praise*—Start the close with a well-intended compliment concerning the prospect's business position, opinion, and/or understanding of the presentation: "It is obvious that your profitable business is continuing to grow faster than the industry. You also seem to clearly understand how this growth will affect the problem we are discussing today. With this in mind..."

- *Implied Consent, Assumption*—Make an assumption that the prospect will buy: "John, let's arrange for the insurance company underwriter to review your file and determine how much coverage you can get. Would next week on Wednesday be okay for the necessary medical examination?" Or, "Mary, I think we should submit our proposal for $400,000 to the XYZ Insurance Company. Will your business be paying?"

- *Benefit*—Repeat (in summary form) the advantages of your proposed products and services. Be positive when summarizing the benefits. Your attitude stimulates agreement from the prospect. After noting the benefit, try saying: "You have agreed that these benefits are important to you, providing a cost-effective solution to a very real problem. With this in mind, I suggest you take the steps to put the insurance in place. Does this seem like the right thing to do?"

- *Minor Point*—Ask for a little decision, rather than a decisive "Yes" or "No." Some prospects find it difficult to make a direct buying decision. By asking for a decision on a minor point or side issue, you help relieve pressure and get the sale completed. For example: "Should the key person insurance just cover Fred and Mary, or do we need to also cover Bill?" Or, "Would you like this program to include a disability benefit?"

Presentation Problems

It is rare for a sales presentation to go problem free. Be prepared to adjust to the typical problems that may come up during a presentation. The two most common problems are interruptions and bad environment.

Given that many of your prospects are busy people, interruptions during the presentation are likely to occur if you're at the prospect's place of employment. If an interruption occurs, your first response should be to determine if the prospect needs privacy. If the interruption is a personal or confidential matter, it is professional on your part to ask (either with words or a gesture) if the prospect would like you to leave the room. While the prospect may want you to stay, the offer to leave is appreciated as a sign of sensitivity and courtesy.

While the prospect is dealing with the interruption, organize your thoughts on how you will restart the presentation. The following steps are advisable:

- Be patient and quiet. Don't jump back into the presentation immediately after the interruption. Silence can be a very powerful tool for regaining the prospect's complete attention.
- Before continuing, briefly summarize the key point(s) you were discussing prior to the interruption.
- Ask a question to test if you have regained the attention of the prospect.
- If the prospect is now "with you," go on with the presentation.
- If you cannot regain the prospect's interest, the interruption may need more of the prospect's attention and it may be best to reschedule the presentation.

Most experts agree that the best place for the sales presentation is a quiet room where you can control or significantly restrict interruptions. If you have an office or a conference room, you can effectively set the stage for a professional presentation. Many agents insist that all sales presentations take place in their office and will seldom attempt to make a presentation in an uncontrolled environment. Yet this may not be feasible or desirable for your practice at this time.

Guidelines If Held in Prospect's Office

A few suggestions may be helpful if the presentation is to take place in the prospect's office:

- Have a scheduled appointment for a sales presentation.
- Ask the prospect if it would be possible to hold any calls.
- Confirm the amount of time needed. Seek agreement. Stay within your specified time frame.

Using Visual Aids

Though an insurance solution cannot be physically demonstrated, visual aids can be used in a sales presentation to

- emphasize key points (problems and solutions)
- create a professional image
- reduce confusion or misunderstanding of technical matters
- hold the prospect's attention

These goals are best achieved if the visual aids are an integral part of the complete sales presentation. Successful presenters suggest:

- If the aids involve equipment such as slides or overheads, be sure to test the equipment prior to the presentation.
- Visuals should be simple, clear, and straightforward.

Steps to Improve Closing
• Be sure the prospect understands the problem and the solution.
• Have available a few "tailored" closes. Different types of people respond better to different kinds of closes.
• The expert needs facts.
• The egotist needs praise.
• The indecisive needs leadership.
• Be prepared for the first "no." This is a normal part of the sales process.
• First use a "trial close" to check your prospect's attitude toward you or the proposed solution.
• Look for and respond to buying signals.
• After each close, be quiet. Silence is powerful!
• Control the visuals. Don't let the prospect go directly through the visuals. Maintain control of the presentation.

AFTER-SALE SERVICE

As with personal insurance, there is service to provide after the business insurance sale. Some of the service steps are familiar to you. For example, the policy is to be delivered and explained. The purpose of the insurance is to be retold. Ownership and beneficiary provisions are to be reviewed for appropriateness and accuracy by you and the business owners.

Other Actions to Be Taken

In addition, there are special actions to be taken after the sale. For example, a corporate resolution may be needed to show the corporation's intent in purchasing the insurance. Or perhaps a buy-sell agreement needs to be drawn up by the firm's attorney.

The firm's attorney and accountant generally need to know that the policy has been delivered and have a chance to review it. Your company likely provides checklists of actions to be completed following a business insurance sale. Some of the actions will be for the business owners to take, some for the attorney or accountant, and some for you.

Future Meetings

After the sale, tell your clients about the need for future meetings. At the very least, an annual review is important, if for no other reason than to learn about any changes that may affect some aspect of the insurance planning. Plan to ask the following questions in the annual meeting.

- Has a new owner joined the firm? If so, what impact will the additional owner have on the existing insurance-related plans? For example, will the new owner be part of the buy-sell plan? A key person to be insured?
- Have any owners left? What impact will that have on existing plans?
- Is there a new second business, or plans for one?
- Are the owners changing to a different form of organization (for example, changing from an S corporation to a limited liability company)?
- Is an owner planning to retire?
- Are the owners thinking about adding special executive perks or adopting new group coverage?
- Has the value of the business increased?
- Has there been an increase in the value of a key person?
- What insurance-related needs are next in line of priority? Is now the time to explore one of those unmet needs?
- Have disability needs been discussed?
- What estate planning would be prudent?
- What work remains to be done with the owner's personal insurance?

Tell your client to contact you if any one of the above events occurs. Keep your own list of dates to contact clients. For example:

- birthdays
- group renewal date
- buy-sell anniversary
- pension anniversary
- new legislation affecting businesses

Life Insurance Illustrations

Virtually all life insurance contracts contain guarantees regarding the policy's face amount, cash values, amount of premium, and how long that premium is payable. The advisor should mention these guaranteed values to the prospective client when a policy is being sold.

In addition, the advisor should provide a policy illustration showing nonguaranteed values. The illustration is an insurance company's estimate of how this particular insurance policy might perform over time if a given set of assumptions occurs. These assumptions are based on four nonguaranteed risk elements:

- mortality experience
- investment performance
- policy lapse rates
- expenses

It is most unlikely that actual future performance would exactly match all current assumptions over a number of years. It is therefore safe to remind clients that a sales illustration would never accurately portray a policy's actual performance.

CASE HISTORY: THE RELUCTANT BROTHER

Agent

Maureen Douglas has been selling life insurance for about 5 years.

Prospects

My prospects were three brothers who owned and operated a gasket manufacturing plant. I knew one of the brothers, and I had met their father who, at age 68, still kept a hand in the business he founded. The brothers were in their late 30s and early 40s.

Approach

My telephone approach to one of the brothers, Jack, was for personal insurance. I approached him on the idea of an estate analysis. Jack said he wasn't interested. "The business will take care of my family," he said.

A couple of years ago, this kind of response would have thrown me for a loop. After all, it does seem logical enough that a thriving business would be able to provide adequate income for the family of one of the owners who died.

It's not quite that simple, however. Although it's possible for a business to provide income to a deceased owner's family in a situation like this, these things require planning.

Without planning, the family is likely to own stock that they cannot sell and that does not provide any income for them. In essence, stock in a closely held corporation like this is virtually useless unless it represents more than 50 percent of the ownership of the business. A majority owner can typically call the shots when it comes to hiring relatives, setting salaries, and declaring dividends.

I replied to Jack, "If you want your business to care for your family, it's doubly important for you to see me. You and I have to sit down and do some serious talking." I like to use this you-need-me approach. It points up my role as a problem solver and has a strong tendency to disturb the prospect.

My approach worried Jack. He asked me to explain what I meant. I told him that I didn't want to talk casually on the telephone about a matter that was so serious and complex.

My firm stand and serious demeanor paid off. Jack eventually conceded, and we arranged an appointment.

Initial Interview

After ascertaining that this was a corporation with all of the stock owned by the three brothers and their father, the interview picked up where our phone conversation had ended.

I said, "You and your brothers apparently get along together very well. Under your father's leadership, you make a good team. However, you have to consider a few very important and significant questions. For example, what do you want to happen to your portion of the ownership when you die?"

Jack said he wanted his wife to own his shares.

"And what would happen if one of your brothers dies?" I asked. "Would you want his widow in here to help you run the business?"

Jack's negative reply was most definite.

I continued, "How do you think your brothers would react to your widow coming into the business as a part owner?"

The light began to dawn on Jack. We discussed the fact that simply owning stock in the business wasn't the answer. Most closely held corporations don't pay dividends, and their business was no different. The wives of the owners didn't have any experience in this particular manufacturing business. In addition, they had no desire to run the business. You can't just pay somebody a nice salary for doing nothing.

We made a few assumptions. First, the surviving brothers would want to have full control of the business if one of the brothers died. Second, the family of a deceased brother wouldn't really want to become active in the business. They would just want to be assured of a source of income to maintain their standard of living. Third, if the father died there would be no serious consequences to the financial well being of the business. Each of the three sons probably would inherit a third of his stock.

Although I explained briefly to Jack what I had in mind regarding an insured buy-sell agreement, I cut the discussion short and asked, "When can you, your father, and your brothers meet with me to discuss just how things would be arranged?"

Second Interview

All of the owners and the bookkeeper were present at the second interview. Prior to this interview, I had told myself to proceed as though this were the very first interview with any of the family members. That way I would not be leaving out any important facts simply because they had been discussed in the previous interview with Jack.

I outlined what I call my "Business Stabilization Plan." I explained the essential provisions of a buy-sell agreement, discussing the reasons why such an arrangement is so important to the future of the business and the welfare of the owners' families.

Toward the end of the interview, I asked for a copy of the articles of incorporation and the three most recent balance sheets and income statements. I learned that there were 800 shares of stock. The father owned 425 shares; each son held 125 shares. The bookkeeper estimated that the going-concern value of the business was about $1,200,000.

The father's will provided that the sons would divide his shares equally. There were no other children. Before I left I obtained agreement about what they wanted to see happen at the death of one of the brothers. I also obtained permission to discuss matters with the firm's attorney.

Planning

The attorney told me he had never worked on a buy-sell agreement but that he was anxious to do so and would check with others to be sure it was done properly. I told the attorney how to get in touch with my home office's counsel in case he wanted to ask any questions.

Closing Interview

I prepared two basic proposals. One was a ledger sheet for $200,000 of permanent insurance on the life of each of the brothers to cover his approximate interest. The other was for term insurance.

I felt that the sale actually had been made after my initial interview with Jack. I felt more certain of this after the next interview because two of the brothers and the father seemed enthusiastic about the idea.

The third brother expressed reluctance, saying he didn't think that such formal plans were necessary within the family. He also seemed concerned about how much this was going to cost.

Prior to the closing interview, I called Jack to ask if there was anything special I should do to relieve the fears of the reluctant brother. It turned out that the reluctant brother had misgivings about dealing with a woman on business matters.

At one point in the closing interview I found an opportunity to say something that I hoped would let the reluctant brother see this insurance as ultimately fulfilling personal and family needs, as opposed to being exclusively business insurance.

If the reluctant brother's objection was based primarily on my involvement in what he saw as a strictly business situation, then perhaps seeing it largely as personal insurance might help him accept the idea of my being the agent.

I said, "Although the immediate purposes of this plan are to stabilize the business and to effect a smooth transition of ownership of the business, its ultimate purposes are to assure the families of a continuing source of income and maintenance of their current standard of living."

Although the reluctant brother never did raise his real objection during this closing interview, neither did he raise his two previous objections. Happily for all of us, he finally nodded his assent when agreement was sought to proceed with this plan.

Comments

My business stabilization presentation contains two main elements:

- Problems caused by death that tend to destabilize a business. This focuses primarily on the fact that there will be opposing desires and opposing objectives at death.
- On the one hand, the heirs of a deceased owner primarily will be seeking income. On the other hand, the surviving owners of the business need to maintain control so that they can continue to do everything possible to make the business successful.

These differences are normal and logical. The result, however, is that the objectives of the heirs and those of the surviving owners are not compatible. This causes a certain degree of tension and possibly dissension or outright hostility.

A buy-sell agreement automatically gives each of the parties what they are seeking. The family gets money on which to live. The surviving business owners gain full control of the corporation and can run it as they wish without outside tension or dissension.

Funding the Buy-Sell Agreement

Although a buy-sell agreement removes dissension and therefore tends to stabilize the business, it will not work unless it is funded adequately. My business stabilization plan discusses the funding aspects of a buy-sell agreement.

In addition to the life insurance solution, I also cover the other alternatives in sufficient detail. These include the possibility of

1. borrowing the money from a bank when death occurs,
2. an installment sale between the heirs and the surviving owners where the purchase price is paid by the corporation to the heirs over a number of years from business profits, and
3. making deposits beginning now into a sinking fund which will accumulate until one of the partners dies.

CHAPTER REVIEW

Key terms and concepts are explained in the Glossary. Answers to the Review Questions and Self-Test Questions are found in the back of the book following the Glossary.

Key Terms and Concepts

IRC Chapter 14
attribution of ownership rules
Section 303 Stock Redemption
business valuation methods
book value
capitalization method

sales method
price/earnings method
disability buyout
business overhead expense
key employee disability

Review Questions

1. Describe two characteristics that distinguish family-owned businesses from other closely held businesses.
2. Briefly describe the main target of Internal Revenue Code Chapter 14 with regard to buy-sell agreements.
3. Briefly explain the purpose of Section 303 of the Internal Revenue Code.
4. What role does life insurance play in a Section 303 redemption?
5. What factors should be considered when determining the value of a business?
6. Why is a proper valuation important for a business?
7. Briefly explain the traditional methods used for business valuation.
8. Briefly describe three problems that generally occur when a business owner becomes seriously disabled.

9. Name three uses of disability insurance for business purposes.

10. Name four issues that must be resolved in drafting a disability buyout agreement.

11. Name four sources of funding a disability buyout agreement.

12. Explain how a business overhead policy works.

13. Explain the tax treatment of premiums paid and benefits received for a business overhead policy.

14. What is the primary goal of the closing interview, and what is the ultimate goal of the closing interview?

15. Name three buying signals.

16. What is an open-ended question? Give an example.

17. What is a trial close? Write three questions that are examples of a trial close.

18. Briefly list three categories of closes.
    The following questions pertain to the case study.

19. What was the agent's approach, or the reason for seeing her to get the appointment?

20. What happened in the initial interview?

21. What happened in the second interview?

22. Who is the Reluctant Brother?

23. What is a Business Stabilization Plan?

Self-Test Questions

Instructions: Read chapter six first, then answer the following questions to test your knowledge. There are 10 questions. Circle the correct answer, then check your answers with the answer key in the back of the book.

24. Using the straight capitalization method to determine the value of a business, how much capital is required to produce $10,000 a year at a capitalization rate of 15 percent?

    (A) $150,000
    (B) $ 66,667
    (C) $ 15,000
    (D) $ 1,500

25.   Premiums paid for a disability buy-out policy are

      (A) fully deductible as a business expense
      (B) partially deductible as business expense
      (C) not tax deductible, but the benefits are received tax free
      (D) not tax deductible, and the benefits are taxable when they are received

26.   A business overhead expense policy

      (A) covers operating expenses when an owner is unable to work due to
           a disability
      (B) pays the owner a specified monthly benefit if disability occurs
      (C) includes coverage for the cost of inventory, capital expenses, and
           lost profits
      (D) covers the owners' salary during a period of disability

27.   The benefit that can be received from a business overhead policy is:

      (A) the actual amount of expenses incurred with a maximum monthly
           benefit specified in the policy
      (B) unlimited amount based on actual expenses incurred during a period
           of disability
      (C) the fixed monthly amount stated in the policy
      (D) subject to a monthly deductible as stated in the policy

28.   The straight capitalization method of valuing a closely held business

      (A) averages a company's balance sheet value over 5 years
      (B) divides a company's historical assets by current liabilities
      (C) divides a company's earnings by a reasonable rate of return
      (D) averages a company's publicly listed stock value over 2 years

29.   Section 303 of the Internal Revenue Code pertains to

      (A) stock redemptions to pay estate tax and other final expenses
      (B) cross-purchase plans at death
      (C) gift taxes on the transferred property at death
      (D) the estate's ability, if qualified, to extend the payment of estate taxes
           for a period of years

30.   The proceeds of a Section 303 Stock redemption are generally

      (A) not taxable
      (B) taxable as a capital gain
      (C) taxable as ordinary income
      (D) considered a dividend distribution for tax purposes

31. The valuation method that is often the easiest to compute and determines owner's equity by subtracting liabilities from assets is called the:

    (A) sales method
    (B) book value method
    (C) straight capitalization method
    (D) comparative price/earnings method

32. Which of the following statements regarding the valuation of a business for estate tax purposes is correct?

    I. A buy-sell agreement specifying a selling price established in an arm's length transaction will establish an estate tax value that likely will be acceptable to the Internal Revenue Service
    II. A buy-sell agreement with a lifetime first-offer provision is one of the factors that is likely to establish an estate tax value acceptable to the Internal Revenue Service.

    (A) I only
    (B) II only
    (C) Both I and II
    (D) Neither I nor II

READ THE FOLLOWING DIRECTIONS BEFORE CONTINUING

The questions below differ from the preceding questions in that they all contain the word EXCEPT. So you understand fully the basis used in selecting each answer, be sure to read each question carefully.

33. All of the following statements regarding disability buy-out agreements are correct EXCEPT

    (A) To avoid potential legal disputes, the buy-sell agreement should define disability in the same manner as does the disability policy used to fund the agreement.
    (B) Most disability buyouts provide for a waiting period of a year or two.
    (C) A partnership is automatically dissolved if a partner becomes disabled.
    (D) A disabled corporate owner has no inherent or legal right to receive a salary.

Learning Objectives

An understanding of the material in this chapter should enable the student to

1. Define and give examples of a key person.

2. List and explain problems resulting from the death or disability of a key person.

3. List the benefits of key person insurance.

4. Describe the procedure for estimating the value of a key person.

5. Describe the tax status of key person life insurance regarding premiums, proceeds, and cash value.

This chapter focuses on key person insurance. The loss of a key person can be devastating to a business, especially a smaller one. This chapter discusses the need for key person life insurance, the problems created by the death or disability of a key person, and how to identify and place an economic value on that person or persons. The chapter ends with a review of the tax characteristics, prospecting and sales ideas relating to key person coverage.

KEY PERSON LIFE INSURANCE

key person life insurance

Key person life insurance is one of the two most popular business insurance sales concepts, the other using life insurance to fund a buy-sell agreement. This chapter takes a detailed look at key person life insurance, an important component in business insurance planning.

What Is Key Person Insurance?

Good business planning dictates the need to provide adequate insurance to protect against loss of tangible assets such as buildings, inventory, and equipment.

Good business planning should also recognize the need to insure the intangible assets most important to the success of the business: its key people. Key people are those who contribute substantially to the profitability of the business. They may or may not be owners of the business.

Key person insurance is used to indemnify the business should one of the key people die or become disabled. Insurance can reimburse the business for economic losses it will suffer because of the loss of a profit maker. Every successful business has at least one man or woman who is a key person—a profit maker. Many businesses have more than one. Key person life insurance is owned by a business and can be used for many business purposes.

Key person coverage is life or disability insurance on the life of a key man or woman—typically an owner of the business—intended to offset some or all of the estimated financial loss which would result from that person's death or disability. The business is the applicant for the insurance, pays the premiums, and is both the owner and the beneficiary.

Key Person Defined

A key person is any person who contributes substantially to the financial well being of a business, or whose premature death or disability would result in economic loss to the business.

For example, Harry Dickson, the president of Clark and Brown, Inc., has made the company a strong profit maker, established its A-1 credit rating, and currently directs its research and expansion programs. Although the company made little or no profit prior to Harry's appointment, it is projecting profits of $650,000 in the current year. The profits are largely attributable to Harry's management and product skills. Clark and Brown, Inc. purchased a $650,000 policy on Harry's life. In the event of his death, the life insurance company will pay $650,000 to Clark and Brown, Inc.

Key person insurance most often insures the owners of a business. It is frequently an add-on sale to a buy-sell sale. After the owners agree that an insured buy-sell agreement is needed, you make a transition to the key person need by asking them, "Will the death of one of you affect the company's profits?" The cash values of the key person policy may be used at retirement as supplemental retirement income for the insured. This double-duty usefulness is a persuasive concept. A major reason for buying key person insurance is for debt protection. It provides a financial buffer by paying off current debts.

The Universal Need for Key Person Insurance

The need for life insurance on key people is not limited to any one type of business organization or to any certain kind of business enterprise. The need is all-inclusive. Modest sole proprietorships, partnerships, and corporations have needs for key person insurance just as much as do the largest organizations.

The need exists in every type of business and industry. Businesses need cash at the death of a key person to offset lost income and lost profits, to pay off indebtedness, and to hire and train a replacement person. It is difficult or impossible for most small businesses to come up with large amounts of quick cash when a key person has died. If the financial advisor calls now, when everyone is alive, tax-favored money can be assured through the "commonplace miracle" of life insurance.

Key Person Case Examples

The owner of a small but successful midwestern company that publishes genealogical books and supplies has an employee who has risen quickly to the position of sales manager. The manager's enthusiasm, creative sales training procedures, and ideas for new product lines inspired a company expansion program that was financed through a bank loan of $250,000. A financial advisor persuaded the business owner that insuring the manager's life would be financially prudent. The insurance would help to protect the business against the loss of profits that would almost certainly result from the death of this key person. The owner's initial purchase was a $250,000 death benefit under a permanent life insurance plan. Within two years, the coverage was increased to $1,000,000.

Another case involved a middle-aged attorney who left private practice to join a rapidly expanding research corporation. It was soon obvious that the attorney's talents included finance and management as well as law. She was named a vice president. After 2 years she had increased profitability to such an extent that the corporation insured her for $500,000, to replace lost profits in the event of her death.

Three brothers own a western farm equipment business as equal stockholders. This corporation is growing by leaps and bounds, due primarily to the selling talents of one of the brothers. He knows the company's farm equipment and machinery thoroughly, and he knows the needs of the western farmers who are the company's customers. This company came to the attention of a financial advisor who had never before written a business life insurance case. He sold the brothers on the prudence of buying $200,000 of insurance on the key brother. Within 3 months, he also installed a buy-sell plan for $1,000,000.

Growing Acceptance of Key Person Insurance

More and more each year, business owners are being convinced of the value of insuring key persons. At the end of World War II, comparatively few of the large corporations in the United States owned substantial amounts of cash value life insurance. Today there are probably well over 1000 large companies listing $300,000 or more of life insurance cash values on their balance sheets.

Many companies show lesser amounts, and undoubtedly many more unintentionally obscure their key person life insurance by listing cash values among unidentified "miscellaneous assets."

Reasons for Growth

The most important reasons for this growing momentum in the field of key person life insurance include the following:

- Businesses are experiencing an increasing awareness of the profit-making value of key men and women.
- Financial advisors are fast becoming aware of the immeasurable potential of this market.
- Competition for experienced and capable key men and women for responsible executive positions has made business owners keenly aware of the financial value of the human asset.
- Businessmen and businesswomen are more net-worth conscious than ever before. They are interested in anything that has real profit potential.
    - For example, business owners appreciate the fact that a small part of earnings, when diverted into cash value life insurance premiums, provides a very substantial increase in surplus (retained earnings) through proceeds payable upon the death of a key person.

- Depending on the company's after-tax profits on sales, this amount could very well be equivalent to sales of as much as 50 times the proceeds. For example, $100,000 of life insurance proceeds would be equal to the net profit on sales of $5,000,000 if the company averages 2 percent net profit on sales.

• Business owners can be shown that permanent life insurance is an excellent way of increasing cash reserves for future emergency and collateral needs, usually without conflicting with the federal tax rules on excessive accumulation of retained earnings, discussed elsewhere in the text.

• The low cost of key person life insurance can be demonstrated to business owners. If the person dies, proceeds always exceed the premiums paid on the policy. If the person lives, the cash values often catch up with or exceed total premiums paid over time.

• Financial advisors are discovering that key person life insurance is a good approach to business owners. The key person approach often opens the door to other sales such as deferred compensation, group life and health programs, buy-sell plans, and pensions. Just as often, key person insurance leads to personal insurance on the owners, key persons, members of their families, friends, suppliers, and customers.

Identifying Key People

Every successful business has at least one person whose talent, knowledge, ability, experience, and leadership is responsible for the continued success and growth of the business. Therefore, every business is a potential prospect.

Owners

When you think of key people, think first and foremost of the owners of the business who are active in managing it. They are almost always key people. After all, it was their skill, talent, knowledge, and expertise that made the company a success. More often than not, key person insurance is on the lives of the owner(s) (as contrasted with persons who are not owners).

Professional Groups
When thinking of business insurance markets, don't limit your thinking to just mercantile and manufacturing businesses. Consider also professionals. The following professional groups are excellent prospects for business life insurance:

- Physicians
- Chiropodists
- Therapists
- Management Consultants
- Physicists
- Chemists
- Actuaries
- Pharmacists
- Advertising agencies

- Survey agencies
- Dentists
- Lawyers
- Engineers
- Architects
- General insurance agencies
- Technicians
- Urban renewal specialists
- Highway safety designers

Others

However, key person insurance is not limited to the owners. A key person is any person whose death or disability could mean a serious credit situation, a loss in sales, an increase in costs, or any one of a number of events that could result in substantial financial loss, insolvency, or business failure.

A key person doesn't necessarily have to have an executive title or be in a management position. One example of this occurred as an advisor was conducting a fact-finding interview with the owner of a mail-order business. The firm employed only a few dozen people, but it did a tremendous volume of business.

When the advisor requested copies of the firm's financial statements, the business owner said, "I'll need to ask my assistant to get those for you. I don't know where they are kept."

Asking what other kinds of functions the assistant performed, the advisor learned that this individual coordinated all of the mail orders, did all of the bookkeeping, and handled the publishing and distribution of the firm's catalogues. The business owner said, "I don't know what I'd do without her!"

The advisor helped the business owner realize the value of the assistant and see that the assistant's death or disability would be a financial and operational shock to the business. The business owner eventually purchased life and disability income insurance on the assistant's life, with the business as beneficiary of the policies.

Business Failures

Several studies substantiate the assertion that businesses fail largely because of human shortcomings. Dun and Bradstreet, for example, has conducted several studies of business failure, including the accompanying survey of over 12,000 business failures.

None of these businesses had simply closed their doors. On the contrary, they had ceased as a result of bankruptcy or due to court-ordered receivership or forced reorganization. Some had voluntarily left the marketplace, leaving unpaid creditors, while some had settled with creditors out of court.

The study revealed the following causes for business failures:

- 44% failed because of incompetence
- 16% failed because of unbalanced experience
- 17% failed because of lack of managerial experience
- 15% failed because of lack of experience in a particular line
- 1% failed because of neglect
- 1% failed because of fraud
- 1% failed because of a disaster such as fire, flood, or burglary
- 6% failed for unknown reasons

Of the over 12,000 failures in this analysis, all but 7 percent were caused by factors involving the human element. In other words, 93 percent of the failures were due to known incompetence, inexperience, or human frailties.

It seems logical to assume, then, that if business failures are due primarily to poor management, then business successes are due to competent management. The finest business in the world will produce profits only if there are competent people to manage it. In other words, the real source of business profits is not capital or physical assets, but key people with the skill, experience, and good judgment to manage the business successfully.

The significance of these statistics is not so much in the fact that human shortcomings caused business failure. Rather, it is that human expertise is responsible for business success. Every successful business has one or more people who are responsible for the company's success. One of your jobs is helping your business-owner prospects become more aware of the organization's key people and their financial value to the firm.

Questions to Ask

Ask questions such as the following to pinpoint key people in the firm:

- *Whose death or disability would create a void that could not be filled from current personnel?*
- *Whose death or disability would upset the normal operations of the business?*
- *Whose death or disability would impair the firm's credit standing?*
- *Whose death or disability would upset the financial control and management of the company?*
- *Whose death or disability would mean a loss of customers?*
- *Whose death or disability would mean loss of a specialized skill?*
- *Whose death or disability would halt or delay a sales campaign, or an expansion program, or some other type of special project?*
- *Whose leaving to go to a competitor would hurt you?*

The next step is to focus on the most important need for insurance on a key person and discuss that person's value.

PROBLEMS CREATED BY DEATH

Just as the loss of a key piece of machinery can cause serious financial consequences to a business, so too can the loss of a key person. When a key person dies, several problems are likely to occur. Unless the business is in a strong financial condition, it may not be able to survive these problems.

Disruption of Management

The key person was responsible for a certain phase of company operations—an expert in his or her particular duties. Now, suddenly, someone else must step into these management shoes.

Usually, this is a slow and costly transaction. It could be particularly severe if death occurs during a major expansion program, or during an economic recession, or during any one of many other conditions which require the special attention of the particular key person.

A few years ago, the president of a major corporation stated that the business had lost a million dollars when a vice president died. He said, "Our corporation has spent at least $2 million in research experiments in this vice president's department, under his direction and control. He was the only person who fully understood the details and knew how to maximize the profit potential of the research. So, when he died, we lost a lot. I'd say we lost half of our anticipated $5 million profit. In another sense, we also lost half of our $2 million cash investment."

Impairment of Credit

A business whose credit is largely dependent on the ability and reputation of one person would have serious financial problems at the death or disability of that individual. Creditors will question whether the business can continue to meet its debts. As a result, they may press for payment and adopt a wait-and-see attitude about further credit. The lifeblood of the business may be shut off just when it is needed most.

Loss of Profits

When a key person dies, profits will be adversely affected, either because income decreases, expenses increase, or both. How much depends on the circumstances of the particular case.

Specific drains on profits following the death of a key person might result from the loss of that person's special abilities and reputation, the loss of customers "controlled" by that person, and the cost of hiring and training a replacement.

In many cases, the death of a key person results in the loss of valuable customers and clients. They may drift away because of the uncertainty or confusion that has been created by the adjustments that inevitably follow a death, or they may be enticed away by aggressive competitors.

Replacement of the Key Person

Most key people have spent a lot of time and effort in acquiring the knowledge, experience, judgment, and reputation that have made them valuable persons.

Many businesses are so small that there is no understudy at all for the deceased person. Where there is such an understudy, the understudy will be months getting up to speed. In addition, the understudy's duties must continue to be performed, and that position must also be filled.

Often it is necessary to go outside the company to find a replacement. This means incurring new costs such as advertising expenses, higher salary, and training costs. In addition, the company must absorb the costs of the mistakes that this person will inevitably make. Hiring an outside replacement also results in delay, disruption, and loss of efficiency.

Loss of Confidence

The death of a key person can cause loss of confidence in the firm by persons, customers, and suppliers. The firm's remaining persons may become concerned about the continuance of the business. As a result, some may leave for new jobs with competitors or may even start their own businesses, possibly taking customers with them. For persons who remain with the business, their morale and loyalty may be weakened if it looks like the business may fail. This can mean decreased productivity.

Customers who worry about the ability of the business to continue providing its products are also likely to look elsewhere to satisfy their needs. Suppliers will be concerned about the ability of the business to pay its debts.

LIFE INSURANCE SALES CONCEPTS

After having discussed the financial losses which are likely to arise at the death of a key person and obtaining the owner's agreement, you will want to show that life insurance is unequaled in protecting against these losses.

The following concepts can help you demonstrate the unique value of life insurance in meeting the business needs that arise at a key person's death. In general, they contrast life insurance with other possible methods (borrowing, sinking fund, using profits) of providing cash to meet the problems that follow death.

Double-Duty Dollars

Instead of draining a firm's working capital, life insurance delivers additional new working capital precisely when it is urgently needed. In addition, it generally arrives as tax-free income. Unlike a regular sinking fund, life insurance delivers the exact amount promised—regardless of when the key person dies.

Life insurance has "living benefits," too. It strengthens a company's credit standing, provides retirement funding, and serves as a source of emergency dollars through its loan provisions. Thus, the premiums paid for key person life insurance are really "double-duty" dollars. In addition, you might call it "key person extra expense coverage." It provides money to cover the added expenses that come about when a key person dies.

"Interest" Only

Key person life insurance allows a business to create an indemnity fund by making annual deposits that are a small fraction of the policy's face amount.

For example, the annual premium for $100,000 of permanent insurance for a 30-year-old key person may be about $1,000—approximately one percent of the face amount. At age 40, the premium for the same amount of insurance is roughly $1,900. This is 1.9 percent of the face amount. At age 50, the premium of approximately $3,000 is 3 percent of the face amount.

Continuing this analogy further, it can be said that the business pays an annual amount equivalent to only interest on the face amount, while the insurance company pays the "principal" at the key person's death. Contrast this with borrowing cash at the death of a key person. If the business borrows the $100,000 from a bank, it must repay this sum and pay interest of perhaps 10 percent, or more. Isn't it better to pay one to 3 percent per year for an asset than 10 percent annually on a liability that needs to be repaid?

Discounted Dollars

Closely allied to the "interest only" concept is the idea that key person life insurance allows a business to buy an indemnity fund at discounts as high as 97 or 98 percent.

For example, consider a $100,000 policy on the life of a 30-year-old key person. If this person dies within the policy's first year, the $1,000 premium will have bought $100,000—a discount of 99 percent. If the person dies in the policy's twentieth year, the business will receive $100,000 for a total premium payment of $20,000. This represents an 80 percent discount (ignoring the time value of money). The same $1,000 per year invested at 6 percent after tax would be worth only $39,993 after 20 years.

Capital Transfer

The capital transfer concept demonstrates a viewpoint about life insurance premiums. It says, in essence, that a business does not really spend money when it purchases key person life insurance. Instead it transfers money from one pocket to another.

For example, suppose you are recommending a key person life insurance policy with a $5,870 premium. The accompanying table (Figure 7–1 Capital Transfer: From One Pocket to Another) depicts the balance sheet transactions that would result.

As you can see, the $5,870 premium reduces the cash account of the business. This reduction is offset, in varying degrees in varying years, by increases in the cash surrender value of the policy. Indeed, this is the accounting procedure specified by the American Institute of Certified Public Accountants.

Table 7-1 Flow Chart Diagram of Key Person Life Insurance

Annual Premium $5,870

Capital Transfer: From One Pocket to Another

	Assets				Liabilities	Owner's Equity
	A	B	C	D	E	F
	Ongoing Cash Flow (Cumulative Premium)	Annual Increase In Cash Value	Cumulative Value (Cumulative Column B Cash Value)		Retained Earnings. Annual Change (Column B minus $5,870)	Retained Earnings Cumulative (Column E Cumulative)
Year 1	$ 5,870	$ 2,527	$ 2,527		$(3,343)	$(3,343)
2	11,740	6,099	8,626		229	(3,114)
3	17,610	6,837	15,463	NO	967	(2,147)
4	23,480	7,391	22,854		1,521	(626)
5	29,350	8,002	30,856	C	2,132	1,506
6	35,220	8,659	39,515	H	2,789	4,295
7	41,090	9,395	48,910	A	3,525	7,820
8	46,960	10,201	59,111	N	4,331	12,151
9	52,830	11,086	70,197	G	5,216	17,367
10	58,700	12,052	82,249	E	6,182	23,549

The cash value of the insurance is carried on the asset side of the balance sheet as an "other asset." Thus, the annual increase in the policy's cash surrender value increases the other asset account.

After a couple of years, there is little net cost for the insurance because the decrease in the cash asset is offset by the increase in the other asset account. After a few years, there is a positive annual impact on net worth. That is, cash value increases more than the premium paid.

When the key person dies, the proceeds of the policy will be paid to the business income tax free. Both the cash account and net worth will be increased by an amount equal to the difference between the proceeds received and the amount already credited to the *other asset* account (the cash value of the policy).

PROBLEMS CREATED BY DISABILITY

Many of the same problems that result from the death of a key person also occur with disability. In fact, it may be a double problem because, with disability, the firm may be in a position of paying both the disabled person and a replacement. The absence of the disabled owner or key person often means that important business functions are likely to go undone, sales can fall, cash flow can drop, and profits can dwindle. As these problems grow, pressure for a formal resolution of the situation mounts. A desire to find a temporary substitute, or even replace the disabled person, becomes increasingly evident.

If the potential length of the disability is unknown, there can be considerable hesitancy to hire a replacement at all, leaving business plans in limbo. If there is any hope that the disabled key person will return to work, the company may delay taking action even longer. The injured or seriously ill owner or person may express a strong desire to ultimately return to the business. Whether realistic or not, hope of recovery makes a disabled person hesitant to admit that the disability could go on for many years or that it could be permanent.

The longer the disability continues, the worse the situation can become. Relationships can start to deteriorate, friendships can begin to fall apart, trust can disappear, and everyone involved is usually frustrated and discouraged, maybe even resentful.

Regardless of the type of business organization, a prolonged disability that strikes a business owner or key person can threaten the very existence of the firm. Disabled sole proprietors can soon find themselves totally out of business. Long-term serious disability can deal a crippling or fatal blow to partnerships and closely held corporations as well.

The Probability of Prolonged Disability

The probability that a business owner or other key executive will suffer a prolonged disability before retirement is greater than the probability of death during the same period.

The following table compares the odds of incurring a long-term disability with those of dying. Notice that even at age 62, the odds are still 2.1 times greater that a disability will occur than a death!

Table 7-2 Death versus Disability Rate			
At Age	Persons Per 1,000 who Die at Age Indicated	Persons Per 1,000 Disabled 90 Days or More at the Age Indicated	Ratio of Disability (90 Days or More) Greater than Death
27	1.42	9.58	6.70
32	1.74	11.40	6.59
37	2.46	14.37	5.84
42	3.73	15.88	4.26
47	5.80	19.78	3.41
52	8.86	24.19	2.73
57	13.60	31.98	2.35
62	20.18	42.78	2.10
Source: Commissioners Disability Table			

You can use this table to show the importance of disability income protection. Here are two approaches:

- *"Business owner, if you had an illness, injury, or a rare disease, would you have an income? Where would it come from? How much would it be?"*

  (Wait for responses from the prospect.)

"A lot of people do not realize that the odds are pretty high when it comes to becoming disabled. For example, here is a comparison with the chances of dying in any given year..."

- *"Do you own disability income insurance?"*

  (If your prospect says no, show this table and continue.)

  "If you are like most business owners, you are protecting your business and your family against the financial consequences of your death—which is wise—but you are not protecting them against a peril that has an even higher probability of occurring during your working years. Have you seen any statistics that compare the likelihood of death against the likelihood of disability? Let me show you. What is your age?"

Multiple Owners

As the number of owners in a business increases, so too do the odds of at least one long-term disability. This is a serious matter with potential major consequences for the owners.

Bad Odds

The following table highlights the odds that disability will strike a company with multiple owners.

Table 7-3 Probability of at Least One Long-Term Disability* Prior to Age 65						
	Number of Owners					
Age	1	2	3	4	5	6
25	53.7%	78.6%	90.1%	95.4%	97.9%	99.0%
30	52.2	77.1	89.1	94.8	97.5	98.8
35	50.3	75.3	87.7	93.9	97.0	98.5
40	47.7	72.7	85.7	92.5	96.1	98.0
45	44.3	69.0	82.7	90.4	94.6	97.0
50	39.4	63.2	77.7	86.5	91.8	95.0
55	32.1	53.8	68.6	78.7	85.5	90.2

*Disability lasting at least 90 days

Source: Commissioners Disability Table

A sole business owner aged 40 has over a 47 percent probability of incurring a prolonged disability before retirement at age 65. In a two-owner business where both owners are aged 40, the odds that one of the owners will have a disability lasting at least 90 days exceed 72 percent. When three owners are all aged 40, the odds of prolonged disability rise to over 85 percent!

Remember that many small- and medium-sized businesses have just one, two, or three owners or key people. The success of these businesses usually depends on those people. The loss of just one as a result of a serious accident or illness can mean serious financial consequences for the firm. Use Table 7–3 to demonstrate your point that disability is not a remote peril and that disability insurance is no more a "luxury" than is fire or life insurance. It is a solution to a real and serious risk that can threaten the existence of the business.

TAXATION OF KEY PERSON INSURANCE

Life Insurance Taxation

Following is a summary of the tax aspects of key person life insurance.

- *Proceeds Are Income Tax Free*—As a general rule, the entire lump sum payable at the insured's death is exempt from federal income taxation. However, C corporations with 3-year average annual gross receipts in excess of $7.5 million are subject to the alternative minimum tax (AMT). (For corporations in existence less than 3 years, the initial qualification for exemption from the AMT involves having average annual gross receipts of no more than $5 million, with the respective number of years the corporation was in existence to be substituted for the 3 years.) This would mean paying 15 percent tax on the amount by which death proceeds exceed the premiums paid on the policy. AMT does not apply to S corporations. The AMT is explained in more detail in Chapter Four.

- *Premiums Are Not Reportable Income to the Key Person*—When a key person insurance policy is purchased with the business as owner and beneficiary, the premiums are not taxable income to the insured. No economic benefit is deemed to have accrued to the key person—even if he or she is the controlling shareholder in a corporation.

- *Inside Buildup Tax Free*—The cash value buildup in a key person life insurance policy is generally not subject to current federal income tax. However, corporations subject to the AMT may find that any excess of cash value over the premiums paid is reportable.

- The business would have reportable taxable income if a key person life insurance policy is surrendered for cash exceeding the aggregate net premiums paid. Only the excess is reportable.

- A number of court rulings have determined that key person insurance by a corporation serves a legitimate corporate purpose. Therefore, accumulations arising from such insurance are not subject to the penalty tax on excess accumulated earnings.

- *Premiums*—For federal income tax purposes, a business cannot deduct the premiums it pays on key person life insurance. This follows the general rule that a business is not allowed to deduct premiums paid for insurance if the business itself owns the policy or is either directly or indirectly a beneficiary under the policy. In the case of key person insurance, the business not only owns the policy but is the beneficiary as well.

- In a properly arranged key person insurance policy, death proceeds are not taxable in the insured's estate for federal estate tax purposes. This assumes that the business-not the individual insured—held all incidents of ownership. However, if the insured is an owner of the business, the policy proceeds will be reflected in establishing the estate tax value of the insured's business interest.

Disability Insurance Taxation

Disability insurance for a key person involves two types of coverage: to replace the key employee's income during a period of disability, and to indemnify the business for the loss of the key employee's services due to disability.

Salary Continuation

Income tax law says a plan is necessary to gain favorable tax treatment for continuation of salary during a disability. If the payments to the person are to be tax deductible, the plan must be established according to IRC Section 105 as a salary continuation plan before the disability begins. Under such a plan, the payments made to the key person are considered wages and are fully deductible as a business expense under Section 162 of the IRC. Without such a plan, payments are not allowed as a business expense and are therefore not deductible. This, of course, would make such payments very expensive. For C corporation owners who are key persons, any salary payments without a formal salary continuation plan could be considered dividends and be subject to double taxation, once at the corporate level and again at the individual level.

Sole proprietors or partners and owners of S corporations are not permitted to take a tax deduction for any premiums paid for disability income insurance on themselves. However, premiums paid for disability insurance are tax deductible by these organizations for disability insurance on persons who are not owners. The persons are not required to treat these premium payments as taxable income, but benefits are taxable when received.

The business that wants to establish a plan to continue the salary of a disabled key person will find no more economical or certain way of funding that obligation than through disability income insurance.

By insuring the firm's wage continuation plan, money for salary comes from the insurance policy rather than from the firm's regular income. This frees up the firm's money for such purposes as hiring and paying a replacement.

If it is not needed for hiring a replacement, it will be much needed for other business purposes because there is always a readjustment and settling-in period following disability of a key person where reduced profits or no profit is anticipated.

Key Person Disability Insurance

Since key person insurance is owned and paid for by the business, and any benefit payments would be received by the business itself, the premiums are not tax deductible. This follows a general principle that you cannot get a tax benefit for insurance at each end of the process. Therefore the benefits paid would be income tax free to the business.

Summary of Federal Income Taxation of Key Person Life Insurance

Key Person Insurance

Key person insurance is life insurance that is bought, paid for, and owned by a business on one of its key persons. The business itself is the beneficiary of the policy.

Premiums—The premiums paid by a business for key person life insurance are not income tax deductible. This is true for all kinds of businesses. It is true no matter who the key person is. It does not matter whether or not the key person is one of the owners.

Proceeds—In general, proceeds of a key person life insurance policy paid to the business at the insured's death are free from federal income taxation. There are two main exceptions to this general rule. One happens when a C corporation is subject to the corporate alternative minimum tax, in which case it may have to pay some tax on the gain in the policy at the insured's death. Another exception happens when there has been a "transfer for value," in which case part of the death proceeds may be subject to federal income tax. These exceptions will be covered later in this course.

Cash Value—In general, the cash values of a key person life insurance policy accumulate free from federal income taxation. One exception to this happens if the insurance is owned by a C corporation that is subject to the corporate alternative minimum tax, in which case it may have to pay some tax on the gain in the policy. This exception will be discussed later in this course. The corporate alternative minimum tax does not apply to partnerships, sole proprietorships, or S corporations.

If the key person policy is a modified endowment contract (MEC), the same rules apply as with personal uses of life insurance. That is, policy loans or withdrawals will be taxable to the extent of any gain in the policy, on an income-first basis. This means that a distribution from a MEC in a gain situation will be subject to current income taxation.

SOLUTIONS FOR THE LOSS OF A KEY PERSON

The ideal solution to the problems created by the death or disability of a key person would be immediate replacement with a person of equal qualifications. This solution is rarely possible, even in large companies with well-established systems of understudies. Death and disability usually are unexpected and always come at the "wrong time," before the replacement is ready to assume full responsibilities.

In small and medium-sized businesses, training and maintaining a second line of management in anticipation of the death or disability of a key person usually is financially impossible. Without understudies, the consequences of losing a key person are quick and often financially disastrous. The real solution to the problem, then, is cash—sufficient cash to indemnify the business for its financial loss and to keep the business solvent until it recovers from the inevitable shock of losing one of its most valuable assets.

Four Sources of Cash

There are four possible sources that can be used to provide the cash needed to offset the financial loss arising from the death or disability of a key person:

- Current profits

- Borrowing
- Uninsured sinking funds
- Life and disability insurance (insured sinking funds)

Using Current Profits

While it's possible that a large financial loss may be absorbed by business profits in the year of death or disability, this is not a dependable or prudent plan. The entire business is on the line.

Would an owner drop the fire insurance because profits might be able to absorb the loss? Hardly. It is prudent, sensible, and wise for a business to insure its most valuable assets.

Borrowing

A business can borrow money to offset the financial problems caused by a key owner's death. However, this isn't usually practical for the bank or the business.

The business has just lost a key profit maker, so it's not too good a time to incur new debt. The bank knows this too and isn't as likely to make the loan until the business shows strong signs of being financially stable following the key person's death.

Even without these concerns, borrowing isn't normally the most desirable alternative, primarily because it's an expensive solution. In addition, it lacks the certainty of the insurance solution and the debt-free aspects of any sinking fund—whether insured or not.

Using a Sinking Fund

Anticipated financial losses may be funded using a sinking fund. For example, the business might set aside a certain amount from profits each year over a period of years during the life expectancy of the key person. This plan has one serious and obvious weakness. Death or disability might strike soon and the money will be needed before there is enough time to accumulate it. There is no assurance that the key person will live even to the end of the first year of such a plan. In addition, why use 100-cent dollars? Why not use discounted dollars?

Using Life Insurance, an Insured Sinking Fund

The anticipated losses may be offset by the proceeds of key person life insurance funded by premiums paid during the key person's lifetime. This is the surest, most economical, and most practical method of all. It is the only plan that automatically provides cash at the very time it is most needed, no matter when death may occur.

Key Executives
"Business owner, all the machinery in your plant is heavily insured because production depends on your machines. Is your business as well insured against human failure as it is against machine failure?"

THE BENEFITS OF KEY PERSON LIFE INSURANCE

Key person insurance provides many valuable benefits to the business that insures its key men and women.

Provides Indemnification

Key person life insurance provides cash to indemnify the business for the financial loss caused by the death of an person.

Provides a Lifetime Reserve Fund

Key person insurance can provide a constantly increasing cash reserve fund. The policy's cash value is an asset of the business. This fund is a ready source of cash for business opportunities or to use as working capital when ordinary lines of credit are stretched to the limit. It is a stable emergency fund, available regardless of the firm's credit standing and at favorable interest rates.

In times of economic stress, banks tighten up their loan requirements and increase interest rates, but an insurance contract provides an immediate source of cash whether the times are good or bad.

Many businesses and business owners have weathered financial storms by borrowing on their insurance when banks would not extend credit. The life insurance reserve fund is free from care and reinvestment worries. In current life insurance contracts, the cash values are accumulating at competitive money market rates of return. This reserve fund is generally not subject to the surtax on unreasonable accumulation of earnings imposed on by Section 531 of the Internal Revenue Code.

Strengthens Credit

The very existence of key person life insurance is an indirect reinforcement of the general credit position of a business. The fact that the business had the foresight to insure against the hazard of the financial loss of a key person reassures bankers and other creditors as to the character and stability of the business. Banks are more inclined to extend credit when they feel that their loan is on more solid ground. Key person life insurance can also be used as collateral for a bank loan if it is cash value insurance.

Increases Net Working Capital

At the death of the key person, thanks to the miracle of life insurance, there will be a much-needed infusion of cash into the business. More specifically, in accounting terms, the firm's net working capital will be increased. As you recall, net working capital is the excess of current assets over current liabilities.

Other Potential Uses

The cash values of key person life insurance may provide or supplement a retirement income plan for the key person if he or she lives to a certain designated retirement age. Another use of the proceeds of key person life insurance is to finance the continuance of a portion of the deceased key person's salary to the spouse for a reasonable period of years. Naturally, this means purchasing a larger policy at the outset, or diverting the proceeds from their intended use.

VALUATION OF KEY PEOPLE

How much is a key person worth to a business? The estimate of a key person's monetary value to a company is arbitrary to a large extent, although based on tangible, profit-producing factors. As far as possible, the human asset should be valued as any other business asset is valued: on the basis of the income it produces.

Before discussing how to approximate a key person's key value, look at this from a sales perspective. You want to get your prospect thinking about the financial loss resulting from death of a key person. Try to arrive at a specific dollar amount so that your prospect will be aware of the severity of the financial impact of death and can have a dollar amount to insure.

You will be asking the prospect questions such as:

- How much of a financial loss do you think you would suffer if Key Person had died last night? What are the best- and worst-case scenarios?
- What is your ballpark estimate of Key Person's value to the business?
- How much cash would you want coming in to replace Key Person for a year or so?

contribution to earnings

replacement cost

Along with this line of questioning, you should be familiar with the following two methods of approximating a key person's value:

- contribution to earnings
- replacement cost

Contribution to Earnings

One method of determining the value of a key person is the *contribution to earnings* method. Estimating a key person's contributions to the net profits of a company depends in part on the type of position held by the person. If the person is in a marketing job, sales records can help provide a basis for the estimate. If the individual is an executive with varied duties, it will be more difficult to set an accurate and objective value. Most key person insurance is on owners themselves, so they will be setting values on themselves.

opportunity cost

One method used to calculate a key person's contributions to earnings is shown in the following table. The steps are:

1. Determine the firm's average net profits before taxes as shown on its income statements for the last 5 years.
2. Estimate the proportion of profits attributable to invested capital. This can be done by taking the average net worth shown in the balance sheets of the previous 5 years and calculating the income that it would have produced if it were invested elsewhere at a reasonable rate of interest (*opportunity costs*).
3. Deduct the interest produced by the net worth (Step 2) from the average annual profits (Step 1). The result represents the earnings attributable to management.

4. Multiply Step 3 by the estimated percentage contribution to the success of the business made by the key person.

5. Multiply the result of the calculation in Step 4 by the number of years required to fully train a replacement for the deceased key person.

Funding Methods to Offset the Financial Losses That Occur at the Death of a Key Person (Cost of Each Dollar)			
Number of Years to Key Person's Death	If You Borrow the Money (10% Interest)[a]	If You Pay Cash[b]	If You use Life Insurance (Approximations)
1	$1.10	1.00	3 cents
2	1.10	1.00	6
3	1.10	1.00	9
4	1.10	1.00	12
5	1.10	1.00	15
10	1.10	1.00	30
15	1.10	1.00	45
20	1.10	1.00	60

Taking this 'cost of each dollar' one step further, talk with your prospect about how much this hypothetical person had to earn, before income taxes, to net this $1.10, or $1, or 3¢ per year. If we assume a 33% income tax, the person who decides to borrow money at the key person's death has to earn $1.55 to net $1.10 after taxes. The person who pays cash must earn $1.50 to net $1 after taxes. The person who buys life insurance has to earn about 4½¢ a year to net 3¢ after taxes.

[a] Assumes the loan is repaid in one year. The amount would be greater with a longer repayment period. Interest rates will vary; 10 percent is used only as an example.

[b] This assumes the availability of cash when it is needed.

Here again, determining how much of the contribution-of-management should be allocated to a particular key person is up to your prospects. In general, it depends on answers to such questions as the following:

- *How much of a profit center is this key person compared to the other key people?*
- *Is the key person engaged in any unfinished business which would be impaired in the event of his or her death?*
- *Would the key person's death result in the loss of customers attracted to the firm by his or her personality and ability?*
- *How much of the key person's compensation is for judgment, experience, and talent?*
- *Would the key person's death impair the credit standing of the firm? To what extent?*

Valuation of Prospect "A" Using Contribution to Earnings Method	
Average net profit before taxes for last 5 years	$400,000
Less rate of return on average net worth for last 5 years (Assume 10% × $800,000)	−80,000
Equals annual earnings attributable to management	320,000
Times estimated contribution of Prospect A to success of business	× .50
	160,000
Times years needed to fully phase in replacement Prospect A	× 4
Total Valuation	$640,000

Replacement Cost

There is no set rule for determining the replacement cost for a key person. Some of the factors involved are the extent of lost profits to be replaced, time required to get earnings back to pre-death level, existence of an understudy, time required to hire and train a replacement, availability of individuals with similar qualifications, and salary considerations.

One method of calculating replacement cost is shown here. It is similar to the contribution to earnings method, but from a different perspective.

1. Estimate how much annual profit will be lost when the key person dies. Or, put differently, how much profit will have to be replaced as a result of the key person's death.
2. To this amount, add the annual cost to hire a replacement for the key person.
3. From this total, subtract the salary saved because the key person died.
4. Multiply this result by the number of years it will probably take for profits to return to what they were before the key person died.

The result is the monetary cost it will take over a number of years to replace the deceased key person.

Valuation of Key Person Smith	
Using the Replacement Cost Method	
Annual lost profit when Smith dies	$350,000
Plus annual cost to hire replacement	+100,000
Annual gross replacement cost	450,000
Less salary saved because of Smith's death	−150,000
Annual replacement cost	300,000
Times years for profit to return to normal	× 3
Total replacement cost over 3 years	$900,000

Administrative Considerations for Key Person Insurance

There are several administrative aspects to consider with the sale of key person insurance.

Authorization

If your prospect's business is a corporation, its board of directors should pass a resolution authorizing an officer to apply for key person life insurance. Generally, the firm's legal counsel is the one to draw up the resolution. No similar authorization is needed for sole proprietorships and partnerships.

The authorization is needed in a corporation primarily to document the action for tax purposes. In this case, the purpose is to help show that the cash value accumulation is for a reasonable and necessary business purpose, so that it will not be subject to the accumulated earnings tax.

The minutes of the directors' meeting and the facts stated in such minutes will vary from case to case, but a typical resolution might read as follows:

Resolution from Board of Directors
Whereas, Leslie R. Doe is now and has been for many years Vice President and Sales Manager of the corporation, and as a result of Leslie's experience, special abilities, and fine reputation the profits for the stockholders have been consistently well above the average for the industry; and
Whereas, the termination of the service of Leslie R. Doe by reason of death would result in the loss of Leslie's experience, special abilities, and profit-making ability to the corporation; and
Whereas, the corporation wishes to make secure its financial position in the event of the death of said Leslie R. Doe and to indemnify itself against losses to its earning power, which would result from said death;

Therefore, It is Hereby Resolved: That the President be authorized and directed to take such action and execute the necessary documents to secure a life insurance policy or policies from the Blank Life Insurance Company on the life of Leslie R. Doe in the total amount of $____, on the ____ plan, with the corporation to be the beneficiary and the exclusive owner of said policy or policies. The treasurer is hereby authorized and directed to pay all premiums on such policy or policies as they become due.

Further Resolved: That this resolution be shown in the corporate minutes as an official act of the board of directors.

Insurable Interest

insurable interest Legal decisions in the various states definitely indicate that a business has an *insurable interest* in the life of a key person whose death would mean a financial loss to the business. These decisions pertain to all businesses, whether they are organized as sole proprietorships, partnerships, or under a corporate form. In addition to the various court decisions supporting this view, a number of states have enacted specific statutes establishing the insurable interest of a corporation in the life of an officer or stockholder.

The authoritative legal encyclopedia *Corpus Juris Secundum* states the case as follows:

A corporation has an key person insurable interest in the life of its president, general manager, principal stockholder, or other person or officer where by reason of his ability, knowledge, skill and experience, the success of the business of the corporation is largely dependent upon his efforts, and the policy is taken out in good faith for the purpose of protecting the corporation against loss in the event of his death.

Good News
"Prospect, I have good news about the cost of life insurance. In recent years, the cost of insurance to protect your business against fire, theft, or liability has been escalating rapidly. Yet during that same period, the cost of life insurance has declined steadily as mortality has improved

This statement is equally applicable to other types of business organizations. It is a general rule that if an insurable interest exists at the time a life insurance policy is issued, the policy can remain valid as long as the premiums are paid, even beyond the termination of the person's services.

When a Key Person Leaves

When a key person leaves the employ of a business, the firm may take a paid-up policy or surrender it. In fact, the firm could continue to pay the premiums if it so desired, even if the insured is no longer an employee. The tax results won't change, even if the insured is no longer employed by the firm. If the insured dies, the proceeds are received by the firm free of federal income tax.

Sell Policy to Former Person

Alternatively, the business can transfer ownership of the policy to the former person. This usually means selling the policy at a price near to the cash surrender value.

If the insured does not pay for the policy, the cash values are reportable by the insured as ordinary income in the year of transfer, with a deduction of the same amount for the business.

To execute a proper transfer, the policy owner completes either an absolute assignment form or a transfer of ownership form provided by the life insurance company. If the business is a corporation, the transfer should be authorized by the board of directors.

Note that the death proceeds will be exempt from federal income taxes if the transfer is made to the insured. A transfer to the insured is a specific exception to the general rule (transfer for value) that death proceeds are partly subject to federal income tax when a policy is transferred for valuable consideration.

Transferring the policy is often a practical solution for the insured as well as for the employer. The insured probably pays less for the policy than the total premiums paid by the company to date and pays premiums at rates of a younger age. It is a gesture of goodwill on the employer's part. A policy transfer is especially valuable if the insured is now substandard or uninsurable.

Rights of the Insured

The insured key person has no rights in the policy. Upon leaving the company, the key person usually cannot compel the business to transfer the policy. That choice rests entirely with the business itself. Most often, the insured key person is an owner-person of the business, so has some influence over such decisions.

Use of an Existing Policy

Under certain circumstances, a business can purchase an existing personally owned policy from the key person and then use it as key person insurance.

The tax-exempt status of the death proceeds will be retained if, at the time of transfer or purchase, the business is a partnership of which the key person is a partner or a corporation of which the key person is a stockholder or an officer.

However, the proceeds will be subject to tax under the transfer-for-value rule if the policy is purchased by a sole proprietorship in which the insured is not the sole proprietor, or by a partnership in which the insured is not a partner, or by a corporation in which the insured is not a shareholder or officer.

Type of Policy

The type of contract used will ultimately be decided by the business owners. They will want to consider such factors as how long the life insurance will be needed, how much premium they are willing to set aside, what living needs will be served by the insurance (funding a supplemental retirement plan, for example), and their attitudes about different kinds of insurance and risk factors.

Permanent insurance will have a favorable impact on the balance sheet. Term insurance is attractive in that it offers a low initial premium. However, term does not meet the need that most businesses have for a sinking fund for such purposes as expansion, emergencies, lifetime stock-purchase transactions, and salary continuation plans.

In addition, businesses—as with individuals—are tempted to drop term insurance when it starts to get expensive. When that happens, of course, the insurance has been only an expense, with no retrievable cash values. And it starts to get expensive just when the risk of death increases dramatically.

Corporate owners who buy key person insurance on themselves may tend to view it as personal insurance paid with corporate dollars. The same perception sometimes encourages them to use corporate dollars to buy insurance on other family members who are persons of the corporation, even though these others are not owners and even though they are clearly not key persons of the company.

Sure Thing
"Business owner, I know that going ahead with this key person insurance is a serious decision for you. "All of us rather routinely insure our homes and our businesses with fire insurance, but then we are unsure whether to insure a key profit maker in a business we own. "Yet the chance of a key person dying is much greater than the chance of a building burning. In fact, for a 45-year-old person, the chances of death in any given year are 14 times greater than the chance of fire. At age 50, the odds are 17 to 1. At age 55, the odds are 23 to 1. "So we're talking about insuring a hazard that is probably more serious than fire, more likely to happen in any given year than fire, and ultimately, a hazard that is certain to occur sometime."

This tendency to view key insurance as personal insurance can lead business owners to name personal beneficiaries, as opposed to naming the corporation itself as beneficiary. This error in judgment might happen at the time of the sale or it might occur later using a change of beneficiary form.

If the IRS discovers such a situation, they will want to know if the premium was reported by the owner as additional personal salary. The IRS may go even further and hold the premium to be a dividend.

In either case, the income tax consequences could be severe because the owner would have to pay additional income tax, plus interest and penalties, on the additional amount deemed as income. If the premium were deemed to be a dividend, the corporation's income tax would be affected as well because salaries are deductible corporate expenses but dividends are not.

An even greater risk is that the IRS will treat the death proceeds as income, possibly a dividend (Revenue Ruling 61-134). This potential tax trap gives rise to a question that you can ask in your approach or early in a fact-finding interview: "Corporate Stockholder, who is the owner and who is the beneficiary of the life insurance your company is paying for?"

If you uncover a situation where a personal beneficiary has been named, you will have performed an extremely valuable service. This is precisely the kind of service that builds trusting relationships and opens doors for you.

Key Person's Cooperation

The business is not obligated to use the insurance proceeds for any specific purpose. No agreement between the key person and the business is necessary, but the key person, as the insured, must sign the application for insurance.

Selling Key Person Life Insurance

The accompanying chart (Number of Firms with Various Insurance Coverages) shows the results of a survey of insurance coverage conducted by the McGraw-Hill Company. Only 87 (13 percent) of 667 companies surveyed had key person insurance. It is obvious that there is plenty of opportunity for you in this market.

While all kinds of businesses need this coverage, perhaps your strongest prospects will be businesses where management is in the hands of a few individuals and where a small number of people are thus performing tremendous volumes of work. Often these businesses have no formal management training programs and no surplus funds from which to meet the emergencies created by the death or disability of a key person. Look also for businesses where one or more of the owners are required to personally guarantee any business loans.

During your approach or fact-finding interview, you may want to ask: *"Business owner, have you (or any of your co-owners) been required to give a personal guarantee for a business bank loan?"* If the answer is yes, you have the strongest possible basis for a key person life and disability sale.

Number of Firms with Various Insurance Coverages (Out of Total of 667 Firms Surveyed)		
Key Person Insurance	87	13%
Wind, Tornado, Flood	298	47%
Burglary	358	54%
Public Liability	547	82%
Workers' Compensation	617	93%
Fire Insurance	645	97%

Prospecting for Key Person Sales

Large businesses usually hire trained specialists to head each operational department. Small businesses depend upon the knowledge and talents of a few individuals. In either case, the financial advisor should look for more than one key person.

Often the success of a business is due to the combined efforts of a team. For example, the president, treasurer, sales manager, and production manager may work very closely together to ensure the profitable operation of a given business. Over a period of years, the team learns to work together.

Suddenly, one member dies, retires, or becomes disabled. Not only must the business replace this key person, but it must also secure someone else who will prove as effective on the team. Not only is there a particular job to be filled, but, even more important, the fine teamwork balance must be restored. This process may take years.

Frequently the services of particular individuals have greater value to the business at one period than at another. For example, during a downturn the sales manager might be the most important individual. In a period of expansion, much might depend on the ability of the treasurer to raise money. The guiding genius of the president may be responsible for the profitable operation of the business under changing economic conditions.

In the majority of cases, key person insurance will be sold on an owner. Certainly the owners of most businesses are also the key management people. It would be a mistake to spend a lot of time talking to these owners about insuring their persons until the potential for insuring the owners themselves has been explored.

In many small businesses, key person insurance is likely to be only on owners. In other companies, additional key persons can be identified. For example, the following list includes executives and persons who often are found to be key men and women in their respective businesses:

• President	• Sales manager
• Executive vice president	• Advertising manager
• Treasurer	• Buyer
• Financial expert	• Plant manager or superintendent
• Controller	• Technical expert
• Chief engineer	• Tax expert
• Public relations director	• Department managers
• Research engineer or inventor	• Branch managers

In some firms, you also can look for opportunities to place business insurance on the lives of persons who are family members of the owner.

Sales Material. Most life insurance companies have materials that can be useful in the area of key person insurance. These materials generally include preapproach letters, sales tracks, and illustrations. If you would like to use the two letters in this chapter, be sure to get approval through your company compliance procedures.

Dear (Business Owner):

A well-known public accounting firm has made this statement:

"During every year there occur many deaths of business executives who could not well be spared. Avoiding the realm of affection and spiritual value, and staying within the realm of things economic, there is no way of avoiding the conclusion that these deaths represent tremendous losses."

Fortunately, life insurance offers a way to protect profits and offset the financial loss of key people. I will stop by in a few days to arrange an appointment to show you how

Cordially yours,

(Advisor)

Note : As with all preapproach letters, get approval from your company before using this.

Special Business Situations

Sometimes special business situations reveal a need for key person life insurance. Among these situations are the following:

- Key person life insurance to pay off loans is an excellent and exciting idea. It can cover substantial indebtedness in the form of bonds, notes, or ordinary current liabilities. In fact, probably more key person insurance is sold because of loans than for any other reason. Businesses that rely on credit almost always are required by bankers to assign life insurance on the key person to the bank. This is especially true with loans from the Small Business Administration, which requires insurance .

  This can generate two sales: (1) key person life insurance to be assigned to the bank and (2) life insurance to indemnify the business for the loss of the key person.

  Try saying this to a prospect: "Your banker recognizes you as a key person. The insurance you just bought will indemnify your bank if you die before paying off your loan. Shouldn't we ask the insurance company to issue at least a like amount to indemnify your business (or family)?"

- Expansion programs—If a key executive were to die during such a period, the result might be not only the failure of the expansion but also the bankruptcy of the firm.
- Dominant individuals—Look for situations in which one or more key individuals are the dominant factors either from the viewpoint of ownership or management or both.
- Situations where there is a dependence on the specialized technical ability, inventions and research, or experience of certain persons.
- Situations where the success of the enterprise is due to the personal contacts and personal goodwill of certain owners or persons.
- Businesses where there is a substantial investment in physical assets, plant, equipment, and the like. Earning power might be affected seriously by competition and other disrupting factors.
- Business situations where there is a great element of risk. The more risk involved in the business, the more its success is dependent on the skills of its key people.

Dear (Business Owner):

Business leaders have long recognized that the real profit makers are people—not machines. Physical assets can contribute to profits, but people are the most important factor in business success! More and more, business owners are acting to protect their companies against the loss of a key person.

Consider the following judgment of a United States Court:

"What corporate purpose could be considered more essential than key person insurance? The business that insures its buildings and machinery and automobiles from every possible hazard can hardly be expected to exercise less care in protecting itself against the loss of two of its most vital assets-managerial skill and experience." (From a unanimous decision, U.S. Court of Appeals, 3rd Circuit; The Emeloid Co., Inc. v Commissioner, 189 Fed. 2nd 230, 1951.)

This is a strong case for key person protection. I think you would find it both interesting and profitable to hear more about this plan for business security.

With this in mind, I plan to call on you soon to arrange a mutually convenient time to discuss this important topic.

Sincerely,

(Advisor)

Preapproach

You will probably find that a general-needs or total-needs approach works well with all prospects. Your immediate aim will be to arrange a fact-finding interview, after which you can focus on key person insurance or some other specific need.

However, some financial advisors do focus on one particular need in the preapproach. Generally this involves using a specific-need letter and following up with a specific-need approach. After developing a degree of rapport with the prospect, the agent will typically start discussing total needs and will ask for a fact-finding (information-gathering) interview. The accompanying sample letter can be used for this method.

Follow-Up

If you use a letter, go see the prospect within 2 or 3 days after the prospect has received the letter. During this course, unless you are making massive mailings to businesses, we urge you not to use the telephone as a follow-up to preapproach mailings. Bring your priority list with you in case you need to fall back on a familiar sales idea.

"Business owner, my name is Chris Agent, of the ABC Company. I sent you a letter a few days ago concerning one of the vital problems of every successful business. In my letter, I promised to stop by. I'm busy, and I know you are. Is now a convenient time to spend 10 minutes discussing a topic of vital importance?"

Opening Interview

The goal of the approach is to capture your prospect's interest so you can have a fact-finding interview. The best way to do this is with thought-provoking ideas and serious questions. After a moment of pleasant greeting, you can say something like:

"Most business owners are so thoroughly wrapped up in their work that they put off doing things that don't have to be done, things that don't have a sense of urgency, or things like planning for what to do if an owner dies or becomes disabled. Let me ask you some questions to show you the kinds of things I mean." (Then ask one or more of the following questions.)

Show your prospect the accompanying chart (667 businesses) and say:

"Most businesses have carefully evaluated insuring all of their physical assets and liabilities, but often overlook insuring the most valuable assets-the assets that make the profits-the continuing production of key people against loss by disability or death." (Explain the chart's significance, namely, businesses insure assets but tend to ignore insuring profit-making people.)

- *Which of your key people have you thought about insuring?*
- *What plans do you have to find and train a replacement in the event of the death or disability of a key person?*
- *If you or one of the other key people should die or become totally disabled, would your profitability be affected?*
- *If you or one of the other key people should die or become disabled, what impact would that have on your business credit?*
- *How would the profits of this business be affected by your death or total disability?*
- *Is your company setting up reserves for the depreciation of its human assets?*
- *Here's an excerpt from a unanimous decision by a U.S. court on the importance and value of business management. (Have the following statement neatly typed on a sheet of paper and lay it before your prospect. Proceed to read as follows:)*

> . . .What corporate purpose could be considered more essential than key person insurance? The business that insures its buildings and machinery and automobiles from every possible hazard can hardly be expected to exercise less care in protecting itself against the loss of two of its most vital assets-management skill and experience. (3rd Circuit, The Emeloid Co., Inc. vs. Commissioner, 189 Federal 2nd 230, 1951.)

"Prospect, this has had a profound impact on thousands of business owners. They realize that human life is the greatest asset any business has. Can we talk about this now?"

When your prospect is interested in the concept of key person coverage, your next step is to identify the key people in the firm and then the most important owner.

Questions presented earlier in this chapter can help you identify each key person and make a rudimentary estimate of their financial value to the business. Remember, too, to ask about any existing key person insurance coverage. Then arrange an interview with all who will participate in the decision.

Potential Problems When a Person Dies

When a key person dies, there will probably be

- a costly interruption of business
- a reduction in business earnings
- a serious threat to business credit
- a very serious problem in selecting and training a competent successor

---

A Sample Outline for a Key Person Sales Interview
The Human Asset in Business Life Insurance for Key Persons

1. Management is more important in business today than ever before-due to increased competition, rising costs, high taxes, government regulations, and narrowing profit margins.

2. If a business is succeeding, this is primarily because of the experience and ability of the people who operate it.

3. The death of a key person destroys irrevocably all of his or her profit-making value to the business.

4. Modern business practice dictates that all risk of loss should be offset as far as possible by some form of insurance, such as fire insurance, workers' compensation, burglary, fidelity, boiler explosion, sprinkler leakage, plate glass, use and occupancy, automobile damage, and liability. It is logical, therefore, that the human asset should likewise be insured to protect the business against the greatest loss it can possibly suffer.

5. Life insurance is the best instrument of modern finance for offsetting such a loss because:

   a. It will indemnify the business at once for the loss of profit-producing ability.

   b. It will provide cash to buy the services of a successor.

   c. It will provide cash to liquidate outstanding notes, bonds, bank loans, mortgages, or other liabilities.

   d. It will provide a fund from which dividends can be paid, if desired, while earning power is impaired.

   e. The increasing cash and loan values of the policies are a special asset during life, entirely segregated from working capital and tax favored under federal income tax regulations.

6. The ownership of key person life insurance stabilizes the entire business because it shows bankers, customers, and creditors that the company is determined to protect itself against the loss of its most valuable asset.

7. The loyalty, efficiency, and peace of mind of executives and other key persons are increased because of the guaranteed continuity of the business in the event of the death of a key person.

The three things that clients typically want to know about the financial aspects of a key person proposal are these:

First, how much is the annual premium? This affects their cash flow and is therefore important to them. Earnings have to be high enough to pay the premium.

Second, when is the break-even point on an annual basis? That is, in what year is the annual increase in cash value greater than the annual premium? The business owner wants to know this because the annual drain on cash flow will have stopped. The shorter the time, the happier the owner will be. Annual profitability is what the owner works for.

Third, when is the break-even point on a cumulative basis? That is, in what year does the cumulative cash value exceed the cumulative premiums? This is significant information because it is the turning point where the policy begins to add to the balance sheet's net worth, since the inception of the policy.

Sales Presentation Script

An outline of a sample sales presentation is shown on the following pages. This presentation assumes that you have established a relationship of trust and openness with your prospect and that your fact-finding interview has uncovered a key person insurance need. Although this sales presentation deals specifically with the death of a key person, it can be adapted to cover the disability need.

Following are a few brief sales-oriented concepts to introduce your prospects and clients to key person insurance.

Income-Producing, Human Asset

"Business owner, have you ever thought of your value from a strictly monetary point of view? That is, calculating how much you're worth in dollars and cents as an income-producing asset for yourself and your family?" (Wait for some reaction.)

"Establishing a business owner's value is a three-step process. The first step is to make a quick estimate on how much annual yield you could expect if you invested in a conservative mutual fund. For example, if you invested $100,000 in a conservative mutual fund, it might give a 10 percent yield of $10,000.

"The second step is to see how much the same $100,000 would be earning if it were invested in your business instead of in a mutual fund. For example, maybe it would return $40,000 a year.

"The third step is to examine the difference between the two yields, because this difference represents the value added by your knowledge, skill, and time. In my example, you add $30,000 per year ($40,000 less $10,000). In other words, you are worth four times the $100,000 investment. In this example, your value as an income-producing asset would be equivalent to a $400,000 investment at 10 percent.

"I propose that we do a rough calculation to estimate your value as an income-producing asset. Then we can consider insuring that value against the risk of death—protecting your business and your family against that loss of income."

Fire Versus Life

"Prospect, business owners today consider it sound business to insure all of the physical assets of their businesses against fire and other common hazards. You have an extensive package of fire and liability insurance on the business, don't you?"

(Wait for agreement.)

"A fire may never happen. Death certainly will—eventually, to everyone. Physical assets destroyed by fire can be restored, but the untimely death of a truly valuable key person may be a disastrous loss to the business. If insuring physical assets is important, isn't insuring human assets vital?"

A Sample Proposal

Key Executive Life Insurance on Chief Financial Officer

The ABC Company

$750,000 Death Benefit

AT DEATH OF KEY PERSON, TAX-FAVORED CASH WILL BE PAID TO THE ABC COMPANY TO

1. increase retained earnings, stabilize the credit of the company, and carry on the business

2. replace the lost earning power of the company during the readjustment period

3. help obtain the best possible person to replace the deceased person

ADVANTAGES OF THIS INSURANCE DURING THE LIFETIME OF THE KEY PERSON INCLUDE:

4.   The regularly increasing cash values will strengthen the financial picture and the credit of the company.

5.   The accumulating cash values constitute a uniquely valuable surplus fund of emergency cash-liquid, safe, separate from the working capital, always available, and free from federal income tax.

6.   Owning this life insurance can help attract high-grade persons and inspire loyalty among officers and employees because of the increased guarantee of the stability and continuity of the business in the event of the death of valuable executives.

VALUABLE ADDITIONAL USES INCLUDE:

7.   Cash values may be used directly to provide or supplement a retirement income for a key person. Alternatively, the death benefit can be used to help the company recover the cost of providing a supplemental retirement benefit to key executives.

8.   At the death of a key executive, the policy proceeds may be used to finance the continuance of salary to the decedent's spouse.

Business Problems Death Can Cause

"Let me outline the specific problems that such a death might cause."

Place before the prospect a list of the four main problems, neatly typed on a plain sheet of paper. Discuss each point briefly. Use questions wherever possible. You may prefer to personalize the four-point list by putting in the name of the business owner in place of the words a key person. This paints the picture dramatically. Then continue:

"Prospect, one or more of these problems is almost certain to confront every business when a key person dies. I am willing to talk about the specifics of these problems with you, if you are willing to consider them. Okay?" (Wait for a response.)

Prospect Concerns and Advisor Responses

The following are some common questions or concerns and signs of reluctance that can arise during the key person life insurance sale, and some appropriate responses. Study them carefully, memorize the answers you find to be most effective, and use them as stepping stones to help the sales process advance.

Prospect Concern: We can accumulate our own indemnity fund.

Advisor Response: Yes, you can. Can we talk about the pros and cons of doing that? A serious aspect of your question deals with time. Can you guarantee that the key person will live until the fund is completed, and that future earnings will continue to be as strong as they are now? For example, what would happen if the key person dies next year, or any time in the early years of your indemnity fund? Would you have only the amount accumulated? Key person life insurance is the only kind of sinking fund that is automatically completed when the key person dies—no matter when that may be. But even if the key person lives until the indemnity fund is completed, wouldn't it be better business and more profitable to conserve your business reserves for working capital and build your needed indemnity fund with discounted dollars?

Prospect Concern: We don't need key person life insurance because our equity in this business is more than adequate.

Advisor Response: I know that your business is very successful, and I am not surprised that you have a healthy equity. But can we talk about the wisdom of using your equity? Even if the company has enough cash to absorb the shock after the death of a key person at some unknown time in the future, it would mean selling assets. What assets would you sell? Wouldn't it be more profitable to conserve your after-tax surplus dollars by using tax-favored life insurance dollars?

Prospect Concern: We don't need key person life insurance.

Advisor Responses:

1. Why do you say that? (Your prospect will raise another objection to which you can respond.)
2. Today your management team is intact, everything is running smoothly, and profits are good. But if your key person died unexpectedly tonight, what would happen then? You have all your physical assets insured against hazards that may never happen. But death is sure to come. When it comes unexpectedly, the damage to earnings can be great, even disastrous. Isn't it just good, sound business to insure against that hazard too?

***Prospect Concern** : If necessary, we could borrow money to tide us over the readjustment period.*

Advisor Responses:

1. This might be so. But can we talk about the wisdom of that course of action? (Wait for a response.) If you borrow the money, you will have to pay 100 cents on the dollar—not only 100 cents for every dollar of principal, but also 100 cents for every dollar of interest. With the plan I am proposing, you pay an annual amount equal to only 2 or 3 percent of the indemnity fund. In effect, you put up only a reduced interest amount—and you never have to pay one cent of the principal.

2. That's possible. But can we talk about the reliability of that course of action? (Wait for a response.) Your company can borrow the money if economic conditions are right when the money is needed (1) if your company is running as smoothly and successfully as it is today, and (2) if the bank is generous with a company forced to borrow to absorb the financial shock of a key person's death.

3. Yes, you probably could. But can we look at this pragmatically? (Wait for a response.) Do you want to risk your business by mortgaging future profits at the expense of working capital?

***Prospect Concern**: Dollars invested in our business will earn more than dollars invested in life insurance.*

Advisor Responses :

1. This might be true in a narrow sense. Can we talk about it in a broad sense too? (Wait for a response.) Isn't the same thing really true of the premiums for fire insurance? They would make a better profit invested in the business, too, if you never had a fire. But an uninsured fire could hurt your business seriously, so you must have protection. An uninsured death of a key person would hurt even more seriously. Isn't it just good business to protect yourself against the greatest danger?

2. Prospect, this is not an either/or proposition. The money you put into insuring your key people is an investment in your business. And literally, too, the policy's cash value is available if you need it for business purposes.

***Prospect Concern**: We can't afford it.*

Advisor Response: Prospect, this is a key point, and we should discuss it carefully. Key person insurance is like fire insurance and every other kind of insurance you have on your business. You really can't afford to be without any of it-the risk is too great. Key person coverage protects you against a far greater loss than fire. You may never suffer a fire, but death is sure to come-sooner or later.

Prospect Concern: *We can't afford it because we are just getting started in business.*

Advisor Response: Prospect, I understand what you're saying. But look at it this way. Your current financial position really makes key person life insurance even more essential. It is the only way you can be certain that the death of a key person will not cause the business to fail before it gets well underway. Isn't it good business sense to insure your investment?

Prospect Concern: *Business conditions are too uncertain right now.*

Advisor Responses:

1. Would you be interested in making them less uncertain? That's why so many businesses have turned to key person life insurance—to take the uncertainty out of the future by guaranteeing cash indemnification in the event of the death of a key person and by accumulating cash reserve funds for use in emergencies.

2. Yes, they are. That is why key person life insurance is so valuable. Today you have an able and experienced management team that can handle those uncertain problems. But what would happen if that team was suddenly broken up by death? That could be disastrous, especially if it happened when general business conditions were bad.

Prospect Concern: *We want to talk it over with our lawyer and our accountant.*

Advisor Response: Naturally. I always suggest a joint conference among all of us so that this matter can be considered from every angle. Could we phone them now so we can arrange it?

Prospect Concern: *Premiums are not deductible as a business expense.*

Advisor Response: Fortunately, you're right. I say fortunately because if the premiums were tax deductible, you can be sure that the proceeds would not be treated favorably for purposes of the federal income tax. I personally think it's far better to give up a deduction on the modest premiums than to have the entire proceeds subject to ordinary income tax.

Key Person—Fact and Feeling Finding

Here is a track to follow in discussing key person insurance with a business owner. Use it, for example, in conjunction with "Areas of Possible Interest" that you can use as an approach. The following track consists primarily of a series of questions. Don't rely on your memory. Use a written list of questions. Write down your client's responses as they are given.

This line of questioning will become second nature to you, and can be used in any situation dealing with key person life insurance. Specifically, it can be used as follows:

1. **Fact Finding** *:* When you are talking with a business owner and using the "Areas of Possible Interest" list as a fact finder. Ask these questions when you come to key person indemnification. They include both fact and feeling questions.
2. **Single Need** *:* If you have come in on a single-need approach, this is a good exploratory track to run on with key person life insurance.
3. **Disability Income** *:* The same track can be used for disability income insurance, with slight variations. For example, instead of talking about a lump-sum payment at death, you would talk about monthly income payments upon disability of a key person.

Assume that you are already talking with your prospect, and key person insurance is the next subject you want to discuss.

"...Besides you, Business owner, are there other key people—people whose death or long-term disability would have a substantial impact on profits?"

"...Who are they?" (You're looking for names and functions. Make notes of this information.)

"...Am I right in assuming that you are the main cause of profitability...the primary key person?" (The responses from here to the end assume that the owner has responded yes to this question. Adjust the following as appropriate if the response was different.)

"...Are any of your key people insured as key people?" (Assume no.)

"...What do you think would probably happen to your firm's normal operations and profitability if you had died last night?"

"...How much lost income and added expense would this be over a year's time if you had died last night?"

"...How would that impact your business and family?"

"...What would you want to see happen at your death regarding the business, its profitability, its survival, and your family's welfare?"

"...Would a substantial infusion of cash to the business at your death have that desired result?"

"...Would more than a year's worth of financial assistance be needed for the business to get back on its feet? If so, how long would it be needed?"

(OR, instead of the last question, pick up here.)

"...Let me tell you the best part..."

> *"...How would you like your company to supplement your retirement income, at no extra cost to you or the company?"*

> *"...Here's how. If you live to retirement age, the company will not need this key person policy any longer, and can cancel it, then use the policy's cash values to pay you a retirement benefit every year, so long as the cash lasts."*

Knowing this line of questioning will help you conduct a meaningful fact-finding/feeling-finding interview regarding key person insurance. In time you should make changes, additions, and deletions so that it serves you even better.

Here are a couple of other "power questions" that you may want to memorize and use as the occasion seems to call for it.

- *What would happen to the company's profitability if you took a year's vacation and could not keep in touch by phone or letter or in person?* (This is what disability could cause for longer than a year, or what death can do permanently.)

- *Have you ever stopped to think about the fact that you conscientiously insure the assets that appear on your balance sheet, while you haven't insured the people responsible for the even-more-important bottom-line profit on your income statement? Don't you think you should at least look into it?*

Your Most Important Asset

Following are selected statements with one common theme: that people are the most important assets a business has.

Paul T. Babson, Chairman of the Board of Standard and Poor's Corporation, one of this country's largest financial reporting organizations...

"The success or failure of a business enterprise is more dependent on management than any other factor-and the crux of successful management is key people."

Charles M. Schwab, the late president of Bethlehem Steel Company and one of the greatest business leaders this country has ever produced...

"I have always likened industry to a three-legged stool. One leg represents capital, the second leg represents labor, and the third leg represents management. I have also been of the opinion that the greatest of these is management, and have based my belief on an experience of 51 years in industry. Whatever we do in business, management is the thing that will make it successful."

Andrew Carnegie, a famed industrialist and businessman...

"Take away my factories, my plants; take away my railroads, my ships, my transportation; take away my money; strip me of all these, but leave me my people, and in 2 or 3 years I will have them all back again."

James J. Hill, the great railroad builder...

"It is ten times easier to assemble a million dollars of capital than to find the right people to manage the capital assembled."

Thomas N. Carver, noted Harvard economist...

"Every investment is, in a strict sense, betting on a person."

Nation's Business magazine...

"Finding and retaining personnel of excellent quality shapes up as one of the biggest challenges your business will face in the next few years. All signs point to vigorous competition for persons with the right abilities and the capacity to handle progressively more demanding jobs."

William Feather, famous publisher and author... "Profits are made by men and not by machines."

Credit Bureau of the Federal Reserve Board of Atlanta...

"In our opinion, 95 percent of the elements of success in any business originate in the personality of the management."

U.S. Court of Appeals...

"What corporate purpose could be considered more essential than key person insurance? The business that insures its buildings and machinery and automobiles from every possible hazard can hardly be expected to exercise less care in protecting itself against the loss of two of its most vital assets-management skill and experience."

CASE HISTORY: KEEPING IN TOUCH

Agent

Martha Perkins, CLU, has been in the financial services business in a major urban center for 10 years. She began working with the prospect she describes in this case shortly after she had made the successful transition from teaching to financial advisor.

Prospect

About 18 months after I had entered the financial services business, my manager gave me approximately 100 three-by-five index cards with the names and addresses of local businesses and with the name of a key person in each company.

My manager had indicated that it was now time for me to expand my practice beyond the personal market and into business-related sales. Since this was my only source of business contacts, I began talking to the people on these cards immediately.

My prospect in this case was Edward Johnson, the president of a small, closely held corporation. As I was to learn, Mr. Johnson was 60 years old and had recently remarried. He had three children from his first marriage, but none of them were dependent on him any longer, and none worked in his business. He had no grandchildren.

Preapproach

I initially sent Mr. Johnson a preapproach letter and followed up with a telephone call in which I asked if he had received my letter. When Mr. Johnson replied that he had done so, I asked for an opportunity to meet him and tell him about my work. Mr. Johnson was very amiable on the telephone although quite reluctant to meet with me.

I tried to handle Mr. Johnson's objections but was unsuccessful in getting him to schedule an appointment. I then asked Mr. Johnson if he would object to my keeping in touch with him, and he was quite agreeable to that.

Using my prospect filing system that automatically brings the names of prospects to my attention on a regular basis, I called Mr. Johnson perhaps eight or more times over the next 12 months. He was always willing to take my calls and was always very nice, but he continued to be reluctant to meet with me. My persistency finally paid off when Mr. Johnson agreed to an interview.

I was stood up for this meeting through no fault of his, and a second interview was quickly arranged. In retrospect, I believe that being stood up the first time worked to my advantage because Mr. Johnson did not want to put me off any longer or stand me up a second time.

Initial Interview

This interview was the key to my ultimately making the sale. It was one of my typical initial interviews in which I simply introduce myself, give my background, begin to ask questions, and try to create some interest and some doubt.

My colleagues accuse me of being too conversational in an interview, and I accept that opinion. I am really not trying to do anything other than establish rapport and understand where my prospect may have a need.

We met in a conference room down the hall from Mr. Johnson's office. I was flattered that he was willing to leave his office and a ringing telephone so that there would be no interruptions. He was curious as to how I had entered the business, so we spent some time discussing my background. We also spent some time talking about his interest in the stock market. He was doing quite well in the stock market. I complimented him on that, and then I told him a story that I believe was the emotional key to making the sale.

Earlier on the same day, I had met with the controller of a small business who was in his mid-50s and had worked for a family-held business for 28 years. The principal stockholder had recently died without up-to-date plans for the continuation of the business, and the heirs had decided to sell the company to a large national concern.

The new owners promptly dismissed everyone at the company and replaced them with their own people. The controller's uncertainty about his future had caused him to become quite emotional during our meeting. I had never seen anyone react like that since I had begun my new career, and I was still upset by the conversation.

As it turned out, Mr. Johnson had several people working for him of whom he was very fond. He began to realize that their situation could be imperiled should something happen to him. This led us into a discussion of the problems surrounding the death of a major shareholder.

By gently probing for information, I learned that Mr. Johnson owned 90 percent of the stock of the corporation (the remaining 10 percent was owned by several key persons) and that he received a salary of $150,000 as its president. In addition, he owned several pieces of real estate in partnership with his brother. Mr. Johnson earned approximately $50,000 on these outside investments. His total assets were worth about $2,600,000.

I had promised Mr. Johnson that our first interview would take no more than 30 minutes. As our time drew short, I attempted to schedule a fact-finding interview. Mr. Johnson felt he first needed to clear up some details concerning his real estate partnership with his brother. He agreed to meet with me in 3 months.

Fact Finding

I met with Mr. Johnson in his office, and he had his administrative assistant hold his calls. Because it was clear from our prior conversation that Mr. Johnson had a substantial estate, I had brought a copy of a completed sample estate analysis that I planned to show as an example of the kind of work I did and as a lead-in to completing a fact finder.

For some reason, Mr. Johnson seemed hesitant to cooperate fully in providing the information I needed. In fact, at one point he said, "Maybe I shouldn't really care what happens when I die. I'll no longer be around to deal with the problems."

Although I didn't intend to do so, I became visibly irritated with this statement. I replied that if Mr. Johnson didn't care about his taxes perhaps he should consider writing a check to the IRS now as a prepayment. I then asked him whether he felt he didn't pay enough now while he was alive.

This seemed to startle my prospect. He indicated that he did see a need to do something about his problem but that if I wanted to do a complete gathering of information, I had better come back in a week and bring someone who was an expert in the field.

He intended to take the advice of his controller who was very knowledgeable about insurance and all other aspects of finance and taxes. I quickly realized that what he really meant to say was that I was too inexperienced to handle this case alone.

I asked a senior agent in our office to come with me when I returned to Mr. Johnson's office. The other agent established rapport with my prospect and his controller right from the outset. We learned that the controller was very conscious of the dangerous situation that existed should my prospect die and was keenly interested in finding a solution.

We used our agency's fact finder, and my suspicions that Mr. Johnson was underinsured were quickly confirmed. He had only $400,000 of insurance to cover a corporate buy-sell agreement that would now cost $1,400,000 to fulfill.

The value of Mr. Johnson's company had risen significantly since the buy-sell agreement had been signed. The agreement specified that the stock would be redeemed by the corporation in the event of Mr. Johnson's death, and his key persons would gain control.

The advisor who wrote the $400,000 policy to fund the buy-sell agreement had never called back to update the coverage, and the agreement was now seriously underfunded. In addition, Mr. Johnson had no funding to cover his real estate interest in the partnership with his brother.

The Close

A closing interview was held some 6 months after the fact-finding interview because Mr. Johnson had been forced by pressing business matters to reschedule our interview on two separate occasions.

As is often the case, the closing interview becomes an opportunity to answer any questions and objections because the real "closing" had been done during fact-finding. Our solution to his most pressing problem was to supplement the existing $400,000 of insurance with $1,000,000 of additional coverage.

Our sale was made because we were able to show Mr. Johnson and his controller just how tenuous both the corporation's and the family's situations would be should my prospect die without adequate funding for his buy-sell agreement. In fact, the controller actually helped make the sale as he was one of the key persons who would control the company at Mr. Johnson's death.

Post-Sale Service

When we delivered the new policy, we explained it in detail to both Mr. Johnson and his controller. At that time, we also laid the foundation for a later sale of $350,000 of corporate-owned insurance on the controller to fund a supplemental retirement plan.

Several months later, we took two additional applications for $250,000 each to cover my prospect and his brother in their real estate partnership. The total commissions on all of the business written as a result of this one prospect have been in the neighborhood of $50,000.

Over the years, we have been in touch with these people on several occasions. They have been through some tough economic times and are now recovering from that.

During the tough times, the flexibility of permanent life insurance proved very helpful to Mr. Johnson's business as he used policy loans for a premium payment and even as a source of additional working capital for the company. All of the loans were repaid as soon as the company recovered from its problems.

Lessons

I have come to understand four important things as a result of this case:

- Keeping in touch with a prospect lets that prospect know he or she is important to you. Do not consider this "pestering" your prospect.
- Emotion often sells life insurance.
- Do not be afraid to get involved in a case that is over your head. Working your way out of difficult situations makes you a better agent.
- Do joint work. Fifty percent of a commission is a lot more money than 100 percent of no commission.

CHAPTER REVIEW

Key terms and concepts are explained in the Glossary. Answers to the Review Questions and Self-Test Questions are found in the back of the book following the Glossary.

Key Terms and Concepts

key person life insurance	opportunity cost
contribution to earnings	insurable interest
replacement cost	

Review Questions

1. Describe a key person.

2. Name three reasons why a business might find it advantageous to insure the life of a key person.

3. In a corporate situation, who would be the owner, beneficiary, and premium payer of a key person life insurance policy?

4. List five serious consequences that can be caused by the death of a business's key person.

5. Name four sources of cash to offset financial loss arising from the death or disability of a key person.

6. List five benefits of insuring key people.

7. Briefly describe two methods of establishing a value on a key person.

8. Why should a corporation's board of directors pass a resolution authorizing its decision to purchase key person life insurance?

9. What rights does the insured person have in the key person policy?

10. What type of policy can be used for key person insurance? What are the benefits of each?
    Term insurance? (yes/no)
    Permanent insurance? (yes/no)

11. What is a potential problem if the beneficiary of a key person policy is the spouse of the insured?
    The following questions pertain to the case study, Keeping in Touch:

12. What did the advisor think was the emotional key to this sale?

13. What were some of the prospect's objections and how did the advisor overcome them?

Self-Test Questions

Instructions: Read chapter seven first, then answer the following questions to test your knowledge. There are 10 questions. Circle the correct answer, then check your answers with the answer key in the back of the book.

14. When a business owns a key person life insurance policy

    (A) cash value will be an asset of the business
    (B) premiums are tax deductible
    (C) the key person must report the premium as a taxable benefit
    (D) the cash value portion of the death benefit will be taxable to the business

15. Which of the following methods can be used for determining the value of a person for key person life insurance?

    (A) unit benefit
    (B) contribution to earnings
    (C) endorsement system
    (D) defined contribution plan

16. The beneficiary of a key person life insurance policy should be the

    (A) spouse of the insured
    (B) estate of the insured
    (C) spouse or estate of the insured
    (D) business or employer

17. A key person life insurance policy

    (A) generally requires that the business continue to have an insurable interest in the key person for the duration of the contract.
    (B) can never be transferred to the key person if he or she leaves the firm, but must be surrendered for its cash value instead
    (C) must be specifically issued for that purpose.
    (D) can be any type of policy, although permanent policies are frequently used because of their favorable impact on the balance sheet.

18. Which of the following is true regarding key person life insurance?

    (A) Cash values can be used by the business.
    (B) Death benefits are taxable income if payable to the business.
    (C) The policy must be sold to the key person upon leaving the firm.
    (D) None of the above.

19. In which form of business is key-person life insurance appropriate?

    (A) partnership
    (B) S corporation
    (C) sole proprietorship
    (D) all of the above

20. One generally accepted way to determine the amount of insurance to own on a key person uses the

    (A) salary test
    (B) length of employment calculation
    (C) estimated cost to replace that employee
    (D) personal financial liability of the employee

21.   Which of the following statements is true about key person insurance?

   (A)   C corporations can deduct the cost of premiums on a key person life insurance policy.

   (B)   Premiums paid by an S corporation for key person life insurance are income tax deductible if the key employee is one of the owners.

   (C)   In the case of partnerships subject to the alternative minimum tax, some tax would be due on the gain in the cash value of a key person policy.

   (D)   In general, proceeds of a key person life insurance policy paid to an unincorporated business at the insured's death are free from federal income taxation.

22.   Which of the following statements regarding the income taxation of key person life insurance is correct?

   I.   Premiums are deductible by partnerships but not corporations.
   II. Premiums are generally not reportable by the key person.

   (A)   I only
   (B)   II only
   (C)   Both I and II
   (D)   Neither I nor II

READ THE FOLLOWING DIRECTIONS BEFORE CONTINUING

The questions below differ from the preceding questions in that they all contain the word EXCEPT. So you understand fully the basis used in selecting each answer, be sure to read each question carefully.

---

23.   All of the following statements regarding key person insurance are correct EXCEPT

   (A)   Key person insurance is bought, paid for, and owned by the business on a key employee

   (B)   Premiums for key person insurance are not deductible to the business

   (C)   Unlike key person life insurance, Key person disability insurance is deductible to the business

   (D)   If a transfer-for-value takes place, part of the death proceeds may be subject to federal income taxation

Learning Objectives

An understanding of the material in this chapter should enable the student to

1. Define estate planning and its importance to the business owner.

2. List issues that necessitate estate planning for the business owner.

3. Name and describe three ways property can be transferred.

4. Describe the federal estate tax in one sentence.

5. Identify key characteristics and types of wills and trusts.

6. Explain what is included in a persons estate for estate tax purposes.

7. Describe the federal gift tax in one sentence.

8. Describe three situations where life insurance can be useful in estate planning.

This chapter focuses on the estate planning needs of the business owner. A discussion of basic estate planning concepts, issues that necessitate estate planning for the business owner, and the calculation of federal estate and gift taxes are covered. Because many successful business owners will face estate transfer issues and will benefit from estate planning, this chapter concludes with a review of major estate planning concepts.

ESTATE PLANNING FOR THE BUSINESS OWNER

estate planning What is an estate? An estate is a person's possessions or property. More narrowly defined, an estate is the assets and liabilities left by a person at death.

You might ask why estate planning is discussed in a basic course on business insurance. The answer lies in two facts. First, much of estate planning focuses on passing property to the next generation. And the main purpose of business continuation is also passing a business to the next generation. Second, estate planning involves all kinds of property, including any businesses or portions of businesses a person owns. Very often, the biggest asset in a business owner's estate is the value of the business. Therefore, business continuation and estate planning are closely interrelated.

This chapter provides an overview of some estate planning concepts and planning fundamentals, the benefits of estate planning, trusts characteristics and types, and vehicles available to transfer property. We will also examine the federal taxes imposed on the transfer of property: gift taxes on lifetime transfers and estate taxes on transfers that occur following death.

Life insurance has an important role in several aspects of estate planning. For example, life insurance is used to create an estate, pay debts of an estate, provide liquidity for the estate, and equalize bequests to family members. In addition, life insurance provides funding for buy-sell agreements designed to transfer ownership of a business at death.

Estate Planning Defined

Estate planning is a process aimed at accumulating and retaining wealth, and disposing of it according to the client's wishes. Estate planning can be defined as an organized effort to give heirs the maximum amount of wealth, consistent with maintaining the business owner's own financial independence, security, and financial objectives. Estate planning can also be described more simply as the creation and distribution of wealth.

The main focus of estate planning is the desired action to be carried out for clients at their death, but it is more than death planning. It is also a process that has lifetime objectives.

Another way to view estate planning is to consider it a process with the following actions:

1. establishing lifetime objectives
2. deciding what the business owner wants to happen to assets during life and at death
3. trying to make sure that the business owners wishes are carried out

Differs from Financial Planning

Estate planning is different from financial planning. Financial planning is strongly focused on lifetime planning, emphasizing what will happen while the client is living, rather than on what happens after death. Financial planning is also much more focused on such things as the use of assets, asset allocation, and planning for life's contingencies such as the education of children and retirement. Financial planning is generally more focused on income taxation, whereas estate planning is focused more on gift and estate taxation.

Differs from Life Insurance Planning

Estate planning differs from planning someone's life insurance. Estate planning is broader and more encompassing, including tools such as wills and trusts, and involving advisors such as tax attorneys and accountants.

Benefits of Estate Planning to You

Your involvement in estate planning can be important to you in a number of ways, all of which pertain either directly or indirectly to increased sales.

- **Prestige and Confidence**—You will find that your prestige and reputation will generally be enhanced when people begin to think of you as an estate planner or as a person who is knowledgeable about estate planning subjects. This usually means more referrals and more repeat business, because people see you as a well-rounded professional.

- **Receptivity of Prospects**—Many prospects find the subject of estate planning intrinsically interesting. This applies especially to gift and estate taxation. For you, this means prospects with open and receptive minds.

- **More Interviews**—Prospects who would not grant interviews for any other reason are often open to an approach based on estate and gift taxation, or tax savings.

- **Larger Sales**—With estate planning sales, the face amount is usually larger than in most other family situations. Prospects for estate planning are usually able to afford the premiums to support the larger purchases.

- **Follow-on Sales of Business Insurance**—Many business owners are prospects for estate planning. If you work at all in the business insurance area, you will find that estate planning is a good next step because it provides benefits for the business owner and protects you from inroads by other financial advisors.

- **Persistency Improves**—When people trust you and turn to you for advice on more and more of their financial affairs, the persistency of your insurance in force will generally increase.

- **New Business Through Annual Reviews**—As the client's estate continues to grow, as laws change, and as the client's situation changes, you will have regular opportunities for repeat business.

Vehicles of Transferring Ownership

vehicles of transferring ownership

Here are three facts that show the interrelationship of estate planning, business, and life insurance:

- First, much of estate planning is the process of deciding what to do with assets in the estate at the death of the business owner.
- Second, the biggest asset in a business owner's estate is usually the business itself.
- Most business owners want the business to continue. This often means establishing a buy-sell agreement and funding it with life insurance. Or, if the business is not to be sold, it may mean using life insurance to provide liquidity to pay estate taxes and to provide a financial inheritance for the heirs.

Life insurance can be used to fund a plan that will pass *ownership* of the business to the spouse or to the next generation or that will pass *the value* of the business to the spouse or to the next generation.

Legally, the rights of a property owner are described as the rights of "possession, enjoyment, and disposition." Disposition in this context means the transfer of property ownership. The property can be personal property, real estate, the value of a business, or almost anything else. There are basically six ways for a business owner—or anyone else—to transfer ownership:

1. **By Gift.** The owner can give it away. Gifts are discussed later in this chapter.
2. **By Contract.** This usually means selling property. But life insurance is a contract too. So are annuities. Life insurance and annuities "send" money to the beneficiaries.
3. **By Joint Ownership.** Joint ownership means two or more people owning the same property. Some forms of joint ownership provide that one owner's portion of ownership is automatically transferred at death to the other owner(s).
4. **By Will.** A Last Will and Testament is a common way of transferring ownership at death.

5. **By Intestacy.** If the decedent left no will, ownership of the decedent's property would be transferred according to the intestacy laws of the state.

6. **By Trust.** Trusts are written agreements that often involve the transfer of property ownership during life or at death.

At death, real estate passes according to laws of the state *where the property is* located. All other property (personal property) is subject to the laws of the state *where the individual lived.*

Contracts

A contract is an agreement to exchange one thing for another. Legally, a contract is an agreement between two or more competent persons to perform a specified act on which their minds are in mutual agreement, for a legal purpose and for a valuable consideration. The word "contract" does not necessarily mean a lengthy legal document with thousands of words of fine print. A verbal understanding can be a contract. A contract is struck, for example, when you offer a friend 10 dollars for his ticket to a ball game and he agrees.

When real estate is transferred, the contract is known as a deed. Merchandise or personal property of many kinds might be transferred under a contract called a bill of sale. If the transfer involves a business interest, the contract might be called a buy-sell agreement.

Life insurance itself is a contract. For estate planning purposes, life insurance has extremely important roles as a vehicle of transfer and a method of creating funds. A business owner's use of life insurance for estate planning purposes might include

- funding a buy-sell agreement
- insuring a key person to keep the business solvent for the family
- providing liquidity to pay estate taxes
- providing liquidity to pay death-related expenses
- providing liquidity so that the business will not have to be sold to pay debts
- creating a fund to equalize bequests to children
- creating a fund for the spouse when the business is given to the children
- creating a fund to provide an income to the family

Joint Ownership

joint ownership Among the common vehicles of transfer is joint ownership. This method of distribution is important to know about because joint ownership is so common, and because so few owners understand fully its advantages and disadvantages.

It isn't unusual for prospects to think that they do not need a will because "everything is going to be in joint ownership with my spouse." This ignores such things as specific bequests, charitable bequests, and minimization of estate taxes. A will is especially important to business owners because continuation of the business may depend on its existence.

Kinds of Joint Ownership. There are three different types of joint ownership:

- joint tenancy
- tenancy by the entirety
- tenancy in common

The property title defines how the property is owned, what happens when an owner dies, whether it can be transferred by will, and so forth.

joint tenancy *Joint Tenancy.* When two or more persons jointly own title to an entire property, provided that they came into ownership at the same time and as a unit, the property is held in joint tenancy. This applies as well to property owned for business purposes. Each joint tenant can be said to own 100 percent of the property. No matter how many owners there are, each owns 100 percent of the property—or more precisely, the unit of owners owns it.

When one owner dies, the other owner or owners automatically continue to have title to the entire property. For example, if there are five joint tenants, and one dies, the four surviving owners continue as a unit to own 100 percent of the property. The heirs of the deceased owner have absolutely no claim on the property. Property held in joint tenancy cannot be willed because the joint tenancy contract controls who will own the property following an owner's death.

tenancy by the entirety *Tenancy by the Entirety.* A special kind of joint ownership usually exists when husband and wife own property. This kind of joint ownership, generally called tenancy by the entirety, provides an insight into how joint tenancy came about.

When a man and woman marry, they are considered as one entity, or one individual unit. They carry this oneness with them in much of what either of them does. They often carry it with them in the purchase of property, and so they own the property in oneness. Neither has the right to give away his or her half because neither owns half. They both own it all in oneness. This applies to real estate owned by the two of them, including real estate they own for business purposes.

When either dies, the other continues to own the property. No one can will away such property (without the written consent of the other) because that person did not own it; the marriage unit owned it. No member of the unit can will any of it to heirs; rather, the surviving members automatically continue as a unit to own the property.

tenancy in common

Tenancy in Common. The other basic type of property ownership is tenancy in common. There are three essential differences between joint tenancy (mentioned above) and tenancy in common:

- Tenants in common may pass on their shares of ownership by will to whomever they wish (at death or during life) or may let the ownership interest pass by intestacy.

- Tenants in common have individual and specific degrees of ownership. Instead of the unit owning all the property as in joint tenancy, each tenant in common will own a partial interest in the total property. For example, where three persons are tenants in common, one might own 5 percent, one 10 percent, and one 85 percent.

- People may be tenants in common regardless of when they acquired ownership. (By contrast, joint tenancy and tenancy by the entirety require a unity of time; all must become owners at the same time.)

Planning Is Needed. Joint ownership might be an excellent means of transferring property in one case and a very poor method in another. The average person is unaware of the many complications that can arise because of a "simple" joint ownership. With proper advice from a qualified attorney, the objectives of the owners can be translated into effective arrangements.

You will find it worthwhile to acquire a working knowledge of how joint ownership is treated under your own state's laws. It will provide a source of motivating questions for the complacent prospect.

There are three other points to keep in mind regarding trusts and joint ownership:

- These subjects are complex and they are a lawyer's job. Do not give legal advice.
- A reasonable knowledge of these subjects is helpful to you in fact-finding situations so that you can ask intelligent questions and be aware of possible solutions and pitfalls.
- Property held in joint tenancy or tenancy by the entirety supersedes the will. That is, it doesn't matter what the will says. The property title will prevail.

Wills

will   ***You are a Catalyst.*** As a financial advisor, you are in regular and close contact with clients and thus are uniquely positioned to assist them. You can focus the attention of the client on the dangers and uncertainties of not having a will and on the necessity of having one done properly.

Wills are especially important to business owners because

- they usually have large estates
- without a will, partnerships and proprietorships do not have authority to continue the business

Point out how the client's family can be served best by careful planning and by having a proper will made. The cost is generally modest, especially compared to the cost of not having one.

Legal Requirements of Wills. While the exact legal requirements vary from state to state, the concepts are consistent throughout the United States. This section will provide a brief overview of those requirements. Technically, one who makes a will is a "testator," if male, or "testatrix," if female.

Testamentary. By definition, a will is testamentary in nature. That means that the will, by its own terms, expresses intent to dispose of the property at death. Many court cases have been fought over whether a written document found after the death of an individual was intended to be a will. Clearly, that is the first requirement—the person making the will must intend that the written instrument take effect at death and dispose of property.

Witnesses. Generally, a will must be in writing and signed at the end by the testator, who must have signed in the presence of subscribing witnesses. The witnesses, in turn, must have signed in the presence of each other and in the presence of the testator. Most states require two witnesses to a will. A few states require three witnesses. While most states require written wills with a minimum number of witnesses, there are some exceptions in some states. Because such exceptions do exist, you should become aware of the general rules, and the exceptions to the general rules, in the states where you live and work.

probate In most states, once a testator has died, a petition is filed to have his will accepted for probate. In order to have the will accepted, the witnesses to the will must come forward and execute documents that this instrument, in fact, is the will of the testator. This procedure is known as "proving the will" (*probate*).

Often it is difficult, or even impossible, to locate the witnesses, or to get them to go to the courthouse to go through the probate process. When witnesses have been located but live too far away to go to the courthouse, very cumbersome and inconvenient procedures apply. If the witnesses have died or cannot be located, even more inconvenient procedures apply. If these requirements seem unnecessarily burdensome, remember that the purpose is to protect the beneficiaries from mistake or fraud.

Self-Proving Wills. In order to deal with these problems regarding witnesses, a number of states have adopted "self-proving" wills. These are wills with special affidavits, which are notarized by the testator and the witnesses. Properly executed self-proving wills can avoid many of the difficulties associated with locating the original witnesses and having them execute the necessary documents for probate. Self-proving wills are accepted at face value, and can be validated without the witnesses being present.

Permanent Nature of Wills. Wills generally must be written on something permanent, but there is no requirement that they be written on paper. There is one reported case of a will written on the side of a barn being accepted for probate. On the other hand, one case did not accept a will carved in a cake of ice—it was not permanent

Competency to Make a Will. The law specifies who may make a will-usually any competent adult. In most states, adult age is 18; in a few states it is age 21.

Because a testator must be competent at the time he or she makes a will, anyone who has been judged legally incompetent may not make a valid will, unless a court has judged that his or her competency has been restored.

State of Domicile. Many legal requirements change from state to state. Which state's law must be considered? That depends. A person's personal property is disposed of under the law of the state in which he or she resides (is "domiciled") at the time of death.

However, a person's real property is disposed of according to the law of the state in which the real estate is located. If a person died while domiciled in Florida, and owned a home in North Carolina, the will must be admitted to probate in the courts of both states. And that means that it must comply with the laws of both states.

Of course, it is legally possible to have two wills, one to cover Florida law and one to cover the real property in North Carolina but complications may result.

Wills usually are written to be the final document, nullifying all prior wills. Therefore, if a person intended to have two wills exist at one time, great care would be required in order to coordinate the two.

Will and Property Title Must Agree. If you want property to be owned and distributed in a certain way, it's important to make sure that your wishes (as expressed in your Last Will and Testament) and the property title agree. Otherwise, there will be conflicting instructions at your death, with your will saying one thing and your property title another. It is also crucial that your beneficiary designations tie in accurately with the estate plan's goals.

Limitations on Disposition of Property. You may think that individuals can dispose of their property by will in any way they please, to whomever they wish, with whatever conditions they might want to apply. Generally this is true, but the law does impose certain limitations on what can be admitted to probate, and on what disposition individuals can make of their property.

Surviving Spouse. The most significant limitation governs how a testator's spouse is treated. The law generally will not allow a testator to completely disinherit a spouse without the consent of the spouse.

Moreover, the spouse of a deceased testator usually has the right to "elect against the will" of the deceased spouse if the share of the estate left to the survivor is not equal to a specified minimum share established by state law.

Example of Surviving Spouse. For example, some states allow a surviving spouse to elect to take one-third of the probate estate. If a testator's will leaves the spouse one-fourth of the estate, the spouse is not required to accept that bequest. The spouse may elect to take a full one-third. The balance of the bequests in the will then must be adjusted to conform to the reality of the spouse's elective share.

Of course, if the spouse is content to accept what the will provides, then there is no problem. The key point is that unless the will leaves the surviving spouse the minimum share established by law, the spouse is free to accept the bequest or to ignore it and claim the minimum amount that the law provides.

Surviving Children. The provision for a minimum bequest generally applies only to a surviving spouse. The law does not require a testator to leave any minimum amount to any other person or organization.

A testator may generally omit all children from a will or favor one child over another. After the spouse's minimum share rules have been satisfied, the testator is free to dispose of the balance of an estate to anyone he or she pleases. No one has a legal standing to complain. The law does not create concepts of fairness, and assumes that the testator can determine what is best based on personal circumstances.

Public Policy regarding Wills. The law will not allow a condition to attach to a bequest if it would violate public policy. For example, if a person left an entire estate to a favorite son, but only on condition that the son never again speak to any of his brothers and sisters, the law would not enforce the condition. To do so would be against public policy.

Nor would the court enforce a condition that a bequest to a daughter is subject to the daughter's divorcing her husband. Requiring people to act in a way that directly attacks family relationships is contrary to public policy and will not be enforced by the courts.

Just as the courts will not enforce a condition that attacks family relationships, neither will they accept a will, or condition in a will, that is illegal. A condition to a will bequest that the beneficiary must commit some criminal act will not be enforced.

Contracts and Agreements regarding Wills. Within limits, it is possible for a person to contract away the right to freely dispose by will. The most common occurrence of this contract right is with prenuptial (before marriage) agreements, which may contain provisions by which one party or the other, or both, agrees to dispose of their property in certain specific ways.

Alternatively, prenuptial agreements may contain provisions by which one party or the other, or both, agrees to accept a property disposition without regard to the elective share that the law provides. In this case, such a person would be making an advance waiver of the right to elect against a will having an inadequate provision for the spouse.

Prenuptial agreements are used for a number of reasons. One fairly common situation involves second marriages in which one or both of the parties have children by a prior marriage. In this case, the parties frequently want to be sure that their children benefit from their estates in certain ways. A prenuptial agreement is a good way to do so.

Such agreements also may be attractive to people of means who are concerned that a pending marriage may be based on financial interest as much as affection. From another perspective, both parties to a marriage may agree that the financial rewards to be afforded by the marriage are a very real consideration. In this case the prenuptial agreement would be the means of guarantee the intended financial consideration of the marriage.

Modification and Revocation of Wills. A will, by its very nature, is revocable. It is intended to speak only at the death of the testator. A will can thus be amended or revoked at any time before death. Of course if individuals become legally incompetent after executing a valid will, they no longer can revoke or amend the will unless they regain competency.

New Will Generally Revokes Old. Wills usually are drafted so that they revoke any previously executed will. This avoids the problem of coordinating a current will with one or more former wills. The simple solution is to start over from scratch. Executing a replacement will is the most common method of revoking a will. It is also possible to revoke a will and not leave anything to replace it.

Explicit and Formal Revocation of a Will. A revocation should be done with all of the formalities of executing a will itself.

Consider these possibilities, all taken from real situations:

- Mrs. Smith tells her best friend that she intends to revoke her will entirely. After Mrs. Smith's death, her will is found among her belongings. Did she revoke it? When? How? What is the evidence, other than a statement that she intended to?

- Mr. Watson died, and his entire family knew he had a will. The attorney had a carbon copy, and most members of the family had photocopies. The witnesses were available to give testimony regarding the original will and the photocopies. But the original will could not be found, and Mr. Watson's only son said that his father had told him that he intended to revoke his will (so that the son would inherit everything). What really happened? Did he revoke it? Did he want to?

- Miss Brown told her sister, Ida, that she was going to "cut that no-good boyfriend right out of my will." After Miss Brown's death, they found the original of her will. A square hole, about six by eight inches, was in the middle of the second page of the will. When a copy of the original was located, the missing portion turned out to be a bequest to the boyfriend. Who cut the hole? When? What was intended? Did Miss Brown revoke that part of the will, or amend it?

These problems are not really uncommon. Substantial resources are expended attempting to straighten things out and find out what the testator really wanted. Carelessness can be as devastating here as it can in executing a poorly drawn will.

codicil   ***Codicils Are Amendments to Wills.*** Wills usually are amended by a device known as a "codicil." A codicil is just an addendum, or add-on to the will. A codicil must be executed in the same manner and with the same formalities as required for a will: it must be in writing, signed at the end, and all of the witness provisions apply.

It is not sufficient for a testator to haul out the will, scratch out the undesired provisions, and write in new ones. That does not constitute a valid amendment to a will. Countless problems have resulted from family members locating a will of a deceased relative and finding additional handwriting all over the face of the will.

What did the testator intend? Was he attempting to amend the will? Was he making notes to discuss with his lawyer or someone else? Was he attempting to revoke the will? These are natural consequences of someone's attempting to short cut the legal requirements and not having a full appreciation of the legal requirements.

As always, help your clients to know that caution and competent, trained legal counsel is the only proper way to proceed.

State Intestacy Laws

intestacy   One professional estate planner often speaks to groups of investors and businesspeople on the topics of business and estate planning. He starts his talk by asking those present, "How many have an estate plan that is in writing and is legally effective to dispose of your estate?"

Regardless of the number of those present who raise their hands, the speaker chides those who do not. He does not chide them for not having a written estate plan, but rather because they do have one and are not aware of it.

Then he points out that the legislature of each state has written out a detailed and comprehensive estate plan for each individual who has not prepared a plan. This state-provided plan covers all possible contingencies. It is thorough and complete. It was designed to fit everyone, and therefore, of course, it fits no one and is known as the *Will of Intestacy.*

Every state has made legal provision for people who die without a will, who have invalid wills, or who have property that is not adequately disposed of by will.

Laws of Descent and Distribution. These provisions are known variously as laws of descent and distribution or laws of intestate succession. The purpose is to see that no property is without a legal owner. Such laws contain complex, detailed, and complete instructions on who is to receive property not covered by a valid will.

Example—Consider the following example from a typical state. Each provision is followed by comments in parentheses to let you see how these intestacy provisions fall far short of a real will.

- If the decedent left a spouse and no children, the entire estate goes to the surviving spouse. (What if the decedent had wanted to provide some funds to help aging parents, or a disabled brother, or any other special bequest? Without a will, these wishes would remain unfulfilled.)
- If the decedent left children and no spouse, then the entire estate goes to the children, equally. (Often, decedents want to provide bequests to children on the basis of need, not equality. For example, give more to the poor single-parent daughter with four

minor children than to the millionaire single son. Without a will, it will not happen.)

- If the decedent left a surviving spouse and children who also are children of the surviving spouse, then the spouse gets two-thirds and the children share the remaining one-third, equally. (Often a spouse wants to give all income to the surviving spouse. Minimization of estate taxes often suggests other arrangements. But it will not be done without a will.)

- If the decedent left a surviving spouse and children who are not children of the spouse, then the children and the spouse make up a group whose members each get an equal share. (Would the decedent have wanted each child to get the same as his second wife?)

- If there is no spouse and no children, then the proceeds go to any grandchildren, or great-grandchildren, and so on. (In this situation, or any of the others, no room is left for the decedent who wanted even some small bequest to be made to a favorite charity, church, synagogue, or school.)

- If there is no spouse, no children, no descendants, then all proceeds go to the decedent's parents in equal shares. (This ignores special people and existing circumstances. For example, the decedent may have wanted to give some to a mentally retarded niece or to a battered spouses' home, rather than to already wealthy parents.)

- If none of the above are living, then all proceeds go to first generation children of the decedent's parents (that is, the decedent's brothers and sisters). (Again, all special wishes are precluded.)

No Personal Preferences. The "Last Will and Testament" on the accompanying page is based upon typical terms of state intestacy laws. These state-provided, one-size-fits-all estate plans are detailed and complete, so they do a fairly good job of distributing an estate. But that is not the point. The real question: Does this legislative estate plan do the job the individual wants? By luck, by chance, by sheer coincidence, has the legislature of the state in which an individual happens to be living at the time managed to come up with exactly the estate plan that this individual would select or design if given the chance? Almost certainly the answer would be no.

LAST WILL AND TESTAMENT

Being of sound mind and memory, I do hereby publish this as my last will and testament.

FIRST, Although my surviving spouse will need all of the financial help possible, I give my surviving spouse only one-half of my possessions; I give my children the remaining half.

SECOND, I appoint my surviving spouse as the guardian of our children. But as a safeguard—despite utmost confidence in my spouse's judgment, I require that a report be given to the probate court each and every year and an accounting rendered of how, why and where money was spent for proper care of the children.

(A) As a further safeguard—despite my utmost confidence in my spouse's integrity—I direct that the necessary time and money be spent to obtain a Performance Bond to guarantee to the probate court that proper judgment will be exercised in handling, investing and spending the children's money.

(B) As a final safeguard—despite my desire to free my surviving spouse from undue burdens and potential harassments—when our children become of legal age, I give them the right to demand and receive a complete accounting of all financial actions taken with their money.

THIRD, Should my spouse remarry and subsequently die having made no will, the new spouse shall be entitled to one-half of everything my spouse possessed. Should my children need some of this share for food, clothes or other support, the new spouse may simply, and quite legally, refuse to spend any of it on their behalf.

(A) At death, the second spouse shall also have sole right to decide who is to get this share; my children may be legally excluded.

FOURTH, Should my spouse predecease me or die while any of our children are minors, I do not wish to exercise my right to nominate the guardian of our children. Rather, I direct my relatives and friends to get together and argue about it. If they fail to agree on a guardian, I direct the probate court to make the selection. If the court wishes to appoint a complete stranger, that will be all right.

FIFTH, Under existing law, there are certain legal ways to lower the amount of federal estate taxes payable at my death. Although my spouse and children could put this tax savings to good use, I would rather give the money to the Internal Revenue Service.

I witness whereof, I have set my hand to this last will and testament.

This day_____   19___

_____

WITNESSES: SIGNATURE

The real truth is that your prospects do care what happens to their accumulated assets during and after their lives. They really do care who benefits, and in what way, from what they have accumulated. Because they care, because they have wants, likes, and dislikes, they cannot truly be comfortable with an estate plan written by a state legislature which never asked them any questions about their personal desires and needs.

Choice of Guardian. Property is not the only item at risk. People who take the time and trouble to have an attorney draft a will also have the opportunity to make a legal declaration of what provisions they would like made if they should die while their children are still minors.

A parent whose will designates a preferred guardian of minor children can be reasonably certain that such designated person will be named guardian unless the court finds something drastically wrong with the individuals.

Community Property States. Nine states have a special system of property ownership that applies to husband and wife, called community property. Its provisions vary from state to state. The intestacy laws mentioned earlier in this chapter do not necessarily apply in these states. To become familiar with the community property laws in your state, visit a library, or a bank's trust department, or a law office, and ask for literature on the subject. The nine states with community property laws are California, Louisiana, Texas, Washington, New Mexico, Arizona, Idaho, Nevada, and Wisconsin.

Trusts

trusts   Business owners who have substantial income and wealth are likely to have a greater need for establishing trusts. A trust is a legal relationship in which one person holds property subject to an obligation to keep it or use it for another person's benefit. The "persons" are not necessarily individuals. They may be "legal persons" such as corporations or institutions.

trust principal   *Four Elements of a Trust.* The four elements of a trust are

- a grantor
- a trustee
- a beneficiary
- a trust principal (or trust corpus)

trustee

beneficiary

A trustee holds property for the benefit of another person. This arrangement separates the legal interest from the beneficial interest. Typically, this might involve ownership of property by the trustee (the legal interest), with income from the property being given to the beneficiary (beneficial interest).

This section will provide an overview of how trusts are created and operate, several different types of popular trusts, and some examples of how they can be used.

Creation of Trusts. Trusts can be created in a number of different ways. The most common method is known as an "express trust," so called because the person creating the trust expressly wishes the trust to come about. However, it is possible for a person to create a trust without intending to, and without knowing that a trust has been created.

For example, suppose a mother gives her son a sum of money with instructions to purchase a home for her and the son buys a house and puts title in his name. The resulting relationship is that the son is a trustee, holding the house for the benefit of his mother.

The same result applies if someone planning a vacation turns over his or her checking account to a friend, with instructions to take care of routine bills during the time the traveler is away. That checking account does not belong to the friend to spend for himself. Rather, it is held in trust for the benefit of the traveler, and the friend can be required to account to the traveler, in full, for the way in which he or she has handled the traveler's funds.

grantor

Trust Agreement. The trust agreement typically takes the form of a contract between the person creating the trust (the grantor) and the trustee, who will have actual legal ownership of the cash or property that is in the trust. In the written document, the grantor states what is being done and what is to be done by the trustee.

Typically the grantor recites that he or she is transferring a certain amount of cash or stipulated property to the trustee, with instructions as to what the trustee is to do with the property and with the income from the property. The trustee usually signs the agreement, thereby acknowledging the terms of the agreement and agreeing to be bound and guided by them. In short, the trust agreement is a true two-party agreement, or contract.

living trust

Living Trust. Living trusts, sometimes called *inter vivos* trusts, are a practical way of passing property on to heirs without the costs and time delays of probate.

In a narrow sense, a living trust is generally established as a way to avoid both the cost and the public nature of probate. By transferring ownership of all a person owns to the living trust, he or she avoids probate, and therefore avoids the costs, the time lag, and the public-record aspects (lack of privacy) of probate.

A living trust is broader than this, however. It is more like a will, except that it bypasses probate. An attorney prepares it. The grantor retains full control to revoke or amend it at any time. The living trust often includes decisions about what the grantor wants to happen if he or she becomes disabled or dies. The grantor decides who will receive property at death and names someone to be responsible for distribution of the property. The grantor can also name someone to take care of him or her if he or she can no longer take care of him or herself.

Everything that will pass through the living trust must have its title changed. The grantor changes the titles and account names of all titled property from his or her name to the name of the trust. This includes real estate, cars, checking accounts, stocks, and other investments. Most personal property does not have formal title documents, so the trust instrument simply uses wording that sweeps all of the non-titled personal property into the trust.

Life insurance automatically bypasses probate and therefore bypasses the cost and time delay of probate. The only way that life insurance becomes part of the probate estate is if the policy owner names his/her own estate as beneficiary of the proceeds.

Pour-Over Will or Trust. A pour-over will is a short will often used with a living trust, stating that any property inadvertently left out of your living trust will go into it at death. The property will then be distributed as part of the living trust plan.

Typically, after a decedent's debts have been paid and various other property has been distributed according to the terms of the decedent's will, the balance of the property—whatever has not been paid out as an inheritance or to clear debts—is paid into an already existing living trust. At that point, the terms of the living trust take over, and the corpus of the trust is distributed or retained according to the wording of the living trust.

Testamentary Trust

testamentary trust   In contrast to a trust created with an agreement, a person also can create a trust by writing all of the proper terms into a will. This is known as a testamentary trust, because it is created through the Last Will and Testament of the testator.

A testamentary trust becomes effective only when the testator dies. Before then, the testator is free to change the terms of the trust or to abolish it altogether. Obviously, the creator of a testamentary trust does not "participate" in the trust after its creation in the sense that the creator of a living trust does.

Revocable and Irrevocable Trusts. The distinction between revocable trusts and irrevocable trusts is substantial. This distinction is magnified when estate tax and gift tax concepts are applied.

revocable trust   *Revocable Trust.* As its name implies, a revocable trust is one in which the grantor has the legal power to revoke. However, the term usually is used to refer not only to the power to revoke, but also to the power to alter, modify, or amend the trust.

irrevocable trust   *Irrevocable Trust.* An irrevocable trust is one that the grantor cannot alter, modify, amend, or revoke. It is permanent and final from the day it is created.

Of course, all testamentary trusts are, by their very nature, irrevocable. Since the trust comes into existence only on the death of the testator, there is no way to revoke it. Accordingly, the distinction has meaning only with respect to living trusts.

Distinction Between Trusts is Important to the Estate. Estate and gift tax laws attach special significance to the distinction between revocable and irrevocable trusts.

When grantors transfer cash or property to a trustee under an irrevocable trust, they are making a completed transfer. If the trust is for the benefit of anyone other than the grantor, then he or she has made one or more gifts and all gift tax rules apply. In making the transfer to the trustee, the grantor parts with all control over the transferred property.

It is the completed transfer element that brings the gift tax rules into play. Unlike the transfer to an irrevocable trust, a grantor's transfer of cash or property to a trustee under a revocable trust has no tax significance. Because the grantor can revoke the trust and reclaim the cash or property at any time, there has been no completed transfer.

Grantor Trusts. Revocable trusts are generally grantor trusts. A grantor who retains certain interests in a trust he creates is treated as the "owner" of the trust. For income tax purposes, the trust is ignored, and all tax items are reported directly on the income tax return of the grantor. However, the grantor-trust rules reach beyond just those trusts that the grantor can revoke at will.

Grantor As Owner. The tax law specifies that a grantor will be treated as the owner of a trust for any of the following reasons:

- **Reversion to Grantor:** A grantor is treated as the owner of the trust if it's likely that the trust property will revert to the grantor or to the grantor's spouse. This would be the case where, for example, Adam creates a trust to pay income to his mother for the rest of her life, and at her death the trust property is to be returned to Adam. Adam's "reversionary interest" is the right to have the trust property revert back to him. Adam's ownership of this reversionary interest causes the income of the trust to be taxed directly to him.

- **Right to Revoke:** The grantor is treated as the owner of a trust if the grantor retains the right to revoke the trust.

- **Control of Enjoyment:** The grantor is treated as the owner of a trust if the grantor has the power to control beneficial enjoyment. For example, assume the grantor reserves the right to decide, on a year-to-year basis, which beneficiary from a group of allowable beneficiaries is to receive the income from a trust. This is a reserved right to affect beneficial enjoyment, and will cause the grantor to be treated as the owner of the trust.

- **Benefits to Grantor:** A grantor is treated as the owner of any trust income that can benefit the grantor or the grantor's spouse, such as being used to pay for insurance premiums on the life of the grantor or the grantor's spouse.

- **Self-Serving Rights:** The grantor is treated as the owner of the trust if the grantor retains certain administrative powers. The grantor could exercise these powers in such a way that it is self-serving or potentially self-serving.

- **Incidents of Ownership:** The grantor is treated as owner if he or she has any incidents of ownership in the property. This means that there is an element of ownership or degree of control over the property.

In addition to these basic rules causing the grantor to be treated as the owner of a trust (or part of a trust), it is possible for someone other than the grantor to be treated as the owner. Of course, if a third party is treated as the owner, then a third party is taxed directly on the items of income, deduction, credit, and other tax attributes flowing into the trust.

These rules treating grantors (or others) as trust owners can apply to the entire trust property or to a portion of it. For example, if the trust document provides that, on termination of the trust, one-fourth of the trust property would revert to the grantor, then the grantor will be treated as the owner of one-fourth of the trust. That means the grantor will report on a personal return one-fourth of all tax items flowing into the trust.

Funded and Unfunded Life Insurance Trusts. A life insurance trust is simply a trust into which a life insurance policy has been placed. Such an insurance trust can be either funded or unfunded.

A funded insurance trust is provided with cash and securities, the income from which is used to pay the premiums on the policies held in the trust. An unfunded life insurance trust is not funded with cash or securities to pay the premiums, and therefore someone other than the trustee pays the premiums.

Basic Trust Income Taxes. An irrevocable trust that is not a grantor trust is a taxable entity. It is like a person or corporation in that it has its own tax identity and must account for, and pay tax on, its own income.

Generally speaking, a trust computes its taxable income and calculates its income tax like a person. However, it does enjoy one deduction not available to individuals—the distributions deduction. The general rule is that a trust is entitled to a deduction for distributions properly paid to beneficiaries of the trust.

simple trust   *Simple Trust.* For income tax purposes, the term simple trust means one which is required to distribute *all of its income* currently, and which does not have any provision for charitable contributions. For any year in which the trust distributes principal from the trust, it loses its status as a simple trust

complex trust   *Complex Trust.* A complex trust is any trust that is not a simple trust.

The income tax rules affecting irrevocable non-grantor trusts can be summarized as follows:

- A trust is taxable on its own income.
- In computing its income, a trust gets a deduction for any income required to be distributed during the year, whether or not the income is actually distributed.
- The trust is entitled to a deduction for other income actually distributed during the year, whether required or not.
- Generally, a trust will end up paying tax on its capital gains, unless it actually distributes the capital gains during the year. Then it gets a deduction for the gains distributed.
- The beneficiaries of a trust do not necessarily pay tax on all distributions from the trust. Rather, they pay tax on the amount of the distribution that qualified the trust for a deduction.

Example of a Complex Trust —Assume that a trust is required to distribute all of its income currently to the son of the deceased grantor. The trustee also has the discretion to distribute any additional amounts to the son or to the widow of the deceased grantor. During the year the trust earned $8,000 of income. It paid out $10,000 to the son and $5,000 to the widow. The tax results are as follows:

- Because the trust actually distributed more than its income for the year, it is a complex trust this year.
- The trust had $8,000 of gross income and an $8,000 distribution deduction. Thus, it had no taxable income.
- The son received a $10,000 distribution. Of that amount, $8,000 is taxable and $2,000 is a tax-free distribution of trust principal.
- The widow received a $5,000 distribution during the year. As she is not required to receive any income, and, as all of the income actually went to the son (as required by the trust document), there is no income to go to the widow. Thus, the entire $5,000 paid to her is a tax-free distribution of principal.

Sprinkle Power. Because taxation of trust income tends to follow the distribution of that income, a "sprinkle" power can be a valuable and flexible tool.

Generally, a sprinkle power is a power given to the trustee, or to another third party, to decide who gets what income from the trust on a year-to-year basis. The trust document will limit the group of beneficiaries among whom the benefits may be "sprinkled."

With such a power, the trustee may, for example, distribute all income to the spouse one year and to the youngest college student in the family the next. Or he may split the income between them. The trustee may even decide to make no distribution in one year.

Trusts and Gift Taxes. A transfer to an irrevocable trust, with someone other than the grantor as beneficiary, is a completed gift for gift tax purposes. Depending on the terms of the trust document, a transfer to a trust may constitute a number of gifts, all made simultaneously.

EXAMPLE

Consider these examples:

- A trust agreement provides that all income is to be divided equally among the grantor's three children until each child reaches the age of 35, at which time that child's share of the principal will be distributed outright to the child. A transfer to this trust is three separate gifts, one to each child. Each gift is a gift of present interest, qualifying for the annual gift tax exclusion. So, the grantor could exclude up to $39,000 ($13,000 per recipient, indexed for inflation annually). And if the grantor's spouse joined in the transfer, the exclusion could be as high as $78,000.

- The trust document specifies that all of the income is to be paid to the grantor's mother for as long as she lives. On the death of the mother, the trust is to terminate and the balance of the trust property is to be distributed to the grantor's brother. Here, a transfer to the trust constitutes two gifts-one to the mother and one to the brother. The gift to the mother is a gift of the income interest in the property. The value of the gift to the mother is determined from IRS-designated actuarial tables and is directly related to the mother's age (life expectancy) at the time of the transfer.

Since this is a gift of a present interest, it qualifies for the annual gift tax exclusion. The grantor must include in a gift tax return the value of this life interest, to the extent it exceeds the annual exclusion.

The gift to the brother is the remaining value after the gift to the mother has been calculated. Because the brother will not be able to enjoy the gift until after the mother has died, this is a gift of a future interest, and it therefore does not qualify for the annual exclusion. Thus, the grantor must include the full amount of this gift on a gift tax return for the year.

charitable trust

Charitable Trusts. If a gift to a charity is going to be an outright donation, a trust instrument is generally not needed.

On the other hand, some situations require the use of a trust to be eligible to receive a deduction for the charitable contribution. For example, if you want to donate $1 million worth of stock to your alma mater today, but want to have all the dividends paid to you for the next 10 years, you would need a trust to get any federal tax deduction.

Turning the example around, you may want to give the income from $1 million worth of stock to the university for 10 years, and then have full ownership of the stock revert to you after those 10 years. This situation would also require a trust to get any tax deduction.

The general rule is this: Without a qualifying trust, a charitable deduction is not allowed to the donor if the charity can merely use the property or can merely benefit from the property. Again, if certain kinds of trusts are used, then certain deductions will be allowed.

The two principal forms of trust for charities are charitable lead trusts and charitable remainder trusts. Both types are irrevocable trusts, meaning that they cannot be revoked nor can the terms be changed.

Your wealthy prospects may be interested in such trusts for two reasons. First, the donor can contribute assets (stock, land, and so on) that have a very low cost basis but can get a deduction based on the current fair market value. Without a trust, the owner would be subject to substantial capital gains tax. With the trust, however, there would be no capital gains tax to the owner. The charity pays no tax either way.

The second reason for wealthy clients being interested in such trusts is that the income paid from the trust to the donor is normally much larger than the amount of dividend income typically paid on stock that was donated to the trust.

Charitable Lead Trust. A charitable lead trust is created to pay income to a charity for a period of time. At the end of that period, the trust terminates and the trust property reverts to the heirs (or to some party other than the charity).

The value of a charitable lead trust is that it provides the grantor with a current year's charitable deduction equal to the present value of the future stream of income, which the trust will be paying to the charity.

The value is determined using IRS-designated actuarial values and present-value tables. These tables assume an interest rate (discount factor). As a result, the present value of a series of payments to be made in the future is less than the sum of all of those payments.

For example, if a trust provides for payments to a college of $10,000 a year for 10 years, the present value of those payments would be 6.1446 times one payment, or $61,466. The 6.1446 figure is the present value of $1 received for each of 10 years, assuming a 10 percent discount rate—a number obtained from present value tables in any basic finance book. The $61,466 is the grantor's charitable deduction for the year in which the trust is funded.

All income earned by the trust is taxed to the grantor. The grantor will not receive annual charitable contribution deductions as the trust actually pays the required amount to charity. The grantor accepts a lower deduction amount in exchange for the ability to get the deduction all in the first year. Alternatively, the grantor could forego the income tax deduction and be taxed on the income. If the remainder was presently gifted to a third party, the value of the gift is greatly reduced. The third party will enjoy the asset's appreciation in value. This appreciation will not be taxed to the donor.

Charitable Remainder Trust. Charitable remainder trusts are the opposite of charitable lead trusts. Under a charitable remainder trust, income goes to the heirs (or other noncharitable beneficiaries) for a period, and the remainder is then paid to a qualifying charity. The grantor is entitled to a charitable contribution deduction for the value of the remainder interest that will go to a charity.

With a charitable remainder trust, the charity gets the benefit of the trust property at some time in the future—either after a specified period has elapsed, or after designated persons have died. In determining the amount of the charitable contribution deduction, the value of the contribution to charity is the value of the total property, less the value of the income interest that will be paid before the charity obtains the property. Once again, IRS-designated actuarial and mortality tables are used.

Crummey trust   *Crummey Trusts.* A Crummey Trust is an irrevocable trust with special provisions that are designed to take what otherwise would be a future-interest gift, and therefore not eligible for the annual exclusion, and turn it into a present-interest gift, which is eligible for the annual exclusion. Although we are calling it a Crummey Trust, it is more appropriately called a Crummey Power in an irrevocable trust. Very often, it is an irrevocable life insurance trust or ILIT.

To see the benefits of a Crummey trust, it is helpful to look at what normally happens under a non-Crummey insurance trust. A typical life insurance trust (whether Crummey or non-Crummey) is created to purchase insurance on the life of the grantor. Typically, under both, the grantor does not place income-producing property in the trust. Instead, each year he or she makes contributions to the trust, and the contributions are used to pay the life insurance premiums. The trust usually has provisions to receive the insurance proceeds at the death of the grantor and invest them, with income from the investments to be paid to the grantor's spouse and children.

Under non-Crummey insurance trusts, each contribution to the trust is a gift of a future interest, because the spouse and children will not begin to enjoy their interest in the trust until some time in the future, following the death of the grantor. Therefore, under non-Crummey trusts, the grantor cannot get an annual exclusion for these gifts to his spouse and children, because only gifts of present interest qualify for the annual gift tax exclusion. So, under non-Crummey trusts, the full amount of each contribution must be considered as a taxable gift.

To make the gift one of present interest, the trust can grant what is known as "Crummey powers." Such powers usually give one or more beneficiaries the immediate and unqualified right to withdraw each contribution during a specified period of time following the contribution. A typical Crummey power would allow the beneficiary to withdraw each year's contribution within 30 days after the contribution had been made, but hopefully the beneficiary does not exercise the power. The trustee must give the beneficiaries annual notice of this withdrawal right. If the beneficiary does not exercise the power, the contribution is made a permanent part of the trust. Of course, the trustee then uses the fund to pay the insurance premium.

Buy-Sell Trusts. Although not formally known as Buy-Sell Trusts, any trust established to facilitate the performance of a buy-sell agreement is a buy-sell trust. The life insurance proceeds would be paid to the trustee who acts in a fiduciary capacity, making sure the terms of the written agreement are carried out by all parties.

Summary of Ownership Transferring Vehicles. Remember that a trust is what the lawyer and the grantor make of it. In essence a trust is simply a set of written directions giving someone authority to handle certain property in a stipulated manner.

Flexibility is virtually unlimited. Discretionary powers given to the trustee can be as broad or as stringent as desired. There can be one or many beneficiaries, properties, and purposes. Over the years certain varieties of trusts have stood the test of time and flourished. As tax laws change, new concepts evolve. Some stay; some disappear.

Trusts are certainly not a cure-all for every financial problem. Many of the ideas that center on their use would have limited appeal, since they would not be of great help to people without property they can spare.

Nevertheless, prospects—especially business owners—will be interested of trusts. They will wonder if there is some way for them to save money or achieve their objectives through the use of trusts.

The answer depends on many factors and should be determined finally by experts. But the financial advisor who can discuss the questions intelligently is going to establish a lot of prestige and is also going to clear the path to other solutions for other problems—solutions that can be financed best by life insurance.

THE CLIENT'S MOTIVATION FOR ESTATE PLANNING

People are motivated by a variety of reasons to have estate planning done. Some reasons are primarily feelings-based or emotional; others are primarily fact-based or logical.

Emotional Concerns

For most people, their interest in estate planning starts with one or more of these feelings or emotional reactions:

- **Death**—With advancing age, people gain an awareness that they are getting older, and that death isn't as remote as it once was. This awareness may have been triggered by the recent death of a brother or sister. Or maybe the serious illness of a co-worker. Or a major operation of a neighbor.

- **Affairs Not in Order**—At some point, many people get a vague but disturbing feeling that their affairs are not in order. They have the uneasy feeling that they have not given much thought to what they want to happen to their wealth and possessions at death, or which relatives are to get what, or how they will get it.

- **Ignorance about Solutions**—Many people get a feeling of ignorance about how things are taxed at death. They don't know about such things as gifts, inheritance, and trusts. Perhaps they have read an article in the business section of the newspaper or in a financial magazine. They may have listened to a radio or TV talk show about financial matters, and are concerned with the potential results of their own ignorance and inaction.

- **Worry about Old-Age Issues**—At some point, many people get an uneasy feeling that some planning should take place regarding such old-age issues as government programs, nursing homes, long-term care, what happens to fringe benefits when retirement comes, or what is left for the family when death strikes.

- **General Uneasiness**—Many of these emotional reactions can come together and give an unsettling feeling that their own ignorance can result in gaps in protection of the family, inefficient use of assets, and higher taxes than necessary. Perhaps they also feel that they will not leave enough to their children, spouse, or other relatives.

- **Who to Trust and How to Start**—Prospects may not know where to start, whom to turn to, whom to trust, or how much they will be charged. A lawyer? A life insurance agent? An accountant? A financial planner? If so, what kinds? Generalists? Specialists? What kind of specialists? Where do you find them?

These vague fears are useful motivational insights. Your clients and prospects do have these thoughts, fears and questions. It is up to you to try to tap into these unspoken concerns. Let your prospects and clients know that their feelings are not uncommon. There are ways to solve many of these questions and ways to minimize their concerns. These are genuine areas of concern. Ask your clients if they have talked recently about these kinds of things.

Sample Estate Approach

For example, as a way of approaching the subject, you might ask your clients about their own parents. You may use a line of questioning such as this:

"Client, are your parents still alive?"

(If yes:) *"Are they well? Do they live at home?*

"Do you know if they have their financial affairs in order? Have they done any estate tax planning? Have they made living trusts or living wills?"

If any of the parents have died, these questions can be put in the past tense. For example, *"Did they have their financial affairs in order? Did they have living trusts, or did everything go through the time and expense of the probate process?*

"What about you, Mr. and Mrs. Prospect? Have you put your financial affairs in order?"

(If the response leaves an opening, continue:)

"I'm thinking about issues that arise with age: retirement, dependable income for life, illness, wills, living wills, long-term care, money for your children, death taxes, and even the question of whom to talk to about these things. Are any of these topics important for you?"

(If yes.) *"I'm more than willing to spend some time with you to talk about some of these topics. How do you feel about that?"*

You could be shorter and more direct than this, and simply ask your prospects if they have talked recently with anyone about estate planning, if planning for the surviving family is important to them, or if they have done any tax planning. If they ask what is involved in estate planning, you are on the right track with potential estate planning prospects.

Logical Concerns

In addition to the generalized feelings mentioned above, there may also be specific logical concerns that cause people to do estate planning. These concerns are often hot buttons that prompt clients to look into estate planning.

Turn these concerns around and you can think of them as specialized goals or objectives, or focal points of the estate planning process. Following are descriptions of several of these specific concerns.

- **Inadequate Liquidity to pay the Federal Estate Tax**—In sizable estates, the federal estate tax will often represent the primary liability of the estate. Cash will be needed at death to pay these taxes and other estate settlement costs.
- **Where to Get Money to Pay Debts**—Federal estate taxes and estate settlement costs are not the only liquidity needs. People today are highly leveraged (in debt). They owe lots of money and have lots of bills. This is especially true of business owners.

Whatever the causes of an estate's liquidity needs, life insurance is almost always the most suitable, surest, and least expensive method of providing this needed cash.

Quite often, the only other alternative source of liquidity is an unsatisfactory one: raising cash by selling assets that the family does not want to sell. This often means selling precious assets such as family heirlooms, the family home, or a family business—often at discount prices because of the pressure from other family members and from the IRS.

Of course, a family could borrow against the estate assets to get money quickly to pay taxes, debts, and other estate settlement costs. However, this is an expensive way to provide cash. They have to pay interest on the borrowed money, and they have to repay the principal amount as well.

However, if they do borrow substantial amounts from the estate, life insurance on that person's life can protect the estate's value if that person dies while the loan is outstanding.

- **High Taxes Shrink the Estate**—Without planning, most wealthy people pay much more than necessary in federal estate taxes. This means that the children and other heirs will get less.

For example, say that someone has a $5 million estate. Assume that without planning, IRS will get $300,000 in federal estate taxes and that the family will get the balance of $4,700,000. If taxes can be reduced by $200,000, the heirs will get $4,900,000 instead of $4,700,000.

Think of it as estate shrinkage. The more Internal Revenue gets, the less the family gets. With planning, however, these federal estate taxes can often be reduced substantially with little or no compromising of the overall objectives of the estate owner and the estate owner's family.

- **Is the Estate Too Small?**—Another potential problem is that the size of the estate is not large enough to accomplish the estate owner's wishes. In general this may mean two related things. *First*, the lump-sum amount of money and/or property left to the family members is too small. *Second*, the amount of income is inadequate in the event of retirement, death, or disability.

  Life insurance is the ideal solution to such problems. Life insurance creates the beginnings of a sizeable estate with the stroke of a pen, and it mushrooms into reality just when it is most needed, at the time of death.

- **Avoid Foolish Mistakes**—Estate owners want to be sure that their existing resources are being used wisely, that they are not doing anything foolish with their major assets, and that a variety of insurance coverages are in place to protect existing assets from various risks.

- **Who Gets What, and When?**—The estate owner will be wise to decide questions about the disposition of his/her property. Typically, this means deciding which family members will receive an inheritance, how much will they receive, and if it will be in cash or in property.

  Also to be decided is the question of whether it is best to transfer property during life or at death. When during life? When after death? Immediately, or perhaps when the recipient reaches a certain age, gets married, or some other contingency?

  How should the transfer be made—by gift, by sale, or by trust? How should these transfers be made to minimize estate taxes, gift taxes, and income taxes? Are there potential penalty taxes associated with the manner of transfer or the timing of transfer taxes?

- **Who Will Own the Business When I Die?**—What will happen to ownership and control of the business when the owner exits because of death, disability, retirement, or simply turns major control of the business over to one or more family members? Many business owners want to pass the business on to the next generation and it is this goal that interests them in estate planning.

- **What Will Inflation Do to My Dreams?**—Inflation can cause a serious reduction in purchasing power during retirement and during the family's dependency period following death. Assets and income can shrink. Two tactics can offset the impact of inflation: diversification of assets and carrying adequate amounts of life insurance.

- **How to Handle Charitable Bequests?**—Charitable bequests are not uncommon for people who have accumulated substantial wealth during their lifetimes. Life insurance, by its very nature, allows people to multiply the size of the ultimate bequests while receiving tax deductions for the premiums paid.

Estate Tax Exemption Equivalents for Applicable Credit Amounts		
EGTRRA 2001 increases the exemption equivalents from 2006 through 2009. In 2010, the estate tax is repealed for one year, but it is scheduled to be reinstated in 2011, as it existed prior to EGTRRA.		
Year Dying	Applicable (Unified) Credit Amount	Exemption Equivalent
2009	$1,455,800	$3,500,000
2010	N/A	N/A
*2011	$345,800	$1,000,000
*The "sunset" provision of EGTRRA causes the estate tax to reappear in 2011.		

Prospects for Estate Planning

Here are several issues that often point to a need for estate planning.

- **If Subject to Estate Tax**—One who is subject to the federal estate tax is a prospect for estate planning. This includes anyone with a net estate value of more than $2,000,000. Net estate value means total assets minus total liabilities.

  Someone who is on the way to having a net estate value of $2,000,000 can also be considered a prospect for estate planning. For example, someone with $1,000,000 of life insurance and home equity of $500,000 could be a prospect. Inflation alone will probably build the net estate value beyond the current value. Also, someone who will be receiving a sizeable inheritance may be an immediate prospect for estate planning.

- **High Wage Earners**—High wage earners are not only likely to have estates valued over $2,000,000; they are also likely to be able to pay the premiums for substantial amounts of life insurance that may be needed to provide estate liquidity.

  In addition, high earners will earn vast amounts of money over a lifetime, and they will want to protect those future earnings. The only way to protect future earnings against death is through the purchase of life insurance. The only way to protect the earnings against disability is through the purchase of disability insurance. Through life insurance these people can create an estate before they earn it. Buying life insurance is a wise and prudent decision for people with high incomes.

- **Business owners**—Business owners often meet both of the preceding criteria. That is, they are likely to have sizeable and rapidly growing estates, and sizeable incomes.

  The business is part of the business owner's estate for federal estate tax purposes. For example, if the business owner owns two-thirds of the business, then two-thirds of the value of the business is included in his/her estate value.

  Ownership of business life insurance is another estate planning issue. Ownership by someone other than the insured person is sometimes advisable with regard to such things as split dollar plans, group life insurance, and buy-sell plans.

Using a Will to Approach a Business Owner

As a financial advisor, you are in a unique position to do a real service for your clients, your prospects, yourself, and for local attorneys as well. The service is this: encourage your prospects and clients to go to an attorney and make a will.

Attorneys are prohibited in various ways from soliciting business for themselves. You can do them a favor by pointing out to your clients and prospects the value of making a will. In addition, you will make yourself some good friends in the ranks of the attorneys. They in turn may direct some of their clients to you for insurance needs.

You will be doing yourself a favor in another way too. By using a will approach, you will have a valuable way of getting people to think about their wants and needs, some of which can be satisfied with life insurance.

- **Children**—Estate planning becomes especially important in the mind of the estate owner when there are children. The estate owner wants to get assets from his/her generation to the next generation with as little shrinkage as possible. This means reducing the amount given to the IRS, and keeping administrative and probate costs to a minimum, yet not thwarting the owner's own plans or security.

  It is also important to help the client exercise care in naming children as beneficiaries. Today there are many "blended" families and adoption is quite prevalent. A careless naming of beneficiaries could inadvertently exclude stepchildren or adopted children. Inquiring about the status of children calls for tact on your part, and advice from your home office on how to word the beneficiary designations. The same degree of care applies to the client's naming of beneficiaries under his/her will and in any trust agreements.

- **Important If No Kids**—Even if the estate owner has no children, the desirability of estate planning is nonetheless likely to be important for most people of wealth or high earnings. This is true for two reasons. Most people keep wanting more of everything, including savings, possessions, and overall net worth. Second, people do not want to give money to the IRS if it can be avoided.

- **Grandchildren**—When there is a very large estate, and when there are grandchildren, there is often a need for special planning because of the generation-skipping transfer tax.

- **Charitable Givers**—Someone wanting to make a substantial gift to a charitable organization would probably be a prospect for estate planning. The gift might be made at death, or during the donor's lifetime. Life insurance can be a valuable tool in the charitable giving arena.

Steps in Estate Planning

Estate planning can be viewed as a four-step process:

1. Analysis phase
2. Structuring phase
3. Accumulation phase
4. Disposition phase

Analysis Phase

The analysis phase is designed to determine where the client is, what the client's goals are for both the near future and for long-range, and what ultimate disposition is to be made of the client's property. For the most part, this phase asks two questions: Where am I now and where do I want to be in the future?

The analysis stage is part of the estate planning process when problems are identified and goals are set. Here the fact finder/feeling finder comes into play as clients tell you where they are and where they want to be. The difference between the two is the problem that needs to be solved.

Structuring Phase

Next comes the structuring phase, also called the implementation stage. During this phase the client puts into effect the instruments and structures needed to carry out the estate plan, normally with the help of an attorney. The estate plan employs a number of tools: wills, trusts, gifts, property ownership, contracts (including life insurance and annuities), and the laws of intestacy.

Accumulation Phase

Following the analysis and structuring phases, the client enters into the accumulation phase of estate planning. This phase began long before the client sought help. In one way or another, the client has been accumulating wealth for some time. For many people, life insurance is the primary accumulation vehicle when it comes to the size of the estate at death.

For business owners, the primary estate assets are likely to be the business itself and the life insurance. In some cases, the life insurance also serves to safeguard the business and its value. This is generally the role of key person insurance and of insurance used to fund a buy-sell agreement.

For some of your prospects or clients, inherited wealth is a major source of their wealth. Their parents died and left them a sizeable inheritance or sizeable amounts of cash from life insurance policies.

Also consider a person's home as a major vehicle of accumulation. For most people, their home is usually the largest or the second largest asset, with life insurance being the contender for top spot when it comes to leaving money to others at death.

Personal property, stock, bonds, mutual funds, other investments, and vacation homes are all sources of accumulated wealth.

Disposition Phase

For estate planning purposes, the disposition phase usually means two different things. One is the transfer of wealth, such as large gifts during lifetime, charitable contributions during lifetime, and transfers at death. Secondly it means the normal consumption that begins with retirement. When wages or earned income stop coming in, this can begin a time of disposition of some of the estate. The disposition phase is what the client, you, and the other professionals worked so diligently to achieve during the first three phases. Now, it is hoped, the client not only has the means to enjoy retirement years, but also has the comfort of knowing that the accumulated wealth will be passed on in the desired manner.

FEDERAL ESTATE TAXATION

Estate planning is sometimes seen simply as an attempt to avoid estate and gift taxes. This narrow focus can lead to a bad estate plan; you should be on guard against such tendencies. Nevertheless, a basic understanding of the methods used to reduce gift and estate taxes will enable you to provide better service to your business owner clients.

Federal Estate Tax

federal estate tax   The federal estate tax is imposed, at graduated rates, on the right to transfer property at death. The federal estate tax return (Form 706), if required, must be filed and the tax paid by the executor of a deceased person's estate within 9 months after the decedent's death. Time of payment may be extended for "reasonable cause."

A Progressive Tax

The estate tax has graduated rates, and therefore takes a proportionately bigger bite out of larger estates than it takes from smaller ones. This is known as a progressive tax. The federal income tax system works the same way.

Measured by Estate's Value

The estate tax is measured by the current value of property transferred at death. For purposes of this tax, the concept of "transfer" is much broader than you normally would expect. The starting place is the decedent's "gross estate," which encompasses all property and rights to property in which the decedent had an ownership interest at death.

Taxable Estate

When the value of a decedent's gross estate has been determined, a number of adjustments and deductions can be applied to determine the "taxable estate."

Tentative Tax

The taxable estate is multiplied by an appropriate rate (taken from the federal estate and gift tax rate table) to arrive at a tentative estate tax.

Final Tax

Any available credits are subtracted from the tentative tax to arrive at the final estate tax. Here is the formula :

Gross Estate	
– Statutory Deductions	(marital deduction, charitable gifts, debts, funeral expenses)
= Taxable Estate	
× Tax Rate	
= Tentative Tax	
– Miscellaneous Credits	(including state death taxes)
– Unified Credit	
= NET TAX DUE	

What's Included in the Gross Estate

gross estate   What makes up the gross estate? For practical purposes it is everything the decedent owned in any way on the date of death. More specifically, it includes but is not limited to, the following categories of property.

probate estate   • **Probate Estate**—This is all property which passes by will or which passes under the laws of descent and distribution. Usually the probate estate is all the property owned by the decedent outright, only in his or her own name, and not jointly with any other person.

- **Jointly Owned Property**—Many prospects mistakenly believe that jointly owned property is not subject to estate taxes. The gross estate includes a decedent's interest in jointly owned property. In the case of a husband and wife who own property as tenants by the entireties, each is treated as owning one-half the property. The value of other jointly owned interests may depend on the nature of the joint ownership or the relative ages of the joint owners. In any event, a prospect cannot avoid estate tax by placing property in joint names.

- **Transfers With Retained Interests**—One way to avoid estate tax on the value of something is to get rid of that something. Often this is done by gift. If the gift is made fully and irrevocably, with "no strings attached," it works. Occasionally, however, an individual will make a transfer of property and retain certain rights or powers regarding the transfer. Congress has declared that keeping such rights or powers to the gift is equivalent to keeping the gift itself. Therefore, for estate tax purposes, such transfers are not considered gifts.

- **Gifts In Contemplation of Death**—Certain gifts made within 3 years of death are brought back into the gross estate for purposes of computing the tax if there are any retained or reversionary interests or any right to amend, alter, revoke or terminate the gift. This means that the transfer (gift) was incomplete, since a grantor must relinquish irrevocably all power and control over the property. "Strings are attached" which require estate inclusion of the gift to the grantor.

- **Pension Plans, IRAs, Annuities,** and so on.

- **Life Insurance**—Generally, life insurance proceeds on the life of the decedent are included in the gross estate if one of the following is true:

  1. The decedent had any incidents of ownership in the insurance contract.
  2. The proceeds are payable to or for the benefit of the estate.
  3. The decedent owned the policy and transferred ownership within 3 years of death.

Valuation of the Estate Property

The law requires that an estate be valued at its fair market value on the date of death or at the alternative valuation date 6 months later.

Fair Market Value

fair market value   Fair market value is the price which a willing buyer and a willing seller would agree to, neither being under any compulsion to buy or to sell, and both having reasonable knowledge of all relevant facts.

One of your functions as a financial advisor is to let prospects know that they may have a problem. Estate owners are sometimes lulled into a false sense of security. They think they have no estate tax problem because they think the size of their estate is too small to be taxed. They overlook inflation of the assets' value. They overlook any appreciation of the assets' value. They think the value of the property for tax purposes is the amount they bought it for, but this is not correct. The value for tax purposes is the *current fair market value* at date of death or on the alternate valuation date of 6 months after death. This knowledge can sometimes enable you to disturb the prospect about the likelihood of estate taxation.

Under EGTRRA 2001, the basic rules for valuing estate property are slated to change. The Act provides that the step-up or step-down to fair market value basis rules for property transferred as a result of death will be replaced with a modified carryover basis system for 2010. The basis of the person receiving the property will be the lesser of the decedent's adjusted basis or the fair market value of the property on the date of death. However, a step up in basis is retained for up to $1.3 million of a decedent's property, and in the case of transfers to a spouse, a step up in basis will be available for an additional $3 million of property. Nonetheless, because of the sunset provision for EGTRRA, the current (fair market value) rules for valuing an estate's property will be reinstated in 2011.

Valuing property may be easy, such as in the case of listed stocks and bonds. However, a business or closely held corporation owned by the decedent can be difficult to value. Such valuation problems account for most of the litigation in the estate and gift tax area today.

As mentioned earlier in this text, one important role of buy-sell agreements is that the IRS will accept the value established in the agreement if certain guidelines are met.

Statutory Deductions

After the gross estate has been established and valued, certain deductions are allowed to reduce the estate that will be subject to taxation. The allowable deductions fall into following categories:

- **Death Costs**—The decedent's estate is entitled to a deduction for the costs of the decedent's funeral, and for the expenses associated with the decedent's last illness. This may include doctor's fees, hospital charges, medication, and similar costs.

- **Administrative Expenses**—The estate is also allowed a deduction for the costs of administering the estate. As a rule of thumb, many estate planners use a figure of 5 percent to 8 percent of the estate's value as the approximate cost (executor and lawyer) of administering the estate. This includes court costs, executor's commissions and fees, legal fees, appraiser's fees, accounting fees, and certain other costs, claims, and obligations.

- **Debts**—Unpaid mortgages and other indebtedness on estate property is deductible.

- **Charitable Bequests**—The estate is allowed a deduction for the full value of estate property that is left to qualifying charities. Generally, these are the same charities for which a deduction is allowable for federal income tax purposes. There is no limit on the amount or percentage of the gross estate that can qualify for the charitable deduction. Generally, in order to qualify for the charitable deduction, a gift or bequest to charity must transfer to the charity full and immediate ownership. Exceptions do exist, however, for certain "split interest" bequests. Allowable split interests are charitable remainder trusts, charitable lead trusts, and pooled income funds.

- **Marital Deduction**—The most significant estate tax deduction, in terms of total dollars, is the marital deduction. Generally, an estate is allowed a deduction for the full value of all estate property that passes to the decedent's surviving spouse. This deduction is available only if the surviving spouse is a U.S. citizen.

Under current law the full value of all property passing to the surviving spouse qualifies for the marital deduction. In fact, it is referred to as the "unlimited marital deduction."

For married couples, although this tax might not be imposed until both have died, it will be imposed eventually. The greatest impact will be on well-to-do single people, including widows, widowers, divorcees, and people who have never married. For them the tax cannot be postponed.

Marital Deduction

marital deduction   The marital deduction is allowable for the value of property
                               that "passes" to the surviving spouse at the time of the
decedent's death. For estate tax purposes, this concept of "passing" is quite
broad and can include

- a gift (devise or bequest) by will
- inheritance under the laws of descent and distribution
- joint-ownership property by survivorship rights
- property passing due to the exercise (or non exercise) of a power of appointment
- proceeds of a life insurance contract
- a lifetime transfer which is "pulled back" into the gross estate for any reason
- benefits paid to a spouse under a qualified retirement plan

Notwithstanding these rather broad concepts of "passing" and transfer, not all
property interests will qualify for the marital deduction. To qualify, a property
interest must be includible in the surviving spouse's gross estate on the
eventual death of the surviving spouse.

Terminable Interest Rule

qualified   Property that won't be included in the surviving spouse's
terminable   gross estate generally will not qualify for the marital
interest property   deduction in the first estate. This is the "terminable
                               interest" rule.

QTIP—However, a special election can be made if the surviving spouse
gets all the income from the property for life. This special election allows the
terminable interest to qualify for the marital deduction, and is called a QTIP
(qualified terminable interest property) election.

The QTIP involves a written trust. The trust gives the surviving spouse all of
the income plus the principal, *if needed*. The major advantage to the QTIP
trust is that after the surviving spouse dies, the property passes down to
the children, rather than being diverted to a new spouse. In this manner,
the person creating the trust is assured that his/her *children* will receive the
property after the surviving spouse dies. The main "catch" in this special
election is that the full value of the property must later be included in the
surviving spouse's gross estate.

Rate Schedule for Computing Estate and Gift* Tax	
If the amount with respect to which the tentative tax is to be computed is:	**The tentative tax is:**
Not over $10,000	18% of such amount
Over $10,000 but not over $20,000	$1,800, plus 20% of excess of such amount over $10,000
Over $20,000 but not over $40,000	$3,800, plus 22% of excess of such amount over $20,000
Over $40,000 but not over $60,000	$8,200, plus 24% of excess of such amount over $40,000
Over $60,000 but not over $80,000	$13,000, plus 26% of excess of such amount over $60,000
Over $80,000 but not over $100,000	$18,200, plus 28% of excess of such amount over $80,000
Over $100,000 but not over $150,000	$23,800, plus 30% of excess of such amount over $100,000
Over $150,000 but not over $250,000	$38,800, plus 32% of excess of such amount over $150,000
Over $250,000 but not over $500,000	$70,800, plus 34% of excess of such amount over $250,000
Over $500,000 but not over $750,000	$155,800, plus 37% of excess of such amount over $500,000
Over $750,000 but not over $1,000,000	$248,300, plus 39% of excess of such amount over $750,000
Over $1,000,000 but not over $1,250,000	$345,800, plus 41% of excess of such amount over $1,000,000
Over $1,250,000 but not over $1,500,000	$448,300, plus 43% of excess of such amount over $1,250,000
Over $1,500,000 but not over $2,000,000	$555,800, plus 45% of excess of such amount over $1,500,000
Over $2,000,000	$780,800, plus 46% of excess of such amount over $2,000,000 in 2006; $555,800, plus 45% of excess of $1,500,000 in 2007-2009; repeal of estate tax for 2010

The Tentative Tax

After all appropriate deductions have been made, the remaining balance is the taxable estate. Initially, a tentative tax is calculated on this amount, determined from the accompanying tables.

Estate Tax Credits

After the tentative tax has been calculated, all available credits are subtracted. The balance remaining after these credits is the net estate tax due. The law provides several credits, only two of which are discussed in any detail here. The principal credits are:

- Applicable Credit Amount
- credit for state death taxes
- gift tax credit
- credit for estate taxes on earlier transfers
- credit for foreign death taxes paid

The Applicable Credit Amount

applicable credit amount Each person is entitled to a credit applied against taxes resulting from both lifetime and after-death transfers. This credit is known as the Applicable Credit Amount, and it is first used to offset gift taxes, with any remaining portion of the credit to be applied against estate taxes. After the passage of EGTRRA, the Applicable Credit Amount remained the same for both gift and estate tax purposes in 2002–2003 only. Starting in 2004, the credit increased in step-rate fashion for estate tax purposes, while for gift tax purposes it remains at the 2002–2003 level through 2009. During 2002–2003, a donor was able to exhaust the total credit while making gifts, leaving nothing to offset estate taxes at death. However, starting in 2004, the credit became larger for estate tax purposes than for gift tax purposes. It is now impossible for a donor to fully exhaust the Credit by making gifts. Even if the amount of the Credit allocated to satisfying gift tax liability is fully used, a certain amount of the Credit will still remain for use against estate taxes. (See the Gift and Estate Tax Tables.)

State Death Tax Credit

There is also a credit for state death taxes. A number of states impose an estate tax, much like the federal estate tax. It is imposed on the estate of the decedent, and the personal representative of the deceased has the principal burden of making sure that the tax is paid. Like the federal tax, it is usually calculated using graduated rate tables, but at lower rates. State estate taxes are frequently payable even if no federal estate taxes are due.

A number of other states impose an inheritance tax. Unlike the estate tax (which is taxed to the estate), an inheritance tax is imposed on the person who receives the inheritance. The tax is determined from rate tables published by the state. Inheritance taxes often have different rates for different recipients, each depending on the nature of the kinship (spouse, parent, sibling, and so on) between the recipient and the decedent.

The federal estate tax allows a credit for state estate taxes properly paid to a state. However, the full amount of the state death tax is not necessarily the amount of the credit. The maximum allowable credit is related to the value of the taxable estate, and is determined by using a table published by the U.S. Treasury Department.

EGTRRA 2001 reduced the State Death Tax Credit by 25 percent in year 2002, 50 percent in year 2003, and 75 percent in year 2004. For years 2005–2009, the State Death Tax Credit will be replaced with a deduction for state death taxes. Then in 2010, the credit will be abolished along with the repeal of the estate tax. If the sunset provision of EGTRRA is allowed to transpire, the credit will be reinstated in 2011 as it existed prior to EGTRRA. (See table below.)

EXTENSION OF TIME TO PAY ESTATE TAX-IRC SECTION 6166

IRC Section 6166   Because estate taxes must be paid in cash within 9 months after the date of death, the estate must either have cash on hand or sell assets to get cash. Owning adequate amounts of life insurance is not only a safe and economical way of having cash on hand to pay taxes, but it is also a way of providing the estate's representative with flexibility. Estates lacking liquid assets also lack flexibility and options. Often they are forced to sell the home, farm, business, or other valuables to raise cash. This is not always necessary when certain farm or business interests are part of the estate. If stipulated conditions are met, the estate can qualify for an extension on the payment of taxes. Of course the business, including farms, might have to be sold anyway, but at least the extension buys time and allows for the possibility of paying taxes out of income instead of from the sale of the business.

Qualifying for Section 6166

An estate can qualify for this extension if its interest in a closely held business exceeds 35 percent of the adjusted gross estate. Adjusted gross estate is the gross estate value minus administrative expenses of settling the estate.

If two or more businesses are involved, the 35 percent test can be met by aggregating the values and treating them as one business, provided the decedent had at least 20 percent ownership of each business.

Extended Payment Plan

IRC Section 6166 allows payment of federal estate taxes attributable to the business to be stretched over a maximum period of 14 years. Only annual interest needs to be paid during the first 4 years, then tax and interest over the next 10 years.

The interest rate is geared to a level of 45 percent of the prime rate for the 10-year payment period, and a special 2 percent interest rate applies to tax on the first $1,330,000 (year 2009) of business value for the 4-year deferral period. The $1,330,000 is indexed for inflation so the rate may increase annually.

Advantages of Section 6166

- produces low interest on some of the unpaid balance
- minimizes the need for immediate liquidity to meet the portion of the tax attributable to the business
- provides time in which to sort out future business directions

Disadvantages of Section 6166

- The IRS requires security for the payment of the taxes. The executor is personally liable unless a lien is placed on estate assets.
- Can the business survive 14 years, especially if a key person dies?
- What happens to the business's credit if there is an IRS Lien?
- The deferred amount is only the portion of tax due on the business interest. Tax on other estate assets cannot be deferred.
- The estate must remain open for the full extension period. This can be costly.
- Certain events, such as transfer or sale of the business or delinquent payments, may accelerate the payment schedule.
- The low 2 percent rate applies only to the tax on the first $1.2 million attributed to the business. This rate may change periodically.

The Role of Life Insurance

Life insurance can provide the lien property (the death proceeds) thereby avoiding all the drawbacks of tying up other prime assets.

The estate can take advantage of the low interest rate and still have use of the money. In effect, the heirs can use Uncle Sam's money to create income.

FEDERAL GIFT TAX

federal gift tax   Federal gift taxation is intimately related to and integrated with federal estate taxation. As with the estate tax, the gift tax is a tax on the transfer of cash or property, measured by the value of the property transferred. The gift tax is calculated on an amount known as "taxable gifts." A gift tax return, and the gift tax due, if any, is required each year for which a donor has taxable gifts.

Annual Gift Tax Exclusion

annual gift tax exclusion

present and future interest gifts

There is no taxable gift if the amount of the gift to any one person is valued at no more than $13,000 in 2010 and the gift is of a present interest. A gift of *present interest* means it is a completed gift; "no strings attached" and it can be used and enjoyed now, without restriction. Tax-free gifts can be given to any number of people provided that each gift is valued at no more than $13,000 and is a gift of a present interest. The *annual gift tax exclusion* is indexed for inflation; adjustments will occur in $1,000 increments.

Split Gifts

The law permits a married couple to file joint gift tax returns. Regardless of which spouse is the donor, if the other spouse signs the return, they have made it into a joint return. The effect of filing a joint gift tax return is that each spouse is treated as having made one-half of each gift. This is particularly significant in taking advantage of the annual exclusion. If married, each spouse can join in making a tax-free *"split gift"* valued at $26,000.

Taxable gifts made during life generally do not require an out-of-pocket payment of taxes until their cumulative total exceeds $1 million, the lifetime exemption equivalent for gift tax purposes. Up to the $1 million exemption equivalent, each taxable gift simply reduces the Applicable Credit Amount.

One Rate Schedule for Both

The gift tax is calculated from the same graduated rate schedule used in computing the estate tax. These two taxes use a unified rate schedule and are assessed at the same rates. This relationship applies until the year 2010, at which time the estate tax is repealed but the gift tax is not.

The gift tax is levied on gifts transferred during an individual's life. A number of changes have been made to the gift tax by EGTRRA 2001. The top gift tax rate (as well as its identical estate tax counterpart) was gradually reduced over the period 2002 through 2009. However, in 2010, the top gift tax rate will be substantially reduced from its 2009 level (for example, from 45 percent to 35 percent). Also in 2010 the estate tax is to be repealed. In 2011, because of the EGTRRA sunset provision, both gift and estate taxes will revert to the way they were prior to the passage of EGTRRA.

Both the gift and estate taxes use a unified rate schedule through 2009. For gift tax purposes, the Applicable Credit Amount remains at $345,800 through 2009, while for estate tax purposes the Applicable Credit Amount increased in step-rate fashion from its 2002–2003 level of $345,800, to $555,800 for 2004-2005, to $780,800 for 2006-2008, and to $1,455,800 for 2009.

Cumulative Lifetime Taxable Gifts

Even though the tax is calculated each year, one does not get the benefit of going to the bottom of the rate schedule and starting over each year, as is the case with income taxes. The law works with a concept of cumulative taxable gifts.

Under this arrangement, each year the current taxable gifts are added to all prior taxable gifts in earlier years. A tax is calculated on this total, and the donor then subtracts the tax paid in earlier years. The difference is the tax on the current year's gifts.

Obviously, the effect of working with a cumulative computation is to push each year's gifts into higher and higher tax brackets. The first $13,000 taxable gift the donor ever makes will be taxable at 18 percent. However, this taxable gift, if layered on top of, say, $115,000 in previous gifts, is pushed into the 30 percent tax rate. This device prevents individuals from keeping gift taxes down by stringing their gifts out over a long period of time.

Applicable Credit Amount

After the gift tax for the current year has been calculated, the donor can utilize his or her Applicable (Unified) Credit Amount to eliminate any tax actually due (unless there is not enough Credit available to offset the tax). As the donor uses the Credit ($345,800) to satisfy gift tax liability, the Credit is reduced by the amount used, and it is not replenished. Any balance is available for use against gift taxes in later years. If any Credit remains at death, it is available to use against the estate tax.

Taxable Gifts

The tax is calculated by applying a tax rate to the donor's taxable gifts. To arrive at taxable gifts, the donor starts with gross gifts.

For this purpose, a gift generally is defined as any transfer of money or property to another, gratuitously, without full and adequate consideration in money or money's worth. However, the government wants to be sure that the transfer is not really payment for property or for services, past or future. If so, it would be taxable compensation or other taxable payment to the recipient. For this reason, many cases involving gift taxes are litigated in court over the question of whether the transfer was indeed a gift.

Once it is established that a transfer is a gift, it must be valued at fair market value. However, determining a donor's taxable gifts is not merely a task of identifying and valuing all of his or her gifts. The law permits too many adjustments and special rules for that to be the case.

The Marital Deduction

As with estates, there is an unlimited marital deduction for gifts. After the gross gifts for a year have been identified and listed, the donor is permitted to deduct the full value of all gifts given to the spouse of the donor.

Gift Tax Example

Consider the married couple with three married children. Assume that they also have five nieces. By taking advantage of the annual exclusion and the split-gift provisions, the donor spouse could give $26,000 to each child ($78,000 total), and $26,000 to the spouse of each child ($78,000 total), and $26,000 to each of the five nieces ($130,000). In this situation, the donor can give away $286,000 each year and not incur any gift tax or ultimately any estate tax. This can be a tremendous planning device and one that your wealthier prospects might like to learn about!

Not only do the gifts avoid gift taxation; they also reduce the size of the donor's estate and therefore reduce the size of the eventual estate tax. Nor are the gifts considered to be taxable income to the recipients.

BUSINESS OWNERS PLANNING FOR LIQUIDITY

Life insurance plays an important role in estate situations where liquidity is needed. This often occurs when cash is needed in an estate that is tied up in a farm or other closely held business that the heirs do not want to, or cannot, sell.

The need for liquidity might include cash to pay funeral expenses, state taxes, debts, attorney's fees, and accountant's fees. It would also include federal estate taxes in many situations, some of which are described below.

Planning Idea #1: Unmarried Business Owners

Unmarried business owners with estates valued at $1 million or more will generally be faced with estate taxes because no marital deduction is available. For business owners who are widows, widowers, or divorcees, where will the tax money come from if the plans call for having the business continued by the owner's adult children or other heirs? Unless there are liquid assets in the estate, the business might have to be sold. Life insurance is ideally suited for providing such liquidity.

Planning Idea #2: Need For Liquidity-Second-to-Die

While the estate of a married person might escape estate taxation, the day of reckoning will ultimately come when the surviving spouse dies. If not remarried, this survivor's estate will then be faced with the need for liquidity so that the business or farm can be passed along to the next generation instead of being sold to pay taxes and make bequests.

Liquidity can be obtained by insuring either of the spouses. If the insured spouse is the first to die, no estate taxes will be due, so the proceeds can simply be invested and earmarked for liquidity at the later death of the surviving spouse.

If, on the other hand, the insured spouse is the second to die, the proceeds would be payable at that time and used soon after to pay estate taxes and provide general liquidity for the estate.

Another possibility would be to use a policy that jointly insures both husband and wife but is payable only at the death of the second to die.

Planning Idea #3: Business Left to Adult Child

Another opportunity for life insurance to do what it does so well and so uniquely is when the business will be left to an adult child rather than the spouse.

For example, if a $3 million business is willed to daughter or son, the only available offset is the Unified Credit. The marital deduction cannot come to the rescue for property left to children. The federal estate tax could be more than $1 million.

Where will the money come from to pay the taxes? Insurance on the life of the business owner will provide the needed cash to pay the estate taxes. To keep the insurance proceeds out of the taxable estate, the policy owner must be someone other than the insured business owner.

Planning Idea #4: Life Insurance to Equalize Bequests

In addition to insurance for federal estate tax purposes, this same situation also gives rise to another important use of life insurance. If one child will receive the $1 million business, will mother and father want to leave $1 million of value to each of the other children as well?

If so, life insurance can do the job superbly. Simply insure the business owner for the amounts needed. If there is only one child, giving the business to the child may leave too little for the surviving spouse. Here again, life insurance provides money at exactly the time it is needed, and in the amounts desired.

Planning Idea #5: Two Estate Planning Roles for Life Insurance

In estate planning situations, it might be helpful to think of life insurance as serving two possible roles. One is the traditional role of creating an estate, using life insurance as the source of income for the heirs. The other role is that of helping to conserve an estate by using life insurance as a source of liquidity—an offset against debts, taxes, and expenses that would otherwise deplete the existing estate or force the sale of assets that the heirs want to retain.

Insurance is great for liquidity, but it can increase the value of the estate and thereby increase estate taxes. This can be avoided, if it fits the overall plans, by having someone else, or an irrevocable trust, own the insurance. The "someone else" is often an adult child or other close relative.

In estate planning situations where the estate owner will likely have an estate tax liability, the estate owner's life insurance is often put into an irrevocable trust. The estate owner no longer owns or controls the insurance, and the insurance therefore escapes estate taxation.

The irrevocable trust is usually a Crummey trust. Crummey trusts are important because they allow up to $13,000 of annual life insurance premiums to be paid from the trust but avoid being subject to gift taxation if they are gifts of present interest. (The $13,000 is the annual gift tax exclusion discussed earlier in this chapter.) The policy is sometimes a second-to-die policy because quite often there are no estate taxes to pay upon the first spouse's death.

Other common estate planning tools are the "A" and "B" trusts, also known as bypass or credit shelter trusts. They are designed to avoid the overqualified-marital-deduction problem for the first spouse to die. This technique places an amount equal to the unified credit exemption into the bypass trust, thus eliminating estate tax on those assets in both estates. The balance of the decedent's assets will go into the marital trust tax-free using the marital deduction. Those assets will be subject to estate tax at the death of the surviving spouse.

One other related concept is that estate planners generally agree that the essence of lifetime giving is to give away assets that are likely to appreciate substantially. This is done so that the eventual estate value will not be so high, and therefore neither will estate taxes. With this rule as a guide, what better asset to give away than life insurance which appreciates so substantially at death. Giving it away can be done in many ways, but giving it away through a Crummey trust provides the additional gift tax advantage. That is, amounts up to $13,000 per donee can be given to the trust each year and later be used to pay the premiums on the life insurance policy, without having to be reported for gift tax purposes.

Growing Estate Values

The dollar amounts used in the preceding examples can cause a false sense of security for people whose estates are less than the amount of the Unified Credit. It is therefore important to remember that estate size can grow rapidly as a result of a combination of factors such as inflation, higher earnings, inheritances, and real growth by investments, especially business interests.

CASE HISTORY: CHARTING A COURSE

Agent

Gary Cannon works for a multiline insurance company. Age 35, married with one son, Gary has a degree in mathematics and science and was a pilot for a corporation prior to entering the insurance business 2 years ago.

Background

I work primarily within a county of 47,000 people, including the town with a population of 20,000. It was long a rural community and county but is fast becoming an industrial/medical center for this part of the state. Land values have increased rapidly, causing many farm families to have need for estate planning.

Prospect

The Cooks had some of their vehicles and property insured with my company. Patricia Cook worked at a local bank as a bookkeeper; she was 56 years old. Tom, age 59, was a farmer and retired mail carrier. Their two children were married and living away from home. I became aware of the fact that they owned a great deal of acreage and were leasing out some of their land—not just any land, but the land which was now a large shopping complex. This told me, of course, that they had not only an estate of substantial size but also a sizable and reliable income.

Preapproach

I had never met the Cooks but I had a "required rewrite" of some of their farm property insurance, so I sent an approach letter that I've been using for about a year now. (See sample.)

Approach

Prior to phoning the Cooks I studied their file closely and found that by combining some policies I could increase their coverage considerably without increasing the cost. Mrs. Cook handled all of the insurance, and after going into a little detail of what I wanted to do, she agreed to meet me in my office during her lunch hour.

Having people come to my office not only seems to create an attitude of professionalism, but saves me many miles of travel and cuts nighttime interviews to almost none.

Interview

Prior to her arrival I thoroughly reviewed her auto and property insurance and had all recommendations and costs ready. When I showed her that we could increase the auto liability to $100,000/$300,000 and farm liability from $25,000 to $300,000, as well as increase other coverages at only a small cost to her, she was very pleased. She said she had been concerned about the liability limits in view of their good fortune in leasing the property.

I then asked her whether they had ever considered the need for estate planning. They had, but didn't know where or how to start. After telling her what estate planning could mean to them and their family, I outlined the procedure I would follow in helping them accomplish this.

- All information pertinent to the plan is assembled: a detailed listing of assets and liabilities, copies of deeds and their wills, and a statement of what they desire regarding disposition of their property.

- When this information is assembled and computed, I tell the prospects what will happen under their present arrangement insofar as distribution and taxes are concerned.

- If the prospects then indicate a desire to pursue the planning of their estate, it is agreed that I will get the accumulated information to an attorney specializing in estate planning.

- After the attorney has studied the information, the prospects, the attorney and I get together to finalize the program. If insurance is needed for liquidity or carrying out other aspects of the plan, I carry out that part of it. If no life insurance need is indicated, I have nonetheless provided a valuable service to people who have other insurance with us. And either way, I have gained a center of influence, a source of referrals.

Mrs. Cook agreed to the procedure. I assured her that she and her husband could stop at any point, without cost, until the services of an attorney were required.

Proceeding

Between each step I reviewed with Mr. and Mrs. Cook where we were in the process and what the next step would be. When the program was finalized, it was felt that $200,000 of permanent insurance on each would provide the necessary liquidity. Because of their income situation, the cost of the insurance did not pose a major problem. They paid a monthly premium and I arranged for medicals to be performed.

Comments

The Cooks were very pleased with what had been accomplished on their estate plan. They were able to see a savings of about $300,000 in potential estate taxes that would have been due at death of the last-to-die spouse. They not only agreed to a regular review schedule of their estate plan, they have since suggested my services to other people for all lines of insurance we offer.

Sample

My letter to the Cooks, mentioned earlier, went as follows:

> Dear Mr. and Mrs. Cook:
>
> I am scheduling meetings with each member family who is taking advantage of our insurance services. It has been our experience that an insurance review every couple of years helps keep your protection up-to-date. We want everyone to have a better understanding of what their insurance covers and what their needs may be. This free service normally takes about 30 minutes of your time, but I will be glad to spend as much time as you like and discuss any insurance problems you may have.
>
> I will be calling on you Monday evening between 7 and 9 P.M. to arrange a time that will be convenient for you to come by my office and discuss your insurance coverage. Our records show that your phone number is 555-9876. If this number is incorrect or if you know that I cannot reach you Monday, please call me at 555-1234.

I am looking forward to seeing you.

Very truly yours,

Gary Cannon

CHAPTER REVIEW

Key terms and concepts are explained in the Glossary. Answers to the Review Questions and Self-Test Questions are found in the back of the book following the Glossary.

Key Terms and Concepts

estate planning	revocable trust
vehicles of transferring ownership	irrevocable trust
joint ownership	simple trust
joint tenancy	complex trust
tenancy by the entirety	charitable trust
tenancy in common	Crummey trust
will	federal estate tax
probate	gross estate
codicil	probate estate
intestacy	fair market value
trusts	marital deduction
trust principal	qualified terminable interest property
trustee	applicable credit amount
beneficiary	IRC Section 6166
grantor	federal gift tax
living trust	annual gift tax exclusion
testamentary trust	present and future interest gifts

Review Questions

1. Briefly describe the six ways property can be transferred.

2. Name the four elements of a trust.

3. Briefly describe a living trust.

4. What legal rights does the grantor of a revocable trust have?

5. Name three kinds of joint ownership.

6.
   a. If property is owned in joint tenancy, can it be willed?
   b. If property is owned as tenants by the entirety, can it be willed?
   c. If property is owned as tenancy in common, can it be willed?

7.   What is estate planning?

8.   Name the four steps of the estate planning process.

9.   List four emotional reasons why people become interested in estate planning.

10.   List six issues that often point to a need for estate planning.

11.   Briefly describe the federal estate tax.

12.   Give a one-sentence description of what makes up a person's gross estate for purposes of the federal estate tax.

13.   List five categories of deductions that can be used to reduce the gross estate.

14.   List five credits that can be used to reduce the tentative estate tax.

15.   Name and describe two situations where life insurance can be useful in estate planning.

16.   Briefly describe the federal gift tax.

SELF-TEST QUESTIONS

Instructions: Read chapter eight first, then answer the following questions to test your knowledge. There are 10 questions. Circle the correct answer, then check your answers with the answer key in the back of the book.

17.   The person creating a trust is known as the

   (A) grantor
   (B) corpus
   (C) trustee
   (D) trust officer

18.   Federal taxes on the transfer of property at death are called

   (A) accumulated earnings tax
   (B) inheritance taxes
   (C) estate taxes
   (D) income taxes

19.   Section 6166 permits

(A) a partial tax-free stock redemption to pay estate taxes

(B) a legitimate way to increase the marital deduction for estate tax purposes

(C) deferring and spreading out the payment of estate taxes attributable to a business interest

(D) (D) a way to average dividends received over a 10 year period to lower income tax due

20.   Estate planning can be viewed as a four-step process that includes

(A) an analysis and an accumulation phase

(B) an income tax and an estate tax phase

(C) a gifting and a disposition phase

(D) a lifetime and a death-time phase

21.   A gift that is given without limits or restrictions, for complete control or enjoyment to someone is called a gift of

(A) reversionary interest

(B) life estate

(C) present interest

(D) future interest

22.   Life insurance is normally transferred to the beneficiary at the death of the insured by which of the following methods?

(A) By will

(B) By intestacy

(C) By contract

(D) By Trust

23.   Implementation of planning tools takes place in which phase of estate planning?

(A) analysis

(B) structuring

(C) accumulation

(D) disposition

24. Which of the following statements is (are) correct regarding life insurance death proceeds passing directly to the beneficiary?

    (A) It passes by will
    (B) It passes by intestacy
    (C) It passes by right of survivorship
    (D) It passes by right of contract

25. Which of the following is (are) correct about joint ownership?

    I. Tenancy in common can only be established at the time of property purchase.
    II. Tenancy in common passes automatically at death to the joint tenant(s).

    (A) I only
    (B) II only
    (C) Both I and II
    (D) Neither I nor II

READ THE FOLLOWING DIRECTIONS BEFORE CONTINUING

The questions below differ from the preceding questions in that they all contain the word EXCEPT. So you understand fully the basis used in selecting each answer, be sure to read each question carefully.

26. Emotional concerns that cause prospects to undertake estate planning include all of the following EXCEPT

    (A) worry about old-age issues
    (B) awareness that friends are dying
    (C) a feeling that their affairs are not in order
    (D) inadequate liquidity to pay estate settlement costs

Current Coverages and Business Data

Advisor		Agency	Date
Name of Business		Telephone	Fax

Business Address

Contact person, title	Nature of Business	# of owners	# of employees

Fiscal year	Date incorporated

__ Sole proprietorship   __ C corporation   __ Limited liability company   __ Professional partnership
__ Partnership   __ Limited partnership   __ Professional corporation   __ S corporation
__ Nonprofit organization   __ Family limited partnership

Current group benefits:	Yes	No	Carrier	Cost	How are amounts determined?	Satisfied with results?	Anniversary
Hospital/surgical	__	__					
Major medical	__	__					
Group life	__	__					
Pension, profit sharing, 401(k) plan	__	__					
Disability income	__	__					
Long-term disability	__	__					
Dental	__	__					

Does the business have any of these individual benefit/plans?

	Yes	No	If no, has it been considered? Still interested? More info?
Salary continuation plan	__	__	
Section 162 bonus	__	__	
Cafeteria plan	__	__	
Deferred compensation	__	__	
Group carve out	__	__	
Key employee life insurance	__	__	
Buy-sell agreement (insured?)	__	__	
Payroll deduction products	__	__	

If yes, pick up copy of bill, booklets, agreements, and details. Complete appropriate areas below.

Does the business own life insurance on any employees or owners?

Employee	Title or Duties	Amount	Type	Purpose

Employee census: Obtain a census of employees showing name, duties, sex, birth date, employment date, salary or hourly pay, marital status and percentage of ownership (if any).

Appendix B: Confidential Transfer-of-Ownership Analysis

Name of firm:_____

Address and phone:_____

Type of business:_____

Date: _____

1. What are the names of your business associates?_____
   _____
   _____

2. What are their proportionate shares of ownership and profit?_____
   _____
   _____

3. What are their duties?_____
   _____
   _____

4. What are their ages?_____
   _____
   _____

5. What is their general health?_____
   _____
   _____

6. Any dependents (number and relationship)?_____
   _____
   _____

7. Do their wills dispose of their business interest?_____
   _____
   _____

8. To whom will their share of the business pass upon their deaths? _____
   _____
   _____

9. If the ownership interest held by a business associate will not pass by contract or by Will to you:

   a. Would you be willing to be in business with your business associate's heirs? In this situation you may do all the work and get only part of the profits._____

   b. Would you agree to take in an outsider who may be inexperienced and untried?_____

   c. If you are not willing to do any of these things, are you prepared to bargain for your dead business associate's interest, or to liquidate the business if no agreement can be reached?___
_____

   d. If you are willing to run these risks, how will you raise the purchase price?
      From capital?   _____
      By borrowing?   _____
      Through life insurance?   _____

10. If your business associate's interest will pass to you:

   a. Is there a formal ownership transfer (buy-sell) agreement?_____
   b. When was the agreement signed?_____
   c. By whom was it drawn?_____
   d. When was it last reviewed?
   e. Does it provide specific performance?_____
   f. How is the purchase price determined?_____
   g. How is any balance that may be due payable?_____
   h. Must your business associate give you first option to buy if he or she decides to sell while living?_____
   i. Does the agreement cover the hazard of permanent disability?_____
   j. How do you plan to have the purchase price on hand when needed? From capital? By borrowing? _____
      Through life insurance?_____
   k. If through life insurance, _____
      On whose life insurance? _____
      Who pays the premium? _____
      Who is the beneficiary? _____
      Who holds the policy? _____
      Who owns the policy? _____

11. When may I examine your:
      Articles of partnership or articles of incorporation?   _____
      Buy-sell agreement?   _____
      Will?   _____
      Balance sheets?   _____
      Income statements?   _____
      Tax returns?   _____

Appendix C: Estate Analysis

Personal Data

1. Full name: _____

2. Home address and phone:_____

3. How long at this address?_____

4. Other addresses for past 10 years:_____

   _____

5. What state or place do you claim as domicile?_____

   _____

6. Shall we use your home or business address for mailing purposes?_____

   _____

   _____

7. Date of birth:_____

8. Do you have a birth certificate: _____

9. Are you married?   _____Yes _____No

   When?_____Where?_____

   a. Full birth name of spouse: _____

   b. Date of spouse's birth:_____

   c. Place: _____

   d. Does your spouse have a separate income? _____

       Source: _____

       Should this income be considered in your personal investment plans? _____

   e. If your spouse is not currently employed, does your spouse have a profession or occupation
       to which he or she could turn to make a comfortable living, if necessary?_____

       Describe the nature of the profession: _____

       _____

       _____

       When did your spouse last work? _____

       Does he or she plan to go back to work?   _____Yes _____No

   f. Does your spouse have a will? _____

10. Have you or your spouse been married before?   _____Yes _____No

    If so, give names, dates, and places: _____

    _____

    Are there any children by former marriage?_____

    Is the former spouse dead or alive?_____

    Did the former spouse remarry? _____

11. Do you wish for your spouse to participate in decisions involving financial commitments or a reorganization? _____

12. Children: _____Yes   _____No

    Name   *Date of Birth*   *Place*

    _____
    _____
    _____
    _____

    a. Are there any adopted children? _____
    b. Is it possible that there will be additional children? _____
    c. Whom would you nominate as guardian for the children other than your spouse? _____
        _____

    d. *Child's*   *Spouse's*   *Names and Ages*
        Name   *Name*   *Occupation*   *Income*   *of Grandchildren*

        _____
        _____
        _____
        _____

    e. For each child who is not married, indicate the child's present occupation and income:
        _____
        _____

13. a. Are you making definite provisions to send your children to college? _____
        How? _____
        What college? _____
        Estimated annual costs: $_____
    b. If it is found practical to establish a special trust fund for your children's education, would you want your spouse to have complete control of this money, including the right of dissipation? _____
        _____

14. Do you have any other special plans for the future of your children (or grandchildren) which should be considered at this time? Explain: _____
    _____

15. Outside of your immediate family (spouse and children), are there any other persons who are wholly or partially dependent of you for support?   _____
    Name: _____
    Relationship: _____
    Dependent for income tax purposes: _____

Date of birth:_____ Nature and amount of dependency:_____

_____

16. Additional family data:

Dependent	Name	Age	If Deceased, Cause of Death
Client's Father			
Client's Mother			
Spouse's Father			
Spouse's Mother			
Brother			
Brother			
Sister			
Sister			
Brother-in-law			
Brother-in-law			
Sister-in-law			
Sister-in-law			

17. Who is your employer? _____

18. Business address and phone _____

19. What is the nature of your business? _____

20. Occupation and duties: _____

21. How long engaged in this capacity? _____

22. Previous occupations during the last 5 years: _____

23. What is your Social Security number? _____

    What is your spouse's Social Security number? _____

    Have you been covered under Social Security for the maximum, continuously since January 1, 1951, or age 22, whichever is later? _____

    If not, indicate dates (or years) excluded, if known: _____

    _____

24. Have you ever served in the Armed Forces? _____

    Branch of service: _____

    Any service connected disability?_____

    Are you receiving monthly compensation or retired pay? _____Amount? $_____

25. Do you have a safety deposit box? _____ Where:_____

    Number:_____ How titled: _____

    Purpose: _____

26. Excluding life insurance premiums, income taxes, savings and investments, about how much do you need every month for actual running expenses of your family and home? $_____

27. a. Barring accident and disease, about what do you estimate will be your average annual income from all sources for the next 5 to 10 years? $_____

b. What has been your average annual income during the past 5 years? $_____

c. What is your total net income currently? $_____

28. a. For each person a day will come when, by choice or otherwise, he or she must close their office door forever. When that day comes, you must be financially able to greet it. Assuming you have a choice, at what age would you like to be financially able to slow down if you should desire, or to retire from active practice of your business or profession?

_____

_____

b. Each of us has an obligation today to the "old, white-haired person" that we will be one day. Our obligation can be met only by our resourcefulness and thrift during our productive years. In this respect, about how much do you want as a guaranteed pension to enable you to play golf, travel, raise flowers, or do whatever you may desire at that time? $_____

29. a. What is the status of your health? _____

b. What is the status of your spouse's health? _____

c. Are your children all in good health? _____

d. Have you or any member of your family ever been declined, postponed, or rated for life insurance? If so, indicate name of family member, companies, and dates: _____

e. Have you ever received or claimed indemnity benefits of a pension for any injury or sickness?_____

Company:	Date:	Nature of illness:

f. If you become disabled and are unable to work, how much guaranteed income will you need? $_____

g. Have you or your family been examined by or submitted a non-medical application to any life insurance company in the past 90 days? _____

30. a. What is your principal banking connection? _____

Address: _____

Personal contact:

b. What brokerage firms have you been using? _____

_____

Address: _____

31. For identification purposes, list names and address of two business and two personal references:

_____

_____

_____

_____

Insurance and Benefits

32. What is the total insurance in force on your life, including group? $_____

Face Amount	Company	Owner	Beneficiary	Plan	Year Bought	Cash Value as of (date)

Spouse's insurance coverage and benefits? (List the coverages. Show life insurance face amount, cash value and who is owner.)

_____

_____

_____

_____

_____

33. Do you own cash value insurance on others? _____Yes _____No
    Insured: _____
    Company: _____ Policy Number: _____
    Present cash value: _____
    Who pays the premium? _____
    Purpose? _____
    Owner: _____

34. Do you own any annuities?_____Yes _____No
    If yes, what is the current value? _____

35. a. Is the property and liability insurance on all of your assets titled in the same name or names
       as the owner of each asset?_____Is your full equity insured in each case?
       _____

    b. Do you have long-term care insurance? _____What company? _____
       Deductible amount? _____Elimination period:_____
       Benefit period?_____

36. Are your spouse's feelings about the value of insurance similar to yours?_____
    _____Yes _____ No
    If not, how would you characterize his/her feelings, compared to yours?_____

    _____

    _____

37. Vested interests (for example, pension, profit sharing, deferred compensation, IRA or Keogh, or inheritance not yet received): _____Yes _____No
    Owner: _____
    Description: _____
    Present value: $_____
    Comments: _____
    _____
    _____
    _____

38. Does your company provide you or your family with any employment benefits such as a pension or profit sharing plan, stock option arrangement, deferred compensation, or insurance plan? _____
    _____

    If so, name and address or person to contact for details:_____
    _____

Estate Planning Information

39. Have you made a will? _____
    When was it executed? _____
    Are the witnesses local? _____
    Are the witnesses still alive? _____
    Were any children born since the will was drawn? _____
    Did you earmark specific assets for payment of taxes, debts, and expenses of administration?
    _____
    Where is the will kept now? _____
40. Have you made any unintentional gifts such as the purchase of property in joint names?_____
    If so, did you file a gift tax return?_____
41. Is your personal life insurance trusteed?
42. Are you creator and beneficiary of any trusts? _____Yes _____No
    Who is beneficiary?_____
    Who established the trust? _____
    Date trust terminates: _____
    Does beneficiary have power of appointment? _____
    Present trust income: $_____
    Present value of trust: $_____
    Comments: _____

43. Have you utilized trusts to
    a. increase your current spendable income? _____
    b. reduce estate taxes? _____
    c. reduce inheritance taxes? _____
    d. reduce probate costs? _____
    e. for other reasons? _____
44. Have you given anyone a power of attorney? _____
    Date executed: _____ Date revoked: _____
45. Have you executed any documents which affect your privilege of transferring property (for example, irrevocable trusts or stock agreements)? _____

46. Do you or any members of your family anticipate any inheritance or gifts? _____
    Sources and amounts: _____
47. a. In relation to your will, do you have any special wishes or objectives? _____
    b. Do you have any favorite charities, persons, or institutions to whom you would like to leave a bequest? _____ Name: _____
       Item or amount _____
    c. Do you want to make special provisions for any dependent persons?
       Explain: _____
48. When you die, your executor will need cash to take care of funeral and medical expenses, pay current bills, and take care of your family and their immediate needs until your will is probated. Do you at all times maintain a cash fund specifically earmarked for these purposes? How much is it? _____
49. Proper use of the marital deduction will reduce your estate tax liability. However, this involves giving your spouse control over your estate when you die. Which is more important to you:
    a. retaining complete control and paying a higher tax or _____
    b. giving your spouse some control and possibly paying a lower tax? _____
50. Some people give away money in order to reduce taxes. Still others make gifts in order to help loved ones or charity. Have you formed any opinion as to the possible personal benefits to be derived from such a program? _____

Investments

51. How do you presently invest your savings (cash or near cash <u>investments</u>)? _____
    _____
    _____
    Is this part of a planned investment strategy? _____
    If so, what is the purpose of this plan? _____
    What is the nature and value of this savings? _____

52. Checking accounts and numbers:

	Current Value	*% You Contribute*

   a.   In your name _____

_____

   b.   In joint names with spouse _____

_____

   c.   In spouse's name_____

_____

53. Savings accounts:

   a.   In your name _____

_____

   b.   In joint names with spouse _____

_____

   c.   In spouse's name _____

_____

54. Cash on hand: _____

_____

55. U.S. Bonds: _____

   a. In your name _____

   b. In joint names with spouse _____

56. Securities, including mutual funds: _____Yes _____No

Description	*Objective*	*No. of Shares*	*Titled**	*Cost*	*Market Value*

*For the purposes of estate analysis, it is important to know how property is titled, that is, is it owned individually or jointly? Name(s) of owner(s)?

57. Natural Resources (Gas, Oil, Coal, Etc.): _____Yes _____No
    Titled: _____
    Type: _____
    Location and name of company: _____
    Present market value: $ _____

58. Copyrights, Patents, and Royalties: _____Yes _____No
    Titled: _____
    Description: _____
    Value $ _____ Income $_____
    Comments: _____

59. Mortgages Owned: _____Yes _____No
    Titled: _____
    Location: _____
    Present balance: $_____ Resale value: _____
    Payments: $_____
    Comments: _____

60. Notes Receivable: _____Yes _____No
    Titled: _____
    Maker: _____
    Present value: $_____Terms _____
    Comments: _____

61. Livestock: _____Yes _____No
    Titled: _____
    Describe: _____

62. Leasehold Interests: _____Yes _____No
    Titled: _____
    Describe:_____

63. Real Estate (other than your primary and secondary residences): _____Yes _____No
    Titled: _____
    Address:_____
    Commercial-residential-unimproved:_____
    Present market value: $_____
    Mortgage balance: $_____Equity: $_____

64. Residence: _____
    Title: _____
    Address: _____
    Present value: $_____Mortgage: $_____Equity: $_____
    a. Do you consider your present residence a permanent home for your family?
        Comments: _____

65. Summer/Winter Home: _____ Yes _____No
    Titled: _____
    Address: _____
    Present value: $_____Mortgage: $_____Equity: $_____
    Comments: _____

66. Automobiles:_____
    For Car A: _____
    Titled: _____
    Who drives? _____
    Year:_____ Make_____ Value $_____
    For Car B: _____
    Titled: _____
    Who drives? _____
    Year:_____ Make_____ Value $_____

67. Boat: _____Yes _____No
    Titled: _____
    Description: _____
    Value: $_____

68. Airplane: _____Yes _____No
    Titled: _____
    Description: _____
    Value: $_____
    a. Have you ever flown as a pilot or crew member?_____
       When? _____
       Comments: _____

69. Household and Personal Effects: (including rugs, draperies, furniture, antiques, sports equipment, clothing, jewelry, furs, paintings, and hobby equipment)_____
    Titled: _____
    Present depreciated replacement value: $_____
    Comments: _____

70. Do you have any outstanding liabilities? _____Yes _____No
    a. Bank loan: $_____at _____
    b. Margin account: $_____Company: _____
    c. Insurance loan: $_____Company: _____
    d. Personal note: $_____ to _____
       Terms: _____
       _____

71. From an investment plan point of view, what is your opinion of the current economic outlook?

    _____

    a. Was the present arrangement of your assets designed with this opinion in mind? _____
    b. Has your opinion of the economic outlook changed during the past 5 years? _____
       If so, was a corresponding change made in your investment program? _____
    c. On a scale of 1 to 10 (10=highest priority), how satisfied are you with the results you have achieved from your investment program during the past 5 years? _____
    d. d.On a scale of 1 to 10, what are your major investment objectives? _____
       (1) Safety of principal? _____ (2) Current income? _____
       (3) Deferred income? _____ (4) Capital gains? _____
    e. Based upon your opinion of the current economic outlook, about how much money do you feel you should maintain in cash or its equivalent? $_____
    f. Have you formed any opinion on the merits of professional managment of security investments? _____

    _____

Business Interests

Find out if the business is a sole proprietorship, a partnership or a corporation, and then proceed with question 72, 73 or 74. Then go on with question 75 to the end.

72. Proprietorship
    a. Name and kind of business: _____
       Book value: $_____ Market value: $_____
       Would there be a purchaser at the latter price? _____
       Have you calculated the tax liability created by your business? _____
    b. Who are your key people?_____

       _____
       Ages of key people: _____
       Are they in good health? _____
    c. In the event of your death, do you want your family to inherit your business or would you prefer that the business be sold? _____
       If you want the family to inherit the business: Do they possess the talent for effective management? _____
       If you want the business sold: Have you considered the problem of finding a prospective purchaser? _____Who? _____
       If there is no purchaser, can you nominate the logical person to buy your business?_____
       Who? _____
    d. Are you aware that your personal assets are subject to the claims of business creditors?
       Comments: _____

73. Partnership
    a. Name and kind of business: _____

    _____

    Names of Partners   *Age*   *Ownership*

    _____
    _____
    _____
    _____
    _____
    _____

    Your interest:
    Book value: $_____ Market value: $_____
    Do you feel there would be a purchaser at the latter price? _____
    Are all the partners in good health? _____
    b. In the event of your death, do you want your family to inherit your interest in the
        partnership or would you prefer that your interest be sold? _____
        If you want the family to inherit the business: Has your partner agreed in writing to go into
        business with your spouse when you die? _____
        If not, are you aware that the business must be liquidated? _____
        If you want the business sold: Do you have a buy-sell agreement in writing_____
        Sale price: $_____
        How is it funded? _____

74. Partnership
    a. Name and kind of business: _____

    _____

    Names of Partners   *Age*   *Ownership*

    _____
    _____
    _____
    _____
    _____
    _____

    Your interest:
    Book value: $_____ Market value: $_____
    Would be a purchaser at the latter price? _____
    b. Is there more than one class of stock? _____
        If so, give percent of ownership of each stockholder: _____
    c. Who are the non-stockholder key persons? _____

Are all the stockholders in good health? _____

d. In the event of your death, do you want family to inherit your stock in the corporation or would you prefer that the stock be sold? _____
    If you want the family to inherit your stock: Has any member of your family been groomed to replace you? _____
    If yes, who? _____
    If not, do they possess the talent for effective management? _____
    If not, whom would you nominate to run the business for them? _____
    Is it likely that the corporation will pay a regular dividend for the benefit of your heirs?

    _____
    If you want your stock sold: Do you have a buy-sell agreement which guarantees a market for your stock and which assures the surviving stockholders that no outsider can buy into the firm except with their approval? _____ Sale price: $_____
    How is it funded? _____

e. Are you aware that the Internal Revenue Service may establish its own valuation of your stock for tax purposes? _____

f. Are you aware of Section 303 of the Internal Revenue Code which provides special tax relief for stockholders such as in closely held corporations? _____

g. Are there any transfer restrictions on your stock? _____
    Explain:_____

h. Are you aware of the possible income tax pitfalls in corporation stock redemption plans? __
    Comments: _____

75. a. Are the executives or key members of your firm insured for the benefit of the firm? _____

    _____
    Details: _____

76. Which of the following employee benefit plans is the business:

Already Using	*Interested In*	
_____	_____	Group Life Insurance
_____	_____	Group Health Insurance
_____	_____	Group Disability Income
_____	_____	Group Carve Out
_____	_____	Salary Continuation
_____	_____	Deferred Compensation
_____	_____	Selective Bonus (IRC Section 162)
_____	_____	Postretirement Death Benefit
_____	_____	Individual Retirement Accounts
_____	_____	401 (k) Plan
_____	_____	Premium Only Plan/Flexible Spending Account/Cafeteria Plan
_____	_____	Pensions

Already Using	*Interested In*	
_____	_____	Profit Sharing
_____	_____	Tax Deferred Annuity
_____	_____	Split Dollar
_____	_____	Salary Savings/Payroll Deduction
_____	_____	Key Person Insurance
_____	_____	Supplemental Executive Retirement Plans (SERPs)
_____	_____	Simplified Employee Pensions (SEPs)
_____	_____	Business Overhead Expense Insurance

Which do you feel is most important to you now? _____

What are two areas you think I can assist with? _____

How much can you and the business put out each month to handle these needs? _____

What are your objectives for this business providing security for you and your family? _____

_____

77. We would like to remind you that our analysis and planning may involve certain legal interpretations and recommendations. In this respect, we can neither give legal advice nor prepare the legal documents that may be necessary to implement your plan. Instead, we must rely upon an attorney of your choice, who will be compensated by you. We also can neither give you accounting advice nor prepare accounting/tax documents. Instead we rely upon your accountant.

    a. Name of attorney: _____

        Address: _____

        Telephone: _____

    b. Name of accountant: _____

        Address: _____

        Telephone: _____

78. Can you think of anything we have overlooked which should be considered in our planning? ___

_____

79. We have attempted to bring to light all of the information surrounding your financial affairs together with your innermost thoughts and objectives, in an effort to guide us in the intelligent arrangement of your financial plan. Although it may be somewhat repetitious, tell us in summary form the things you want most to accomplish for your family and your business. (List in order to relative importance.)

_____

_____

_____

_____

_____

Chapter 1

Answers to Review Questions

1. Sole proprietorships cannot have more than one owner. The proprietor is ultimately responsible for everything: the responsibility is not shared with anyone and the liability is unlimited. It is the simplest form of business organization. There are no formal or legal requirements to form or terminate the business other than permits or licensing in local jurisdictions.

2. A limited partnership requires at least one limited partner and one general partner. General partnerships have no limited partners. Limited partners have limited liability and no participation in management of the company. General partners have full management responsibility and unlimited liability.

3. Publicly held C corporations are traded on the stock exchanges; closely held corporations are not. There is a union of ownership and management in closely held corporations, but there is no ready market for its stock. The limited liability for closely held corporations may be true only in theory, since creditors may require the personal guarantees of owners.

4. Neither S corporations nor partnerships are taxed as separate entities. Both are pass-through forms of businesses. All earnings for both must be reported on the personal 1040 forms of owners.

5. The following are characteristics of limited liability companies: unlimited membership, non-resident aliens may be owners, may have different classes of ownership, transfer of ownership requires consent of other members, members' financial liability is limited, and the LLC is taxed much like a partnership.

6. Comparison of Five Types of Business Organizations:

    a. A corporation pays corporate tax on income over expenses, before paying dividends to stockholders.

    b. The life of a C corporation is perpetual (unlimited)—not affected by the death of a stockholder.

    c. The life of an S corporation is perpetual (unlimited)—not affected by the death of a stockholder.

7. The 10 forms of business are: sole proprietor, general partnership, limited partnership, professional partnership, family limited partnership, limited liability company, C corporation, S corporation, professional corporation, personal services corporation.

8. A business does not have to stay locked into the form of business it initially chooses. At virtually any time it can change to another form of business. While there will be advantages and disadvantages of making such changes—and perhaps tax consequences as well—owners are generally free to change form when they want.

9. A C corporation pays federal income tax as an entity.

10. A general partnership is easily created (written or oral). Each partner has equal authority and shares profits equally unless otherwise agreed. A partnership entity pays no taxes (pass-through income and loss) and allows pooling of capital and talent. Disadvantages include unlimited personal liability for one's own acts as well as those of other partners and the firm. The personal assets and partnership assets can be subject to the claims of creditors. Death of a partner ends the partnership automatically. A corporation offers limited liability to stockholders, continuity of existence (death of a shareholder will not automatically end the corporation), ease of transferability of interest (this can also be a disadvantage) and the ability to raise capital by offering new shares for sale. Corporations can offer owner-employees tax-deductible fringe benefits and a corporation is taxed separately from individual owners, which can be an advantage or disadvantage. There is no ready market for the stock and the limited liability may be marginal in a closely held corporation. Double taxation of dividends and increased level of initial and going regulation are also disadvantages of corporate form.

Answers to Self-Test Questions

Question	Answer
11.	D
12.	A
13.	D
14.	A
15.	C
16.	C

Question	Answer
17.	A
18.	D
19.	B
20.	C

Chapter 2

Answers to Review Questions

1. Ten day-to-day concerns of business owners include: being profitable, obtaining credit, maintaining efficient production and service operations, cash flow, competition, providing service, resolving personal problems, public relations (consumerism), personnel and labor relations, economic trends, government regulations, changing markets, technology, and tax laws

2. Money is the essential ingredient to the survival of a business when an owner dies.

3. An ownership transfer plan is a written agreement among the owners of a business to buy a deceased partner's share of the business at a stipulated price, or with a predetermined formula to obtain the price. It is another name for a buy-sell plan or agreement.

4. The death of the business owner can lessen working capital and cash flow, jeopardize credit, and cause a loss of goodwill. Suppliers and creditors may come to call for the money owed to them. Employees may leave because the future of the business is uncertain.

5. Three financial statements used by business owners include: balance sheet, income statement, and cash flow statement (or cash budget).

6. Assets are the values of all rights and property owned by the business.

7. Liabilities are the debts of the business.

8. The owner's equity is the portion of the value of the business that the owners own. Assets minus liabilities equals owner's equity.

9. The bottom line of an income statement shows the company's net profit (or net loss) after taxes.

10. The eight categories discussed for each plan are: objective, owner, income tax aspects to business, income tax aspects to employee,

income tax aspects to deceased family, estate tax aspects, premium payor, and beneficiary

11. The objective of key employee life insurance is to provide protection to offset losses to a business due to the death of a valuable employee

12. Premiums are not deductible for buy-sell agreements, but the death proceeds are not generally taxable

13. The covered employee is the owner of a Section 162 plan.

14. Bob took time to establish rapport and collect facts. He approached the prospect with a personal insurance concept, the guaranteed insurability rider. He involved the mother in the sales process and she was supportive of the purchase. He then introduced the idea of the business paying the premium.

15. The business will pay the premium so the premium is considered compensation to Steve as an "executive bonus". He must pay income tax on the bonus amount. The premium is tax deductible to the company as compensation paid.

The following questions pertain to the case history, One Approach to Business Owners.

16. Three alternatives for business owners regarding disposition of the business at the death of an owner include:

   a. Keep it. This means keeping that ownership portion in the family.

   b. Sell it. Sell the business as a going concern

   c. Liquidate it. Sell the assets of the business after shutting down the business.

17. The question suggested in the textbook for approaching business owners is: "What do you want to happen to the business when you die or retire?"

18. If you get over your level of knowledge in talking to a business owner, you may simply stop the interview, gather what you need, and come back at a later date with an expert.

Answers to Self-Test Questions

Question	Answer
19.	B

Question	Answer
20.	A
21.	D
22.	C
23.	A
24.	B
25.	B
26.	B
27.	A
28.	C

Chapter 3

Answers to Review Questions

1. Sources of business prospects include current clients, business patronized by you and your family, referrals, centers of influence, tips clubs, community involvement contacts, observation, cold calls and cold canvas, lists, reference books, directories, newspapers, and public records.

2. Attributes of centers of influence include high prestige in the community, in their industry or profession, or in organizations to which they belong; interest in your success, and ongoing access to a wide circle of successful people.

3. Endless-chain prospecting is a natural outgrowth of <u>referred-lead prospecting.</u>

4. This is a personal choice and there are no right or wrong answers. See the helpful list of directories and other sources in Chapter 3.

5. Ways in which a business and personal approach to prospects differ include: time and timing (They are at work and work time is important. Do not call at busy times), focus on needs and wants (maximizing profits and solving problems), accessibility (getting through the gatekeeper—often the prospect's assistant/secretary), your attitude (be confident of your valuable service), and specialized approaches (know your strengths and use them).

6. The purpose of the preapproach is to precondition your prospects to expect your request for an appointment and be receptive to it.

7. Two preapproach prospecting methods include using letters and the telephone to contact prospects.

8. Advantages and disadvantages of using the telephone as an approach and prospecting tool:

   • advantages: quick, convenient, inexpensive
   • disadvantages: people may find it easier to say no on the phone than they do in person, technologies such as caller ID and answering machines, and legal restrictions such as "Do-not-call" lists.

9. Four factors that influence how well you are received include: appearance, manners, what you say, and how you say it.

10. This is a personalized application of what is discussed in the chapter as well as your own experience and company training.

11. This is a reference to a buy-sell agreement, cleverly put in an effective way to create interest and make the concept less technical.

12. This is an opinion question. Many advisors find it an effective method to find new prospects. The owner can be met face-to-face on a drop-in basis—an advantage when you are not be able to reach the prospect by phone. It is time-consuming and can be frustrating at times, but usually yields positive results.

13. It is not necessary for the legal agreement to be completed before the insurance is applied for or issued. But this case study demonstrates clearly that the advisor should diligently follow-up with the client to be sure that all necessary documents have been implemented.

Answers to Self-Test Questions

Question	Answer
14.	B
15.	D
16.	B
17.	A
18.	B
19.	C
20.	A B

Question	Answer
21.	A
22.	A
23.	C

Chapter 4

Answers to Review Questions

1. Buying is a decision to purchase a good or service resulting from a 4-step process: recognize problem, desire solution, decide on solution and make purchase. It parallels the sales process: discover problem, show consequences, offer solutions, and help buy now. The advisor must assist the buyer through this process. Do not offer solutions before discovering problem, collecting and analyzing facts. The advisor must recognize where buyer is in the buying process. People like to buy, not to "be sold".

2. It is during the fact-finding process that the prospect's problems are identified and are made so clear that the prospect decides to do something to resolve them. Fact-finding lays the foundation for recommendations. Trust and the credibility of the advisor are reflected in how fact-finding is conducted. It also is the basis for the continuation of the sales process.

3. Fact Finders found in this textbook include:

    - Appendix A ("Current Coverage and Business Data") is an all-purpose business fact finder.
    - Appendix B ("Confidential Transfer-of-Ownership Analysis") is for buy-sell situations.
    - Appendix C ("Confidential Questionnaire") is primarily for estate planning situations, with questions 72 to the end applying to business situations.
    - "Areas of Possible Interest" is a general purpose fact finder.
    - "Brief Fact Finder/Feeling Finder Regarding Disposition of a Business at Death" is for buy-sell situations.
    - "Key Person Fact Finding and Feeling Finding" is a key person fact finder.
    - The 15 segments of "Areas of Possible Interest" are each mini fact finders—one for each of the 15 topics.

     • The "Prospect Files" questions in Chapter 6 can serve as a general-purpose business fact finder.

4. The advisor must determine who is the decision maker and get in front of him or her. The advisor must make sure to the extent possible that all decision-makers are present at advisor presentations. Decisions are made in basically one of three decision styles: authoritarian, consultative and participative, based on how much the decision maker allows input from others. Social style tells us that people behave in one of four characteristic styles: driver, expressive, amiable or analytical. Recognizing a person's style helps you to develop rapport and address your response to what is important to that individual.

5. Five typical outcomes of the death of an owner of a loosely held corporation are:

    a. Liquidate: the surviving owners, along with the estate executor, sell the firm's assets, pay debts, and split any remaining funds among themselves.

    b. Heirs and surviving associates sell the business as a going concern to outsiders.

    c. Heirs become owners and active employees.

    d. Heirs sell their share to outsiders. Surviving owners retain their ownership.

    e. Heirs sell their share to the surviving owners.

6. The alternatives at the death of a partner are quite similar to those at the death of an owner in a closely held corporation.

7. When a sole proprietor dies, one of the following outcomes may typically occur:

    • the business may shut its doors and be liquidated by the estate executor

    • the business may be continued by the estate's executor until it can be sold as a going concern

    • the business may be transferred by will to a specified individual, usually a family member

    • the business may be sold to an individual or group under the terms of an agreement made prior to death.

8. Problems that may confront a sole proprietorship at the death of the sole proprietor include:

   - The executor and heirs may not be familiar with the business on a day-to-day basis and are not likely to devote full time to it.
   - Employees may leave, lose incentive, and be concerned with their jobs.
   - Creditors may push for payment.
   - Goodwill may be lost.
   - The value of the business may fall as a going concern or may result in a liquidation sale.
   - Courts or legal problems may delay sale, also causing the value to fall.

9. The death of an owner in a small or one-person corporation would not dissolve the corporation, but forced liquidation would be likely. A partnership would end and would need to be reorganized. Loss of management in a small firm would most likely be very disruptive, and profits and cash flow may fall. Heirs may want cash from the business, or to take part in a corporation. Whether the deceased held a majority or minority interest would effect position of surviving owners and heirs.

10. If the deceased was a majority shareholder, the executor or family controls the corporation and would have control of the operation of the company. If a minority interest shareholder died, his/her heirs could provide their "nuisance value" to survivors but would not have a controlling interest, and would be subject to decisions of majority shareholders. Minority owners would have a right to vote and receive information about the operation of the company, and could demand that measures be taken for their interest, which could cause friction, bad feelings and possible legal actions.

11. One effect of the death of a business owner on heirs would likely be a loss of income to the survivors. There would be no salary or dividends expected. The business may be impaired and unable to provide income, but there would be no reason to do so anyway outside of previous agreements. The choices for the family are discussed in answer 4-4.

12. In the fact-finding interview, the advisor asked some pointed questions designed to make the prospect realize the need. The prospect feels she would leave the business to her husband if she

died, but she is made to realize he is not prepared to run it. Her key people would probably leave.

13. The value of the business was determined by using the industry standard of seven times earnings (profit of $60,000 × 7 = $420,000). If no buyer was established, liquidation value would only be $75,000 ($100,000 assets - $25,000 debt).

14. The solution proposed in the closing interview involved the owner loaning key employees part of the premium for life insurance on her life, to be paid to her husband at her death. Employees would also contribute part of the premium.

Answers to Self-Test Questions

Question	Answer
15.	C
16.	B
17.	D
18.	B
19.	B
20.	C
21.	B
22.	D
23.	A
24.	B

Chapter 5

Answers to Review Questions

1. Benefits of a funded buy sell agreement to owner's heirs:
   - estate gets money to pay taxes and costs
   - estate distribution is planned
   - a purchaser is established
   - estate is settled more quickly
   - estate tax value and fair price are set
   - cash is assured

Benefits of a funded buy-sell to surviving owners:

- eliminates the pressure to help heirs financially
- eliminates potential conflicts with heirs
- provides funds to buy interest and assures control

2. Three types of buy-sell agreements are:

- cross-purchase agreement—agreement between owners to purchase the business interest of others upon death
- stock redemption agreement (entity plan)—business agrees to purchase owners interest upon death
- wait-and-see agreement—agreement allows type of buy-sell to be determined after the death of an owner

3. Five sources of funding a buy-sell are:

- accumulated capital in a sinking fund
- borrowed funds
- installment payments from an owner's personal funds
- installment payment by the business from future profits
- life insurance

4. Some major points that should be included in a buy-sell agreement include:

- the parties to the agreement
- purpose of the agreement
- commitment of the parties
- lifetime transfer restrictions (right of first refusal)
- method of determining purchase price
- funding
- transfer of the business
- modification or termination of the agreement

5. The benefits of using life insurance to fund a buy-sell agreement include:

- the event (death) creating the need creates the solution (cash)

- the annual outlay is relatively small compared to the potential benefits
- the full amount needed is available immediately
- there can be competitive return on products
- cash value can have alternative uses if it insures lives to retirement
- estate planning is aided by having an insured plan
- existing assets remain intact to heirs
- the buyout is predetermined, so disputes are avoided
- the plan allows all involved to go forward with confidence

6. The federal income tax treatment for buy-sell agreements is as follows: premiums are generally not tax deductible under any plan, but the death proceeds are generally received by beneficiary income tax-free (except if proceeds are subject to corporate AMT or the transfer-for-value tax).

7. Alternatives to insurance when an owner is uninsurable include:

- buy personal in-force life insurance of the uninsurable, if practical and available
- start a sinking fund
- create an installment sale agreement through personal or company funds
- borrow when necessary
- place key person insurance on insurable owners to supplement funding through death proceeds or cash values outside of previous agreements.

The choices for the family are discussed in answer 4-4.

8. The advisor presents himself by saying, "I see myself as a problem-solver." My job is gathering data to develop well-founded recommendations." He thinks that business owners should have a financial advisor on their team of advisors.

9. In fact-finding, the advisor focuses on what the prospect wishes to happen in the event of death or disability and what business continuation plans they have.

10. According to this advisor, fact-finding is the opportunity to pinpoint problems, find the prospective client's hot button, and disturb the prospect about these problems.

Answers to Self-Test Questions

Question	Answer
11.	C
12.	D
13.	D
14.	A
15.	B
16.	C
17.	C
18.	D
19.	A
20.	D

Chapter 6

Answers to Review Questions

1. In a family-owned business, in contrast to other businesses,

   - all or most owners are related family members
   - usually the owners want to pass ownership to their children at death or retirement
   - both spouses may rely on the business as their source of income
   - at death, complications often arise regarding control of the business

2. The main target of IRC Chapter 14 is an owner of family corporations (or family partnerships) who transfer some stock ownership that is expected to appreciate in value while the owner nonetheless retains operating control of the business. In brief, IRS does not want to give a tax break to a transfer that does not, as a practical matter, have an impact on who really controls the business.

3. The purpose of Section 303 is to give a tax break so that a family business won't have to sell the business to pay the estate tax.

Section 303 allows an income tax-free partial stock redemption of a closely held business if certain conditions are met.

4. Part of the proceeds of a key person life insurance policy can be used to fund the partial stock redemption. The insurance can provide funding for a Section 303 Stock Redemption so that illiquid assets do not have to be sold.

5. In valuing a business, factors offered by the IRS include: the nature of the business, business history, economic outlook of the business, earning capacity, goodwill, sales, stock sales, market price of comparable businesses.

6. The buy-sell agreement requires a business value. A fair value must be determined to treat the owners and heirs equitably. A properly valued business can set the estate tax value, which may save the owner's estate considerable money and the heirs considerable delay and aggravation.

7. Traditional methods of valuing a business include:

   - book value of owner's equity
   - straight capitalization which is based on the earning capacity of the business
   - sales method, which looks at arms-length prior sales of the business
   - price/earnings analysis, which involves comparing the market value of the business to similar businesses, taking into account majority or minority interest into the valuation

8. When a business owner becomes seriously disabled, the business can be deprived of the services of the owner and the income and profit produced by the owner. A replacement may have to be hired and paid. There is likely to be a severe financial drain on the business' income. Other owners and employees have to work harder to make up for the loss of the disabled owner's services.

9. Three uses of disability insurance for business purposes include:

   - key employee disability insurance
   - funding a disability buyout
   - business overhead coverage

10. In drafting a disability buyout agreement, items to be resolved include:

- the definition of disability
- when the buyout will occur
- whether or not the buyout will be mandatory
- how the disabled owner's business interest will be valued for the buyout
- what funding source will be used

11. Sources for funding a disability buyout include: current income, an uninsured sinking fund, borrowed funds, or disability buyout insurance.

12. Business overhead expense insurance pays operating expenses when the owner is unable to work because of a disabling injury or illness. It will allow the business to operate until the owner can return to work. It is a reimbursement policy, and pays for actual incurred expenses.

13. Premiums for disability business overhead expense insurance are tax deducible to all forms of business as a business expense. The benefits received are taxable. However, because the benefits reimburse deductible business expenses, the tax impact is erased.

14. The primary goal of the closing interview is to help the prospect see and acknowledge the problem, its size and its urgency. The ultimate goal is to have the prospect take action to solve the problem.

15. Examples of buying signals include: the prospect asks questions, the prospect seeks an opinion, or the prospect becomes friendly and relaxed. Body language and nonverbal signs are important in detecting buying signals.

16. Open-ended questions are questions intended to get the prospect to talk. Standard questions— who, what, when, where, why and how—are good ways to introduce open-ended questions such as "How do you feel about retirement?" or "Why do you feel that way?" These questions are designed to obtain subjective and detailed information, especially about a person's feelings, attitudes and beliefs.

17. A trial close is a question to helps the advisor determine if the prospect is ready to buy or is interested in a proposed idea, without asking directly. Examples would include "How does this concept sound to you?" or "Do you think this is important?" or "Does this feature fit your need?"

18. Categories of closes, or closing techniques, include: choice, praise, implied consent, benefit, and minor point.

19. The approach was by telephone for personal insurance on the idea of estate analysis. The advisor explained that planning was needed if the prospect planned to use the business to care for his family.

20. In the initial interview, fact-finding and establishing the need for a buy-sell agreement occurred. The advisor asked disturbing questions about what would happen if one of the owners died.

21. In the second interview a presentation was made to all owners and the bookkeeper. The "Business Stabilization Plan" was presented. The advisor got more specific information about the number and value of the shares and the business and got permission to see a family attorney.

22. The reluctant brother was the "Third" brother, who did not think this was necessary to have formal plans and was concerned about the cost.

23. A "Business Stabilization Plan" is a plan to overcome problems caused by death—in other words, a buy-sell agreement.

Answers to Self-Test Questions

Question	Answer
24.	B
25.	C
26.	A
27.	A
28.	C
29.	A
30.	A
31.	B
32.	C
33.	C

Chapter 7

Answers to Review Questions

1. A key person is any employee who contributes substantially to the financial well being of a business. Their death or disability would result in an economic loss to the company.

2. Insuring the life of a key employee can provide cash at the death of the key person to offset lost profits; it can pay off indebtedness; a permanent policy can serve as a cash reserve; and it can provide cash while the business hires and trains a replacement.

3. The corporation is the owner, beneficiary and premium payor of a key person policy.

4. Serious consequences of the death of a key person include: disruption of management, impairment of credit, loss in profits, need to replace the key person, and loss of confidence by customers, suppliers and employees.

5. Sources of cash to offset the loss of a key employee include: current profits, borrowing, uninsured sinking fund and life and disability insurance (insured sinking funds).

6. Benefits of insuring key people for a business include:

    *   provides indemnification
    *   provides a lifetime reserve fund (permanent insurance)
    *   strengthens credit
    *   increases net working capital (upon key employee death)
    *   can supplement retirement income
    *   can continue a portion of the deceased's salary to the spouse or other heir

7. Methods for valuing a key employee include the contribution to earnings method, which estimates a key person's contributions to net profits, and the replacement cost method, which is an estimation by the business owner of the cost to replace that key person's contribution to company profits.

8. By passing a corporate resolution authorizing the purchase of key person insurance, the firm has a much better chance of avoiding the accumulated earnings tax.

9. The insured person in a key person insurance policy has no rights. The owner and the beneficiary is the business.

10. In insuring a key person, both types of insurance, term and permanent, would be appropriate, based on the total needs analysis of the business's situation. Permanent will provide cash value benefits, but the cost is considerably more, at least initially. Term will be initially low in cost, but will increase over time. How strong is the cash position of the company, how long do they need the insurance, how long is the employee expected to remain with

the business, and so on are questions that would need to be answered to address the question of which type of insurance would best suit the prospect's need.

11. Naming a person as a personal beneficiary makes the insurance personal insurance. If the IRS discovers that personal insurance was paid for with company money, they will insist that the premiums be reported by the insured as taxable income.

12. The emotional key was her story about the company she had visited earlier, where the principal stockholder died and the heirs sold the company to a large national concern. The new owners dismissed everyone at the company and replaced them with their own people. The owner prospect cared for his employees and didn't want this to happen to them.

13. In the fact-finding process the owner said, "Maybe I shouldn't really care what happens when I die." The advisor became irritated and asked if he would like to prepay the IRS now rather than later. It appears the prospect's hesitation stemmed from his lack of confidence in this inexperienced advisor, so she called in an experienced advisor to work with her.

Answers to Self-Test Questions

Question	Answer
14.	A
15.	B
16.	D
17.	D
18.	A
19.	D
20.	C
21.	D
22.	B
23.	C

Chapter 8

Answers to Review Questions

1. Ways that property can be transferred include: gift, contract, will, joint ownership, trust or intestacy.

2. The four elements of a trust are a grantor, trustee, beneficiary, and trust principal (or corpus).

3. A living trust is a revocable trust that is like a will, but it avoids the time lag, the expense and the public aspects of probate.

4. The grantor has the right to revoke, alter, modify, or amend the revocable trust.

5. Types of joint ownership include: joint tenancy, tenancy in common, and tenancy by the entirety.

6. Joint tenancy and tenancy by the entirety cannot be willed, because the property automatically passes to surviving tenant at death, but any tenancy in common can pass by will.

7. Estate planning is a process aimed at accumulating and retaining wealth, and disposing of it according to the client's wishes. More simply, estate planning is planning for the creation and distribution of wealth.

8. The four steps of the estate planning process are: analysis, structuring, accumulation, and disposition.

9. Emotional reasons for an interest in estate planning are: the thought of death, one's affairs not being in order regarding death planning, ignorance about death-related issues, worry about old-age issues, general uneasiness about the future, how to start the process, and who to trust with the process.

10. A prospect for estate planning is a person who is subject to estate tax, is a high income earner, has high potential earnings, owns a business, has children or grandchildren, or wants to give to charity.

11. The federal estate tax is a tax on the right to transfer property at death.

12. The gross estate includes all property and all property rights owned in any way by the decedent.

13. Deductions that can reduce the gross estate include: death costs, administrative expenses, debts, charitable bequests, and the marital deduction.

14. Estate tax credits that can reduce the estate tax include: the unified credit, the state death tax credit, the gift tax credit, a credit for estate taxes on earlier transfers, and credit for foreign death taxes paid.

15. Life insurance can be used in estate planning to provide liquidity for living expenses, debt liquidation, estate equalization, funds to pay estate tax, funding for business succession, and charitable giving.

16. The federal gift tax is a tax on the lifetime transfer of property.

Answers to Self-Test Questions

Question	Answer
17.	A
18.	C
19.	C
20.	A
21.	C
22.	C
23.	B
24.	D
25.	D
26.	D

accumulated earnings tax • the tax on the portion of a corporation's income that is beyond the expected needs of the business. The tax base for the calculation of the accumulated earnings tax is called accumulated taxable income.

accumulated taxable income • the portion of a corporation's income that is beyond the expected needs of the business and therefore the tax base for the calculation of the accumulated-earnings tax

acid test ratio • an indication of a company's strength and how well it can cover its short-term obligations. This is a comparison of current debts with "quick assets" or near-cash assets (cash, marketable securities, and net receivables) found by dividing near-cash assets by total current liability. This test eliminates inventories, goods in process, and other current assets that might bring less than their stated value.

adjusted book value • an approximate fair market value that is arrived at by adjusting the value of assets and liabilities as carried on the books, adding a value for goodwill to the value of the firm's tangible assets

administrator • a representative of the decedent, appointed by the court in the absence of a duly appointed executor, who is designated to hold legal title to the estate's property

alternative minimum tax • an income tax that attempts to make certain C corporations pay a fair amount of tax despite deductions, credits, and other tax preferences that reduce their regular income tax to a small amount

alternative minimum taxable income (AMTI) • the amount of a corporation's income that determines if the alternative minimum tax must be paid. The base is calculated by adding certain tax-preference items to the corporation's normal taxable income.

annual gift tax exclusion • There is no taxable gift if the amount of the gift to any one person is valued at no more than $13,000 in 2010 and the gift is of a present interest. A gift of *present interest* means it is a completed gift with "no strings attached" and can be used and enjoyed now, without restriction. The *annual gift tax exclusion* is indexed for inflation and adjustments will occur in $1,000 increments.

applicable credit amount • a credit to which every decedent's estate is entitled that can be applied directly against the estate tax (formerly called the unified credit). *Compare* applicable exclusion amount, which shelters taxable transfers from payment of gift and/or estate taxes by the applicable credit amount.

approach • No matter what method you choose for contacting prospects, you are seeking to achieve one primary goal: getting an appointment. When you have secured an appointment, you have an important commitment from the prospect. When you meet a prospect in person, it is the time to demonstrate your credibility and ability to be of service. It is time to determine whether the sales process will continue after this initial meeting.

assets • the values of all rights and property owned by the business, typically divided into current assets, fixed assets, and other assets. Intangible assets are business assets that are not considered easily appraised and are thus not included as assets on the unadjusted balance sheet (for example, customer relationships or production know-how).

Areas of Possible Interest fact finder • This one-page fact finder asks "What interests the business owner?" You can use this list as a focal point and/or giveaway piece of literature on cold calls, as a pre-approach mailer with a cover letter saying that you plan to stop by, or as an abbreviated fact finder on your initial interview. You can also use it to show your prospects the kind of work you do.

articles of incorporation • a document registered and filed with the state, describing such aspects of a corporation as the name and location, its purpose and powers, and the capitalization of the corporation. The corporation's legal existence is established by the filing of the articles with the appropriate state authority.

asset sale • the sale of a corporation in which the buyer may pick and choose the assets of a company he or she wishes to purchase, and the purchaser will gain a new cost basis for the assets. This type of sale may require action by the shareholders of the selling corporation, such as a majority (or super majority) vote by the shareholders of the corporation.

attribution of ownership • stock owned by one individual or entity but considered to be owned by another individual or entity for the purpose of determining how a particular transaction is taxed (also referred to as constructive ownership)

balance sheet • a formal statement of the assets, liabilities, and owner's equity on a given date

blockage discount • a discount allowed by the IRS when a large block of corporate stock is valued for estate tax purposes, reflecting the fact that the market would be depressed if a large block of corporate stock was offered for sale in a brief time frame

book value • a type of business value equal to the excess of assets over liabilities; not considered the "real" value, or fair market value, of the business. Adjusted book value is an approximate fair market value that is arrived at by adjusting the value of assets and liabilities as carried on the books, adding a value for goodwill to the value of the firm's tangible assets.

business continuation (succession planning) • the process of planning for the continuation of a business in the case of the death, disability, or retirement of the owner

business life cycle • the natural progression of a business from a start-up venture in survival mode, through a growth and success stage, to a mature and thriving business that needs to address issues of management transition and succession of ownership

business-overhead-expense insurance • disability insurance that provides reimbursement for certain specified expenses to allow the business to remain viable until the disabled owner returns to work

business valuation • the process of assigning a value to a business or a formula to determine its value for the purpose of federal income and estate tax, and for buy-sell arrangements

business valuation methods • book value, capitalization method, sales method, price/earnings analysis

buy-sell agreement • an agreement between business owners or between business owners and employees regarding business continuation. Upon the death of one of the owners, the surviving owners or employees will buy the deceased owner's interest, and the deceased owner's heirs will sell that interest to the surviving owners or employees. This is also called an *ownership transfer plan*.

buying cycle • buying is the decision people make when they want a service or a product. In reaching this decision, people go through a process with four basic steps: 1. Recognize a problem. 2. Desire a solution. 3. Decide on a solution. 4. Make the purchase.

buying signal • a non-verbal or verbal indication from the prospect that they are interested in some aspect of your presentation or are generally favorable towards your recommendation(s). The advisor must be aware of the prospect's behavior to be ready to respond in the appropriate manner. Examples of buying signals would include the prospect asking questions, leaning forward, moving closer, seeking your opinion, or becoming friendly and relaxed.

bylaws • a corporate document approved by the founders that describes duties and powers of directors and shareholders, the rules for shareholder and director meetings, and other corporate operating matters

C corporation • a body, created by law, composed of individuals united under a common name, the members of which succeed each other, so that the body continues the same notwithstanding the change of individuals who compose it, and is, for certain purposes, considered as a natural person. Its characteristics include limited liability of stockholders, continuity of existence, ease of transferability of interest, and the ability to raise capital through the sale of stock (ownership interest).

capitalization factor • the inverse of the rate of return calculated for the capitalization procedure

capitalization of earnings • one of the most common methods of valuing a closely held business, based on the concept that the value of property is the value of the earnings stream it produces

cash flow • the relationship of actual receipts minus actual expenditures, resulting in the amount of cash on hand, closely related to working capital. Cash needs are matched with projected receipts and expenditures to be able to create a cash budget. Good cash flow is an indication of good management and business solvency.

center of influence • an individual with high prestige in the community, in their industry or profession, or in organizations to which he or she belongs. This person will have more than a passing interest in your business success, and access to or knowledge of a wide circle of successful people on a regular and ongoing basis.

closely held business • a business not traded on a securities exchange whose shares are not generally offered for sale. The business is controlled by a small group of shareholders who generally are engaged actively in the day-to-day management of the business.

codicil • a supplement or addition to an existing will, to effect some revision, change or modification to that will. A codicil must meet the same requirements regarding execution and validity as a will.

complete redemption • a stock redemption that qualifies as a capital transaction if a corporation redeems all the stock owned by a shareholder. This results in complete termination of the shareholder's interest in the redeeming corporation.

constructive receipt • a tax-timing concept that provides that income is taxed when it is available to a recipient without substantial limitations or restrictions.

contribution to earnings method • used to determine the insurable value of a key employee. To perform this calculation, determine the firm's average net profits, select an opportunity cost for investment return, estimate the portion of profits attributable to investment return and net this out of profits, multiply the net profits by the portion made by the key employee, and multiply by the number of years until a replacement can reproduce these results.

corporate liquidation • dissolution of a corporation in which the corporation's properties are distributed to shareholders and the corporate stock is canceled in the process of terminating the corporation

cost basis • what you pay for something, or your investment in a contract or object. It is the starting point for determining a gain or loss for income tax purposes. For tax purposes, this starting point can be its cost, its fair market value at a specified date, or a substituted basis. It can also be adjusted for reasons such as depreciation or the costs of improvements.

cross-purchase plan • a type of buy-sell agreement formed between the owners of a business that commits the surviving owner(s) to buy and the deceased owner's estate to sell the ownership interest of a deceased owner. A cross-purchase agreement can be formed between partners in a partnership, shareholders of a corporation, and members of a limited liability company.

current ratio • current assets divided by current liabilities, an indication of the debt-paying ability of the business and of working capital.

decision making styles • accessibility to the decision maker is critical in sales, but decisions are made differently in different organizations and with different individuals. There are formal and informal decision-making processes, and there are styles of decision-making, differing in the degree of participation by those who are affected by the decision. The text discussed three types of decision-making processes: authoritarian, consultative and participative.

disability buyout insurance • specialty policies designed to facilitate a disability buy-sell agreement by providing for large lump-sum or installment benefits related to the value of the business. These policies, provided by a limited number of insurers, are subject to restrictive financial underwriting and policy maximums.

disability income insurance • insurance that provides income payments at the disability of an insured. If used to fund a cross-purchase buy-sell agreement, the individual owners will purchase disability income insurance on the other owners. If used in an entity or stock-redemption approach, the business itself will buy, pay the premiums for, and be the beneficiary of policies covering the owners.

discounted future earnings (DFE) • a method of valuation similar to the capitalization-of-earnings method but based on projected future earnings

dissolution • the point at which a corporation or partnership ceases as an entity or is dissolved

earnings and profits (E & P) • current or past earnings of a corporation that have not been distributed as dividends to shareholders and are carried on the corporate books

economic benefit • a benefit from a nonqualified deferred-compensation plan that is immediately taxable if the plan is treated as funded with the benefits set aside for the participants beyond the claims of the corporation's general creditors

elimination period • the amount of time that must elapse after the onset of a disability before benefits are paid from a disability income policy or before purchase must occur in a disability buy-sell agreement

entity plan • a type of buy-sell agreement in which the business, as a separate legal entity from the owners, will purchase the interest held by any deceased owner's estate. As parties to the agreement, the owners commit their estates to sell their ownership interests to the business at death. In a corporation, an entity agreement is known as a stock-redemption agreement.

equity split-dollar plan • a variation on the split-dollar arrangement in which the employer's rights are limited to the actual premiums paid by the employer and the excess cash surrender value vesting in the participant

estate planning • an organized effort to give heirs the maximum amount of wealth, consistent with maintaining the business owner's own financial independence, security, and financial objectives. It can also be defined as the accumulation, conservation and distribution of wealth.

executor • a representative of the decedent, named in a valid will, who is designated to hold legal title to the estate's property

fact and feeling finding • lays the foundation for any recommendations to be made by the financial advisor, or any buying decision by the prospect. It is the primary tool used by an advisor to demonstrate the need for the prospect to act. Objectives of fact finding include: build trust and credibility, gather the data to construct a proposal based on the prospect's needs and wants, and get agreement from the prospect to continue with the next step of the process. Objective (fact) and subjective (feeling) information is collected.

fair market value • used as a business valuation technique, the net amount at which a willing purchaser would pay a willing seller, neither being under any compulsion to buy and sell, and both having reasonable knowledge of all relevant factors.

family limited partnership • a partnership in which family members act as the partners, often splitting the partnership income among several people and placing some business income in lower tax brackets.

federal estate tax • is imposed, at graduated rates, on the right to transfer property at death. The federal estate tax return (Form 706), if required, must be filed and the tax paid by the executor of a deceased person's estate within 9 months after the decedent's death. Time of payment may be extended for "reasonable cause."

federal gift tax • is integrated with federal estate taxation. As with the estate tax, the gift tax is a tax on the transfer of cash or property during the donor's life, measured by the value of the property transferred. The gift tax is calculated on an amount known as "taxable gifts." A gift tax return, and the gift tax due, if any, is required each year for which a donor has taxable gifts.

first-offer restriction • a provision contained in many closely held corporation stock certificates requiring the shareholder to offer stock to the existing shareholders first, usually at an agreed price, before selling it to outsiders

funded buy-sell agreement • The most practical and certain way to assure these objectives following the death of an owner is through a funded buy-sell agreement. The funded, properly drafted buy-sell agreement produces the following benefits: it establishes a fair price for the business interest or it clearly specifies a method or formula for determining a fair price, it guarantees the heirs that they will receive cash for the inherited business interest, it assures the surviving business owners that they will have uninterrupted control and full ownership of the company, it helps creditors and suppliers to know today that the company is more likely to survive the problems associated with a future death of a key employee-owner, if properly funded, it provides cash at the exact time needed and in a predetermined, specified amount, and it establishes a value for estate evaluation acceptable to the IRS.

general partnership • a partnership containing only general partners who are typically coequals in the ownership, management responsibilities, and liabilities for the business

gift tax • the federal tax on the transfer of cash or property, measured by the value of the property transferred and payable by the grantor

goodwill • theoretically, the earning power of a business in excess of a fair return on the business's tangible assets; its formula valuation is often used by appraisers and generally accepted by the court.

grantor trust • a common type of living trust in which the grantor is treated as the owner for income tax purposes, typically a revocable trust created as a probate-avoidance device

guaranteed renewable • a policy option providing that the insurer must renew an insurance policy until the insured reaches 65 but has the option to adopt a new rate structure for future renewal premiums

incidence of ownership • some degree of control over a life insurance policy, which would cause it to be included in the estate of a decedent. It refers to a number of rights of the insured or insured's estate in the economic benefits of the policy and is not limited to ownership.

income statement • compares the income earned during a certain period of time—usually annually—with the expenses incurred during that same period. The income statement summarizes income and expense items and measures how successfully the business has been managed. Total income less total expenses equals net income for the period. If expenses exceed income, the deficit is called net loss. Unlike the balance sheet, the income statement is a summary of what has taken place (regarding income and expenses) over a period of time.

income in respect of a decedent (IRD) • income that was earned by a decedent but not constructively received at the time of his or her death

installment sale • a purchase method of installment payments for a business interest, employed when pre-funding is not the option of choice for a buy-sell agreement or if the life insurance funding proves to be inadequate. The buy-sell agreement specifies the details of the installment purchase, such as term and principal amount.

insurable interest • a financial interest in the insured in which there is a reasonable expectation of benefit from the insured's continued life or a financial loss from the insured's death.

intestacy • individual state laws providing for distribution of the property of a person who has died without leaving a valid will

IRC Chapter 14 (intra-family transfers) • tax rules for valuation of interests in family-controlled businesses that are transferred to family members of the owner, wherein the owner retains certain types of interest in the transferred property. The rules are aimed at owners of family corporations (or family partnerships) who transfer some ownership (stock) that is expected to appreciate in value, while the owner nonetheless retains control of the business. IRS will accept the value stated in a buy-sell agreement if the agreement meets four criteria: it is a bona fide business arrangement, not a device to transfer the business to other family members for less than full value, similar to those entered into by persons in arm's-length transactions, and the valuation must be acceptable to the IRS.

joint ownership (tenancy) • two or more persons owning the same property. Types of joint ownership include joint tenants, where two or more persons own an undivided interest in property (If one dies, the other(s) own it automatically and totally); tenancy by entirety, between husband and wife; and tenancy in common, where a tenant owns a divided interest and can pass that interest on to others during life or at death.

joint venture • a business relationship resembling a partnership. Joint ventures may exist between individuals, corporations, partnerships, or any combination for their mutual advantage. Participants bring special skills, knowledge, property, or money to work together on a specific project or projects.

key person (employee) • an employee whose skills, client base, or other attributes make him or her a valuable asset to the closely held business. A loss of the key employee may result in a loss of income and increased expenses.

key person (employee) insurance • life or disability insurance owned by the business to indemnify the business in the case of the key employee's death or disability. This insurance is owned by the company, and the non-deductible premium is paid by the company. In the event of a claim the company would receive tax-free benefits from the policy.

key person (employee) valuation • in replacing a key person consideration must be given to the amount of insurance needed to cover the cost of the loss to the business of the key employee. Two methods available to determine this value are the contribution to earnings and replacement cost methods.

liabilities • claims on asset values of the business by persons other than the owners. Liabilities are the debts of the business on the date that the balance sheet is prepared, generally separated into current liabilities and long-term liabilities.

LIFO/FIFO • measuring methods for inventory. LIFO is the abbreviation for *last in, first out.* FIFO stands for *first in, first out.* Under LIFO, goods most recently bought or produced are treated as those first sold. Thus, goods on hand at the close of the year are treated as those bought or produced earliest. Under FIFO, goods purchased first or produced first are treated as the first goods sold. Thus, goods on hand at the close of the year are treated as those bought or produced latest.

limited-liability company (LLC) • a form of business enterprise in which business owners (members) have liability protection and the company can elect to receive pass-through tax treatment for federal income taxes

limited-liability partnership (LLP) • a partnership in which all partners are sheltered from liability for partnership activities

limited partnership • a partnership composed of active participants (general partners) who retain personal responsibility for business operations, and passive investment partners (limited partners) who are at risk only to the extent of their investment in the business

liquidation • the dissolution of a business upon the death of an owner. Liquidation means selling the assets for cash and bringing business activity to a halt. This may have unfortunate results if the sale is forced or piecemeal. For a corporation, the corporation's properties are distributed to shareholders and the corporate stock is canceled in the process of terminating the corporation.

living trust • Living trusts, sometimes called *inter vivos* trusts, are a practical way of passing property on to heirs without the costs, time delays, and public nature of probate. A living trust is like a will, except that it bypasses probate. An attorney prepares it. The grantor retains full control to revoke or amend it at any time. The living trust often includes decisions about what the grantor wants to happen if he or she becomes disabled or dies. Everything that will pass through the living trust must have its title changed to the name of the trust. This includes real estate, cars, checking accounts, stocks, and other investments.

marital deduction (unlimited) • The most significant estate tax deduction, in terms of total dollars, is the marital deduction. Generally, an estate is allowed a deduction for the full value of all estate property that passes to the decedent's surviving spouse. This deduction is available only if the surviving spouse is a U.S. citizen. Under current law the full value of all property passing to the surviving spouse qualifies for the marital deduction. In fact, it is referred to as the "unlimited marital deduction."

marketability discount • a discount in value of a closely held business, employed if a business interest lacks a ready market and cannot be quickly converted to cash.

member • a holder of an ownership interest in a limited liability company

minority ownership interest discount • a discount in value for a minority ownership interest, based on the lack of power to control the business

noncancelable • the insurer cannot cancel an insurance policy prior to the insured's reaching age 65 and must guarantee the premium rate for the entire period

not essentially equivalent to a dividend • a stock redemption that has undergone a "meaningful reduction" in a shareholder's interest in a corporation. This classification is determined by a subjective test by the IRS, which evaluates the particular facts of the redemption and allows the redemption to be treated as a capital transaction for tax purposes.

open-ended questions • questions designed to obtain subjective and expansive responses, especially where soliciting opinions, thoughts, ideas, values and feelings.

operating agreement • a contract drawn up by members of a limited liability company that states the terms upon which the organization will perform its business or services, similar to a partnership agreement. Modification is generally only allowed by the unanimous vote of the members.

option agreement • a type of restriction used to handle business continuation problems, stipulating that the surviving owners of the business will have the option to buy a deceased owner's stock at a specific price

own-occupation definition of disability • the continuous inability of the insured to engage in his or her regular occupation or profession due to illness or injury

owner's equity (net worth) • the excess of assets over liability (also known as net worth). It is the portion of value to which owners—rather than creditors—have claim. A negative owner's equity on a balance sheet is referred to as a *deficit*. In a partnership balance sheet, the equity or owner's equity figure may be subdivided according to the respective shares of the partners. In a corporation, owner's equity is generally divided into two categories: capital stock and retained earnings.

ownership transfer plan • another term for a buy-sell agreement

par value (face value) • the dollar amount printed on the face of the stock or bond certificate

partial liquidation • a distribution in which the distributing corporation is partially liquidated, qualifying it for treatment as a capital transaction for tax purposes. Qualification is determined by examination at the corporate level, rather than from the point of view of the shareholder receiving proceeds.

partnership • an unincorporated business that is run by two or more persons who act as co-owners of the business for profit. A partnership interest is an intangible personal property right held by each partner once a partnership is formed and holds property. A partnership interest is considered personal property and is treated as such for inheritance tax and succession purposes.

partnership interest • an intangible personal property right held by each partner when a partnership is formed and holds property. A partnership interest is considered personal property and is treated as such for inheritance tax and succession purposes.

pass-through entity • business organizational form whose items of taxable income, capital gain, tax-exempt income, losses, deductions, and credits resulting from business operations generally pass through as individually taxed items in relation to the owners' relative interests in the business. Pass-through entities include partnerships, LLCs (if partnership tax treatment is chosen), and S corporations.

personal property • property other than real property

personal-service corporation (PSC) • a corporation owned by shareholder-employees in which substantially all activities involve services in the fields of health, law, engineering, architecture, accounting, actuarial science, performing arts, or consulting. This type of corporation is subject to a flat tax rate of 35 percent on all corporate earnings.

pre-approach • contacting prospects to arouse curiosity, create concern, or upset complacency in order to make your prospect want to meet with you to hear what you have to say. Success depends on prospecting, attitude, and creating trust and prestige. The purpose of the pre-approach is to precondition your prospects to expect your request for an appointment and be receptive to it. The pre-approach usually occurs after you have a prospect's name but before you ask for an appointment.

presumptive disability provision • a provision that triggers automatic payment of benefits under a disability policy at the insured's loss of certain functions, such as complete loss of eyesight or loss of two limbs

price/earnings comparative analysis • a method of business valuation which uses comparisons of a closely held business to similar, publicly traded companies.

probate • the process of proving a will's validity in court and executing its provisions under the guidance of the court

professional corporation • a corporation whose activities involve the performance of professional services by professionals who are shareholders of the corporation

professional partnership • a partnership whose activities involve the performance of professional services by professionals who are partners

proprietorship • a business enterprise that is formed with one owner, who owns the business assets, manages the business, and conducts business affairs. The business is not a separate legal entity, and assets and income of the business are treated as directly owned by the proprietor.

prospecting sources • the methods for obtaining potential clients. Those discussed in this text include current clients, businesses you patronize, referrals, centers of influence, tips clubs, community involvement, canvassing and lists and directories.

real property • land and anything permanently attached or affixed to the land

reasonable compensation • a compensation test that determines if a deduction from corporate income tax as an ordinary and necessary business expense will be permitted for the total compensation of a shareholder-employee. Amounts determined to exceed reasonable compensation will be treated as dividends, which are subject to double taxation.

recapitalization • a rearrangement of the capital structure of a corporation involving the exchange of all or part of a shareholder's stock for newly issued stock, pursuant to the plan of recapitalization

replacement cost method • for key employee insurance on a key person, the business should consider as a result of the loss of a key person: lost profits to be replaced, time needed to return to pre-death profitability level, time and cost to train a replacement, and the availability and salary of a replacement.

residual disability benefit • a disability plan that provides reduced benefits when the disabled insured suffers a partial loss of earned income, thus giving the insured an incentive to return to work (also referred to *as income replacement or recovery benefit*)

retained earnings • profits that have already been taxed to the corporation. The retained earnings account is part of the owner's equity portion of the balance sheet. Dividends are paid out of retained earnings. If a corporation has no retained earnings, it cannot pay dividends. If a corporation pays out all of its profits as dividends each year, it would have no retained earnings. Retained earnings are also known as *retained income, retained profit, accumulated earnings, surplus, and earned surplus.*

right of first refusal (first offer provision) • a provision contained in many closely held corporation stock certificates requiring the shareholder to offer stock to the existing shareholders first, usually at an agreed price, before selling it to outsiders

S corporation • S corporations share some features with closely held corporations and C corporations. There is generally no federal income tax levied on S corporations. They are pass-through forms of business. The owners of S corporations are taxed on their proportionate share of the earnings of the corporation. Like C corporations, S corporations have continuity of life; each shareholder's liability is limited to the amount of his or her investment; and shares of ownership are readily transferable.

salary continuation • a plan to replace the salary of a disabled business owner or employee, funded either by disability income insurance or by the business itself. When used in conjunction with a disability buy-sell agreement, the payments generally continue at least until the disability buy-sell agreement becomes effective.

sale-or-exchange treatment • a value-for-value disposition of property, in which the seller receives capital-gains tax treatment for federal income tax purposes

sales cycle • the 10-step process of identifying and satisfying the needs and wants of the buyer. This involves the following steps for insurance: selecting, approaching, meeting the prospect, gathering data, analyzing the situation, presenting recommendations, implementing the solution, underwriting, delivering the contract, and monitoring and servicing the plan.

sales method (business valuation) • method of business valuation which considers prior sales as a fair valuation basis

sales ratios • the relationship of sales activities to sales results. These measures, a result of good record keeping, show the amount of prospecting activity on average required to make a sale or to get any other key result. For example, the number of calls to obtain a sale would be calculated by dividing the total number of calls during a period by the total number of sales for the same period.

savings fund • as one alternative to funding a buy-sell agreement, a fund created to accumulate enough money for a key employee or other purchaser to buy the business interest at the owner's death

Sec. 162 plans • executive bonus life insurance plans that avoid the nondiscrimination rules applicable to other fringe benefits by having shareholder-employees and executives who participate in the plan apply for, own, and name the beneficiary on permanent life insurance policies covering their lives. The corporation pays the premiums through a bonus payment to the insurer or as a bonus to the executive.

Section 303 stock redemption • a relief provision of the Internal Revenue Code that applies to estates in which stock of a closely held corporation constitutes a substantial portion of total estate assets. This type of redemption allows distributions to be treated as made in exchange for a capital asset, and therefore eligible for capital-gains treatment, subject to certain requirements and limitations.

Section 6166 installment payments • if a qualifying estate holds a business interest that comprises a substantial portion of the gross estate of a deceased owner of a closely held business, an estate liquidity technique that allows the estate tax caused by the business interest to be spread over a number of years in installments

self-employed businessowner • proprietor, partner (or member in an LLC taxed as a partnership), and more-than-2-percent shareholders in S corporations

sinking fund • as one alternative to funding a buy-sell agreement, a fund created to accumulate enough money for a key employee or other purchaser to buy the business interest at the owner's death

social styles • Individuals have four different social styles or typical ways of behaving in social situations: Driver, Expressive, Amiable, and Analytical. When you adapt to the prospect's social style, you make the person feel at home and less threatened. By listening and observing carefully, you learn how to treat the prospect. Knowing the social style of your prospects will improve your ability to build rapport more effectively. Paying attention to relationship issues will improve your ability to understand the why behind what is taking place and should improve your ability to communicate with the prospect.

sole proprietorship • a business enterprise that is formed with one owner who owns the business assets, manages the business, and conducts business affairs. The business is not a separate legal entity, and assets and income of the business are treated as directly owned by the proprietor.

special-use valuation • an election available to value certain real property by taking into consideration how the property is currently being utilized instead of how it might be used if placed in its best and most profitable use

split-dollar plan • life insurance plans in which the premium obligations and policy benefits of a the policy are split between two individual entities, usually an employer and employee, who share the premium costs while the policy is in effect and split the benefits at the death of the insured or upon termination of the agreement

split-dollar rollout plan • a split-dollar plan in which the arrangement may terminate at some point during the employee's life, with the policy vesting in the employee and the corporation either being repaid for its contributions or providing the policy to the participant as a bonus

stepped-up basis • generally when a taxpayer acquires property through a decedent's estate the basis in the property is the fair market value as of the date of the decedents death. This tax benefit is of great value if the property received has substantial untaxed appreciation, for that appreciation will escape taxation. This occurs when someone inherits a business interest, or as the result of acquiring a business interest through a cross-purchase agreement.

stock redemption plan • a buy-sell arrangement that binds the corporation to purchase a shareholder's interest at the occurrence of certain specified events

stock sale • the sale of a corporation in which the buyer acquires the whole corporation with all its assets and liabilities. In this type of sale the buyer cannot incur direct liability for the corporation's debts, and the sale of stock does not affect the basis of the corporation's assets.

stock-transfer restrictions • a provision in a buy-sell agreement that sets forth any restrictions imposed on the shares of stock subject to the agreement, such as a first-offer requirement preventing a shareholder from disposing of stock to a nonparty without first giving the other parties to the buy-sell agreement the option to purchase the shares at a specified price

syndication • syndications are much like joint ventures in that they are the joining together of two or more individuals or entities. A syndication can be a joint venture, or take the form of a general partnership, a limited partnership, a C corporation, or an S corporation. The limited partnership is the most popular form. Most syndications are the joining together of a relatively small group of investors for the purchase and development of a large financial undertaking, such as the purchase and development of real estate.

tax-free reorganization • the reorganization of a business, such as a sale of assets or stock, which does not incur tax to the seller/selling corporation at the time of the transaction, and in which the seller receives stock in the acquiring corporation at a basis equal to the seller's basis in the property sold

tenants in partnership • a form of property ownership in which each partner has an undivided interest in each specific partnership asset, giving each partner the right to use partnership property for partnership business

termination by operation of law • the termination of a business by the death, bankruptcy, or legal disability of an owner

third party influence • material from a reputable and credible source that can be valuable in establishing prestige, credibility, and support what the advisor is attempting to establish. Various publishing houses have available such items as series of tax letters, legal bulletins, and other mailing pieces that are of interest and value to business owners and executives.

tips club • a group of local salespersons from diverse industries who meet regularly to exchange of information on business prospects. Each member of the tips club shares his or her own expertise and business/social contacts with the group. The resulting exchange of ideas and leads can multiply each member's referred leads. Usually a tips club has only one member per industry.

transfer for value rule • death proceeds must be reported as taxable income when an existing policy has been sold or transferred for a valuable consideration. The taxable income is the death proceeds, reduced by both the amount of consideration paid for the sale or transfer of the policy and the net amount of any premiums paid after the transfer, and is reportable as ordinary income by the beneficiary. To facilitate the transfer of policies in business situations, federal law allows certain exceptions to the foregoing rule. Death proceeds will be wholly tax exempt, despite a transfer for value, if such transfer is to one of the following: the insured person, a partner of the insured, or a partnership in which the insured is a partner, a corporation in which the insured is a stockholder or officer, or the spouse of the insured.

trial close • to "feel the pulse" of the prospect regarding his or her position or buying attitude. By getting clarification on how the prospect feels about an aspect of the sales presentation, the advisor is in a better position to address issues that need to be clarified or reinforced, or to back away from issues that the prospect does not like or want to do.

trigger date • the date a disability buy-sell agreement becomes operative after an elimination period following the onset of the owner's disability

trust • a written agreement involving the transfer and management of property ownership during life or at death by someone for the benefit of another. There are many types that serve different purposes, such as testamentary (by will) or living or inter vivos (during lifetime), revocable (changeable) or irrevocable (cannot be changed), and many others.

wait-and-see buy-sell plan • a buy-sell arrangement in which the identity of the purchaser is not predetermined in the agreement but upon the first death of a shareholder

waiver of family attribution • by meeting certain Internal Revenue Code requirements, the avoidance of having stock owned by a shareholder's family attributed to the shareholder when all the stock is redeemed

weighted earnings • a method for valuing a business where a calculation is made to determine representative earnings in which the most recent year's earnings are given the greatest weight and earnings of the preceding years are given progressively less weight

working capital • the excess of current assets over current liabilities, which indicates the debt-paying ability of the business